Sell Up and Sail

TAKING THE ULYSSES OPTION

Laurel

Sell Up and Sail

TAKING THE ULYSSES OPTION

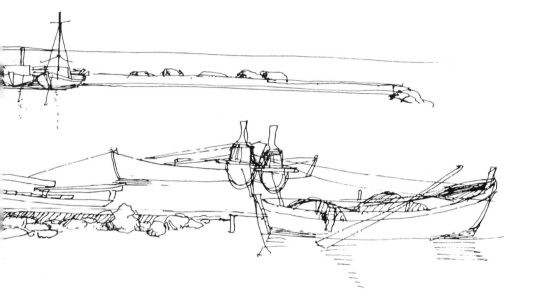

Bill and Laurel Cooper

SHERIDAN HOUSE

This edition first published 1991
by Sheridan House Inc.
Dobbs Ferry, NY 10522

© R. William Cooper & E. Laurel Cooper 1990

Library of Congress Cataloging-in-Publication Data
Cooper, Bill.
    Sell up and sail: taking the Ulysses option / Bill and Laurel
  Cooper. ——
      p.   cm.
    ISBN 0-924486-08-2
    1. Sailboat living.   2. Yachts and yachting.   3. Cooper, Bill.
  4. Cooper, Laurel.   I. Cooper, Laurel.   II. Title.
  GV811.65.C66   1991
  797.1'24——dc20   90-26813
                                                        CIP

Printed in Great Britain

All quotations at Chapter headings and
elsewhere are either by Laurel Cooper, or
Captain John Smith: *A Sea Grammar*, published
in 1627, unless otherwise attributed.

Contents

DEDICATED
To our parents and children,
who let us go.

Acknowledgements

Dr R. Morriss, in charge of manuscripts at the National Maritime Museum, Greenwich
Peter Williams of the Department of Trade and Industry, London
Dr Harold Fore, the Eggs Authority, Tunbridge Wells
Institute of Child Health, Guilford St, London
London School of Hygiene and Tropical Medicine
Derek Bate, Librarian at the Fisheries Laboratory, Lowestoft (Ministry of Agriculture, Fisheries and Food)
Dr Paul Clarke of MASTA (Medical Advisory Services for Travellers Abroad), Keppel St, London
Admiral Epaminondas Caravas, formerly of the Hydrographic Department of the Hellenic Navy
Baysan Curer of Turkish State Marinas
Cdr Cerfessee, USN, Meteorologist at Bermuda Naval Base.
Dr Tom Goedicke for photographs of cat Nelson
Yachting Monthly

For much help and advice with the Health and Welfare chapter we are indebted to:
Dr E. W. J. Brown of Maidstone
Dr Caroline Blackwell, BS, PhD
Professor Donald Weir, MB, CLB, MD, FRCP (Edin.)

And to THE GRAND FLEET (so much larger than anyone supposes) of dedicated long-term cruising people all over the world, with whom no discussion over a mug of coffee or a glass of wine was ever less than absorbing, entertaining, and instructive.

We offer our grateful and admiring thanks.

ΠΑΝΑΓΙΑ

Laurel.

LAMPARAS AT PETRI

Introduction

Not so many years ago the number of people living aboard cruising yachts was small enough for them to be considered very eccentric. The situation is no longer the same.

In 1980 a survey for an Italian marina company produced a figure of four thousand boats which were lived in all the year round, in the Mediterranean alone. Of this number, twenty-five per cent were British and some ten per cent were American. The number grows year by year, and to it must be added the substantial population doing the same thing in the West Indies, the Bahamas and the South Pacific, as well as the American community on the move up and down their East Coast waterways.

The significant words are 'on the move'. We are not concerned with houseboat residents, or even those who live in a yacht in one place. This is about mobility, and we try to go into it quite deeply.

It is about escapism as well. Too many moralists infer the escape is from obligations, but this view begs a lot of questions. Many of us escape from regimentation, from interfering bureaucracy, from cradle-to-grave suffocation: we want to look after ourselves. We are rebels from the Welfare State. We discuss that.

But an urge to go is not enough. To a lifelong sailor the act of setting sail comes naturally and easily. Most people are not so experienced, and we are often asked how we have managed to enjoy fourteen years of early retirement in this way, when many others have set out but have not managed to keep going. A good deal of the answer lies in understanding what you are trying to achieve, in defining your aim, in ordering your affairs to further that aim, and then finally having the capacity to cast off the last mooring and go.

This is not a book on technique — seamanship, how to sail, how to maintain engines — though we do indulge ourselves from time to time. It is about attitudes, about ways of ordering existence on the move.

We are not concerned with obsessive achievers speeding round the world on curried split peas, without touching land except to have their GREAT SAILOR ticket punched at the more spectacular blue-water stopping places. Nor do we have time for bathtub sailors, navigators of barrels or floating bedsteads, or voyagers in re-cycled cornflakes packets and other unsuitable craft. Our advice to nautical loonies is to stay at home, buy a plastic duck and give the rescue services a break.

There are some who for various reasons can be only partially or temporarily committed to wandering. Those with a sabbatical and no time to waste, and others with a semi-annual approach, wishing to live aboard for perhaps six months at a time. Though not suffering from a terminal case of wanderlust as we are, they have a minor infection: perhaps we can help them too.

We are writing for people who are out to enjoy themselves. So we concentrate on those parts of the world to which the live-aboards tend to gravitate, and where our voyaging experiences are more recent.

We write also for dreamers, for most of us were dreamers to start with, and we hope we may encourage them to realize their dreams. There may be those unsure of their ability, of their endurance, or uncertain that the lust is real. Those too who have to cope with the wanderlust in a partner, and how it might affect them. We try to help these people analyse their attitudes in Chapter Two, 'Test your U.Q.'.

The two of us have very different personalities and we see things different ways. To some extent, then, this is two books for the price of one, for we both express (as much between the lines as in them) what drives us on.

Introduction to the Second Edition

Since the publication of the first edition we have taken part in two symposiums on the subject of long-distance cruising organised by *Yachting Monthly*, and have thus enjoyed more than usual feed-back from our readers, to whom we are very grateful.

There is now no doubt that interest in living aboard a cruising boat and sailing far and wide is much greater than we thought. It really is a social phenomenon, but not one that lends itself to formal social research, because the motivations of us all (the sailors) are so diverse. What the social scientists might like to investigate is why, in principle, so many people turn down the easy option of the Welfare State.

In this revised edition we have updated where necessary (Finance and Insurance for example), amplified important subjects like food and health, added 'A Yacht to Grow Old In', and some comments on those topics our readers missed in the first edition.

Since *Sell Up and Sail* first came out we have sold our beloved boat *Fare Well* to people we like, who are going to live on board and travel, as we did. She'll like that.

Our old friend Nelson, the one-eyed cat, died and was buried with honours off the mouth of the Tiber River.

We are now living aboard the Dutch barge *Hosanna* which is as yet unfinished, but we are in sight of our next cruise. If you see us, come and call.

CHAPTER ONE

Why Do We Do It?

'What a greate matter it is to saile a shyppe or goe to sea.'

In 1976 we sold our house, waved goodbye to the family, and took to the sea in a boat we had built ourselves. We became long-distance, liveaboard cruisers, for whom no very accurate generic term has yet been established, though the nearest is perhaps 'Yotties'. Abandoning brick walls and gardens, property taxes, and interference from authorities who continually tried to order what we might or might not do, we took on the less comfortable but much more invigorating life of responsibility for our own actions, health, welfare and safety, and through this self-reliance achieved contentment.

Since then, the interest shown in our way of life has increased to a point where the number of people who wish to emulate us, and others like us, has become almost a social phenomenon. The idea of it seems to appeal to many. Although it is the antithesis to the collective responsibility of the Welfare State, that may be a perverse explanation for its attraction. It may also be why some people find they cannot handle the idea, since there is no doubt that great exchanges have to be made (We prefer not to call them sacrifices).

Sudden change is not good for the system. On a boat you can usually choose to change slowly, to stay a bit or go on as the mood takes you. An Atlantic crossing is a very slow change, giving you time to get used to the climate, and hurling no insults at your biological clock.

Have we not, some people ask, merely exchanged one set of problems for another? Yes, in a sense. We have exchanged the insoluble problems of politics, the pace of life, the battles with bureaucracy, and the appalling proliferation of paper which push one to the edge of madness, for problems of wind and wave and how and where to go next, which we *can* solve. That alone does wonders for your well-being.

When the wanderbug bites you, the symptoms vary from person to person. The acheing boredom and frustration of many of today's jobs — or worse, the lack of any job at all — produce understandable feelings of restlessness, and in some people a desire to travel. Many people in middle life feel that this is something they wish to do before they get too old. The young feel they would like to do it now, before family responsibilities and education become too great a burden. Many feel that it would be a great way to retire. All have differing requirements and expectations. With some, the idea of travel comes at the head of the list; with others, the escape vehicle comes first and travelling in it second. There is a third category to whom the building of the boat is a sufficient release. They dream of going but remain at home, quite content.

There was no doubt in Bill's mind that he wanted to build his own boat, and travel in it. There was a great deal he wanted to get away from: a 9—6 job, very stressful, complications of property and official-dom, winters of ill health, the speed of life, and the trauma of too much change too quickly and for no good reason. I could see his point.

Why a yacht? Because it is a romantic dream that has a chance of coming true: you can build it yourself. And when you've built it, you can travel in it, which is another romantic dream. Building a boat, or acquiring one and refitting it to your own requirements, seems to appeal to something very ancient and necessary in man. Your life, and that of your family, depend on how well you build it and how care-fully you plan the voyage. In a world where someone else is always to blame for any misfortune (and where with luck, you can sue), to take responsibility for your lives firmly on your own shoulders and find out that the burden is bearable brings feelings of worth and confidence.

A yacht has a freedom of travel that no other vehicle enjoys. The sea is, by and large, still free to all to cross from one side to the other, starting and finishing where you please, or to stitch your way round its shores. There are extremely few restrictions and regulations specifi-cally affecting yachts, and what few there are would be complied with by a prudent mariner in any event. Close to land and in harbour, you will find the only restrictions you are likely to meet. In or near big commercial ports you will find one-way systems, parking regulations and choked traffic just as on the busy roads of any city. Away from the big ports restrictions dwindle until they disappear altogether. A yacht marina is merely a specialized commercial port, and you can expect the same sort of restrictions; added to those of a caravan camp (no laundry lines, no barbecues). We avoid them if we can.

God help us if the day ever comes when we are all directed into marinas because commercial interests or overcrowding demand it, or indeed for any other reason. That will be the day when Bill and Laurel start building their kit-form space capsule. (Well, it's got to come, hasn't it?)

Until then, if your aim is carefree mobility, then a yacht is the ideal vehicle. Some people may find eventually that cruising is merely an interval between long stops in one place. Some find a place they love so much they never leave it. Would a caravan have been a better choice? It is certainly cheaper. To use a yacht to stay in one place means that you are not using to the full the expensive and specially designed equipment that was intended to give you mobility: like using the Rolls-Royce as a chicken shed.

If you find, after doing the U.Q. test which follows, that neither sailing nor travelling are really what you want, but that you would like to drop out of the Stress Layer for a while, or forever, and sink down to the quieter levels of the world, afloat or ashore, then it would make sense to search for your place in the sun by land cruising.

This involves driving at an average of fifty miles an hour instead of five knots. You need registration, insurance and a driving licence. In most places where you would feel like staying, caravans are strictly regulated into campsites. If you are not in a campsite, water and sanitation can be a problem. You can not carry much fuel, and yet cannot move without it. You have to stick to roads, of more or less good quality. You are dependent on ferry services to get you across water, and filling stations for fuel, therefore you are at the mercy of strikes and industrial policy. But, yes, it is cheaper. Still, find your small village or town or island, and you will in some ways be less isolated than in a bed-sit in outer London.

We find that in a stay of one month in a tiny port we can, even if not accepted as part of the village, at least lose our tourist status. It takes care and tact, however. Try to change nothing. Watch before you join in. Does Baba Iannis always sit in the same chair in the Taverna? Then don't sit in it yourself. Do the old men like to cluster in one corner and gaze out over the bay? Then don't block their view with a table full of strangers. If the village turns in at half past nine, don't keep them up with noisy chat and laughter, ordering strange drinks that the Taverna has not got. Try to talk a little in the language, to assuage natural curiosity as to your age, marital status, and number and age of children. Don't go on too long, though; they have the whole world to run in their deliberations, don't forget, and if they missed an evening who knows what could happen? Catastrophe.

If Selene brings out her distaff to spin a little in the evening, I go and sit near her with my knitting, and we can exchange wordless admiration without making many waves.

Sense the mood, so that you do not behave inappropriately. One day, when the ferry came in, everybody stopped smiling. We, too, put on grave expressions. The men ran down to the ship and came forth bearing a coffin. The women came down to meet it and fell in behind. It was taken up the little alley beside the Taverna to a courtyard where three old ladies had been wont to sit on the warm stones in the evening. Now only two remained: Eleni had been whisked off to hospital on the mainland the day before, and had died there. She was very old, so faces were grave, but not tearful. 'Poor lady,' said the baker, 'I gave her half a loaf of bread many times. She was too poor to pay me, so I forget always to ask for the money.' Everyone came to her funeral, as she had no relatives left. The village cared for her in death, as they had done in life. Can one ask more?

Some people can. They want to go and spend another month at a different place, learn to understand another kind of village and another sort of people, drinking rum punch on a coral beach or rough red wine in a bodega, or 'island tea' in a Turkish tea house, or cook their stew in fumeroles in the Azores and eat lobster-in-the-rough off paper plates in New England. I cannot think of a better way of doing this than to go with your house on your back like a sea snail, at a speed where your surroundings change slowly and without shock to the system.

> What is this life, if on our cruise
>   We have no time to sit and booze?
> Conversely what, if full of booze
>   We never get to sea and cruise?
> What is this life, I'd like to know
>   If I am always down below?
> And if, upon the starboard tack,
>   The loo is always out of whack?
> And what if I am ill at ease
>   With not a ripple on the seas?
> What is this life? It suits us well.
>   It's mostly heaven, rarely hell.

To have built your boat, or at least lovingly altered and equipped her for such a voyage, is a process which brings in itself many rewards. For us, the real reward was the travelling. We held on to this aim through many black days during the building period.

This is a book for dreamers, but especially for those who would like to achieve the dream. We would like to take the stars out of your eyes, and use them to illuminate practicalities.

While anyone contemplating long-term cruising would be foolhardy to embark without some nautical ability, the effort of acquiring it can be eased by planning and dreaming. Indeed, dreaming may be one of the most enjoyable aspects of the whole enterprise. If you never get beyond the stage of catalogues and cruising books by the Sunday fire, enjoy the book. Just before we sailed, the Lifeboat Coxs'n said to us, 'A lot of people want to do what you're doing. Difference is: you've done it.'

We were dreamers once. Dreams can become a reality. It is hard work, rather than magic, that gets it done.

CHAPTER TWO

Crucial Questions

'Make voyages! Attempt them! There's nothing else.' Tennessee
Williams — *Camino Real*

PART ONE: How Laurel was Persuaded to go to Sea

It was the insidiousness of it that got me.

From the day he retired from the Royal Navy, Bill began the 'one
day we'll both go to sea' gambit. Over the years, punctuated by annual
visits to the Boat Show (I always went with him — I almost always got
migraine), the subliminal mention became less subliminal, and during
his next two careers became friendly persuasion, then gentle insis
tence, and finally downright intransigence.

Not that I disliked either the sea or sailing; far from it, though my
experience, while considerable, was largely on inland waters. I even
liked the Boat Show. But I was entrenched in a comfortable little life
and saw no reason to abandon it in order to get wet, cold and seasick
away from my books, cats and children.

It became clear that if I was not to be shanghaied to sea willy-nilly, I
should have to take certain steps. These were all backwards, and
included countering every stated assumption that I would go by good-
humoured negatives and careful references to 'your boat' and 'your
voyage' and 'when *you* go, I'll have a cottage somewhere for you to
come back to'.

After some years of this it dawned on my husband that I meant it,
and that I did have good reasons for doubting my capacity at sea. With
a sigh, he began to design singlehanded yachts. At this point I realized that he too meant what he said. My bluff called, negotiations
began with frank and free discussions, and meaningful dialogues; and
the next few designs were very different. If I was going, I wanted a say
in the sort of boat I would live in.

The Inevitable Compromise

Bill says now that he built *Fare Well* round my books and my bath. For
the next few years he worked on my sense of adventure and I worked
on his sense of responsibility. We had two children whom we could

15

not leave until it seemed they could do without us. We had cats (one horrid and one super) and a dog. How could Bill leave his tiresome, but very lucrative job? We had a large house that I adored. My life was busy and interesting, and I loved the work I was doing. It was going to be very hard to sell up and go.

Departure

In the end, as so often happens, some decisions were made for us by events. Bill became very ill for a year or two, able only to potter about the half-completed boat; and there was no longer any problem about breaking away from the job — the firm had already filled the vacancy. The children grew up suddenly and moved out, leaving us in a house far too big and expensive on our own. The horrid cat died, and we decided to take the other with us — one of our more brilliant decisions, as was the idea of giving the dog to Bill's widowed father, leading to one of those man-dog relationships worthy of letters of flame.

It began to look as if the sooner we went the sooner Bill would regain his health. There *was* the little matter of finishing a 55 foot ketch, and getting it to sea, but we had been working on that for some time anyway. (It took five years altogether and is quite another story.) Gradually the people who had been saying 'you'll never finish it' began to realize that we damn well would, and that we were damn well going.

It was hard. Morale was sometimes very low. It was as hard as I had thought it would be to sell the house, part with the dog, and say good-byes to family and friends. On the plus side, our son Ben decided to accompany us for a while. A sense of excitement began to grow as we worked, planned and stored ship; and found some pleasant people to share our maiden voyage to Gibraltar. This being, apart from trials, our first trip, and nearly my first ocean trip, Bill had decided to be prudent and take some extra muscle.

When we finally set sail from Lowestoft, six people and the cat Nelson, a burden rolled off my shoulders that I had never been aware of. I smelt the sea, saw the first of many ocean sunsets, and felt a freedom I'd never known before.

I wouldn't have changed places with anyone.

Looking back

I had always loved the sea in rather a romantic and sentimental way. I was born and brought up by the sea, and dipped my toes in it nearly every day of my childhood summers, or sat in the shallows and let the little waves bounce in my lap. You could pee in it without anyone knowing. You could watch the storms from the cliffs and be amazed by the crashing noise of the breakers, the cold hiss and rattle and roar of grating pebbles; even at that distance you must shout to be heard. In bed you could hear the waves above the fitful pelt and spatter of the winter rain. How blissful to be warm in bed, and not out in the dark on the wild sea.

As I grew up I learned to sail, on the Broads of course, as did the young Nelson, but I was seventeen before I even crossed the Channel in a ferry, and the sea was still magic, and dangerous and attractive like an elder brother's motorbike.

That attitude was not very helpful when faced with a life at sea. How would I cope with storms? How would I handle seasickness and exhaustion when we were short-handed? Could I stand my companions (let alone my husband) at close quarters and under stress? It seemed a good idea to find out about this sort of thing while the boat was still a-building. I do not advise anyone less dedicated to leave it as late as this. It is far better to do all this and more before you embark on a project which has a momentum as inevitable as the birth of a child, and to abort which is just as painful and a good deal more expensive.

Getting some sea-time in

My only real sea experience at that time (I discount dinghy racing where you are home and dry after a couple of hours) was a four week cruise in 1954 with Bill, our six-month old daughter and my brother. The yacht was a 5-tonner without motor or loo. I felt that there was some basis for confidence here, as although it was July in the Mediterranean we had had one of those unseasonal summer storms, and a thick fog in the Sicilian Channel shipping lanes to boot. I had by no means disgraced myself, I had cooked, washed nappies, kept watch, steered and been useful. The baby enjoyed every minute. I enjoyed most of it. So far, so good.

I had the great advantage of faith in my captain. Bill is an experienced deep-sea yachtsman, and an ex-professional navigator. He is also a seaman of the old-fashioned kind, which he describes as managing without what you haven't got, and which leads to some amazingly ingenious ways of achieving the aim. I felt I should have confidence in the boat, too; she was strongly built and looked seaworthy, and I was getting to know her by building her. I had had a lot to say about the design, and not just in the galley. The guardrails were to be very strong in case my hip failed me; and on the foredeck we had strong netting to prevent a body slipping through the guardrails. Below, the furniture was built strongly enough to fall against in a seaway without damaging it, the corollary being that such solidity can cause a lot of mayhem to bodies bouncing off it. Despite the numerous handholds that we put everywhere, strong enough to Tarzan around the boat on, I still sometimes ping-ponged off the furniture. Gazing at my doleful bruises, I insisted on more cushions, in the cockpit as well. Bill hates them, but they do cut down injuries, not only mine.

We have mentioned the bath. For anyone with bone-aches a hot bath is a solace greater than any medicine. Salt water can be used. Since it is now believed that more yachtsmen die of hypothermia than drowning, and a recommended remedy for the former is a warm bath, maybe it's less of a luxury than we thought.

I wanted a corner for drawing, and I refused to share the chart table as I knew it would cause friction. I got it, a neat solution that was flexible enough to become a workbench when I started enamelling.

Double bunks were unusual at the time. You spend a lot of your life in bed, you might as well be happy there: we designed the first double bunk we'd seen that could be got at from three sides, instead of being shoved against the ship's side. I heard of some one who had an arm broken by a heavy bunkmate crawling over her in such a bunk, answering a night call. Twice.

Gaining experience

To get more confidence in myself, I went to the National Sailing Centre at Cowes (now alas no more) to learn some navigation (the coastal part of the Yachtmaster's qualification). Bill normally does all this, and to compete with him seemed foolish: if someone can play the Moonlight Sonata should you join in on a penny whistle? But I felt a lot better for knowing something, and it might have become vital.

I gained more experience. When we could we helped friends who were new to sailing by doing short trips round the coast or across the Channel. I began to realize I was not the first in the crew to succumb to seasickness, that pills and sensible precautions to prevent over-tiredness and chilling were better than being frightfully brave, and that I was so hungry I *had* to cook something. I found that a little yacht flying down-Channel before a stiff breeze was great. I discovered that I did not much like going to windward. We remained on speaking terms with our friends. It looked as if things were going to be all right.

The house was sold. I still writhe with pain when I recall this period. Although planning and forethought went into everything we did, it turned out there was still a lot to learn. Most of it we are still learning by pleasurable stages, and a little of it the hard way.

Our happy years of cruising are witness to the fact that we did our homework, and that by the end of our maiden voyage a romantic dreamer had become something of a practical sea-person, and Nelson had enthusiastically embarked on the life of a one eyed sea-cat.

Having described the process whereby I came to accept and eventually enjoy living at sea, there are some relevant questions you should answer.

PART TWO: Test Your U.Q.

> 'Too little thought before you go,
> And you'll be back before you know'

We have devised a test to measure what we shall call your 'Ulysses Quotient' or U.Q. While it should not be taken desperately seriously, it will nevertheless give you plenty to think about. You and your mate may even have your first disagreement over the first question. Ulysses, it will be remembered, roamed the seas for about ten years, looking for his homeland, the island of Ithaca. U.Q. can be described as a tendency to wander off for years in a small boat without actually getting anywhere much. (Though he was probably the worst navigator in history, he did, it is pointed out to us, suffer under the handicap of having an all-male crew!)

The desire, the will, to go cruising is paramount. We realize that nothing we say will stop you if you are determined; whether you are an unskilled, penniless tyro, incapacitated by alcohol and agues, embarking in an unseaworthy boat with a sack of lentils and aiming to be the first member of Depressives Anonymous to round Cape Horn; or a thrifty couple with a small but well-found boat, making well planned voyages that are triumphs of ingenuity, courage and dedication.

However, we want you to enjoy your cruising; and time spent now on thinking and planning will save you money and misery later on. We cannot say this often enough.

You and your spouse, or mate, or whatever, should do the test separately, in private, and without discussions or comparisons until all the scoring is finished. If you would like your children to do it, the same conditions apply: certainly they should join in the discussions which follow. Incidentally, I had better make it clear that I use the word 'Mate' throughout this book to cover: wife, husband, son, daughter, companion, friend, crew, lover, consenting adult — whoever is going with you to be your team mate.

You each (or all) have a lot of decisions to make, and you might as well know what your sticking points are now. They may prove to be immovable, they may need hard work and compromise to find a way round them, they may in time vanish like smoke, but at least you will know what you are up against. Name your enemy and the battle begins.

Note that your scores are nothing to do with winning or losing, or with being right or wrong. The test is an attempt to assess: (1) your present situation, which may of course change, (2) practical considerations which may have a bearing on your future, (3) your abilities and capabilities, and (4) your attitude to mobility. The scoring comes under three different headings: Alpha (A); Kappa (K); and Sigma (Σ). Their significance will become apparent later.

If you cheat — have fun, and carry on dreaming. If you are really keen on the idea, take a good look at yourself, answer honestly, and this could be the first step in your voyage.

The Ulysses Quotient

Section One — Basic questions: Do you really want to go?

(1)   Do you really like sailing?
    (a)   Yes, very much.
    (b)   I don't know, I think I do.
    (c)   I don't know, I think I don't actually enjoy it.
    (d)   No, I don't.
If (a) score A4, if (b) score A1, if (c) score Σ5. If (d) score Σ15, and go to question (Q)3.

(2)   You are faced with a rough sea and a rising wind on a long beat into harbour. Do you:
    (a)   Grin and bear it?
    (b)   Say 'This is what it's all about' and call for eggs and bacon?
    (c)   Get sick and miserable, and let the others get on with it?
    (d)   Get sick and miserable, but try to produce the eggs and bacon?
If (a) score A2, if (b) score A1, if (c) score Σ1. If (d) score A1.

(3)   Have you ever been abroad? If Yes, continue. If No, score Σ4 and go to Q7.

(4)   Do you like travelling abroad? If Yes, continue. If No, score Σ4 and go to Q7.

(5)   When you are abroad, do you prefer to stay in:
    (a)   A pension?
    (b)   A campsite, or boat?
    (c)   A hotel?
If (a) score 0, if (b) score K1, if (c) score Σ2.

(6)   When you are abroad, do you:
    (a)   Like eating local dishes?
    (b)   Enjoy lots of olive oil and garlic?
    (c)   Prefer your normal diet?
If (a) score K1, if (b) score K2, if (c) score Σ2.

(7)   Do you speak any language other than your own (enough to be polite and do some shopping)? Score A1 for each one more than two.

(8)   Can you afford this venture?
    (a)   Yes.
    (b)   In time, or maybe.
    (c)   No.
    (d)   I've just won the Pools.
If (a) score A2, if (b) score 0, if (c) score Σ3, if (d) score what you like!

Discussion on Section One:

(1−2)   These are germane questions. If you are unsure, you had better find out the answers for certain, for your own sake and the rest of the crew. Do this by sailing with friends, in as many different boats and situations as possible. If you ultimately intend to go singlehanded, skip the next paragraphs and go to (3). If you are going to sail with a mate, and your answers to Questions (1) and (2) differ widely from your partner's, the battle lines could be already drawn. If you like ear'oling (sailing with the lee rail under) and spray in your face, and your mate prefers to go over on the ferry, you have a compatibility problem which needs to be resolved. How much can (and will) Salty Sam or Sue throttle back to accommodate the natural fears of less adventurous members of the crew? We have known voyages founder on the fact that the skipper was too harsh, hard-driving and self-punishing. This is fine for racing weekends but unbearable for a long cruise, which ought to be a pleasant experience; and feeble, weedy crews do not contribute to this either.

Willingness is all, however, and much may be learned and achieved with determination. We have mentioned sailing with friends. Some might consider that a flotilla holiday would be the ideal way to do this. We do not. It makes a marvellous holiday and may tempt you into thinking you like cruising; but it is an artificial set-up. You will learn little that is of any use for your purpose, since flotilla sailing has less to do with long-distance cruising than the child licking the basin has to do with making the cake.

For Absolute Beginners there is a starter pack at the back of the book which will help you to be useful even on your first sail.

(3−6)   Do you really like 'abroad'?

We all love the thought of the palm trees, soft breezes, and swaying Hula hula girls. But do you enjoy new tastes and smells, or would you rather have your joint and two veg. and tea like mother made? (for Brits), or biscuits and red eye gravy (for Americans). You can get hamburgers, French fried and Foster's almost anywhere.

Do you find it all interesting and exciting, or do you worry about the drinking water and the loos? Are you happy in a pension, eating with the family and making a stab at the language, or do you prefer a coach tour or hotel where a courier takes care of all the hassle? Are you, in other words, a self-reliant traveller?

(7)   If you are not good at languages, you can always go West, where most of the continent of North America and a good many of the West Indian islands, plus the Bahamas and Bermuda, are populated by people who speak English of a sort. You can also go down to the Antipodes. If you go to the Mediterranean you will have to cope with foreigners on entry to a new country; and you will have to store ship, get water and fuel, and deal with spares and repairs. This will be stressful if you are impatient with people who speak little or no English. The

AGHIOS EFSTRATIOS
EARTHQUAKE DAMAGE

other side of the coin is the fun of it. When I was much younger and prettier, I left our boat *Phoenix* in Syracuse harbour and went looking for a fishhook with my Italian Dictionary. 'Amo?' I said hopefully to the proprietor of the fishing tackle shop. His eyes lit up. 'I love you too!' he said. It was a while before I could get him back to the subject of fishhooks. When Nelson had a skin problem that I suspected to be a fungus, a young German came over to help. 'I hear your cat has the mushrooms,' he said.

(8)   Can you afford this venture? What is enough? Selling your house, if you own it, will provide enough money for a reasonable boat. But it has to be maintained, as you do; you will need to fit her out and store before you go, and you need reserves for contingencies — which may be drastic. Don't count on being able to find work on the way. The next chapter on Finance will give you some idea of probable costs, but a lot depends on whether you are in the Champagne or local beer and wine bracket. Perhaps you need more time to work and save, in order to sail with debts paid, mortgages discharged, some reserves and a light heart.

If you scored all (a)s in this Section, you have crossed the first barrier with ease. If you scored all (c)s someone probably gave you this book as a present. Tough. Enjoy reading it, however. If you came somewhere in the middle, you have some thinking to do. Now go to Section 2.

Section Two — Your job: Can you leave it?

(1)   Do you own your own business? If Yes, go to Q4. If No, continue.

(2)   Are you unemployed or retired? If unemployed score K2, If retired score K2. In either case proceed to Q7 otherwise continue.

(3)   How do you feel about the job you are doing now? Choose any of the following:
- (a)   I have a strong vocation.
- (b)   I really like my job.
- (c)   It's just a job.
- (d)   I'm in line for promotion.
- (e)   I'll be glad to leave.
- (f)   I'm ready for a change.
- (g)   I've embezzled the tea fund and I'd better go.

If (a) score Σ3, if (b) score Σ2, if (c) score 0. If (d) score Σ1, if (e) score K1, if (f) score K2, if (g) score K10. Proceed to Q5.

(4)   Which of the following statements is nearest to how you feel? (Choose one.)
- (a)   I can't let my work force down.
- (b)   It's a family business: I have obligations.
- (c)   I work all the hours God sends, and love every minute of it.

(d)   I used to enjoy it, but it's getting me down.
(e)   It's a good living and I'm content.
(f)   I'd sell if I could find a buyer.
(g)   I'd be glad to be shot of it.
If (a) score Σ2, if (b) score Σ3, if (c) score Σ1 if (d) score 0, if (e) score Σ1, if (f) score K1 if (g) score K3.

(5)   Are you worried that you might lose skills and/or seniority while you are away?
(a)   No problem.
(b)   I'll catch up later.
(c)   Yes.
If (a) score K2, if (b) score K1, if (c) score Σ4.

(6)   If you are a member of an occupational pension scheme, what happens if you give up your job now?
(a)   I get a reduced secure pension on retirement.
(b)   I get a return of contributions but no pension.
(c)   I have no protected rights.
If (a) score K1, if (b) score 0, if (c) score Σ1.

(7)   Can you use your skills abroad? (A skilled craftsman is welcome almost anywhere, but the Professions often erect barriers against foreign practitioners.) See next chapter on Finance.
(a)   Yes
(b)   To a certain extent
(c)   No
If (a) score K2A2, if (b) score K1A1, if (c) score Σ1.

(8)   If in Section One (Basic Questions) you scored: As: more than 6, score a further K1. Ks: more than 5, score a further K1. Σs: more than 6, score a further Σ2
(9)   Are you any of these, or do you hold similar posts: Justice of the Peace, President of the Women's Institute or Townswomen's Guild, Provincial Grand Officer in the Buffs or Freemasons, chairperson or officer of any Clubs or Societies, Mayor, Councillor or Alderman, etc? Score Σ2 for each post you hold. If you hold more than three, score a bonus of Σ3.
(10)   Do you spend more than two nights a week at meetings which are nothing to do with your job? (Here only, your job means what you are paid to do. In all other questions 'job' includes unpaid work such as housewifery, parenthood, voluntary work etc.) If Yes score Σ4.
(11)   Do you spend more than two nights a week at meetings which *are* to do with your job? If Yes score Σ3
(12)   Can you give up the interests in Q 9: (a) Easily (b) With regret   (c) No. If (a) score K1, if (b) score Σ1, if (c) score Σ3.

Discussion on Section Two

(1)   Can you leave it? If you are unemployed, now could be your chance to go until the job situation changes, especially if your skills are such as to enable you to pick up work here and there on the trip. Although 'job mobility' is much in everyone's minds, 'serial professions' as envisaged by Alvin Toffler in his book *Future Shock* are not yet with us: that is, a series of occupations where you will change jobs at around five-year intervals. If and when such flexibility arrives, it will make leaves of absence or sabbaticals between jobs a much more feasible proposition, and probably improve the mental and physical health of all concerned.

(3—5)   If yours are technical skills in a fast-changing field, it will be hard to keep up while you are away. Technical journals are heavy: trusting them to foreign mails is expensive and chancy. We often ask friends to bring them when they visit us, and are smitten with guilt when their heaviest piece of luggage turns out to be full of yachting magazines, a pilot book, *Exchange & Mart*, the Sundays, 'and a few paperbacks' plus several Royal Institute of Navigation Journals.

If you want to keep your options open, then leave of absence, while you find out if you really enjoy the life, is the best answer. Otherwise you face a refresher course of some kind on your return, if there is one. This also applies if by leaving your job you lose status and seniority. It could be hard.

If leave of absence is not possible and you can not take your job with you, you should look on your voyage as early retirement, with the possibility that you might have to return to work later. If your skills are really rare and valuable you should have no trouble finding a job when you come back, and your employer will not care where you have been, so long as it wasn't in gaol. If your skills are less useful, you could face re-training for a new career. In either case, we don't need to tell you that your curriculum vitae (resumé to Americans) would need to be carefully worded. You will clearly be able to provide adequate, not to say impressive, reasons for your absence. The usual pack of lies, in fact. At least your health and vigour should have improved, and you might have acquired a whole new set of skills, but in the present climate you may face great difficulties getting back into the labour market, especially after a certain age.

(6—8)   If you are used to being a person of consequence, consider whether you will be satisfied with being 'just a yottie'. We tend to come a bit lower on the social scale than some of you are accustomed to. There are many compensating and pleasurable feelings of achievement and satisfaction, but these do not scintillate outwardly in other than an air of contentment and relaxation.

And once having tasted real freedom, could you ever again settle to a 9—5 existence? We think we could if the devil drove — but he'd need a big whip.

Section Three — Your health: Are you fit to go?

(1)   Do you feel unwell a lot of the time? If No, continue. If Yes, score $\Sigma 4$.

(2)   Do you have a condition for which you regularly seek medical advice? If No, continue. If Yes, score $\Sigma 5$.

(3)   Do you have a condition which worries you and for which you have not sought medical advice? If Yes, score $\Sigma 4$. If the answers to the last three questions were all No, score K3 and go on to Section 4. Otherwise continue.

(4)   Do you remember your condition:
  (a)   Hardly ever?
  (b)   Some of the time?
  (c)   All the time?

If (a) score K1, if (b) score $\Sigma 1$, if (c) score $\Sigma 3$.

(5)   Would your doctor allow you long periods of self-medication?
  (a)   Yes
  (b)   No
  (c)   He doesn't give a toss.

If (a) score K1, if (b) score $\Sigma 4$, if (c) score 0 and change your doctor.

(6)   Could your condition:
  (a)   Prevent your standing a watch, night or day?
  (b)   Endanger the boat or fellow crew members?
  (c)   Necessitate expensive and/or time-consuming medical attention while on voyage?
  (d)   Cause over-tiredness or require a rigid regime or time schedule?

I your answer to Q6 is No to all three, score K1. If your answer is Yes to (a), (b) or (c), score $\Sigma 2$ for each Yes. If (d) score $\Sigma 1$.

Discussion on Section Three

(1–4)   Are you fit to go? There is no doubt that we go to sea with the most amazing handicaps. We have met unbelievably courageous long-distance cruisers with diabetes, cancer, heart conditions and stroke, amputees, people with imperfect limbs and paralysis; not to mention those souls (perhaps more foolhardy than courageous) who were obese or alcoholic or addicted; to which list we should add several who were clearly bonkers. Nothing short of coma seems to stop us, as long as we are willing and able to 'manage' our disability with long-range advice.

A positive mental attitude will assist one's fellows to make a few (oh, very few) allowances, as will a determination to excel in the things one *can* do, while not shirking those tasks which will cause discomfort but not damage. Realism is of the utmost importance here, and the quality of enjoyment one can expect must be considered as carefully as physical well-being. A long talk with a doctor who understands exactly what long-distance cruising is all about will be necessary. If you have not already consulted on anything that worries you, ask yourself why.

(5—6) At sea you will have to care for yourself. This requires more sense than bravado. A golfing doctor who doesn't understand what is involved will merely tell you not to go: professional people must be cautious about giving advice in unusual circumstances, as they could be held liable for the consequences. Find yourself a yachting doctor to consult. Where do you find him? Offshore at the Yacht Club, of course, where his patients can't get at him! If you are in luck you should get a realistic answer; pointing out dangers to avoid, how to monitor your condition, what drugs or medication to take with you, how to inject yourself safely, and what to exercise and how.

(6) Consider carefully whether you are a danger to the boat or crew. Red-green colour blindness, for instance, is a strong contra-indication since it is of vital significance on a night watch to be able to distinguish red and green lights on shore and on other vessels. A condition that causes you to tire easily, or requires a rigid regime or time schedule, should give you pause; since one of the great benefits of the life is being able to forget time and rigidity. Most of us long-term cruisers don't even know what day it is, and find that getting friends to airports is an unwelcome return to a scheduled world.

A word on drinking. Most of us do this with great gusto, the rum or wine being cheap and the company enjoyable. But note that air pilots are forbidden to drink before and during flying. Naval navigating officers are not so forbidden, but nevertheless have a long-standing tradition of not drinking *at sea*. (Of course when let off the hook you'll find them drinking ashore and sinking a gin; but that's better than drinking at sea and sinking the ship.) Make up your own mind, but the sea is no place for alcoholics. We know of at least one yacht that was lost with all hands, and a good many drownings, of which drink was a contributing cause.

Don't forget that alcohol in the bloodstream increases seasickness! Not a few wild farewell parties have caused a postponement of the sailing day. Nor is it unknown for a yacht, after the gongs, bells and cannons have wished them Bon Voyage, to creep into a bay round the very first headland and drop anchor till their headaches improved.

Now the good news. On a well organized voyage your general health will improve, as the outdoor life and the lack of stress seep into your body and mind. You will probably be cured of your migraine (as I was), your asthma (as Bill was), or your hayfever, tummy cramps, eczema, PMT — anything with its true origins in tension and stress.

Section Four — Your family: How strong is the pull?

(1)   Have you parents, children, or near relatives living? If No, score K1 and go to Q4. If Yes, score Σ1 and continue.

(2)   Are you worried about any of them? If No, score 0. If Yes, score Σ3 for each one.

(3)   Are you the only child? If No, score 0. If Yes, score Σ2.

(4)   Has your mate (if any) parents, children or near relatives living? If No, score K1 and END THIS SECTION. If Yes, score Σ1 and continue.

(5)   Is he/she worried about any of them? If No, score 0 and END THIS SECTION. If Yes, score Σ3 for each one and continue.

(6)   Is he/she an only child? If No, score 0. If Yes, score Σ2.

(7)   What age will your child (children), both yours and your mate's, be when you sail? Will you take them with you? Score as follows:

Taking them	Leaving them
0–5 years: 0	Σ5
6–12 years: Σ1	Σ4
12–18 years: Σ2	Σ4
over 18 and/or independent: K2	Σ1
over 18 and dependent: Σ2	Σ4

(The score is additive, thus if taking a baby and toddler with you score 0; and if you are taking one four-year old and leaving two of 13 and 15 years respectively, score Σ8.)

(8)   Is there someone reliable to care for children remaining at home? If Yes, score K2. If No, score Σ4.

(9)   Do you have children of school age? If No, END THIS SECTION. If Yes,
    (a)   Will you teach them yourself?
    (b)   Will you use a correspondence course?
    (c)   Will you send them to boarding school at home?
    (d)   Will you send them to local schools as you travel? And stay long enough to benefit?
If (a) score K2, if (b) score K2, if (c) score K1. If (d) score 0.

Note:(8)   There is a wide range of possibilities here. Boarding schools fill the bill in term time, but usually other arrangements must be made in the holidays if they cannot join you. Compliant relatives may take your child on for a while; this was a common thing in wartime, and most of us did not seem to suffer from being parked on aunts and grandparents and changing schools at frequent intervals. The criterion has to be that the arrangement is satisfactory to all parties, and you pay their way and extra costs.

Discussion on Section Four

(1–6) You will not enjoy your cruise if family responsibilities lie heavily upon you. It makes sense, therefore, to solve as many problems as you can before you leave, so that on sailing you know that the situation is as stable as can be expected. *Good communications* after your departure are important; apron strings pull in both directions, and your family will sometimes be as anxious about you as you may be about them. Several cruisers we know have a clued-up person back home, who may or may not be a member of the family, to act as a clearinghouse for news; so that one phone call only, and that a short one, need be made. A fortnightly (for instance) 'How's things?' 'Everyone's fine, where are you?' is worth a lot, being positive and up-to-the-minute reassurance. Messages to ring home often go astray, and we find we do better by telepathy, and so do others we've met. I'm not kidding: we always obey any feeling that we ought to go and telephone, as we are so often met with a relieved 'Ah! you got my message.' It wouldn't be quite truthful to say 'What message?' but one always does.

Forwarding mail can be rather a chore. Some member of the family usually takes it on, sometimes quite gladly. Make sure they are reimbursed for any postage, and that they clearly understand what is junk mail to you and what is not, otherwise you might get the bulb catalogues and 'YOU MAY HAVE ALREADY WON' (date of competition expired, of course) instead of a sought-after spare parts list and the *OCC Journal*. Written instructions with the address of the next mail drop are better than blurry orders over a telephone line that hisses and crackles like a radio star.

If you have elderly relatives that you have been in the habit of visiting, it is well worth going along to the DHSS and pointing out that you will not be available after such-and-such a date. The Social Services can often help a great deal, and will do more if prodded: a talk with them may produce Home Help, meals on wheels, and a regular health visit, for instance.

If you think more help is needed, Age Concern can tell you what might be available. A good neighbour can be given the number of your communication link in case of need. The more people who know the situation the better: doctor, lawyer, fellow club members, fellow church members, and reliable neighbours: anyone who could help to hold the fort if need be. Don't forget great-nephews and nieces, and grandchildren, all of whom should be concerned, and encouraged to visit and give what assistance they can. However, they will all expect you (if you are female) to reappear and wave a magic wand if anything goes wrong, and this can be tricky if you are one donkey, two ferry-boats and a bus away from an air terminal. Let alone the expense. If you are male, then it is considered that you have a good reason for what you are doing, and far less pressure is applied.

You may, however, be the only child and your relative may be isolated and friendless. The Social Services and Age Concern will be vital in this case, especially if the idea of moving to sheltered accommodation (for example with a warden) is met with resistance or is not possible for other reasons. What if, after all your efforts, your obstinate 90-year-old tells the meals on wheels lady where to put her gammon and mashed, and slams the door on the Health Visitor as if she were an itinerant brush salesman? What if your old person, in fact, insists on self-sufficiency and independence, in a mountain shack or the middle of Dartmoor? Presumably they do this from choice. You are a chip off the old block, aren't you? You can wish them good luck, and sail; also from choice. Only you can decide, but if things are unstable at home, it is particularly necessary for your peace of mind to have frequent communications, and a reserve of cash to travel home; and this will affect your choice of cruising ground.

Children: Take 'em or leave 'em? Many people have taken their children to sea, from birth to 13 or 14, and few have regretted it. Books written by survivors can frighten you off, but note that the children do survive. Read the many articles written for cruising magazines by parents who find, in the main, that cruising with their children has been an enriching experience. Their tales of sailing to new lands, meeting new people, and how the children develop self-reliance and confidence, and better yet, a stronger family bond, will be an inspiration for you. We have a feeling that crews with children on board take more care.

Section Five — Boat skills: How able a seaman are you?

(1)   Do you own, or part-own, a boat? Or have you in the past? If Yes, score A2. If No, score Σ1.

(2)   Do you maintain, or help to maintain, a boat? (Hands-on, not just paying for it.) If Yes, score A2. If No, score Σ2.

(3)   Are you a qualified Master with a lifetime of experience and over 30,000 miles under sail in your log? If Yes, score A30, and go to Q17.

(4)   Do you potter about in boats? If Yes, score A1. If No, score 0.

(5)   Are you a weekend dinghy or small-boat sailor? If Yes, score A1. If No, score 0.

(6)   Have you cruised locally at home or abroad in a yacht for more than fourteen days? If Yes, score A2. If No, score 0.

(7)   Have you made a passage to a foreign country? If Yes, score A2. If No, score 0.

(8)   Have you kept a night watch by yourself at sea? If Yes, score A2. If No, score 0.

(9)   Can you take a compass bearing? If Yes, score A1. If No, score 0.
(10)   Can you make any of the following: bowline, clove hitch, rolling hitch, fisherman's bend, figure-of-eight knot, sheet bend? If you can do them all *now* score A2. If you can do three of them score A1.
(11)   If your car goes wrong do you:
     (a)   Call in the garage.
     (b)   Have a go at mending it.
     (c)   Read the manual and have a go at mending it.
If (a) score Σ2, if (b) score A1, if (c) score A2.
(12)   Can you cook:
     (a)   Under difficult circumstances?
     (b)   With unfamiliar and limited ingredients?
     (c)   Without getting seasick?
If (a) score A1, if (b) score A1, if (c) score A1. If Yes to all three, score a bonus of A2.
(13)   Do you suffer from seasickness? If No, score A4 and go to Q17. If Yes, continue.
(14)   Is your seasickness controllable or reducible by drugs? If Yes, score A1 and go to Q16. If No, continue.
(15)   Do you recover after 24 hours or so at sea? If Yes, score A1. If No, continue.
(16)   Are you prepared to suffer the occasional day of misery? If Yes, score A1. If No, score Σ10.
(17)   Do you have any of the following skills? carpentry, compass adjusting, diesel and petrol engineering, electrics (AC and DC), electronics, firefighting, fishing, food preservation, haircutting, how to move heavy loads, laundering (by hand), metalworking, meteorology, musical instrument (small), paramedical skills, painting, plumbing, radio, rigging, sail repair, scuba diving, sewing, swimming, upholstery.
Score A1 for each three skills you claim.

Discussion on Section Five

'If there be more learners than saylors all the worke to save ship, goodes and lives must be on them especially in foule weather.'

It seems to us that anyone who wishes to go in for the cruising life will have acquired *some* skills. Such is the availability of experience these days that failure to have done anything so far could indicate a lukewarmth: or maybe you are just dreaming.

Some definitions might be useful. In Questions 1–3 we clearly infer a sailing boat, though if for perfectly valid reasons you are thinking of going in a motor yacht, then adapt the question accordingly. Question 4, on the other hand, could mean any type of boat, which is clearly better than none at all. Questions 5–9 involve many conditions which might be borderline: you must use your common sense. If you haven't any, subtract A 20!

Question 10 is a fundamental. At first we thought it should score very high; then we reasoned that we are not testing seamanship, but a kind of nautical wanderlust of which ability is only a part. Bill would not like anyone to go to sea without being able to do all these knots in the dark, or to drive a motorboat away from its moorings without knowing the bowline at least.

If you are a novice and learn to tie these knots (or make these bends, or bend these hitches: what a rabbit warren old nautical jargon can get you into), then you will be already useful. We have come across many Yachtmasters who make their yachts fast with snowball hitches that melt in the sun.

In (11) we are after your willingness to get stuck into a dirty problem with some chance of solving it effectively. Too many of us dash at a problem without thinking first. Always start with the simplest explanation, because that is often the case. And emulate John Guzzwell who was crewing for the Smeetons when their yacht capsized and was badly damaged rounding Cape Horn. His first re-constructive action was to sit down and sharpen his saw. There are rites of passage in all crafts: preparation before deciding what form the work will take is good thinking time.

Cooking (12) is one of the basic skills of cruising. Skippers are not entitled to hide behind wifey's apron all the time. Poor food is as demoralising as bad weather.

Seasickness (13—16) must be taken seriously, since it can affect the morale and capability of everyone who suffers. A determined effort should be made to discover whether you start to recover after about 18 hours at sea and then are immune for the voyage, as the majority are; whether pills help you; or whether yours is the truly resistant kind, in which case you will probably hate the sea for ever.

The list of skills in (17) are those that we have needed (or lacked) aboard *Fare Well*. (It is not definitive: if we have missed out your special expertise, sorry.) We intend the level of competence to be that of a conscientious amateur. Being a Pro does not score extra, but might improve your earning capacity. Moving heavy weights is an art worth studying if you don't want to get a hernia.

Section Six — Goods and gardens: Can you leave them?

(1) Have you lived in your present house/flat for:
  (a) Less than two years
  (b) Two to five years
  (c) Five to ten years
  (d) More than ten years

Laurel

GIGLIO, ITALY.

If you love your house, score (a) $\Sigma2$, (b) $\Sigma3$, (c) $\Sigma4$, (d) $\Sigma6$. If you are ready for a change, score (a) 0, (b) 0, (c) $\Sigma1$, (d) $\Sigma1$.

(2)   Do you like gardening? If No, score K1. If Yes, score $\Sigma4$.

(3)   Do you like horses and riding? If No, score 0. If Yes, score $\Sigma2$.

(4)   Do you own antique furniture or fine pictures? If No, score K1. If Yes, are you prepared to sell it, or give it to parents/children? If Yes, score 0. If No, score $\Sigma2$

(5)   Do you have a fine collection of anything too big or fragile to take with you: old cars, steam engines, carousels, mangles, Ming china, 13th century armour, books, bird's eggs or pornographic (excuse me, *curious*) literature? If No, score K1. If Yes, are you prepared to sell it, or give it to parents/children? If Yes, score 0. If No, score $\Sigma2$.

(6)   Do you have a sport or hobby that you cannot take with you, e.g. billiards, model railways, pottery, hang-gliding, monumental sculpture or mink breeding? If Yes, score $\Sigma2$. If No, score 0.

(7)   Can you manage without the local library? (a) Yes, (b) With difficulty, (c) No. If (a) score K1, if (b) score 0, if (c) score $\Sigma2$.

(8)   Is there life without TV? Do you watch, per week, (a) 1–2 nights, (b) 3–4 nights, (c)more than 4? If (a) score $\Sigma1$, if (b) score $\Sigma3$, if (c) score $\Sigma5$.

Discussion on Section Six

To some people, possessions are status. It is important to them to have a quality car, a house in the right part of town, and the latest gadget whether this is a Jacuzzi, a microwave oven or a home computer. They get a lot of fun out of their things, and are not likely to be reading this unless escape by yacht becomes frightfully fashionable one year, when they will buy a frightfully fashionable yacht to do it in, and have a lot of fun doing it for a short time before wanting to get back to their other gadgets. In our world, some people travel as light as a soul to heaven: Dan was one of these, he crewed for us from Antigua to Bermuda on his way to Europe and seemed to possess what he stood up in, a tracksuit and some running shoes.

Between these two extremes lie most of us, with a heap of rubbish that we could gladly say goodbye to, some useful odds and ends whose passing we might regret, and a further pile of junk that we cling to fiercely and beyond all persuasion. The more of it you can get rid of, the less hassle you will have on your voyage.

(1) *Houses*   If you are going on a long voyage, your house back home will be a nuisance. Besides, you are probably buying your boat from the proceeds of selling it; since owning no property may give you tax advantages (see Chapter on Finance). Renting it in case you want to

return can cause a lot of headaches: the Hiscocks tried this at first but eventually sold the house as the tenants caused so many problems. We have this spring met a French couple whose summer cruise to Greece had already ended in Fiumicino near Rome: they had to return and sort out some legal difficulty with their house.

We sold ours. It was a wrench at the time, but the wound heals. (2–5) Those possessions that we could not bear to part with we left with various members of the family to mind for us. Funny, I can't remember what some of them are now. A few we took with us. So, we find, did other people; and it is surprising what a variety of objects mean enough to someone for them to find room and make a safe stowage for. We saw a cello on the 26 foot *New Life*, lovingly cradled on the forward berth (the second best cello, to keep in practice) an ice-making machine which worked by burning camel dung or any other solid fuel on *Northern Light*, an electronic piano for writing songs on *Clarity*. We carry my enamelling kiln. Eight year old Ben Lucas on *Tientos* has a most impressive Lego set. *Snow Goose* had a home computer before they got as small as they are now. Chess computers, TVs, guitars and bicycles are run-of-the-mill; golf clubs and tennis rackets rather less so. A dentist we know keeps a neat case of the tools of his trade on board, so do most doctors; indeed anyone with skills might want the wherewithal to use them, with the possible exception of lion tamers and nuclear physicists.

> Beware of Grandsons, Goods and Gardens:
> Here your wife's resistance hardens.

Section Seven — Attitudes: You've got to be crazy.

(1)   Is your dreamboat taking shape? Are you (or your mate) currently:
-   (a)   Buying or building her?
-   (b)   Planning or designing or choosing her?
-   (c)   Still looking for the right one after ten years?
-   (d)   Designing for the tenth time in ten years?
-   (e)   Still building after fifteen years?

If (a) score K4, if (b) score K1, if (c) score 0, if (d) score Σ1, and if (e) score Σ3.

(2)   All of us have fears and uncertainties about such a voyage. Let's look them in the eye. Which one of the following statements is most true for you, concerning:
Keeping a night watch alone
-   (a)   I'll be OK.
-   (b)   I'm a bit nervous
-   (c)   I'm rather nervous.
-   (d)   I'm not keen on the dark.

If (a) score 0, if (b) score Σ2, if (c) score Σ4, and if (d) score Σ7.

Becoming ill on the voyage (you or your mate)
  (a) We'll cope somehow.
  (b) I don't know what I'd do.
  (c) I'm going to first aid classes.
  (d) We'll have a check up before we go.
  (e) He/she would be helpless without me.
If (a) score K1, if (b) Σ1, if (c) 0, if (d) 0, if (e) score Σ2.

Bad weather
  (a) I'm used to it.
  (b) I think I'll be OK.
  (c) I'm a bit nervous.
  (d) I'm very nervous
  (e) I'm scared stiff.
If (a) score K2, if (b) K1, if (c) 0, if (d) Σ1, if (e) score Σ4.

(3) Pick whichever of the following best expresses your situation:
  (a) I'm determind to go.
  (b) I'm looking forward to it.
  (c) I can't wait, but I don't think he/she wants to come.
  (d) If he/she won't come, that's the end of it.
  (e) I love planning, but I'm nervous about going.
  (f) If he/she really wants to go, I suppose I shall have to.
  (g) If we go for a year, he/she might get it out of their system.
  (h) The idea is great, but I can't leave my grandchildren/dogs/
       cats/garden just now.
  (i) I don't think he/she has enough experience yet.
  (j) My friends seem dubious about my going.
For (a) score K4, if (b) K2, if (c) 0, if (d) Σ3, if (e) Σ1, if (f) 0, if (g) 0, if
(h) Σ5, if (i) Σ4, and if (j) Σ2.

(4) How long do you envisage doing this?
  (a) For the rest of your life?
  (b) For a year or two?
  (c) For several years?
  (d) Until you get too old?
  (e) For the foreseeable future?
If (a) score K4, if (b) K1, if (c) K2, if (d) or (e) score K3.

(5) If you are not yet committed to going, how long before you do
commit yourself?
  (a) This year?
  (b) Next year?
  (c) Sometime?
  (d) Never?
If (a) score K3, if (b) K2, if (c) 0, and if (d) Σ5.

(6) Why haven't you already gone?
  (a) I'm really just dreaming.
  (b) For reasons I don't wish to reveal, or am not sure about.

    (c)   I have.

If (a) score Σ5, if (b) Σ4, and if (c) you are fouling up the system!
If your score in this section is more than K15, you are somewhat
imprudent: subtract A4.

Discussion on Section Seven

In terms of partnership, one person is usually the instigator and prime
mover of the Ulysses plan and the other (or others) the more or less
willing follower. *Usually* the man is the instigator, and is going to be
Captain. *Usually* the women and children are followers, and are going
to be mate and crew. To the discussion which follows, it does not
really matter which way round it is, but in order to avoid saying
he/she too often we will go with the majority.

    Trouble is clearly going to arise if the views of the partners are too
divergent. *Now*, before you go to great expense and disruption, is the
time to find out: if you disagree fundamentally about whether to go at
all; or less radically about the kind of boat, the amount of time and
money to be spent, what areas you will travel to, and the standard of
comfort required.

    Women have been home-makers ever since the first cave-wife hung
a skin on the wall of her cave, instead of wearing it or lying on it. The
habit, after 5000 years, dies hard, and it is too much to expect your
wife to live in a production boat, stark as a railway station gents (and
probably smelling rather similar), without letting her cosify it, within
reason. The happiest boats we meet seem to be the ones with the
homely touches. I have seen the look in a woman's eyes when her man
boasts that 'We haven't altered or added a thing since we got her at
the Boat Show: keeps up the resale value, you know.' I am far more
inclined to Hal Roth's view: 'the layout and detailing of the little ship
on which a man lives and travels ought to be as personal as his
fingerprints.'

    I cannot see that curtains, covers, cushions and decor ruin the resale
price. Nor has any production boat designer thought of all the extra
gear you need to live aboard: indeed in many boats it is hard to find
space for the oilskins and seaboots for every crew member. I shall say
more about this later, when we talk about storage.

    If you embark on this life with any hope at all, you have to trust and
have faith in each other. It follows that there should be some basis for
this trust, and that you should set out to acquire skills and experience
that will justify it. It's no good sailing out into the sunset, Captain,
with your manly hand on the tiller and your manly pipe clenched
between your teeth, if your mate quickly concludes that you do not
really know what you are doing or where you are. No good, Lady,
posing like the yachting mag ads, in immaculate whites holding a rope
that obviously goes nowhere, when your Captain needs knowledgeable help. You owe it to each other to learn as much as you can by

sailing together and separately, with friends or by answering 'crew wanted' ads, for long or short journeys, in different kinds of boat with different kinds of skipper.

If you have both been living the nine-to-five life, you will be used to speaking to each other about five to six hours a day: less if you are silent breakfasters, TV addicts or in the darts team. How will you cope with being in each other's company twenty-four hours a day, barring night watches? When in such close quarters, a seventh sense needs to be developed. You should know when another person's space and privacy should be respected, and words that can wait half an hour be left unsaid. Long companionable silences should be easily achieved, and just as easily broken at the right moment. When we have friends on board we find that siestas are a great idea. Everyone separates to their own patch of space, and quiet activities, rest or sleep prevail for a blissful couple of hours. On meeting again later the chat is all the livelier, and the wit keener, for having had a break.

Fears and fancies we all have (2), and they need dragging out into the light where they can be more carefully examined. It is no good saying 'Cheer up, it won't happen!' because it probably will; no cruise is without incident. If you are aware of danger you have already taken the first step to prevent it; but be sure that you are guarding against realities, and not bogies under the bunk. You will reduce unnecessary worry to a minimum if you develop confidence in your boat, your Captain or crew, and your self. Fear is allayed by encountering, and coping successfully, with trouble; this is what experience means. From the statistics, one ought to be far more terrified of crossing the High Street than keeping a night watch, but the first is a known and familiar danger and the second an unknown one. Eventually it becomes as ordinary as crossing the road, and rather less dangerous, though never to be taken lightly.

Illness on the voyage (either oneself or one's partner) is one of the thoughts that perturb us. Why do we not worry as much over becoming ill in our ordinary life at home? Because help would be available, in the form of doctors, hospitals, and friends. We have only to seek advice, and the burden is straight away on other shoulders: all we have to do then is follow instructions. If you wish to have the freedom that the cruising life brings, you have also to accept that you are going back to the pioneer days of being self-reliant.

Having said that; you will certainly be a lot healthier than if you'd stayed at home; and it's surprising how often there is a doctor in the next boat just when you need one. We have come to no serious harm in ten years of cruising, some of it in very remote places. (See Chapter Fifteen for further comment on prevention of illness and accidents.)

I suppose most of us are afraid of bad weather, though some of us are reluctant to admit it. It's no fun at all to have your house bucketting about at all angles, and the corners of your galley attacking you when you cook; and when the cat burrowing on to your lap under your oilskin while you steer is the only bit of companionable warmth you'll get till the weather improves. But if your boat is strong and your Captain capable and prudent, and perhaps above all you have got your sea legs, then it's possibly a little better than two hours in a packed commuter train.

No blame attaches to people who are afraid to go to sea, any more than those who would fear mountain climbing or motor racing, or (in my case) pot-holing: I'm already not too happy on the Underground. Some people do these things precisely because they *are* afraid, and singlehanded too. To such brave hearts we give our admiration, but this book is not for them. Cruising is a game that two or more should play: no sane person goes mountain climbing or deep diving alone, and people who go off on journeys which they mentally label 'One Man against the Elements' or 'Alone in the Southern Ocean' are taking greater risks than we would care to. There is no need to be *that* crazy. Nevertheless, if you want to undertake the life, you must develop a self-reliance that *is* unusual these days. We yotties are felt to be eccentric, a curious cross between hermits, voluntary exiles and adventurers. We feel very normal, of course; and only at gatherings of landpeople do we realize that we are perhaps a bit peculiar — when our answer to the inevitable question 'And where do you live?' is followed by an odd little silence, or a rush of enthusiastic clichés covering extreme social embarassment. If you can't be classified, you are too alien to converse with. If they don't know where to put you in the social order you naturally go to the bottom. It's quite comfortable down there, there's no competition!

So, you do have to be crazy. But at least do it with planning, forethought and prudence.

Summary

Now, write down your scores:

	A	K	Σ
Section One	..	..	..
Section Two	..	..	..
Section Three	..	..	..
Section Four	..	..	..
Section Five	..	..	..
Section Six	..	..	..
Section Seven	..	..	..
Totals for each type of score	..	..	..

Now add up the totals for A and K, and multiply by 100. Divide this figure by your total Σ score: this gives your ULYSSES QUOTIENT, i.e.

$$UQ = \frac{100(A + K)}{\Sigma}$$

where A represents your APTITUDE and ABILITY for cruising, and K represents KINESIS which is the mobility force in your personality, while Σ (SIGMA) represents STASIS which is the inertia in your personality.

If your U.Q. is below 100, you are a static person from a cruising point of view.

If your U.Q. is between 100 and 200, you are moderately kinetic: go with someone who has a higher one.

If your U.Q. is between 200 and 300, you are kinetic: you'll get by.

If your U.Q. is over 300, you have marked kinesis.

If your U.Q. is over 1000, you are a bit weird; why haven't you already gone?

There is a possibility of obtaining a total Σ score of zero, which would lead to a U.Q. of infinity. This is only possible if you are already following the life of a Ulysses, and are thoroughly content. Go on and enjoy it in good health.

PS: If you can't do the arithmetic, you wouldn't be able to work out a sunsight: stay at home.

CHAPTER THREE

Finance

'The Purser doth keepe an Account of all that is received and delivered'

When we were giving talks following the publication of the first edition, we were frequently asked about finance and it is clear that this is a pre-occupation with many prospective voyagers.

Taxation

In the first edition we wrote that the important thing on the income side, assuming you have any, is to be able to stop most of it falling into the hands of governments or assorted middlemen. Since that time taxation in Britain has changed dramatically, the main change being the big reduction in personal taxation level, now standing at 25% basic.

This level is actually less than the Value Added Tax in some countries, and because VAT is much more difficult to evade it is likely the process will continue, or at least not be reversed. There comes a point when the costs of setting up schemes to minimise taxation make the process self-defeating. We do not think it is any longer necessary to devote one's energies to it when there are more enjoyable things to do.

Non-Residence

There thus remains only one important tax advantage to obtaining the status of non-residence, and that is exemption from Capital Gains Tax. So if you have property or business to sell, it is worthwhile starting the process of emigration and obtaining provisional non-resident status. This will need professional advice. Remember that an important factor is to emigrate: you need not immigrate anywhere, that is a completely different thing. The two verbs are quite opposite in meaning, and one does not necessarily involve the other. Tax men can get quite confused about this.

Apart from Capital Gains Tax I do not feel that non-residence is worth the bother unless you are very rich, in which case you will get better advice than we can give. One of the reasons is that when non-resident, susceptible income is taxed from the very first pound: one does not get any personal allowances. There is a complex formula which the Inspector should work out to decide whether you would be better off being taxed as non-resident or as resident (it is too difficult to go into here), and you pay the lower figure.

On what, you may ask? Can one not invest entirely in those magical gilts which are tax-free to non-residents, and thus pay no tax at all? Yes you can, but with inflation at its current 8%, and the yield on long gilts at less than 10%, you are not exactly doing very well. It is better to get 75% of something, rather than 100% of damn all.

Incomes of husbands and wives are now taxed separately. It is likely there will be several changes in the rules because the Treasury never gets anything right first time, but it seems at the moment possible for a husband to be a non-resident and to have all the non-taxable income, while the wife remains resident and has all the inflation-resistant but taxable income in her name. If the husband has a good pension, then the position would be reversed.

At the moment, double taxation arrangements do not seem to be worth the candle.

Do not forget that being non-resident deprives you of the vote, and exempts you from jury service. It also enables you to do some very interesting things with the taxation of motor vehicles which we cannot go into here. Most yotties do not concern themselves with motor vehicles being glad, in the main, to be shot of the beastly things, but some people who settle in the Med do return to the same wintering port year after year, and they sometimes find it worth having a car.

Do not forget that the British old-age pension (or whatever euphemism the current political masters dream up) is very good value. Keep up the voluntary payments if you can: the DHSS has leaflets on what to do.

The exemption from VAT that can be claimed by non-residents when buying goods in Britain for personal export is no longer the great advantage it once was because it is no longer available to EEC countries. You have to give a bona fide residence in a non-EEC country to which the re-imbursement cheque will be sent. Everybody needs an American friend, anyway.

Do not overlook the question of Value Added Tax on your boat. The position will be radically altered in Europe from 1992, when it seems that VAT paid in one country will be equivalent to paying VAT in any or all the EEC countries. This seems to be so convenient that someone will inevitably foul it all up. Don't count on it. In the meantime, if you intend to return to your country of origin after a cruise, it is advisable to get the situation sorted out with the Customs.

Commercial ships are exempt from VAT. We think you don't stand much chance of persuading H.M. Customs that your 35 foot sloop is a car ferry in disguise. But something similar has been done!

For those looking forward, not to settling at sea for life but for having a limited break, finances become different. When the break is for a comparatively short period (say two years), one has to be careful to define what one wants or can achieve. Many try to greyhound round the world, struggling to get their 'I'm a Great Sailor' ticket punched. Because we do not go for this approach does not invalidate it, but the finances will be much the same.

I think that if you are going to be away for a period such as two years, do not dismantle your personal finances, because every major change involves fees and costs. You will not be able to become non-resident of the UK, so your strategy will remain that of a resident. Try to minimise the property (in its widest sense) that could cause problems while you are away. Many will want to keep their residence, but it will need protection, and delegated authority to deal with problems is essential.

In the USA

For citizens of the USA, the main problem in avoidance of US taxation is the possibility of losing citizenship. Having seen examples of correspondence shown me by American friends, I can affirm that the relentless po-faced tone of the USIRS makes the UK Inland Revenue seem like knock-about comedians.

Our American friends still fill in their tax returns and send them off each March, whereas most English do not unless they have a pension. Given American freedom from exchange controls, it is surprising more of them do not look at the prospect of getting better net returns elsewhere, while still retaining the financial strength of the dollar. There are some Scottish mutual funds invested entirely in the USA.

Earning your Keep

Earning one's living locally is theoretically possible but in many cases not wholly practicable. Unemployment is not a British monopoly: many places are far worse off, and elaborate precautions are taken to protect locals from foreign competition. The problem needs looking at in three ways: first, how can one earn in a way that does not upset the locals, wherever one is? Second, what jobs, trades, or professions are generally welcome anywhere? And last, what about the Common Market?

Under the first heading come those various occupations that can be carried out aboard, the income therefrom not being obtained locally. Artists come under this heading, provided they are not seen to sell in direct competition with the locals, though even here there is often a degree of tolerance not evident in most fields. The keynote is discretion; it does not seem to matter how much you make, it is the degree of ostentation involved which is important. We have personal knowledge of this field. Artists in general are very tolerant of one another, respecting genuine talent in any form. The chief source of possible objection comes from the local art gallery or souvenir shop, but sales direct to other foreigners excite little attention. Only Bermuda has really restrictive laws. Places where the artist can make a little something are the West Indies and the Bahamas, where the locals do not do much towards providing a souvenir industry, and where the majority of tourists are comparatively wealthy Americans. Greece is interesting, for it can be chauvinistic or even xenophobic at times, but it is genuinely liberal toward real artists and musicians. However, I suspect there exist several ways in which they could cope with unfair exploitation of this liberality.

Writing is not an easy way to earn, and I do not say this merely to impress the publisher. Best-seller writers live like kings, but a couple of well known novelists living afloat in the West Indies do so modestly. Writing for yachting magazines is hard work, and a very poor return for the time spent. One would need to produce a very large volume of words, like the Pardey family, to make much of a living, and original, worthwhile subjects become harder and harder to find, leading to an inevitable fall in standards. Magazine writing has to be seen as a way of making an occasional bonus.

There is one lady yachtsman who makes very high quality bikinis for the boutique trade. She is now well known, and is a good example of a well-planned, suitable home industry.

I would also put under the first heading the carrying out of services associated with boats for other foreign yachtsmen. I have made some pocket money adjusting compasses, and was fortunate to get the approval of the local Greek Coastguard officer. Persons capable of doing electronic repairs are very hard to find. A good working knowledge of technique, and ability to read a circuit diagram, are required, while electronic parts are often easier to buy retail in less well developed countries.

Those skills which are welcome anywhere are not numerous. Trained nurses are in demand world-wide, but doctors definitely are not; the latter seem to have devised some very nasty restrictive practices. Mechanics can do well in some parts, though often it is a question of a direct job for another yottie, but really skilled men are almost always needed, especially in some West Indian islands. Shipwrighting jobs can be found, though these are usually in the busy season which is when the dedicated cruiser wants to be doing his own boat. This applies also to casual labour; even if found it is likely to be when one would rather be sailing. Qualified teachers can sometimes get work, especially those with a certificate to teach English as a foreign language.

The Common Market

Persons from one member country are supposedly allowed to work in the others. I am only aware of the situation round the Mediterranean coasts, but the French seem to be honouring the treaty. Not unreasonably, they demand that any foreigner working there should pay French taxes and social service dues; however, the bureaucracy is a wilderness for the foreigner to get lost in, and it is necessary to take care. In general I have found French authorities are sympathetic, and fair about unintentional breaches of regulations, but they do not take kindly to attempts to pull a fast one.

If French bureaucracy is difficult, the Italians' is a complete enigma that even the natives do not try to solve. I get the impression that everyone lives illegally, and pays up when, or if, caught! It is a completely undisciplined society, and the illegal work going on is widespread. Italians, however, are the most tolerant and least chauvinist people in Europe.

It baffles me why Greece was ever admitted to the Common Market. On the ground, they show little sign yet of honouring the Treaty of Accession, and I doubt they will ever do so, for there seem to be local exceptions in almost every case and business ethics are certainly not European. The written contract is only a basis laying out within what limits the fraud will take place. There is a system whereby informers get a percentage of the fine, and this leads directly to the existence of the agent provocateur. Be very wary of doing anything that might be wrongly construed. Given the tradition of Greek hospitality it may seem odd to call them xenophobic, but the answer is in the status of the individual stranger. If you are a visitor, a guest, passing through the delightful country, you will be most graciously received and your property will be inviolate. But if you go to do business, you are suspected, resented and usually defrauded.

> It isn't funny
> To run out of money.
> Having some for contingencies
> Avoids stringencies.

Getting Money to Where it is Needed

We now come to the problem of transferring funds and drawing money. In general it is necessary to have a bank account in any country where you have income originating. Transfer from bank to bank is hopeless. Transfer from an office of a bank in one capital city to an office of the same bank in another capital city is not much better. For example, a sum of $7000 dollars sent by the London office of the Bank of New York took 32 days to become available in New York, and that was fast going. Another sum took 53 days to get from the London

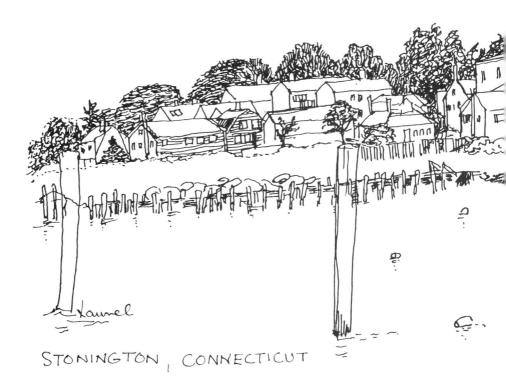

STONINGTON, CONNECTICUT

office of Credito Italiano to one of their offices near Rome. Even Barclays took three weeks to get money from their head office in the City of London to their associate company in Antibes. All of these were telegraphic transfers: I expect I would still be waiting if they had gone by mail. I have since abandoned all forms of bank transfer.

As if to confuse matters further, just before sending this to the publisher, those old-fashioned bankers to royalty, Coutts & Co., have just transferred a sum to Holland for me in two days, which is absolutely astonishing. It seems it *can* be done, perhaps only by bank clerks wearing frock coats. And we must remember that Anglo-Dutch banking has always been good, ever since the burghers of Amsterdam saved the Bank of England from default in 1697, in return for which we took William of Orange off their hands.

Drawing funds for everyday living can be done in several ways.
1. *Eurocheques* can be drawn in Europe, also in Turkey and several unlikely other countries, which are not in Europe, but only on special cheque forms and with yet another card. The cheque is written in the local currency, and the limit is usually just under £100, though some banks will cash two per day. Of course, everybody subtracts a service charge at every stage, which varies from place to place. A good system, this, but one does need the special forms from one's own bank.

2. *Travellers' cheques* are acceptable generally, but beware of cheques drawn on little-known banks—that means little known at the back of beyond. ('Who is this Barclay that he has a bank?' I was once asked.) These also have a ridiculous charge payable when you buy them, though in view of the fact that you are lending money to the bank, unsecured, the public ought to be paid a fee. A big snag with travellers' cheques is that they are difficult to get once one has left one's native banking scene. They can be bought abroad, but if you already have the money, why buy the cheques? Not unreasonably, banks will not send them through the post.

3. *Postcheques* are available to those with a National Girobank account. They come in chequebook form and enable withdrawal of up to £100 daily in local currency at post offices in Europe and the Middle East (with a few exceptions). There should be no commission on each cheque, but 50 pence is charged per transaction. This is possibly the cheapest way of getting funds at the modest level. Apart from Italy, I have found post office queues rather shorter than those in England. They are much the same length in Italy, but service is even slower.

4. *Credit cards* can be used for a variety of purposes, but have limited use for ordinary shopping. Most shops in the scheme are the high mark-up luxury type of shop which we do not patronise. Cards can not be used for

buying diesel oil at marinas, though they can be used to buy petrol at garages, which seems an anomaly, as this would be the most convenient use for such a card. On the whole, for retail use cards are not worth the bother. I started out with a full set, and here are my views on four of them.

American Express This card has a very high annual service charge, but its administration is completely unsuited to the needs of the long-distance sea-going traveller, being more geared to the casual tripper. Like most cards, it can be used for airlines and luxury hotels — so what? I thought it would be useful in the USA, but shops refused it or asked for an extra payment if I wished to charge the purchase to the card. An exception to this was car hire: it is virtually impossible to hire a car without a card, but it does not have to be American Express. When I did charge something, there were so many billing errors that the whole procedure became a nightmare. One advantage of this card is that there exist AmEx travel offices in certain places where one can draw both travellers' cheques or cash in quite large amounts. Unfortunately these centres are mostly in capital cities or major tourist venues which, apart from Antibes, are unlikely to be of much use to yachtsmen.

Diner's Club Much of the above about American Express also applies, except that it is not nearly so widely accepted, and has no travel offices. I gave it up very early. The annual charge is too high.

Visa/Barclaycard has been the most useful. I have used it for drawing cash in both USA and Europe with good results, having once established that one needs a credit limit of more than twice one's normal monthly drawings, owing to delays in payments clearing and getting into the authorizing computer abroad. It is widely used in Europe without much difficulty, except in France where retailers are now using electronic machines which refuse some foreign cards, including British. We have corresponded with Barclaycard for over a year now, and have been repeatedly assured that this is a hiccup which will not continue.

Access/Mastercard is almost as good as Visa, but it is difficult to find co-operative outlets in France, while the Italian outlets limit the amount drawable to £200. Visa and Mastercard give good service in the USA.

With both Visa and Access I have an arrangement with my bank in Britain to pay the accounts on presentation, which keeps one's credit limits up and avoids unnecessary interest charges on otherwise inevitable late payments. One problem with American Express was that they refused this eminently sensible arrangement, expecting travellers to pay within a few days from a position about a thousand miles west of the Canary Islands.

5. *Carry cash* There is a lot to be said for regarding the dollar bill as the perfect travellers' cheque. There is no charge for issuing it, and it is acceptable everywhere, sometimes at a premium. A few years ago in Turkey, the up-market newspaper Çum Huriyet published the black market rates every day. There, is however, no safeguard in the event of loss.

Getting a Large Amount in an Emergency

This is a big problem, but it is not very likely to occur. Possible causes might be a fine by local Customs (however undeserved, it has to be paid before being appealed) or the purchase of a major piece of equipment. Generally major repairs take long enough for money to be remitted by routine means, but it is possible for estimates to be exceeded giving rise to an urgent need.

As a precaution, negotiate the maximum possible credit limits on credit cards, which should be good for £3000 each at the very least, and this gives quite a good sum available at very short notice. Both Visa/Barclaycard and Access/Mastercharge will make personal loans above the credit limit and are very prompt, so it might pay to carry appropriate application forms.

We have already mentioned that AmEx travel offices will cash quite large cheques for card holders. But I don't think this facility alone justifies the high annual charge.

In theory it ought to be possible to draw a certified cheque on the London (or New York) branch of a foreign bank and present it to the local branch of that bank for immediate payment. In practice it just doesn't work out.

Obtaining really large amounts (in this context) is an intractable problem; there is no certain solution that can be applied in all countries. I do recommend keeping a personal relationship with your home bank manager; if there is a crisis an understanding at a personal level can oil a lot of wheels. If you are going to be in one country for a fair time consider opening a local account and be known to the manager. Local advice at a friendly professional level is usually worth it.

All in all, the best way of getting a large amount in a hurry seems to be to get a lot of small amounts by various means and add them together. A nuisance, but effective. If you think it might be necessary, organize the methods in advance.

Banking Overseas

Considering the problem of getting cash country by country, I think it is fair to say the British will generally be astonished at the lack of customer convenience at retail banks in many parts of the world.

The USA

Here, banking is very fragmented and localized; there is no cheque card system, and cheques are not welcome outside a particular bank's locality so Visa or Mastercard are essential for drawing cash. Foreign money is certainly unwelcome anywhere; even the Canadians have trouble. Financially, the country is parochial; it is easier to make transactions between countries in Europe than between states in the USA.

The West Indies

Here one finds Barclays generally very efficient and they will accept UK cheque cards. It is not generally realized that Canada does a lot to help the more backward islands and Canadian banks are common, well organized and helpful. In a world league of bank helpfulness I would put Canada second only to the UK. Apart from the French islands where French banks and currency are used, and there are no significant problems, most islands either use the US dollar as legal tender (the British Virgins, for example) or tie their dollar to the US, and both currencies circulate side by side. Even on those islands with British sovereignty or strong connections, the pound sterling is not welcome, and this applies to the Bahamas and Bermuda too. Before leaving make sure to change local currency into US dollars as it can be difficult to do afterwards.

Europe

French banking is reasonable, and the most appallingly inefficient is in Italy, where modern banking is supposed to have been invented and the system does not appear to have changed since the prototype. Commissions charged are higher, chaos and error abound, and it is one of the few environments in Italy where they are habitually rude to the customer. The best banking services for the tourist are to be found in the more backward countries that are heavily dependent, economically, on tourism. Greece is an example where the service is very good. In Turkey, everything is very polite and correct but takes a long time with much cross-checking. Spain and Yugoslavia are tolerable, but it is useless to try anything out of the routine in Yugoslavia.

Expenditure

Now let us have a look at expenditure. I would like to quote a cost of living figure, but tastes differ so much that it would be meaningless. We have met a couple who claimed to live (exist?) in a small yacht in the Med on about £30 per week for everything (approximate adjustment made for 1986 prices). I would treat this with a little caution because I cannot see how their craft could continue to be maintained properly, though at the time it appeared to be well enough. Such a life-support existence would be feasible if the cruise were short and no maintenance were done; no replacements, no emergencies to be met, no sickness or injury, and few, if any, excursions into the interior, which are certainly part of our life.

In the later chapter on victualling and marketing, Laurel will discuss the relative costs of food and stores from country to country. With a fair sized boat one can take advantage of differentials or bargains and buy some things in bulk. By moving from place to place many costs do average out, except between continents.

The Med is undoubtedly the cheapest area to live in, and within that sea probably Greece and Turkey come off best, followed by Spain, Yugoslavia and Tunisia, then France some way behind and Italy last of all (1984–5). One of the reasons why some countries are cheap to live in is that a lot of imported or luxury goods are not available outside the big cities, which we avoid.

If we are having to budget for food, we allow £30 (1990) per person per week in the Med (the 1976 figure was £11). This will cover all food, wine, refreshments and an occasional meal ashore; except in Italy where restaurant prices are outrageously high for value received. The figure does not include fuel. It is, however, catering on a reasonably liberal scale: we could do it a lot cheaper and still enjoy life.

In the West Indies and the Bahamas, where the economy is dollar based and much is imported from the USA, the cost of living reflects this. One can live cheaply, but a bit primitively, on local breadfruit, eddoes, bananas, fish and rum. And why not? In 1982 our budget for a longish stay in the Grenadines was US $30 per person per week, and in the USA in 1983 it was much the same.

Insurance

The costs of insurance are substantial in the type of boat suitable for living in. In some countries, notably Italy and France, third party cover is obligatory, and there is talk of it becoming so in Greece, and I think anyone not so covered is an anti-social menace. However, there are a lot of yachtsmen who do not carry *full* cover.

We had good value for some years from the gentlemen of Lloyds, who behaved splendidly when we were struck by lightning. However, it became clear to them that they were not writing the right sort of policies, and instead of changing their policies they decided to write none at all. Our brokers (Fenchurch Marine Brokers) obtained reasonable cover elsewhere.

But there is no doubt that it is difficult to get cover for an ocean cruising boat, and virtually impossible if there are only two persons on board. I cannot convince underwriters that they are wrong here; they maintain that a small crew can get tired in poor conditions, but seem to forget that the Battle of the Atlantic was won by men, many of them yachtsmen by inclination, keeping watch and watch for weeks on end in appalling conditions.

If you do get good cover, then keep in touch with your broker. Become known.

It seems to me unlikely that anyone will get good cover in the Med for less than 1.5%., and that rates will be a lot higher elsewhere.

The ocean-going yachtsman badly needs a policy that will insure him against any third party claims, fire, lightning strike, and any structural damage, but excluding cosmetic finishing. It is often the latter that runs away with costs, and it is something most of us are prepared to do ourselves.

One odd feature is that US underwriters charge more for cover in European waters than for cover in the Western Hemisphere, while European underwriters rate the risks the other way round. This strongly suggests that rates are based entirely on personal hunch rather than on statistics.

Syndicates

The majority of craft we come across are manned by a married couple (the word 'married' being interpreted a little loosely), but there are a number of boats being sailed by syndicates, and as these are essentially financial arrangements this is perhaps the place for some comment. There are two broad kinds of syndicate. In the *Running Syndicate* the expenses of running the boat and living aboard are shared, but the boat herself belongs to only a part of the syndicate, perhaps to one person only. In a *Property Syndicate* all the members have shares in the boat, though not necessarily equal shares. It is evident that it is possible to have a combination of the two sorts.

In the first, there is no question of ownership of assets, thus the syndicate is comparatively easy to start, break up or alter as it goes along. Many running syndicates have no formal agreement; they run happily on a shared interest and good fellowship. Given goodwill all round, a break can be just as easy: the person who wishes to leave just packs up and goes. Cautious people might like to have a more positive agreement; I would, but few actually do.

It has to be recognized that the boatowner(s) have the right to withdraw their vessel. But they cannot reasonably exercise this right suddenly in a completely isolated port and thus leave the rest of the syndicate stranded. Likewise, members must not leave the owners stranded, supposing the boat needs a crew to sail. A period of notice needs to be agreed, and it should be expressed in two ways, both in time and in geography; i.e. there should be a minimum notice of say, two weeks, but that the break shall only take place in a reasonably accessible port, to which the vessel should be taken as soon as possible. New members can be added at any time, but I know of problems, where, for example, one member wishes to bring in a marvellous girl he met last night, and the others just do not see eye to eye with him about her value to the syndicate as a whole.

The loose agreement might at least define what types of expenditure are covered, e.g. housekeeping, ship's stores, fuel, repairs, replacements and so on. It should certainly appoint a book-keeper. It should ideally set up a contingency fund to help meet accidents or disaster; the decision to use the fund has to be a majority one, and it should be used only for an item too large to be met out of two (say) months' total contributions. Most people would accept simple provisions like that otherwise there is no point in starting. If disagreement becomes serious, expulsion or dissolution has to follow, even if a somewhat different syndicate re-forms.

In these circumstances the major problem is often the distribution of the contingency fund, especially if it is long standing and/or substantial. In theory it is possible to work out the refunds arithmetically, but a lot of syndicates have fairly frequent changes, and few of them have a computer. One terminating syndicate I knew (a German one), threw a fantastic party, inviting all yachtsmen in the port to drink the fund which was eventually done. The real problem is that goodwill is often thinned on a dissolution.

A running syndicate problem occurred when an aggrieved party considered that a major repair that became necessary arose from neglect by the owner before the formation of the syndicate, and could enhance the value of the vessel after the syndicate broke up. He felt this was a capital matter, not maintenance; the owner thought otherwise. Such arguments cannot be pre-defined, or pre-determined. They are questions that have to answered as and when they occur. All parties to a running syndicate must accept the vessel 'as is, where is', and they have to use their judgement as to future liabilities. Of course, an arbitration agreement would help.

The property syndicate, the second type, is concerned not only with running a boat from day to day, but also with the ownership of, and responsibility for, a very valuable piece of property. In these circumstances an agreement MUST be made in proper legal form, for though there will be no problems if goodwill prevails, the scope for bitterness, anger and nastiness when tempers become frayed after some real, or imagined, injustice or slight is so immense that the exercise can turn into a lawyers' benefit. Better a small fee for legal advice at the start.

The syndicate agreement must, therefore, lay down clearly:

Who is the skipper for purposes of running the ship (there can be only one).
How decisions, other than navigational ones, are reached.
Procedure for changes in the syndicate.
How unforeseen liabilities will be paid, e.g. reconstruction due to previous neglect or hidden defects.
Procedure for final dissolution.
Arrangements for arbitration.

No syndication agreement should ever give any one person a right of general veto. When all goes well, such a right is exercised with tolerance. But if one person gets disaffected, or has a breakdown perhaps, then such a bloody-minded partner can ruin everyone's life. For similar reasons, agreements should contain a clause that in the event of a death the remaining syndicate members have the right to buy out the deceased partner's equity at a valuation arrived at by a stated method. Though all the partners might be the best of friends, this happy relationship may not extend to an executor, or to a legatee of one of these friends. If the capital values are substantial, and exercising the right is liable to cause embarrassment to a partner, then it is possible to obtain a temporary, contingency insurance on a number of lives payable to the survivors on the death of one of them.

I do not think the concept of time-sharing has any relevance to the type of cruising we are considering. Come to think of it, I do not think it is much good for anyone except the organizing entrepreneur.

Marine Mortgages

Though vessels can be bought with marine mortgages, it would need a lot of careful weighing up before sailing off with such a burden. The finance companies would not be overjoyed to see their security, mobile as it is, disappearing to parts of the world where they could well have great difficulty and expense exercising any rights in the event of a default. Even if they granted a loan, it would have to be considered less secure than a loan on a boat owned by a man in a steady job, and who never left the country in her, and this would probably lead to a higher rate of interest.

And how would you pay the regular, very large, instalments? Out of a substantial pension, perhaps, if you are lucky enough to have one — but one is very unlikely to earn that sort of income while actually cruising. It has been done by investing a large sum in property and using the net rental of the property to meet the mortgage payments on the yacht, but this presupposes that the former is greater than the latter. Remember that the finance company is in the investment business too, and in my experience it would be a very special investment opportunity that would make that sort of deal profitable after taking into account all the on-costs of the various arrangements.

To try to earn enough as one goes along to meet mortgage payments is crazy, other than for best-selling novelists, artists who can regularly sell a load of rubbish to the Tate Gallery or hard drug smugglers. The latter will assuredly have their yacht confiscated when they are inevitably caught, so the less equity they have in her the better. They should mortgage to the hilt.

But it must be possible to get some idea of what it will all cost?

I have been persuaded, against my better judgement, to be a little more specific about the costs of wandering abroad. This is, of course, to be on a hiding to nothing, for I will be trying to say how long your piece of string is. On the other hand I do have some data, thanks mainly to Laurel's elementary but effective accounting methods, and I do have a certain amount of both personal and borrowed experience of several boats, so here goes. The jargon may be mathematical, but I will give some examples at the end. We are *forecasting*, remember. Currency is immaterial for this exercise, provided you do not mix them; reckon using the same one throughout.

Let the price or current value of the craft be **P**

Let the building material factor be **B** (see Table 1, below)

Let the rig factor be **R** (see Table 2)

Let the age (boat, not crew) factor be **A** (see Table 3)

Let the physical capability of each of the crew be **E** (see Table 4)

Let the displacement of the boat in tons be **T** (to the nearest whole number)

Let the cost of the sea-going inventory be **F**.

Table 1   Building material factor **B**

Fibreglass (GRP)	1.0	Steel	1.35
Aluminium alloy	1.1	Teak	1.35
Ferrocement	1.2	Other timbers	1.4

Table 2   Rig factor **R**

Sloop	1.0	Wishbone or staysail	
Cutter	1.05	schooner	1.15
Yawl or Ketch	1.1	Schooner	1.2

If craft is gaff or sprit rigged multiply each of above by 1.1. For example a gaff schooner would be 1.2 × 1.1 = 1.32.

Table 3   Age factor **A**

Less than one year	1.0	10 years but less than 20	1.4
1 year, but less than 5	1.05	20 years but less than 50	1.8
5 years but less than 10	1.2	50 years or over	2.6

Table 4.   How about the crew — **E**?

A really fit person well used to manual labour   3.0

Average person 16–40 years, according to fitness   2.0–2.6

Average person 12–15, or 41–60 according to fitness   1.8–2.3

Average person over 60, according to fitness   1.1–1.9

Someone willing and capable, but completely out of condition   0.9–1.1

A partially disabled person but willing and able to keep a lookout, pass tools, brew tea, and give first aid.   0.5–0.8

Maintenance cost

The total annual maintenance cost is divided into two parts, of which one is dependent completely on the ship and her gear, while the other takes into account the capacity of the crew to do things themselves.

Obviously they cannot do everything, or it is very rare that this is the case, and it would require unusual combinations and levels of skills. Our assumption is for an amateur and willing, but not specially skilled, crew. The formula works only for sailing craft because I have no data for motor yachts. The costs of engine maintenance in a sailing yacht are included with the broad assumption that the boat and her engine are proportional to each other in size and condition. Well, I do have to make some assumptions, don't I?

The first part m_1 is:

$$m_1 = 0.02 \, (P \times B \times R \times A + F)$$

which represents maintaining engine, structure, rigging, and replacing them from time to time. It is a long-term annual average.

The second part, m_2 is:

$$m_2 = \frac{B \times R \times A \times T \times 40}{\text{sum of E}}$$

The total expected annual allowance for the ship **M** is given by adding these two, thus: $M = m_1 + m_2$.

If you are still with me, you must be keen, so let us look at some examples; we will take three to show a fair cross-section of types.

A. A 50 year old gaff schooner, built of pine on oak, displacing 36 tons, costing in good sea-going order £30,000 and with an inventory of about £5000. So P = 30,000; B = 1.4; R = 1.32; A = 2.6; and F = 5000.

$$\begin{aligned} m_1 &= 0.02 \, (30{,}000 \times 1.4 \times 1.32 \times 2.6 + 5000) \\ &= 0.02 \times (144{,}144 + 5000) \\ &= 0.02 \times 149{,}144 = £2983 \text{ per annum.} \end{aligned}$$

She will have four young crew: a sporty accountant, and his wife who is something of an athlete, a bricklayer, and his wife who is not too fit. These might rate, in order: 2.6, 2.3, 3.0, and 1.4, giving a total crew worth, from this point of view, 9.3 as E.

Thus $m_2 = 1.4 \times 1.32 \times 2.6 \times 36 \times 40 \div 9.3 = £744$.

One might expect to budget for maintenance, then M = 2983 + 744 = £3727 per annum. (Always round up.)

B. A bermudan steel ketch, 10 years old, displacing 20 tons, worth £50,000 with a £7000 inventory. She is crewed by a 54 year old fit man, his out-of-condition wife, and a 15 year old fit daughter. In this case P = 50,000; B = 1.35; R = 1.1 × 1.1 = 1.21; A = 1.4; F = 7000.

$$\begin{aligned} m_1 &= 0.02 \, (50000 \times 1.35 \times 1.21 \times 1.4 + 7000) \\ &= 0.02 \, (114345 + 7000) = £2427 \\ m_2 &= 1.35 \times 1.21 \times 1.4 \times 20 \times 40 \div (2.2 + 1.0 + 2.0) \\ &= £352 \end{aligned}$$

So her total expected maintenance **M** would be 2427 + 352 = £2779 per annum.

The owner presumably gave up a good job and went from Riches to Rags.

C. A new fibreglass sloop, costing £32,000 with inventory costing £4000, displacement 9 tons. Her crew are an elderly couple; he is 64 and fairly fit, but his wife has arthritis and has difficulty with ladders.

$$m_1 = 0.02 (32000 \times 1.0 \times 1.0 \times 1.0 + 4000) = £720$$
$$m_2 = 1.0 \times 1.0 \times 1.0 \times 9 \times 10 \div (1.2 + 0.7) = £189$$

So her maintenance might well cost £909 per annum.

Since gathering the data for the foregoing the range of electronic gadgets has increased beyond my expectation, and the amount that has to be spent, not only on buying new, but on maintaining what has been installed is showing signs of getting out of hand. All consideration of electronic maintenance is excluded from the above estimates. The more you have, the more you spend, because modern electronics are based on the 'do not repair' outlook. It should read, 'Do not mend; go out and spend'.

Insurance again

If the boat is insured there will be another annual expense equal to the value of the boat with her inventory multiplied by the insurance rate, that is $i(P + F)$, where i is the insurance rate which, as discussed earlier, usually lies between 1.0 and 2.5% depending on cruising areas.

Even if the boat is uninsured, the crew should keep a contingency fund and start this off at the beginning with 1% at least of the boat's value; but they should add to this from time to time. I think it ought to be a budget item of about 0.25% of the boat's value. If the boat is insured, then a sum equal to the excess (the 'deductible' in the USA) should be kept on one side in a realizable investment, or in a deposit account on short call.

Personal Costs

Other costs that have to be met consist of the housekeeping bills, that is feeding the brutes. In 1990, that appeared to lie between £20 and £30 per person per week in the Mediterranean, depending on tastes (it could be more if you lived in luxury), or $35 to $40 per person per week in the West Indies. Again it is possible to go wildly outside the figures, but they are a guide.

What your pleasures are, I have no way of knowing, nor do I think I ought to tell you what ours are. You'll just have to sort this one out for yourself.

There are other costs that have to be budgeted for, and these are particular to the person too. There will be the occasional trip back home to see the folks, which is coupled with buying spare parts, thus mixing sentiment with hard-headedness. You will have expenditure on any property or chattels you keep in the old country. You will perhaps have medical insurance, which is no cheap item. Worldwide cover is expensive.

Obviously, I cannot comment on what allowances you make in 'your bits', but in 'my bits' above I would say that, if you do it all in a thinking way, you should not be more than 50% out. That is not a bad approximation in these circumstances.

CHAPTER FOUR

A Yacht to Live In

'Were I to chuse a shippe for myselfe i would have her sail well yet stronglye built, her decks flush and flat, and so roomy that men might pass with ease.'

The yacht is to be more than just a nautical vehicle: she is to be a home. This puts a very important requirement into the considerations, because many boats that are a joy to sail would make abominable homes, and of course vice versa. From reading accounts written by mile-hungry ocean voyagers, it is apparent that few, if any, spend more than 40 per cent of their time at sea. In our case, over the last six years our average number of days when we were at sea was 95 per year, which is just over one day in four. In our busiest year with three ocean passages it was 118. Many others spend less time at sea, especially those who stay in the Mediterranean where sea-going in winter is, to say the least, uncongenial and even downright dangerous.

It must also be borne in mind that even at sea one is living aboard the yacht, and that is a different thing from doing a fortnight's cruise. A degree of discomfort or inconvenience that is acceptable for a week or two rapidly becomes intolerable over a long period.

Size and Type

With the exception of the idle rich, most of us are subject to financial restraint. The reader has to balance the amount of boat to the amount of money and to the size of the available crew, and the answer has much to do with personal preference.

It is a mistake to try to live in too small a boat. Small size admittedly requires less energy to handle and to maintain, but the extra difficulty of moving about, the unavoidable close intimacy, and the obtrusiveness of all those stores for which there is no locker, make a breeding ground for irritation. I know a couple still living aboard a 25-footer after crossing the Atlantic in her, but they are young and very much in love, as well as being short of personal possessions. A German couple lived in a 24 foot boat with an Alsatian dog. Next year we met them in a 68 foot converted Baltic trader, having gone from one extreme to another.

A yacht that is too big can be a liability, of course. A couple limiting their cruising to sheltered waters under power could expect to cope easily with 75 feet, but one has also to think of mooring fees and maintenance. Surprisingly, gear does not always cost more in the bigger sizes; often chandlery for yachts is fancy, of materials chosen for their looks rather than their strength, and the ability to use fittings made for small tugs or barges can save money in some cases.

Our own *Fare Well* is a 55 foot ketch of about 30 tons displacement. We have sailed her a lot, and Laurel, my wife and mate, and usually sole crew, is a lightweight five-footer with a congenitally dislocated hip. However, our last Atlantic crossing left us both tired, and a severe spring gale off Corsica reminded us both of advancing years. The boat is fine, but we are aging faster than she is.

I feel that for a monohull a waterline length of 33 to 37 feet, a beam of just over a third of that, and not too V-shaped in cross-section will provide a home that can be comfortable, have enough storage space, be easy enough to manage even when years advance, and be reasonably economical to moor and slip.

Multihulls

This is the time to mention multihulls. They certainly give more boat for the money, but they have compensating disadvantages. When heavily loaded, and in our life they always will be, they seem to lose proportionately more performance than a monohull. It is also necessary to go up in size to get enough headroom in the living accommodation. One can get by with a shorter overall length than a monohull, and whereas the latter might run to some 40 or 50 feet, a multihull might provide as good accommodation on 33 or 40 feet. But again there is a disadvantage in the multihull's beam: berthing becomes more difficult, and when it has to be paid for much more expensive, the loading being 50 to 100 per cent. This is a big factor in the Mediterranean; it is less significant in the West Indies where one spends a lot more time swinging to a single anchor, and it is even less significant in the Bahamas where many of the best harbours are closed to the deeper-draughted monohulls. It's horses for courses.

Motor yachts

It is not easy to be a long term liveaboard cruiser in a pure motor yacht, partly because long passages are virtually impossible, and also because one must be much more cautious about the weather. We do know of several, all in the Mediterranean but polarized somewhat between Greek and French waters; in the latter they have the attractive canal system, and in the former there is much scope for short sheltered passages. Another venue is the Intra-Coastal waterway in the USA, but that is rather a special case as, apart from a few Canadians, most

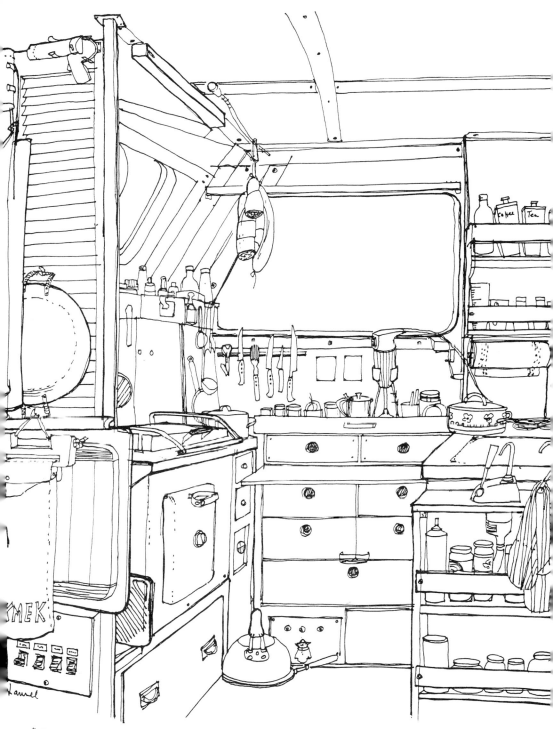

"FAREWELL"S GALLEY

yachts there are in their home waters. As Laurel and I seem to be unwilling to give up this life, maybe motoring will be our eventual mode. Most of the motorboaters we know are older than we are; others feel they lack the confidence to learn to sail.

Of course a motor yacht provides considerably more comfort than a sailing yacht of the same length. I see no reason to adopt a superior attitude to the dedicated motor yachtsman. Typically he runs his boat well and safely, and conforms to cruising etiquette much better than the bare-boat charter people. Long-term cruising is an attitude of mind.

The motorsailer

There is a lot to be said for the motorsailer in the Mediterranean. The powerful engine capable of hull speed into a force 6 wind and short sea is most reassuring in the unsettled weather at the beginning and end of season, while the ability to set a fair spread of canvas on a long passage saves a lot of fuel and gives her a much easier motion. It is having the option of two adequate power systems that impresses me, but I think it important that both are efficient. I wish now that we had installed a bigger engine than our present 62 hp. It's nice to be able to move about the engineroom, but a bit more potential thrust would be a good use for the space.

I hope it is unnecessary to advise against the petrol engine. I notice that a flotilla company operating in Greece has this year introduced boats fitted with these time-bombs. I have swept up after too many nasty accidents involving petrol in boats, and I maintain that even in the hands of the experienced user the system is dangerous. Even in the USA where the low price of gasoline has favoured the petrol engine, there is now a trend away from them. In the Mediterranean it is often difficult to get petrol except in cans.

New Boat or Old?

The process of selection introduces the alternatives: new or second-hand, one-off or a production boat?

This is the time for sweeping generalizations, and we will have plenty. It is a highly opinionated part of the book because it is impossible to be completely objective, for choosing a boat to live in is as subjective as choosing a wife. I suspect that these days it is becoming easier to correct an unfortunate choice of spouse than to change boats.

Production boats make less good homes than one-off vessels.

Professional yacht designers seem to have no idea how to design a yacht for long-term cruising.

Looking at these two generalizations, first go back a few years to the days when a designer would be commissioned by a gentleman to produce a yacht for a specific purpose. The designer would try hard to satisfy his client, and would go to some lengths to find out exactly what was needed. Now and then he must have succeeded, or we presume so, because in those days owners tended to keep the same boat for a longish time.

Nowadays people keep boats for a very short time, and there is less profit for the designer in the modest one-off for a private owner. By designing a prototype for a production run the naval architect hopes for extending royalties and a wider dissemination of his name, for the designer is in the rat-race too. Because this is the market he is aiming at, his general arrangement plan will have more to do with production engineering and market research than with real suitability for the sea. Though the word 'cruising' will appear in the advertising, fashion will dictate her shape and rig, she will have more than a nodding acquaintance with the IOR rating rules, and the marketing men will demand as many bunks as it is possible to get in. Probably, when sold, she will spend most of her life at moorings, and that is about the right place for her.

If one needs a readymade boat I believe in going to the second-hand market, and even then picking a vessel that is capable of some alteration without losing her charm. There are good boats about, and they often have the advantage of a good inventory that saves a lot of money. In general boats from the boards of American designers tend to be more suitable for cruising than those of other nationalities, though the Dutch do not do too badly. The chief differentiating factors are that less attention is paid to rating rules, leading to more attention being paid to stowage, ease of handling under both sail and power, crew comfort and a nice appearance.

If you are building from new, or carrying out any major task and feel you have to have professional advice, then try to find a naval architect who has actually lived in a cruising yacht. They are understandably rare, because one would not make much of a living swanning about the Med, but it is quite an important point, like choosing a land architect who lives in a house of his own design. Have you noticed how most of them seem to live in Georgian houses?

A rare professional designer who qualifies is Bill Arnott Fowler, an Englishman living aboard his *Xicale*, which he designed himself. We last met in Antigua. Of course there may be others, but I have not met any.

If you are trying to buy second-hand, do not expect very much help from yacht brokers. Even if you itemise carefully exactly what you are looking for, you will be sent, for a time, details of craft that are manifestly unsuitable for your purpose, and then shortly you will be sent nothing further. This is because brokers generally do not understand what living aboard is all about, but then it is difficult to do so unless you have actually done it.

Britain is not the only place to look for a boat. There are many starters in this life, who for one reason or another do not get very far. Perhaps they have not done their homework. In any event there are often bargains to be picked up in Gibraltar, the Canary Islands, southern Spain or Portugal where they have been abandoned by a disillusioned crew.

Many yachts winter on the Cote d'Azur if they can afford it, and although most of these are likely to be holiday or luxury craft there is a substantial total turnover, so there are often suitable boats on offer. Brokers are used less in France because of the silly commission rate, and marinas often have many boats with *A vendre* (For sale) signs on them.

An area where liveaboard people are to be found in winter is round Elba and Cala Galera (Tuscany), while the less well-heeled or more dedicated are to be found wintering in Larnaca (Cyprus) or Kus Adasi (Turkey). The Balearics and Alicante are further winter haunts.

In the Western Hemisphere, Fort Lauderdale and vicinity seems to moor as many craft as the whole of Europe put together, and the Chesapeake cannot be far behind. Given the high standard of US cruising yacht design, one should find something there.

English language magazines where suitable boats may be advertised are *Cruising World* (Newport, RI), and *Yachting Monthly* (England). *Yachting World* (England) has a lot of brokers' advertisements, and *Practical Boat Owner* (England) is useful for the smaller sizes.

Buying a Bare Hull

If the extent of alterations required is large, or one's requirements are very esoteric, one should consider buying a hull and then finishing it. This is basically what we did, though I did have some say in the design of the hull too. Completing a hull is not so difficult as may be imagined, and the cost of the bare shell itself is a surprisingly small fraction of the total cost of a professionally built boat, often about one-sixth. This means that there is a lot of work in finishing it, and it is a long time-consuming project. Ours took 4000 man-hours of amateur work. We had a few jobs done by professionals, and in almost every case this work had to be done again by somebody else, often myself. An intelligent and manually competent person with access to a good reference library can out-perform some of the ham-fisted, thick cowboys who menace today's British yacht industry.

> I will arise and go now, and go where the wind is free,
> And a fine keelboat build there,
> Of wood and metal made.
> Nine summers will I sail her,
> With a cat for the company;
> And live content in the awning's shade.

Any serious cruising means being prepared to anchor, with ground tackle and deck gear and structure that are substantial enough to hold in open roadsteads. The yacht's tender needs thought too: it may have to be rowed or motored for some distance across exposed waters when they are a lot rougher than this. (photo Mark Brackenbury)

Weatherliness

'A well bowed shippe so swiftly presseth the water as that it foameth, and in the dark night sparkleth like fire. If the Bow bee too narrow . . . she pitcheth her head into the sea; so that the meane is the best, if her after way be answerable.'

I have already referred to the yacht that is a joy to sail but hell to live in. Understandably, most dreamers and planners contemplate a boat with good performance; yachting editors and cruising correspondents write endlessly about it, recalling with enthusiasm the drenching they got batting to windward for a few hours last weekend. A glorious sail! Yes, but they went home afterwards for a hot bath and change of clothes.

It's a bit different doing it for days on end, trying meanwhile to prepare and cook good meals, to do the maintenance and repairs, and to keep dry clothing. Many dedicated cruisers never beat to windward at all. Our own motto is 'if you have to beat, you're going to the wrong place.' On a long passage it is occasionally necessary to compromise, but we have been known to heave-to in mid-ocean when confronted by an unseasonal heading force 6 and wait for it to change. It is not that our heavy Bermudan ketch will not go to windward (she will, though not very well), it is a question of enjoying life and having all the time in the world to do it. Generally we do not approach closer to the wind than 55°; if we do it is usually for a short leg or to keep a better offing, and even then we tend to run the engine at half revs, which contributes some ever-welcome amps as well as thrust and gets the unfortunate episode over sooner.

High performance

One sometimes finds the opinion that high sailing performance is a potential safety factor. Let us examine this hypothesis. In 36,000 miles of cruising the following have been our 'dangerous situations':

(a)   A fire at sea
(b)   A hurricane
(c)   Damage from a heavy squall, or possibly a waterspout in the Gulf Stream
(d)   A lightning strike
(e)   A shaft coupling disintegrated, leaving a big leak
(f)   I fell and hurt myself in a gale off Cap Corse
(g)   The forehatch was left improperly secured and the forepeak filled with water
(h)   The genoa furling gear failed, and at the same time I allowed the trailing sheet to foul the screw.

In addition we have endured nine other gales of force 8 or over, with no worries other than understandable apprehension.

At no other time in 36,000 miles over ten years were we in danger, and at no time would high performance on the wind have been of any benefit whatsoever. Nor any other high performance for that matter.

Let us contrast that with the racing fleet, which we suppose to be the exemplars of high performance. In the Fastnet Race of 1979 the fleet met a short summer gale of admittedly above average severity, but managed to score a world record for the number of distress signals per square mile of sea. The RYA enquiry served to encourage the already enormous complacency of the ocean racing industry. It concluded that there was no firm evidence that any particular design feature was common to all the sinkings or damage, but failed to bring home that the lightness of construction was a common feature together with the flimsiness of spars and rigging, and even more so the unseamanlike nature of the sail plan encouraged by a rating rule that is dangerous. However, the enquiry failed to take evidence from cruising yachts that were in the area at the time. They, as far as we know, were all able to come through without assistance.

It is significant that a small American cruising yacht sailed through the worst of that storm with the owner, his wife, and two children under four on board, and wrote home that they had 'had a rough passage'. So far as I know the RYA did not seek their evidence, which was that of very experienced cruising sailors.

My opinion is that for safe cruising one should seek well tried and proven dispositions of sail, improved where appropriate by new materials, make everything very strong, and so arrange matters that any sail can be furled or trimmed by one person without recourse to power assistance.

In Mediterranean conditions, where winds are often light and the seas can be unexpectedly and uncomfortably short and steep, we find we use the engine much more than we expected to. The number of engine hours per year has remained fairly constant, and has not increased much with age, but in any case with fridge, running lights and other domestic conveniences some battery charging is needed. In addition, in the Med a lot of passages are of 30 to 50 miles, and if the wind changes or drops (it often does in the evening) there is a strong incentive to set the iron topsail for an hour or so to ensure timely arrival in a good berth before the whole port is full of nasty, noisy, Italian motor yachts.

In the Bahamas and West Indies things are somewhat different. Winds are more reliable, it is easier to sail to an anchorage and/or weigh under sail, and the line of the Windward Islands runs conveniently across the wind, generally giving a comfortable reach in both directions.

Ease of Handling

A constant assumption throughout this book is a short-handed crew. The yacht must handle easily, whether sailing, motoring, berthing or unberthing. It is no good having a beautifully balanced sailing boat if your attempts to back her into an awkward slot in a strong cross-wind leave you tired, cross, and feeling foolish under the eyes of the whole town out for their evening stroll. These things are not incompatible; it is just that some designers, particularly those who have made their name in racing, have never learned how to relate them.

To be able to handle sail quickly, and without too much effort, is vital to both comfort and safety. No matter how much you tell yourself that by keeping alert (or even several lerts) you will never have to do anything in a hurry, sooner or later you will slip up. I have, several times.

We once rounded Cape Malea in southern Greece, leaving it close aboard, ghosting under every stitch of canvas we could set. The cape is a steep cliff some 2,000 feet high and as the Admiralty Pilot warned, on the other side there was a katabatic wind of great force. The log was reading 10½ before I got the mizzen staysail down, and I never did furl the 670 square feet genoa. It would not let me. As we sped south towards Africa at right angles to our intended course, the wind gradually eased and we re-established tenuous control.

On another occasion I fought that *maladetto* genoa for more than an hour at the end of the bowsprit which was dunking me every half minute. With each dunk the sea surged up my trouser legs leaving by the neckhole in my oilskins, and doing unmentionable mischief en route. Real cruising men are pledged to avoid such heroics, so shortly after these incidents we bought roller reefing/furling gear for the headsail.

Good roller gear, which can reef as well as furl a sail, solves a lot of problems, but in the large sizes it still requires a lot of physical effort, though reasonably reliable electrical winding gear is now available. Roller headsails are sometimes held to be less aerodynamically efficient than hoisted headsails. I do not think the difference when the whole sail is set is significant to the cruising yachtsman, while the ability to reef a headsail a little, a lot, or a little bit more or less, more than compensates for marginal losses. The whole system of roller reefing/furling is completely appropriate for short-handed sailing. Jams, snarl-ups and breakdowns are not more frequent than conventional foredeck foul-ups, and the cost of the gear is offset by the fewer headsails required.

It would, I think, be advisable not to follow our example of fitting the headsail roller with a big, 175 per cent overlap genoa. Ours is 670 square feet and a lovely puller, but it is also a bit of a menace on occasions when the wind gets up, as it is difficult for one person to tack it round the inner forestay. For a cutter foretriangle I think the roller headsail should be a slightly oversize yankee. This means that in addition to the forestay about which the roller genoa works there is a need for a twin forestay on which to set a light-weather genoa, but as I like two of everything important this is not much of a disadvantage. There are occasions when the unused forestay gets wrapped into the rolls, usually while rolling up before a strong wind, but one soon gets a technique for avoiding this.

It is impossible to recommend any particular gear because new ones come and go frequently. Unfortunately it is not advisable to seek sailmakers' advice, as most sailmakers either have their own gear or are agents for one or two, and objective advice is difficult to get. Very few people, and I am not among them, have experience of more than one or two different makes; real deep-sea experience I mean. As with all things still in course of development, there are still snags and problems; you just have to use whatever advice you can get and apply your own judgement.

Roller mainsails are not so good as headsails. The long luff of Bermudan mainsails means that the sort set externally to the mast tend to sag away from it, and to add very considerably to the compression strain on the spar without the vibration-deadening effect of the continuous contact via the slides or luff rope. Mainsails that roll inside the mast are available, and I have no intimate knowledge of them, but I would be much concerned about possible chafe of the sailcloth at the mast slot on the sort of voyages many long cruisers habitually make. Foul-up problems are probably not too significant and unlikely to be much worse than with a headsail. But I have noticed one gear, Hood's, to have a serious problem in harbour, when with strong winds the mast slot turns itself into a gigantic organ pipe, and the whole place is disturbed with the hooting of a demented owl. By 1990 this problem seems to have been solved.

Whatever rig you have, make sure there is no sail you cannot furl singlehanded, and quickly too. In these circumstances the divided rig makes a lot of sense, but remember that one cannot furl or reef all the sails simultaneously. Standing rigging should not be the flimsy affair of the racing fleet: it must be able to support full canvas in gale strength squalls, then as sail is reduced things will get better. There is one case to watch which I have found little appreciated nowadays: in gaff-rigged craft when the main is furled before reducing the headsails, there is still great compression in the mast and without the pull of the mainsail hoops to damp vibration it is quite possible to lose it.

The long-distance cruiser's status symbol, especially in France. In my opinion such domes are little use. They soon become scratched and crazed, then more and more opaque. Better to have a proper wheelhouse.

In general a well balanced ketch rig virtually eliminates the need for reefing. We almost never do so because the possiblities are such that one can always find a comfortable way of setting whole sails. An exception is that I have a very deep reef on the main which avoids the need for a trysail. We have used it once in ten years. Our mizzen has no reefing system.

If you have a mainsail that requires reefing, then the system depends on personal preference influenced by size of sail. For short-handed crews slab reefing is dubious above an area of 400 square feet, but sails that big are getting dubious in our context anyway. It is in sloops and cutters that reefing becomes very important, and the frequent necessity of getting up there on the high bit of boat in bad weather is a strong argument against the single-master. Reef points should be avoided: you have to be up there even longer.

All booms but especially main booms should have a stout gallows, not only for stowing in harbour but also with slots in the outboard ends so that the boom can be easily bowsed down to leeward to be worked on. It is far easier and safer to hold onto a rigidly fixed boom than to cling to one that is allowed even a little movement. If the gallows is fitted about two-thirds of the length of the boom from the mast it is possible to arrange a slot on the extreme end, so that the end of the boom when in it is a foot or so outboard of the ship's side, thus

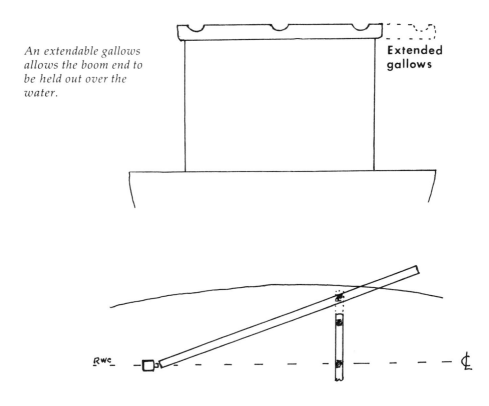

An extendable gallows allows the boom end to be held out over the water.

Extended gallows

RWC

providing a good lifting point for bringing heavy weights on board, or recovering people from a watery environment.

What applies to furling, applies to sheeting too. When one is short-handed, all sheets and controlling cordage of all types should, so far as is possible, be led to a sheltered place, preferably a cockpit. It will not do to have one or more sails flog while you sheet the others. Even a few seconds' hard flogging in a severe squall can demolish a clew.

With roller furling, if heavy weather is expected then over-roll by a few turns. I once left our 8 oz genoa loosely rolled, with perhaps a square foot or so still off the roll. When a Gulf Stream squall hit us in the middle of the night the force was enough to pull all taut and effectively unroll a few feet of sail, which disintegrated in seconds. An 11 oz sail that was set survived in usable state but a conventionally, though hastily, furled mainsail was ripped out of its gaskets and was lost too. One cannot go about continually taking precautions against squalls of this extreme violence of course, but where their occurrence is possible or likely, then one should.

Roller reefing/furling does partially solve a problem of stowage, for sails so set remain above deck and also one needs fewer separate sails. Space below in a long-cruising boat is so valuable that many stow their sails on deck. It is possible to have a sailbag such that a headsail can be put in it while it is still hanked on its stay. It does not look very elegant, making the average yacht look as if she has a nosebag on. It is quite important that all sails should be covered when not in use. Simple light covers will do: all that is necessary is to stop ultraviolet light damaging the synthetic cloth.

Hull Shape

While for most passage-making a deep keel is desirable, except perhaps over the Bahama Banks, there are innumerable little ports and bays where the deeper boats cannot go but where a shallow draught can find most wonderful peace. There are also opportunities for exploring canals and rivers, especially those of France, or the lovely Intra-Coastal Waterway of the US east coast. These factors point the need for a compromise, and I would opt for a monohull draught of 5 feet 6 inches. *Fare Well* was designed for 6 feet and for her size that is quite modest, but she has not ended up that way — and cruising yachts never do, because no one can ever believe the incredible weight of things that they need to carry on long voyages. GOLDEN RULE: IN EVERY CASE, DRAUGHT WHEN CRUISING WITH FULL LIVING LOAD WILL BE AT LEAST 6 INCHES MORE THAN EXPECTED.

Centreboards are not an ideal answer. When the Bollay family took their Rhodes-designed c.b. sloop *Snowgoose* into the French canals they eventually exported a good part of the mineral wealth of the country, which had got itself jammed up the trunking, and it took a lot of getting out. Centreboards can be awkward to manage in larger boats because they have to be heavy to be strong enough to take the big lateral cantilever strains. In smaller boats the draught need not be so very deep anyway, so that centreboards are perhaps an unnecessary complication.

It is worth mentioning that *Fare Well* while drawing 6 feet 7 inches cruised the Bahamas and the full length of the Intra-Coastal Waterway without any serious problems. We found the bottom a few times; once we stuck on a coral head for a tide, but got off unaided by laying out our two bower anchors.

Long overhangs have a sporty look, but are expensive in mooring and construction; they add to the maintenance and contribute little to usable boat. I do not think they are an advantage for our purpose.

The retroussé stern and spade rudder hung right aft pose problems for a cruising yacht. Not only does one lose a commodious locker and some very valuable deck space, but if one berths stern-to, as in most Mediterranean ports, this configuration can be a positive hazard. Lying bows-to is an alternative that has its own disadvantages, which I will refer to under anchoring. The problem with a deep rudder right aft is that quays in the Med (and elsewhere) seldom have vertical faces to their full apparent depth. Very often they are ballasted to just below water level, and odd rocks together with the assorted detritus of centuries extend some distance from the quay. The sloping transom makes passing to and from the quay more difficult, but on the other hand it is a very good site for a permanent bathing ladder.

Twin screws are an unnecessary luxury for sailing yachts in the sizes we are contemplating, but for the pure motor yacht they would make a lot of sense. Although undoubtedly vulnerable in canals, there will be occasions in less frequented parts where the ability to limp home might be a blessing. Away from the British or US coasts help is not so readily available, or even not at all. In some parts we have visited, VHF channel 16 may be of more use for ordering a taxi.

Hull Construction

It is in craft over 33 feet waterline that steel becomes an economical material. Then it becomes possible to have a hull of plate thickness sufficient to stand a variety of abuses, including abrasion and impact. In fact the only short-term danger to a steel hull is the tin-opener effect typified by striking a sharp rocky pinnacle. It is the most effectively resistant material to ice, though that rarely concerns us. Once the plate thickness rises above 4mm, this danger recedes for the speeds we are likely to reach. The bottom of our keel is 1½-inch plate, rounded up at the forefoot, and when we sledded up 2 feet out of the water after striking a coral head at seven knots the scratches on the steel were less than a millimetre deep.

Maintenance is heavier with steel, but it is unskilled labour for the most part, and the dedicated cruiser is there all the time to do it. If the hull is initially shot-blasted to an even grey, then instantly coated with epoxy-based cover to a thickness of half a millimetre, you have a good basis, but it is important to touch up damage to this film as soon as possible. *Fare Well's* initial paint job lasted eight years, and even then only needed redoing near the waterline. I have heard of people who like zinc or aluminium spraying, but I believe this actually weakens the bond of the epoxy to the steel, though there may be some merit in epoxy-zinc as a paint. I think one can get too clever over this problem; the vital thing is to get the strongest possible skin to adhere in the strongest possible way, and any minor damage to the coating below the waterline ought to be taken care of by fitting good sacrificial zinc anodes, the life and effectiveness of which can be periodically checked.

Steel hulls do not leak, except through contrived openings. Similarly, fibreglass hulls ought not to leak, but strength and reliability depends on the quality of the materials and also on the conscientiousness of the laminators; factors which are difficult to assess in a second-hand boat later on in its life. Hulls of this material have been known to crack, particularly where skegs or keels adjoin the hull, and this seems to happen irrespective of the reputation of the yard. The material abrades very easily, which is very important if one visits non-yachty harbours where there are fishing boats with sharp steel projections, like metallic porcupines. It burns easily, and is a poor conductor of electricity which can cause it to disintegrate in lightning strikes, which are much more common in tropical climes. Like steel, it is not habitually eaten by any known animal (except Greek goats), but it does have its equivalent to corrosion, osmosis, which can be difficult to deal with. It is expensive on a one-off basis but this can be ameliorated by using the sandwich method, which has the great advantage of insulating the skin and is therefore an appreciated method of building for the hotter climates.

Ferrocement boats have a bad reputation, which is not fully deserved. The well built hull is very good indeed, but poor technique

A deep rudder hung well aft near the transom is vulnerable when mooring stern-to.

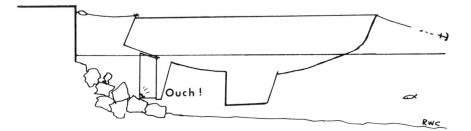

gives rise to nautical disasters. I would consider a hull made by the Wroxham firm of Windboats to be worth a second look, as I have seen some very good work of theirs. As for the material, abrasion resistance is poor compared to metal, though better than GRP. Impact resistance is quite good for boats with a heavy steel reinforcement, but chicken wire, often used by amateurs because it is cheaper, lighter and easier to shape, is very vulnerable. Maintenance is a lot less of a problem than with steel. Ferro is thought of as being the cheapest material for a one-off amateur built hull, but so much depends on standards. In any case the cost of the hull is likely to be between one-sixth and one-fifth of the total cost of building. Resale of these boats is supposed to be difficult, but those with experience tell me they are much like any one-off: it depends on the quality.

A wooden hull has a lovely feel about it, but it presents many problems. All sorts of things eat it, and it rots and grows fungi, problems which are all much worse in warm climates. Hulls built traditionally are subject to leaks. It can be easily repaired in backward communities, though often good hardwoods are hard to come by. Abrasion resistance is moderate, and whereas impact is unlikely to penetrate because of wood's elasticity, it can lead to planks springing, or to distortion with multiple small leaks that can be hell to stem. I have little knowledge of the more recent wood techniques, but I do use a lot of epoxy resin aboard *Fare Well*, and have tried it in various ways on woodwork, so that I have a feeling that its use now as a sealer/adhesive bears examination.

An aluminium hull has some of the properties of steel, but is lighter and not nearly so resistant to damage, a fact that is apparent in many a large repair yard. One of its principal problems is that it is softer than steel and dents very easily. It is vulnerable to electrolytic problems if great care is not taken over the selection of alloys and fittings, and it is by no means unknown for the wrong alloy to creep in because the right one is temporarily unavailable at the yard. It is expensive to build and extremely difficult, not to say impossible, to get repaired neatly outside the major sophisticated yachting venues.

Decks should be made of sheet material and never rely on caulking for their watertightness. If they do, they will leak, which is a catalyst for rot and marital discord.

Long-term Value

Whether a particular yacht will retain or lose pecuniary value depends on many factors. Investment analysts have a lot of trouble accurately forecasting future prices of quite simple things; it seems to me very dangerous to base decisions on projected future assumptions about prices of one second-hand yacht against another. Some points are worth bearing in mind.

A long-cruising yacht will get much more wear and tear than a similar yacht that is seldom out of its shed, or off moorings.

A strongly built boat which is unfashionable today may well be a strong 'character' boat when today's fashionable trade-in models are in the scrapyard, provided hull, engine and gear are in good condition and she's not too massive.

Resale prices are heavily dependant on fashion.

Are you buying a boat for life? If not, how long do you envisage cruising? If over seven years, it seems to me that resale worries should not be allowed to cause sleepless nights. Almost everything I worried about seven years ago seems to have solved itself in the meantime.

The most important thing is to buy a boat that suits you well. You would not buy a car that was a bastard to drive just because someone suggested it had a good resale value. We once knew a couple who had started out to live aboard, and thinking that they might not like it they had chosen a Finnish production boat with a good reputation for being easy to sell. A moment's thought showed its complete unsuitability for long-term living aboard. Of course they did not like the life; they had ruined their prospects by forgetting what was the principal purpose of the boat and instead choosing on other criteria.

If you are not going long-cruising as a completely new way of life, but as a short break of perhaps two years in a working career, your attitude to resale prices will be somewhat different. You will still need to consider your aims carefully in order to live reasonably well, but you would be a hostage to financial fortune to ignore the likely proceeds from the sale of the yacht, which you are unlikely to want to keep forever. It is quite reasonable to forecast two years ahead, and a good broker's advice will be valuable in this respect. Do not, however, pay much attention to his advice on what sort of yacht to cruise in unless you are really sure he knows what living aboard is about: I have never met one who does. Your aim may be different from the aim of a long-term cruiser, but you will still have an aim that is not entirely centred on resale. You make the compromise.

A Yacht to Grow Old In.

> 'The saylers are the antient men ... and nothing but experience
> can poffibly teach it.'

This is a difficult subject to find a name for, mostly because we have all got into the habit of using euphemisms for 'old-age'. My preference for calling spades spades has not changed much since becoming a pensioner, but I discarded the word geriatric because my elementary knowledge of Greek suggests to me that the word really means an old doctor.

When we took part in two symposiums on the 'Sell Up and Sail' concept organised by *Yachting Monthly*, we were very impressed by the strong interest in the subject shown by people who had retired. We were in process of changing to a boat more suitable to our own increasing years, and were somewhat shamed by the ambitions of some of our fellow symposers. It became evident to us that there is a positive demand for boats suitable for retired people to do a lot of sailing in, even if not to live aboard full-time.

This is the time of life when living aboard becomes especially attractive. No more worries about careers, children growing up, and income, because you should have seen to all that by now. The only problems are to do with one's physical capability, and the fact that it can be expected to decline as the years go by. (You can also go bonkers, but many of us are quite a long way down that road already.)

If you are buying a boat to retire into, it is important to project ahead what you can cope with. Certainly your skills will improve to offset failing strength, but there will come a time when skills reach a plateau and strength goes on declining.

It would be unwise to contemplate frequent changes of boat. God knows, it is hard enough to find one super-boat in a lifetime without giving yourself the task of finding several, and every change is expensive. Nevertheless it requires quite a lot of self-discipline to buy a boat that will not perform to the full extent of your present capabilities. If you are not ready to face this prospect yet, come back to the subject in a few years' time.

We say elsewhere that we find production boats not very suitable for the live-aboard. In this we found ourselves at odds with the Editor of *Yachting Monthly*, who is no fool and not inexperienced. It just goes to show that opinions can differ. But note that when a former editor of the rival magazine, *Yachting World*, retired, he wrote that he found the production boat not exactly ideal for old-age, and he had his retirement yacht specially designed to suit him. I didn't like his boat either, but that is beside the point.

We have just faced the problem of changing boats. We do not pretend that our own personal solution is necessarily the right one, but we feel it might help some folk if we described the arguments that led to our decision.

Firstly, prospective old salts should consider their personal qualities. For example Laurel is small, and somewhat lame. Her disability will not improve; rather the opposite. Bill is big and very strong in the short-term sense, but shortness of breath prevents him exerting himself for long periods without resting. None of our problems will improve.

If we were each at 90% of our best-ever capacity when we first set sail in 1976, we are probably now at about 65%, which represents a decline of about 2% per annum. This has to be projected forward. We owned *Fare Well* for about fifteen years; this means that our new ship *Hosanna* ought to be our ultimate if it lasts us another fifteen. What will be our physical capacity then? Probably not very good.

We have known and met a fair number of yachtsmen who have gone on cruising far and wide into very old age, and we have become aware of some of their difficulties. We have helped some with their problems; for example, diabetes, which is only one of the possible scourges of old age, many of which can be coped with until they become really debilitating. Two old salts we can think of clearly went on far too long. It is one thing to rely on other people's help in an occasional crisis, but when one can no longer cope without frequent and almost regular assistance, it becomes time to think about swallowing the anchor, however much it sticks in your throat.

With regard to the boat, the obvious solution to the problem is to settle for a smaller boat than would the younger person. I say obvious because it seems to be everyone's instinctive answer. I don't think it is necessarily the right one. A lot depends on what you think you will be able to handle. Surprisingly, size is not as important as, for example, whether the boat itself acts like a gentleman or a hooligan. Some boats are absolutely intractable.

The process of adapting to decreasing faculties can be approached in two ways. One is to have a boat that will be easily coped with until death us do part, come hell or high water. The other is to have a boat that is comfortable and reasonably sea-worthy, but which will both require and allow one to modify one's cruising range when that becomes necessary. We chose the latter course, but let us consider the first option first.

Maintenance is not so much of a problem because it can be undertaken in slow time. Clearly it is unwise to take on an impossible burden, but apart from that, maintenance should not figure too largely in the argument.

Assuming one is going to come down in size, what is the right size? We have to have good living conditions, so the boat cannot get too small. Small sporty boats need quick physical reactions, something we tend to lose as we get older. Space is needed for the things one likes to have about one, souvenirs, photographs, small treasures and so on.

On the other hand it is desirable that the boat should be of a size that can be pushed or pulled short distances in harbour by old-man power without gut-busting effort, and that her gear should be light enough to be handled without causing hernias.

These two opposing factors bring us to a gross registered tonnage of between ten and fifteen, and sails that do not exceed 300 sq ft each. To get good living comfort in this range one is going to have to sacrifice some speed and sportiness. Good fat lockers lead to good fat boats.

Inside, the accommodation should be arranged so that tired people do not have to step over things, so that a person falling does not fall far, so that edges and corners are padded, and there are innumerable hand-holds. It should not be necessary to demount the table in order to have a restorative nap.

Unless there is a deck-house configuration, which has its points, the

whole accommodation should be on a level, thus avoiding those irritating little three-inch steps that all naval architects seem to think
essential, and which even able crews are always falling over.

There should be a good seat at the galley, and bunks that are not
too difficult to make. A lot of the problems down below become the
lady's problems; she may stay fit longer than her old man (she may well
be younger into the bargain), but how many yacht designers have been
deeply into the ergonomics of an old lady at sea? Going to the loo in
a small yacht arguably produces more broken bones than any other
nautical accident, strong handholds in the head and a sit-down shower
are essential. Even such a simple thing as bed-making can be difficult
with awkward enclosed bunks; fitted bottom sheets and a duvet can
help here.

On deck we come to the real difficulties. Admiral Goldsmith, one of
the earliest dedicated live-aboards, died hauling up his anchor. I had
tried to talk him into having electrics in his boat, but he was adamant.
'Amperes are the curse of mankind' he bellowed at me from a distance
of about three feet. Admirals tend to do that.

I am torn while writing this bit because if I had the chance to choose
a way of dying, this would be it, except for the awful problems it would
leave my devoted crew. But isn't it better for many reasons to have an
electric windlass and a self-stowing anchor? Heart attacks apart, there
are times when, caught perhaps by a squall in an anchorage, one is
obliged to work cables and anchors under trying conditions. Getting
exhausted doesn't help.

Nowadays there are some excellent little windlasses on the market,
led by those made in Italy. Of course they use a lot of amps, but not
for long; most of them pull in at over twenty feet a minute, so weighing
anchor would not normally take more than three minutes. Forty amps
for three minutes is two ampere/hours; not very much is it? especially
as one would almost certainly have the engine running at the time.

Sheet winches do come with electric motors, but the prices are
prohibitive as one needs a fair number of them. It is better to have
geared winches with plenty of power. When getting on it is easier to
give six gentle turns than three hard ones; it takes longer, but so little
in cruising terms. Winches should be just above waist height if worked
standing up, which is the best position for the effort. If you have to
work them sitting down, then even more power is required. Don't risk
straining the back.

The steering position should be in a wheelhouse. There is positive
evidence that old people can be distressingly unaware of the onset of
hypothermia. I know that the evidence applies strictly to very old
persons, but I do not suppose that the condition jumps suddenly to
danger level overnight: its development is almost certainly spread over
quite a period; its onset probably arrives with the pension book.

Do not suppose that hypothermia is unknown in the tropics. Of
course on a starlit night with a gentle force three blowing from the

quarter there is no problem, but during Hurricane Alberto I was wearing a thick sweater down below. (I didn't go on deck; I was too scared.) And remember you don't always stay in the hot climates. In the Med in April or October it can get quite chilly. We lit our wood-burning stove last night, October 19th.

The wheelhouse should have opening windows for the good weather, and a good chair to rest in. In *Hosanna* we have seats from which both of us can see around at the same time, and why not? It is still essential to have somewhere to sit outside, and even to entertain on a small scale, but do not place too much emphasis on sun-bathing; one gets tanned quite well enough without ever going into the direct sun, though the process takes a little longer.

Sail plans must be arranged for ease of handling rather than sailing efficiency. All sheets should come to a cockpit. All halyards or roller furling lines too. It should be possible to douse a sail without having to put on an act like a chimpanzee in a circus. In my view this makes roller sails virtually essential, and means either leaving the spinnaker behind or saving it for when junior pays a visit.

Have really big cleats. Hands and fingers get less agile, and fumbling with irritatingly miniature fittings is bad for one's frame of mind.

Give a lot of attention to lifelines. The aged do not pick their feet up so easily as the young, and we have seen older people tripping over deck fittings; the average deck-level lifeline is a perfect tripwire. It needs some experimenting but a lifeline at waist height may be the best. One tends to crouch a bit in bad conditions, and it might be easier to duck under than clamber over.

Mooring is a pastime which can tax old bones. Though Old Tom will undoubtedly be more experienced than Young Fred, his reaction time will be slower. Ensure a boat that is responsive under power and steers well at slow speed. Even if the boat is less than fifteen tons, one of those miniature bow-thrusters marketed by W.H. Den Ouden of Holland is probably a better buy than a lot of electronic navigating equipment (though I do not discount the value of anything which takes some of the physical burden off a small crew).

A motor-sailer is probably the best type of craft, for one will need a good engine. Consider how you could manage if one of you had to cope on their own. I could just about have sailed *Fare Well* back to the harbour by myself, Laurel would not have had the strength. If the event had arisen then she would have had to motor, and it is essential that the boat has engine power to make headway in a rough sea.

As one gets older one tends to use the motor a little more, whatever one's intentions. I see nothing wrong in this: in my view the prudent mariner is the one who uses all or any of his resources to the best advantage.

So how have the authors solved their problem of the old man's boat?

First of all Bill designed a steel boat in accordance with all that we have said above. We never built it.

We approached the basic problem by considering the cruising grounds we enjoyed the most, and those we had not yet cruised but wished to. Some would require more nautical effort than others; quite clearly some are getting too much to contemplate unless done soon.

Having graded these by degree of ambitiousness we found we had more than a lifetime's cruising ahead of us, and we decided to cut down by removing those such as the China Sea, which are unlikely to become congenial to the casual yottie for some time.

It was about this time that Laurel indicated that she wanted to bring all her library this time, so we threw away our lists and Bill proposed putting in a bid for the *Queen Elizabeth II*.

When the argument settled down again we both went to look over the market in sea-going Dutch barges in their raw, unconverted state. Bill had seen several conversions in the West Indies and in the USA which had sailed there on their own bottoms, and it seemed to him that one of modest size might suit us well. When sea sailing got too difficult we would have all those European canals and rivers to potter about in. In the meantime we would be limited to the fine weather zones in their more reliable periods, but our list was mostly that anyway. We tend towards a quieter life.

When we found a beautiful little barge of 26 metres available for what was virtually the price of her engine, we dealt. It was our intention to cut out 4 metres of length and make a full motor-sailer of her.

After the two of us had driven her in ballast across the North Sea in February in quite rough conditions we became very impressed with what we had bought. Bill looked again at Laurel's pile of books. He decided we could cope with the Little Dutch Barge under power under all but survival sea states, once one or two things were improved. The cost of cutting out 4 metres, if invested, would produce enough income to maintain 4 metres.

So *Hosanna* has ended up whole and entire, with three fixed keels and a sail plan divided into three low masts, and all sails rolling. She has two screws and a bow thruster. And a lot of books.

We are now at Aigues Mortes in the south of France finishing her conversion, and then we will be off to sea once more, and all our readers are welcome to hail us and come over to argue about it.

CHAPTER FIVE

Above Decks

'For a man of warre a well ordered taunt-mast is best, but for a long voyage a short mast will bear more canvasse and is less subject to beare by the boord.'

Nautical Terms

Neither Laurel nor I are sticklers for using a lot of nautical jargon. We are both inclined to talk of our bedroom, windows or ceilings, to give three examples. But there are items or doings which are peculiar to the sea, which are well described by sea terms, and for which no other words are adequate. Sometimes these terms have been debased by yachtsmen using them wrongly; it is my intention, when discussing equipment, to be precise and to go back to the right ones. To avoid confusion, they are defined here.

Passarella: a plank, gangway or brow leading from ship to shore, especially used over the bow or stern in the Mediterranean.

Guardrails are a 'safety fence' running round the vessel; they can be solid rails, or they can consist of wires supported by stanchions.

Lifelines are wires rigged between various rigid parts of the vessel so that crew can hold on or clip harness onto them when moving about. Some people wrongly call these jackstays.

The remaining words concern *anchors*. Apart from names indicating the design, such as Danforth or Bruce, anchors may be described either by their function or by the part of the vessel from which they are used. *Bower anchors* are normally stowed on either bow, and are the normally used anchors by which a ship comes to anchor. A *sheet anchor* is a spare anchor usually kept forward, for use only in very bad conditions. Though it gives rise to an expression much used by politicians, it is not necessarily noted for its size or unusual holding power; generally it was a last resort because it was a bit of a pest to get overboard. A *stream anchor* is one stowed at the stern; let go from there, usually in conjunction with a bower, so that the two anchors and the ship lie parallel to the stream and do not swing with its changes. A *kedge anchor* is an anchor used to point the ship or to move her about. The rope used between ship and kedge anchor is called a *warp*, which is also used to describe ropes used between ship and shore or between ship and a buoy, also for moving the ship. The kedge, which in these days of tugs and bow thrusters has largely died out, was usually lighter than other anchors because it was typically carried away from the ship to be laid by boat; the word does not mean a light anchor but defines the use to which it was put.

The big racing yachts did not want to anchor during a race unless the wind was light and they might have to stem the tide. As their lightest anchor was enough for this purpose they would save weight by landing their bower anchors, and thus the racing fraternity debased the word kedge because that was the way the professional crews referred to their light anchor. In the same way yachtsmen came to refer to the rope on the anchor as a warp, when the correct word is *cable* whether it is cordage or chain. In the US it is often called a *rode*, which is also correct up to a point.

When two anchors (or more) are used we usually say the vessel is *moored*, which strictly means made fast to the bottom. The angle at which an anchor cable leaves the ship is referred to as its *stay*. If it is almost horizontal and enters the water a long way ahead of the ship, it is called *at long stay*. A *short stay* is when the cable hangs down almost vertically.

The amount of cable between the anchor and the ship is called *the scope*. It should not be dependent on the size of the ship but on the depth of water. With chain cable a scope of five or six times the depth of water is prudent, double this for nylon unless a heavy angel is used. An *angel* is a heavy weight lowered down an anchor cable to provide an extra 'spring' to prevent the cable coming up bar-taut and snatching (see p. 92). I have been told some yachtsmen call this a 'chum', and discover this is because some enterprising manufacturer used this as a trademark.

Lastly, watch the word *spring*. Though originally applicable to a rope that carried out the expected function of a spring, it has gone through stages of becoming verb, adjective and probably a gerund too, and crops up in all sorts of places.

Rigs and Rigging

If one discounts the requirement of high windward ability, one brings into question the suitability of the Bermudan rig. Why do so many long-term cruising yachts sport this rig? *Fare Well* is so rigged, and as I designed it so, I suppose I should be able to answer this question. I cannot. It must have seemed the right thing at that time, but then I knew even less than I do now.

For tradewind cruising it certainly is not the best rig. For short-sea sailing when short-handed, the modern type of Bermudan rig with a small mainsail and a very large foretriangle may be very efficient when on the wind on a long tack, but it is far from convenient when putting about, and a period of short-tacking in a largish boat can exhaust a crew of two: the rig can become a monster. The perfect answer does

Can you believe that production boats are sold with navigation lamps tilting downwards like this? Well, they are. Just imagine what the bits you can't see are like.

not exist, because it is a very subjective matter, but I think it pays to look at the question from viewpoints other than maximizing tractive effort per square foot of canvas.

One of these is ease of maintenance and repair, and I will touch on this in Chapter Eight. Another, already mentioned, is ease of management, especially when short-handed or tired, in setting, furling and trimming the sails. On longer voyages there is the important matter of chafe. There is initial cost, as well as cost of maintenance of masts and rigging as well as the sails themselves.

With roller reefing/furling gear, some older rigs that did not prove altogether suitable for yachts, or which never caught on, bear some re-examination. Some years ago, Blue Bradfield cruised the lovely little ketch *D'Vara*, a little over 30 feet, which had an American designed wishbone rig, well sub-divided. He swore by this rig, saying that it gave him any combination or balance he required in any weather conditions. It seems to me that the wishbone mainsail with a down-mast roller system would be effective and easy to manage with the wishbone set aloft permanently.

The spritsail also needs a revival. Being essentially quadrilateral, it could be set on a shorter mast with a vertical roller, and with vangs on the sprit. Shorter masts make a lot of sense when cruising, especially when off to distant parts, but one does need to keep a fair area of sail up aloft where the wind is stronger.

85

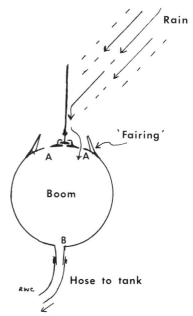

Rain

'Fairing'

A

A

Boom

B

Hose to tank

RWC

Catching rain with the mainsail. The fairing strips trap water next to the sail track where it runs into the boom through holes A, and drains away to the tanks via an outlet B near the gooseneck.

I could like Mr Hoyt's cat-rigged Freedom boats but for the necessity of stepping heavy masts through the deck, which has never appealed to me. I favour the tabernacle; perhaps it is my East Anglian breeding.

A square-sail is a great asset on a tradewind passage, but it must be easily handled. The Dutch sailor Harm set a big one on his old Colin Archer using the 'drawing curtain' method of brailing the sail in from either side to the mast. I am told he did not keep it long, and others have said this way can be a nightmare in a squall. Has anyone yet set a square-sail from a horizontal roller gear inside a hollow aluminium boom? Such a sail, easy to reef and set, would appeal to me.

If one does have a shorter mast, then standing rigging is much simplified. It is possible to save a lot of money from this simplicity, and some of this will come with the sailmaker's bill. Sails made very simply for a rig that is not state-of-the-art (whatever that really means) generally last twice as long and cost half as much as those from fashionable sailmakers with gimmicks, computers, big advertising accounts and another different gimmick next year.

With a boomed conventional mainsail it is possible to have a hollow aluminium boom made with a simple 'fairing' riveted on either side of the track to collect rainwater that falls down the sail and allow it to pass into the boom. A 1 inch BSP hole tapped underneath, close to the gooseneck, allows a hose to be connected and the water fed straight into a tank. One can collect many gallons during a squall.

Mast steps are seen on many long-distance cruisers; they have become, with the windvane, a status symbol of serious cruisers. I have got them, but would not waste money on them again. One does not

LEFT
This fairlead is not only a rope-eater, but one of the crew actually cut her foot on it.

RIGHT
Fare Well's laterally pivoted side davits, an adaptation of the merchant ship type and much more practical than swinging davits. Note the strong guardrails. The fitting at top right takes the awning.

want to go up a mast that often; a 60 foot climb at my age is no light undertaking; and at sea, when rolling, my moment of inertia at that radius is more than I can cope with and still do a job. Instead I use a cloth bag type of boatswain's chair. Nonetheless, a pair of steps conveniently placed below the cap or wherever work is likely to be needed would enable one to steady oneself and thus leave both hands free to work.

Running rigging is a great expense, and I use cordage. Wires are tolerable if turned on to a self-stowing reel winch, but they have disadvantages. First, they have a tendency to spring into kinks which if inadvertently pulled taut, in the dark say, will seriously weaken the wire and also stop it passing easily through blocks or eyes. Second, when minor damage occurs, some of the small wires break and the ends project. The discovery of one of these can be painful and even disabling. Third, it is apparently impossible to find sheaves properly designed for wire rope. I once took part in some elaborate Admiralty tests to discover the best size and section of sheave for wire. It turned out to be a question not of finding the best, but of finding the least worse, but the trials did show a requirement for very large diameter sheaves, and a deep narrow groove of roughly semi-circular section.

Cordage, on the other hand, chafes. It also stretches, but in lengths up to 60 feet or so I have never found this a problem. It cannot be conveniently wound on self-stowing reel winches, and thus it can leave one with lengthy snakes about the deck. These can have their ends washed overboard where they will surely find the propellor; even if it is only trailing, it is doing enough revs to wind wool. (Someone defined a screw propellor as the perfect self-tailing winch.)

This leads on to winches. I believe in the self-tailing type, and have found those little blue rubber gadgets that can be added to existing winches to be less than perfect. This is a department where the money should be found for the proper job. I have always found Mr Gibb's winches satisfactory (which is more than I can say for his blocks), and as they are less expensive and less complex than the racing fraternity's 'this year' choices, I recommend them. They do have one disadvantage: the drums revolve round Tufnol sleeves. As supplied, these are of too fine a tolerance: the Tufnol swells a little and the winch seizes. I have had the Tufnol turned out to a greater clearance (trial and error) and had no trouble since. Also, and this is rare, I think the firm recommends too small sizes for the short-handed crew.

Steering and Safety Arrangements

The chore of steering a boat for long periods is usually eased by self-steering vane gear or autopilots, which I will discuss later. One finds that they are in use for 99 per cent of the time, but the occasion will arise when hand steering becomes unavoidable and a comfortable position is essential.

If I were starting again, I would have a wheelhouse. The open sportscar syndrome becomes less relevant as one matures. The Royal Navy were the last professionals to overcome this juvenility, and it needed the atom bomb with its fallout problems to convert them. For my part, I do not like a wet shirt and a flowing sea. A first-class permanent awning is necessary over the conning position if there is no wheelhouse. Without an awning, the sun will boil your brains or else the rain will drown you. As the rain can also come at you horizontally, we are back to wheelhouses again. Of course the windows should open, and one of them have a substantial watershedding device. The Kent Clearview Screen is good, though in the smaller sizes the clear area is not big enough. There are also some very powerful windscreen wipers on the market.

Even if a wheelhouse is impossible, make sure the cockpit is well fenced in. Some modern designers, obsessed with getting more berths and walk-through headroom everywhere, have put cockpits high up on top of the accommodation. It may surprise you to know that I do not object to this from the point of view of height (it raises one above a lot of the spray), but only because, to keep a racy profile, such yachts are usually given too little cockpit fence, either to keep a sea out or to keep stumbling, tired crew in. If you find a ready-made yacht with a high cockpit but which otherwise suits you, contemplate fitting a strong rail round it. The upper edge of the cockpit coaming should be at least 3 feet where one can stand up to it, but where a seat or bench is in front of it then an extra 6 inches is desirable.

Guardrails become even more important when short-handed or family cruising. In the early days of offshore racing we did not have them all round, and I went overboard one night, so I can be considered one of the few with personal intimate knowledge of this subject because not many of us survive to be able to discuss it.

There are some very expensive 70-footers on the market with guardrails eminently suitable for laundry lines. From 32 feet upwards, the minimum height of the top rail should be 30 inches and the maximum vertical gap a foot. Anything else is a perfect trip-wire. They need to be strong enough to arrest the progress of 200 lbs of body falling across the beam of the boat, assisted by flowing water, and that exerts a very large force indeed. This is not an area to take chances about: one has to consider the extreme case, and remember that a safety device never causes a disaster by being too strong, only by being not strong enough.

Another aspect of guardrails is their vulnerability when mooring. Novices have an irresistible urge to push boats about by heaving on their stanchions, and given the apparent numbers of novices about it is desirable that the rails withstand this deplorable but widespread practice. Modern motor yachts are designed with high freeboard and considerable flare at the deck edge: for the comparatively low-freeboard sailing yacht, these features make mutual fendering very difficult. The ability to fender against one's guardrails is an asset. Fare Well's guardrails are 32 inches high, that is 22 above the gunwale. The stanchions are 1½ × 1½ × 3/16 inch RHS steel welded on at 4 foot intervals, the intermediate rail is welded and the top rail is all teak. They are sufficiently strong to allow the unbraced top of a stanchion to take the sheet lead block of the 670 square foot genoa, and I feel happy about them. Up forward there is a different arrangement with netting, as the foredeck has less impedimenta to interrupt a fall, and netting is nicer to fall into than steel bars. It should be remembered that Laurel has only one good leg and falls about a lot, though oddly enough she is less prone to this at sea.

Harness is very important on deck in rough weather. My opinion is that, given good strong guardrails as a back-up, one can move about better without clipping on to lifelines, but instead use two clips and move from one ringbolt to another. However in small yachts with light guardrails, narrow side decks, and the necessity to do a lot of work on the coachroof, some forms of stout wire lifeline are required. One should extend from cockpit to mast on each side, and another from mast to headsail tack. Wire of 1 inch circumference is about right, but must be made fast to strong fittings. I fear that a falling body could pull the mooring cleats out of some of the production boats I have seen.

There is some thought that cockpit cushions can double as lifebuoys as is sometimes found in the US. This is more a hope than a reality: the time when people are most likely to go over is in rough weather, and it is then that cushions start to fall all over the place, and are either stowed below or strapped down in some way. They then cannot be thrown over at short notice. Let's call them 'Chesapeake (or Broads) lifebuoys', and keep them for inland waters.

There is something to be said for a fair-sized yacht having a folding davit by her midship gangway rail-break. It would not only be of great help recovering heavy weights from the sea, but would be good in harbour for doing ditto from the dinghy.

One of the useful things to have on deck during the above type of emergency is a moderate length (100 feet, say) of light floating rope, about 1-inch circumference. This will not get in the screw, and given two circumstances, that manoeuvring is difficult and the victim is conscious, it is possible to come close enough and turn so that the rope is brought across the victim. If the yacht can be stopped, it is possible to haul him alongside. The rope should have a 3 foot loop at the end, but the person should not normally be towed. Better to let the rope go from on board, and to pick it up again, if you have too much way on.

I believe in use of engine in recovery. My experience is that even when running under spinnaker, the engine at full astern will not destroy steerage way and will save valuable yards while the sail is being furled: a point of importance for short-handed crews. But beware of trailing cordage when furling.

When we commissioned *Fare Well* there was no windvane gear strong enough, so we had a Sharp Mate autopilot which was the simplest I could find. In consequence I know little about pure wind-vanes, except that the Mediterranean's variable winds cause problems for them. Our Sharp has been a good companion; it only let us down once (on the first day out on an Atlantic crossing!) when a diode failed. (No dedicated cruiser should be without a stock of diodes, and a basic understanding of what they do: they are everywhere.) One little peculiarity of our autopilot (and others) is that it occasionally goes barmy and takes us round in a 360° circle before resuming the previous course on its own. We do have trouble running before a big

Note the good strong rail high up on the coachroof on Tientos. *Sensible sailors do not take risks.*

quartering sea, and I believe some vanes are not so good on this point; it certainly is a difficult point of sailing.

Liferafts and Tenders

I suppose most people contemplating long cruises have read with interest, if not alarm, the accounts of yachts lost and the experiences of survivors. One feature that is worth stressing is that an inflatable liferaft is not designed for long-term survival, and there are several cases where persons have been recovered from rigid dinghies after long periods adrift. I am moving back to the view that the best liferaft for a cruising yacht is a good rigid dinghy, even in the severest storm where survival needs an element of luck anyway. The dinghy must have inherent buoyancy, and a stout cover or at least a partial one, and rope-loop handholds below the gunwales. The Panic Bag should be kept in it at sea (and it is the best place for the vegetable locker in any case). It requires no annual service, which is not only very expensive in some countries (it bears VAT in France and Italy for a start), but also difficult to arrange and check, while the dinghy has many other uses.

Which leads us to tenders. Once we had a rigid dinghy and an Avon, but we found that we used the rigid one for choice; and when we met a fellow traveller whose Avon had perished in the sun, we contemplated the inevitable deterioration of this asset and sold it to him. We have never missed it. Our dinghy is a small Norfolk lugsail dinghy, good for pottering up creeks and by-waters, but it is not a heavy load carrier. We hoist it on side davits which I made myself. We have stern davits too, but a stern-hung dinghy is a nuisance in the Med, though a stern-hung inflatable makes a good emergency fender when lying stern-to a quay. The advantage of the side davits is that the dinghy can be turned in and stowed on deck in rough weather or when manoeuvring, where it is much safer and makes an extra locker.

We got rid of our 2hp Evinrude outboard. We used it very seldom, it was noisy, always giving trouble, and in our view had more potential as an anchor than as a propulsion unit. Our dinghy sails and rows very well, and when we are tired we have a very cheap Sears Roebuck electric outboard that ghosts us about at slow speed, needs no maintenance and does not wake the neighbours.

On the other hand, friends have a large Zodiac with a powerful outboard, and they tend to zip into some harbours for a little shopping without berthing the yacht. Unless the harbour is very encumbered I feel berthing is rather less trouble than fiddling about with the dinghy. Once we returned to Gouvia very late at night, formally dressed, Laurel in long skirt and so on. The chap who was taking his dog for a walk and took our lines for us asked where we had been in formal dress. 'To the theatre', we said. 'In a 50 foot yacht?'

Another form of tender is a vehicle. Many dedicated cruisers are advertised by a rusty bicycle on deck; larger boats sometimes have a mini-motorbike, which, if under 50cc does not require licensing in most desirable countries. In some it requires insurance (France is one) but no driving licences. The obligation of a crash helmet is spreading; France and Tunisia insist and there may be others. Motorbikes should have a painted sign 'Tender to . . .' instead of a number plate.

Anchors

The long-term cruiser will have to take more thought to his anchors than the marina-based animal who probably never anchors at all. During 1982 we spent 134 nights riding to single anchor, and a further nine moored with two. We did not drag once, though that event is not unknown to us. We are fitted with two 75lb CQR bower anchors which self-stow over rollers close either side of the stem. To port we have 45 fathoms of $7/16$ inch chain, and to starboard 40 fathoms of $1/2$, both handled by a Simpson-Lawrence 521 electric windlass. This layout owes a lot to big-ship experience, and it means that my diminutive wife can manage anchors and cables in all normal circumstances without any help. Foul anchors are another thing altogether.

To let go, she equips herself with a brake lever and a shipwright's hammer, takes off the brake, taps the friction clutch with the hammer

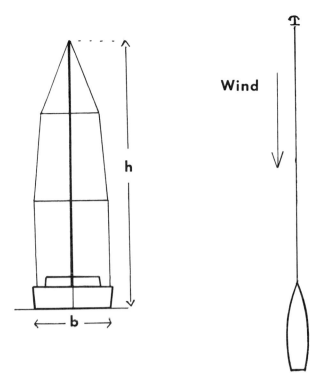

The windage of a sailing yacht even without any sail up is considerable. At anchor she will tend to lie with bows into the wind, reducing the strain on the cable.

to get it to release itself (design fault in the windlass?) and the anchor drops, pulling its chain behind it. The cable is marked by paint at 5 fathom intervals (my job), and at the required scope, usually six times the depth of water, she applies the brake, engages the ratchet, and after watching a little to see if the ship has got her cable she walks aft to join me in a drink. There is no need to (wo)manhandle anything. To weigh, she merely switches on, and when the anchor has stowed itself on its roller, switches off, covers the windlass and we are ready for sea. This installation is not luxury. It is commonsense for short-handed or family cruising; good design is as important on the fore-castle as anywhere, and equally hard to find in production boats.

The Simpson-Lawrence 521 windlass is not ideal, but it is adequate: it has too many dissimilar metals which give trouble unless one carries out unnecessarily complex maintenance routines. If I were fitting-out again I would go to Italy for my windlass. To an Italian, the very thought of actually touching a beastly anchor or its cable is so appalling that considerable effort has been made to avoid it.

The size of bower anchors is very important. Most published tables

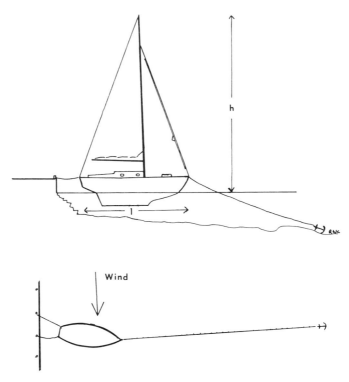

A yacht moored to a quay with an anchor out is not free to swing, and a wind from the side has more windage to act upon and causes far more strain on the cable and upwind mooring lines.

of recommended anchor sizes seem to have in mind the marina animal or the ocean racer, and not the real sea-going yacht. For example, I followed the advice of Simpson-Lawrence, who are not noticeably incautious as a rule, but wish I had fitted larger anchors. Their table:

Length WL	Disp. tons	CQR wt
40ft	25	60lb
45	30	75

In my view, to enjoy peace of mind, one should have bower anchors one size larger than this table. Cable should be in proportion. A 60lb anchor needs $7/16$ inch chain cable, a 75lb needs $7/16$ or $1/2$, and a 105 lb anchor needs $1/2$ or $9/16$.

When moored bow or stern to a quay, and with an anchor out, the wind on the beam has a sort of sweating-up effect on the anchor cable, which in a strong wind can multiply the tension in it several times. Add to this the fact that a wind on the beam acts on a larger area of boat than a wind from ahead, and it is not surprising that anchors of apparently adequate size come home. If you expect to spend much time in the Mediterranean an increase in size of both anchor and cable is desirable. The alternative, which we follow, is to have two bower anchors and use both if a strong wind is expected. The practice of waiting until the wind blows and then laying out a second anchor by dinghy, in an upwind direction, solves the layer's problem but inconveniences others, and is selfish.

If I had thought further ahead I would have fitted a self-stowing stream (stern) anchor with its own capstan or windlass. It would have been useful on several occasions, especially in restricted tideways such as the Intra-Coastal Waterway. We have no kedge, and I see no need for one as there is little point using a lighter, less secure anchor when the heavier, safer bowers can be managed more easily. We have a spare 75lb Danforth which remains unused. If the need arises to send away an anchor in a boat (after a grounding, say) I have always used a bower with enough chain cable; one does not need a lot if it is shallow enough to run aground. On those rare occasions when the wind blows across the swell and rolling becomes a nuisance (it happened in Mustique in the West Indies, and also at Pargos in Greece), it is possible to spring the cable to point ship across a moderate wind.

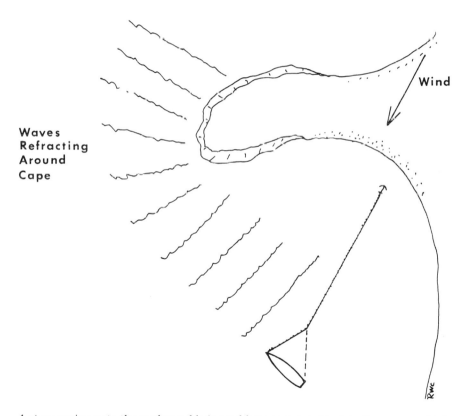

Waves
Refracting
Around
Cape

Wind

A stern spring onto the anchor cable is used here to point ship into the waves, which would otherwise be uncomfortable; however, the wind is now brought on the beam.

95

Choice of anchor type is a personal matter. They are mostly difficult to stow other than as described above. But the criterion of choice should not be a tabulated holding strength in one or two particular conditions, but a good all-round security in most conditions where sea sense indicates anchoring is worth considering. No anchor holds on smooth marble as one discovers at Xania in Crete. Taken overall I have found the CQR satisfactory, but respect that some friends prefer Danforth. Both these anchors were very carefully designed, and perfected after proper trials. Avoid imitations. The Bruce anchor finds favour with some, and it will stow over a roller. I have an idea that it is not so good in the smaller sizes as it is in the larger; perhaps this is another case where one should read the next line in the table. Admiralty Pattern and Fisherman's anchors are really not worth it, except as rock picks.

Cable

I favour chain cable, though with frequent use it does wear off the galvanizing and begin to look dreadful. When this happens, as re-galvanizing is not only very expensive outside the UK, and often very badly done too, turn the cable end for end, wire-brush it and keep it soaked in boiled linseed oil, which is the only suitable oil without a nasty smell. Nylon has advantages, and for the lightweight yacht which is normally in a marina and does not often anchor, it is a good choice. There is on the market a coil of flat-braid polyester which I consider dangerous. Though the principle of rolling up a flat braid is excellent and practical, the material should be of nylon, which is highly elastic, and not of polyester, which is meant to be inelastic. The importance of elasticity in an anchor cable cannot be over-estimated. In doing anchor trials for the Admiralty, I found that anchors were started to drag very easily by a series of jerks; they would not move for a much greater steady tension in the cable. It is the weight of the chain cable in catenary that acts as a very good spring, and if you do want to use the polyester braid I would recommend lowering a weight (called an angel, and it should be about half the weight of the anchor) down the cable to about one-third of the scope from the bows.

One sees reference to nylon being subject to chafe or cut over coral, but I have no personal knowledge of this happening, probably because my friends are sensible enough not to lay out a cable over sharp coral heads, which in any event are not good holding ground. More important is the fact that nylon will abrade over sand and fairleads, especially when strong winds have the ship yawing. Nylon is more awkward to stow coming in than chain, especially as one needs double the scope, and another consideration in the Med especially is the question of security in crowded harbours when other boats are manoeuvring. Nylon cables lead at longer stay than chain

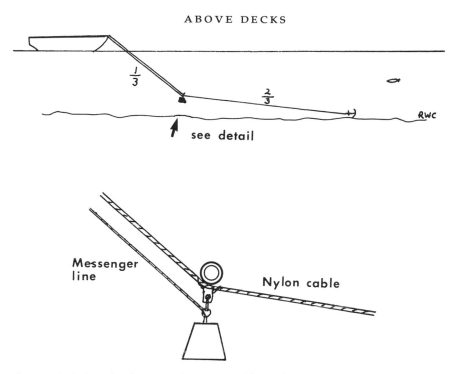

An 'angel' designed to hang on the anchor cable at about a third of the scope out from the bows, with its own light messenger line to lower and retrieve it. The weight should ideally be half that of the anchor.

and thus enter the water much further away from the bows, and are easily cut by a vessel manoeuvring with difficulty. The question of legal liability is not the half of it: the case might well have to be argued in foreign tongues in foreign countries, and that still is not all. The reason why the cutter was in trouble in the first place was probably a strong wind, and the ensuing dance of yachts cut adrift and/or disabled with a rope round the prop soon develops the characteristics of a gang-rape among elephants, with comparable dangers to life, limb and property. Though legal opinion has it as the cutter's responsibility, that is based on big-ship cases heard before the days of nylon cables, and it could be argued that these, at long stay in crowded harbours, are unseamanlike and a contributory factor to trouble.

It is the ease of handling self-stowing bower anchors with a good windlass that makes berthing stern-to a quay the best proposition for craft needing an anchor of about 40lb or more; even though skippers will find it simpler to manoeuvre ahead, rather than astern. If one had a self-stowing stream anchor the case might be altered, but a bowsprit does make boarding difficult and larger boats with normal sheer find the stemhead a little high.

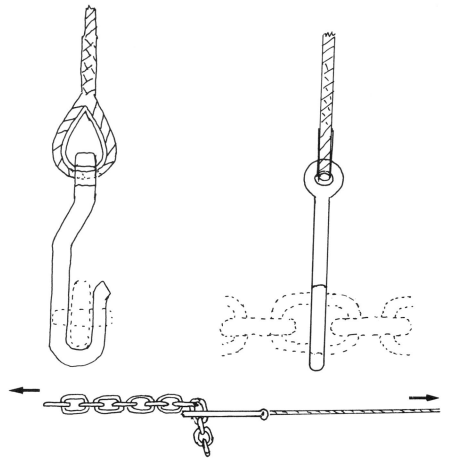

Heavy steel hook for holding chain. No moving parts.

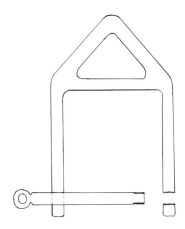

A typical Dan Leno shackle, very useful for joining small chain to large rings, etc but hard to find. Chandlers that supply fishing and commercial craft may be a source.

Fare Well's *folding motor bike in its folded state; it is a Di Blasi. Behind the typically scruffy author one can see the dinghy hung outboard on its side davits, freeing the poop for comfortable living.*

A simple, strong awning on Alan and Pat Lucas' world cruising cutter Tientos. *There is a lot of good sense in this ship.*

Other Matters

Backing into a berth is not as difficult as it appears and is soon mastered by most. Exceptions are yachts with an outward turning, off-centre screw. The secret is to get enough way on, for she will not steer until this is achieved. The speed required depends on the amount of cross-wind, and in very strong cross-winds it may not be possible at all. Most ship-handling textbooks counsel a softly-softly approach until one has mastered the feel of her, but in this case it is not the best approach. The prudent mariner will go off somewhere secluded and do a bit of practice.

I once served in a small warship which had an anchor cable of wire, which wound itself on to a winch. This seems to me to be well worth considering for a yacht.

A recent development has been the introduction of moderately priced (comparatively!) bow thrusters, and I have seen several fitted to luxury yachts which seldom leave moorings. For short-handed single-screw yachts above, say, 30 tons such a device might be a better investment than electronics.

100

A simple board fender, for use against piling, rough concrete or damaging projections.

For serious cruising it is essential to have very strong bitts or cleats, because one is occasionally obliged to berth in harbours where the shelter is not perfect, and a swell or scend will have boats constantly dancing in their berths. Most deck fittings seen on production boats are criminally inadequate; this seems to be the area where the builder goes berserk to save a fiver. The main centreline bitts forward should be strong enough to tow on, and one needs two shoulder cleats fit to spring on. Two midship cleats ditto and two substantial bitts aft, again strong enough for towing. Spring bitts or cleats should be on the gunwale, thus avoiding the need for fairleads which are seldom as good as their name.

In many primitive harbours chafe of ropes on quay copings is a nuisance. A common Med practice is to have a loop of chain at the end of the rope, sometimes with a carbine hook. Unfortunately the size of chain equivalent to the strength of the nylon would be impossible to heave. In any event stand clear of people throwing chain about. A nylon rope of 2 inch circumference (16mm dia) has a breakload of 4000kg, which is a lot more than that of a 9/16 chain and more than

A complete turn round the bollard prevents chafe in the eye of the mooring rope. Not recommended if more than one vessel is on the same bollard.

twice that of the biggest carbine hook. One suggested solution to this problem is to use a soft wire eye at the end of the nylon, or if you wish to use chain, use a picking-up rope of lighter nylon and afterwards substitute the main berthing chain and/or rope which can be quite short.

Fenders seem to be cheaper in England than anywhere else; in the US they are stupidly expensive, and no better. Most people use air-filled plastic fenders, and for lightness and convenience a few of these are more or less essential. But they are not ideal. Hot sun decomposes the plastic material of which they are made and they turn into sticky, grit-attracting balloons. Second, they are expensive; and third, they do not stand up to hard wear alongside rough concrete or chipped stone quays. A couple of motor tyres are advisable for bad conditions, though it is not nice to use them against someone else's topsides. Of course we know that the marks are easy to remove, but some of the fancy brigade get a little paranoid, and there is no point in causing offence. He will be quite happy about the grit-encrusted plastic ones.

'An awning ... spread over their heads ... especially in hot countreys to keep men from the extremity of heat or wet, which is very oft infectious.'

I have mentioned already the need for good permanent shade over cockpit or conning position. In harbour, where one spends most of one's time, temperatures are higher, breezes are attenuated, and some form of living in the open air is desirable in hot or sticky seasons. I designed our poop as a verandah: it is 15 feet long and 13 at its widest point, planked in teak and with very few impediments. It becomes a delightful living room under a big awning, with folding table and chairs.

It is possible to have a simple awning which is, in effect, a sheet with a batten sewn into the hem at either end. When spread over the boom, and with the ends of the battens bowsed down, it is a very cost-effective solution. I prefer a long-term investment of a good heavy cotton awning, roped all round and strong enough to be set over the mizzen boom in all but very strong winds. Our mizzen boom has a sliding gooseneck so that it can be raised up to about 7 feet in harbour, and the awning has hose connections sewn in: in the West Indies, where fresh water is quite hard to come by, there are frequent showers and we can get 15 gallons from a half-hour rain.

We tend to have strong opinions on what is best, but that does not mean other arrangements are intolerable. In fact there are a lot of boats it would be a pleasure to live aboard. Go, find one, get it, and never regret it.

CHAPTER SIX

Below Decks

'On each side of the Stearage roome are divers Cabins ... with many convenient seates or lockers to put any thing in, as in little Cupberts.'

Though there is a natural emphasis on comfort in a long-term cruising boat, it is essential not to lose sight of the requirement that the comfort should extend to comfort at sea, otherwise we will end up with something like a Chelsea houseboat. So important is the ability to maintain efficiency and safety at sea, that the question of comfort, whether in harbour or offshore, has to be fitted round the requirement to survive such rare testing moments that the yacht might be expected to encounter. Important factors in keeping going at sea are minimizing both physical and mental strain; and minimizing the possibility of water entering the accommodation, which in effect will comprise most of the hull.

In my view, watertightness is a vital part of living in a boat. Inevitably one has more possessions on board than the holidaymaker, some of which are perhaps precious even if only for sentimental reasons. Sea water is the great destroyer, and it has allies with which it works. Dampness breeds mildew, mould and rot. And bad temper. Avoid it. It may not always be possible to stop every whit of water entering the bottom, but do get a watertight deck and windows. The aim is to be able to clean one's bilges with a vacuum cleaner, and it is perfectly achievable.

But water will get in. Spray flies, waves do wash over the deck, a moment's inattention when tired and there it goes, down the hatch or skylight. Only a paragon can maintain eternal vigilance and what a bore he'd be to live with. We once had a terrible night beating down the Ionian Sea toward Kephalonia into a rising wind, the spray flying the length of the ship as her head ploughed into each short sea, making us duck rhythmically behind the spray shield to avoid the worst of it. Then, worried because she seemed to be diving a little more deeply than usual, I missed a duck and saw the forehatch lift, only an inch or so but enough to swallow a gallon or two from the water swilling about the deck. We bore away instantly, foregoing the pleasure of mutual recriminations, and investigated the forepeak which is separated from the accommodation by a watertight bulkhead.

I later calculated that there must have been four tons of water in it, and all because we each thought the other had screwed down the bad-weather fastenings. And that was not all: it was a night when Professor Murphy drove home several points. Detritus from the anchor cables had blocked the pumps, but then, there has never been a pump as fast as a frightened man with a bucket. (A joke of course, but with a grain of truth.)

You cannot enjoy living in a yacht with the watertight integrity of a submarine. There is a mean, and how far one goes in either direction depends on the chosen voyages, the chosen times, the chosen crew.

One way water can get below, even in harbour, is on the crew's clothing. A surprising dampness can build up this way over a period of prolonged rain or spray. Another source is condensation, something that yacht designers have yet to appreciate fully. One modern Camper & Nicholson yacht in which a young couple were wintering in Corfu was dreadful: they were unable to use two of the bunks because of condensation dripping from the aluminium window frames. Now this is bad design and it is something to look out for when buying a boat. A palliative is to cover the aluminium with some layers of masking tape, when the top layers will prevent the under ones from hardening out.

The best hull insulation is to cover the interior above the waterline with about an inch of sprayed on, closed-cell polyurethane foam, which is also an excellent protective coating for steel. It is, sadly, flammable and will give off toxic smoke if it does ignite, so it is no bad thing to spray it with fire-retardant paint, which is not completely reliable but does help. We had a fire on board at sea, and I am glad to say that the foam scorched but did not ignite.

Recently, while insulating our new boat *Hosanna*, we discovered that this foam is now available in a highly fire-resistant form. We used this and found it good, so much so that it was possible to make *small* welds on the opposite side of the steel plate without igniting the foam. In these circumstances, this foam is highly recommended for boats that are going to be lived in.

Other insulation methods are to line with glassfibre wool, which does nothing to protect the steel. I saw an old steel ship with natural straw packed behind the linings, which must be highly flammable. In my opinion, the sprayed foam is best in spite of its disadvantages.

Ventilation alone will not cure condensation when the dewpoint conditions are really ripe. In fact ventilation can import dampness when the air outside becomes saturated, so some means of closing off ventilators is desirable.

Designers might well reply to my criticisms of them, that they do not attempt to design boats for living aboard in winter. This is probably true, but it is more of an excuse than a reason, for a yacht should be capable of use whenever its owner wants. Watch that insulation, then: a full inch of it, no less.

Our own solution of the comfort/seaworthiness dilemma was eased by *Fare Well*'s size, but I believe the principle is adaptable further down the scale. It is to recognize those bits of boat that are vital to the navigation, those that are desirable for harbour comfort in winter or summer, and then those that are common to both, such as galley and heads. Then design a layout with a sea-going 'citadel' separated from the rest of the boat, not completely, but so that in bad weather especially there is no need to go beyond it. In our citadel, mostly in the deckhouse which is at half-deck level, we have the galley, chart table, radio, fridge, switchboards, a sea bunk, a small table, tool chests, oilskin locker (big — 21 x 24 inches x full height), and close by but down a ladder, the bathroom. (This actually contains a bath, essential in our case for therapeutic purposes, but it also makes a first-class place to dump soaking-wet clothes.) The deckhouse is also the access to the engineroom, which is beneath it.

In the ends of the yacht (excepting the forepeak and the lazaret) are the saloon forward, and a small guest cabin and our own double bedroom aft. This latter is not a cabin; we use the word 'bedroom'

Laurel.

deliberately to emphasize the comfort and peace of the place, which is the biggest single space in the whole ship.

I do not say that our conception of the best (there is no perfect) layout is the only one, or even the right one for another couple. It has worked very well for us, for a long time, for deep-sea and short-sea cruising and winter living. The only substantial improvement I would make would be to have a real wheelhouse instead of the present shelter.

Others we know have an open-plan layout, one enormous airy space. It's nice for a party, and it suits the smaller yacht. It does suffer from 'one place wet — all places wet', and there is a lack of privacy when one has guests. Some have a small, separate after cabin as guest accommodation. These are very good for children, but having once been a guest in a Seadog ketch where I needed a shoehorn to get myself into bed, I suspect their long-term use for the grown man is a question of hope rather than reality.

A more conventional use for the half-deck deckhouse is to make it the saloon. This certainly looks better on demonstration models at the

Boat Show. It does feel nice to have a light and airy saloon, but in my view it is also nice to have a light and airy galley. Certainly the catering tends to improve if the cook is not condemned to working in an ill-lit, ill-ventilated dungeon. In the climate we aspire to, most of the living is on deck, which is the ultimate in light and airy. In a Mediterranean winter our saloon does have its disadvantages because our side ports are often blocked by neighbouring craft, but it is mostly in the evenings that it is used and it gets dark early in winter.

Now, let us look at the interior in more detail. I will start with the galley because that is the most important bit. The first thing that has to be chosen is the fuel, and this has to be done in conjunction with the heating. There are many good arguments for having only one fuel aboard, one that is easily and universally available, and easy to load. The commonest fuel, and one that most of us are obliged to have in any event, for propulsion, is diesel oil, so let us consider that as a sole fuel.

First, it not only drives the main engine but it can also drive an auxiliary generator if you should want one. It will drive an outboard; unfortunately these are heavy though powerful, and not very convenient. In the low power range one can have a battery-run electric outboard, thus using diesel oil at one remove. There are very good diesel heaters on the market. At the simple end I like the Danish made Refleks heater, which requires no fan and is therefore silent, but of course it heats only the compartment in which it is mounted. I am not so happy with blown-air oil heaters, having seen a serious fire in Antibes which happened when the crew were ashore for a very short time. It is possible in a bigger boat to have proper central heating with a normal oil-fired boiler. Cooking can also be done by diesel. There is a Canadian stove, the Dickenson, but I think the Rolls-Royce job is that produced by Perkins Boilers of Derby, which not only cooks but provides hot running water and some central heating too. It is expensive and very heavy, but the company give the most excellent service.

There is no other single fuel arrangement. To have bottled gas for cooking will save both initial cost and a certain amount of weight, much of which will be lost because of the price, size and weight of the necessary number of cylinders required for reasonable independence from the shore. It will bring problems apart from its propensity to explode, which can be controlled: practically every major country has its own size and design of gas bottles, very often with differently threaded connections. To change bottles at a retail supplier it is necessary to hand in a local bottle. Odd bottles can sometimes be refilled at depots, but then there is the problem of transport, for the depots are seldom conveniently placed for yachts. I remember helping another boat take their bottles to a depot in Greece, and beating a hasty retreat as I observed the workman pouring liquid gas into an open cylinder through a funnel while he was smoking a cigarette. Possibly the mixture was too rich to explode, and the fumes did not rise.

I would think very carefully before opting for gas as the sole method of cooking, except in a small boat when I would agree that it is the only solution. If the boat is big enough to have a powerful separate 240 volt generator, then one can maintain the one-fuel principle by cooking with electricity. This does mean a lot of generating, even in the evening, when it can cause bad feeling among neighbours in a quiet harbour, but it is becoming more and more common especially among charter yachts. One can get a four plate hob, two of which are electric and two gas, and this seems a good way of solving the problem of the late night cuppa, the amount of gas required for this occasional use being very small.

Paraffin is not suitable for the liveaboard. We have small oil lamps in gimbals which we keep lit at night at sea, turned very, very low, when they provide a faint glimmer which allows us to move about without switching on electric lights and spoiling night vision. But refined paraffin is getting very hard to find because rural or isolated communities are changing to liquid gas.

Alcohol cooking is a menace. It surprises me that the Americans have tolerated it for so long, and I am happy to note a trend away from it at last. However, in the last two years I have seen two flaring cookers thrown overboard, so it still goes on.

The lovely old sloop *Diotima* in which the late Admiral Goldsmith lived the life of a dedicated singlehander, (and on the foredeck of which he died, weighing anchor at Monemvasia) had a solid fuel stove which was lovely in winter but noticeably warm in summer. Fuel was never a problem for him. What a lovely little yacht! I last saw her in Hydra, now owned by a Greek sculptor who cares for her.

A particular advantage of having the galley high up is that it enables the sink to have natural drainage, something which can be very useful. The galley need not be large, but it does need planning *by the cook*. When living aboard one needs a rather more varied menu than sea stew forever, so food stowage has to be extended and a more comprehensive range of cooking tools is needed. Even if one does not have 240 volt generators it is worth considering a circuit powered from the DC batteries by either a government surplus rotary converter or an electronic one. It is easy to get 500 watts (or even more if you wish, but the converter prices rise sharply with size), which can be used for a food mixer as well as electric drills, sanders, blow-driers, vacuum cleaners, soldering irons and many other things that ease the chores for permanent residents. Usually this type of appliance is on for a few minutes only, so the battery drain is small. In any event, a 240 volt AC circuit is desirable if one is going to spend a Mediterranean winter on shore power.

Do not rely on all countries having the same wiring practice. The UK system of Earth, Live and Neutral is a good system in principle, but abroad electricians often do not wire up three-pin sockets in a consistent way. It is a good idea to have twin fuses, one on each load-

109

What builders do not provide has to be improvised, but one shouldn't have to use a beer can to adjust a hatch.

carrying wire of your shore power connection, and to have a certain means of completely isolating the ship's AC generator when connected to shore supply. Also, do not rely on the third pin in a shore connection being connected to earth; use a two-wire shore power cable and bond the earth connections of all your shipboard outlets to your own earth.

In Europe generally the supply is 220 volts 50Hz, but voltage at the dockside sometimes falls as low as 170, especially in Italy where I suspect a lot of people tap into the supply illegally. In the US the supply is generally 110 volts 60Hz, but it is possible with some shore sockets to get 220 volts by connecting up the pins in a particular way. Local knowledge is necessary, as the pilot books say, but Americans are very obliging. We found that all our 50Hz equipment worked without any noticeable ill effect on 60Hz, and I suspect that there is considerable tolerance in the design. Motors and clocks go faster: this is possibly what is meant by dynamic America.

Refrigeration is the biggest energy user in the boat, apart from propulsion. There are a few families living without refrigeration, usually in a small boat. When you get acclimatised it is not too bad, as I remember from days of yore. But nowadays I do like a cold beer, and both white wine and rum punch are better chilled. Some say that the only way to take retsina is so cold you cannot taste it. In *Fare Well* we have a top-opening refrigerator of about 3 cubic feet, and beneath and accessible through it a storage freezer of 2½ cubic feet. This has been a good installation, driven by a Canpa-Simpson compressor unit, with a large holdover tank. The control is manual with an externally reading thermometer. I don't much like automatic devices; not only is it something else to go wrong, but the fellow who set it up has probably never lived afloat and would certainly have different values to those I favour. The compressor is driven by 24 volts DC from the battery, so although it is mainly switched on during the daily battery charge, I can top it up with extra cold at other times.

That system sums up the custom-built refrigerator, which has as many variations as you care to give it. The alternative is to buy a conventional household fridge at low initial cost and run it via the AC converter referred to above. The custom-built is probably more energy economical as its insulation is usually better, and cooling the refrigerant is usually by sea water. The domestic system cools by air, which can heat up the accommodation if not ducted out. In the event of major breakdown the domestic system is much easier to replace.

If considering the alternative of an ordinary domestic fridge with power from a convertor of some sort, be careful. The starting loads of most domestic fridges are about ten times their running loads. This means that a fridge with an advertised power drain of 100 watts will need about 1000 watts for a second or two while starting up. This would be enough to blow an electronic power invertor, but the rotary type will take it in its stride. I favour buying American refrigerating machinery; the country is so obsessed by ice that they seem to have solved more of the problems than anyone else.

There are refrigerators working on the absorption method, getting energy from a gas or paraffin flame. I once tried the latter, and though I was quite pleased at the time there is no doubt that the present system is much better. The absorption system can be troublesome at sea because tilting and movement inhibits its operation. Laurel will discuss our use of the freezer under victualling.

Water systems in small yachts are usually manually pumped; the larger boats normally have a pressure system. The best I know of is made by Godwin; like most really good jobs it is bulky and heavy, but again their service is excellent. Power consumption is negligible, and we have running hot and cold via the Perkins cooker. I know of some boats which use a header tank. One has a tall, narrow 5 gal cylinder inside the mainmast with a visual sight glass. The skipper pumps water up each morning and has a very exact check on consumption. Knowing him, I bet he has a lock on the pump! Usually liveaboards use more water than holidaymakers; again it is a question of wanting a higher standard of living for long stays. I would certainly make sure that the yacht has very capacious tanks; most production boats, being dedicated to weekend use, are very poorly fitted. We have 400 Imperial gallons and without any drastic economy measures use about 10 per day. With two guests extra this rises to about 13. For an ocean voyage we exercise a little economy and use 5 on average, laundry day always being an upset to the calculations. Probably tankage of 200 gal is the minimum for comfortable living and water security.

One of the major factors in the accommodation aboard a long-term cruiser is the relationship between bunks and stowage. Ocean racers can get by on half a cubic foot per man, but such an allowance would make for marital discord, and in time a pretty smelly crew. In tropic conditions, when humidity can be high (and the same applies during a scirocco in the Med) the best way of stowing clothes is the hanging cupboard or wardrobe. Though women's clothes are smaller and lighter, the female needs (and demands, and uses) rather more space than a man. If we were to decide on a requirement of 4 feet of wardrobe bar for a couple (and this is a bit on the mean side) it would indicate $2\frac{1}{2}$ for her, and $1\frac{1}{2}$ for him. Generally guests need only about 6 inches each.

The problem is that while living afloat one has to carry on board full outfits of hot weather decent, hot weather indecent or casual, the same for temperate climes, and finally winter garments for both sea and shore which are very bulky. Whereas a man is moderately content to put on a shapeless old sweater to do the winter shopping, most ladies prefer to look a little less like an itinerant scarecrow.

Each person living on board ought to have about 12 cubic feet of good dry locker or drawers for clothing, quite apart from the wardrobe and any oilskin stowage. I like to provide a guest with 2 cubic feet, enough for a two to three week stay.

Food stowage is not such a problem in the Med where one is seldom far from a good market, but in the oceans, or the West Indies or Bahamas, one does need a fair bit of tin space. The bilges are traditionally used for this. Without leaks, one need not go through the old ritual of marking tins with a chinagraph pencil: we don't. Also, with dry bilges tins keep for very long periods, years even. We did once have a labelling problem by stowing tins in the bilge just above the prop. The vibration made the tins rotate slowly and wore off the labels, leaving the tins brightly polished. It took some time to trace the cause for we didn't go down there while motoring.

Tools are very important, and by keeping the boat dry I have had few bad rust problems without taking any elaborate precautions. One has to keep some tools very handy. I have five large drawers, each one sub-divided, in the deckhouse close to the main hatch. There is seldom a hardware store round the corner.

By the same token, spare parts are a problem. Most of the spares we started with are still intact in their wrappers: it has always been something else that has gone wrong. So the quantity carried has grown and grown, and the ship has settled deeper and deeper into the water. It is necessary to make a list of all those gadgets the lack of which would cause severe problems, and these are the spares to carry. Call them class A spares. Class B spares are from those suppliers who are so bad, slow or unreliable that one is obliged to carry them on board. Class C is for those companies who can be relied on to help you out of a hole if their product goes wrong, by sending a spare by a fast and convenient carrier. One should make a policy of buying the products of companies in class A or C: they deserve every encouragement. Unfortunately there are occasions where one has to patronise a mediocre outfit, and the more you do the more spares you have to carry.

Designers seldom give sensible thought to chart stowage. I have seen a claim for a boat to be well endowed in this respect with space under the chart table for 25 charts, which is about half an inch. A yacht's outfit (a full one would be much larger) of charts for UK to the Med, in the Med, Black and Red Seas, the Middle Atlantic, the West Indies, Bahamas and the US comes to a stack 9½ inches high, and is probably the heaviest movable item on board. And quite possibly one of the most expensive, too. Navigational publications for the same areas. i.e. pilot books, tables, almanacs etc, occupy 10 feet of bookshelf; and while it is true that I have one or two old chums among these which are not a great deal of practical use any more, the figure is not far out. There are sixteen Admiralty Pilots alone, and besides these other books of a nautical nature that it is desirable to carry. Catalogues, a few books giving advice on problems, multi-language nautical dictionaries, and instruction books for equipment. To the suggestion that one does not need all these charts or books at once, the answer is that they have to be on board because the ship is one's home. There is no other place: no shed at the bottom of the garden, no convenient storage at Grandma's that one can easily get to.

Other books can be a problem too. People who have been brought up to read seem to need books to keep in practice, and books abhor damp. The worst are those printed on glossy paper, whose pages tend to stick together. Thank heaven Penguin and others publish a good list of paperback reference books.

The frequent mention of dampness leads naturally to ventilation and light. We have already referred to the possibility of moisture coming in the ventilator, but unfortunately other things can get in too. A good wire mesh (which should be of bronze because rats eat plastic) is desirable, to exclude mosquitoes, rats and mice. Laurel will take up this point later.

In really hot weather it is nice to have windows that open (though our steel boat is often cooler down below than on deck, largely because she is well insulated). The problem with opening windows is that they are seldom completely watertight, nor are windows and openings of whatever type. Our fixed windows have aluminium frames, as do the skylights. They all give a little trouble from time to time because the tropical sun has perished the rubber-like compound in which the glass or acrylic is bedded, and one has to come to the conclusion that the aluminium framed opening or window is not really good enough for the long term. Replacing seals is a tedious job,

A desirable aid to ventilation.

and sadly I cannot recommend an alternative system, but we all badly need a better one.

It is not strictly necessary to have windows of the miniature mouse-hole size so often counselled by the old salts in the magazines. I have heard tell of Messrs Camper & Nicholson selling a large yacht to an American who, to demonstrate that their windows were not strong enough, hit them and broke them with a hammer, telling the builders that that was the type of force that they would need to withstand. While having every sympathy with an owner in quest of confidence in his vessel, I feel also for the builders, who had already fitted extra strong glass, which was almost certainly adequate. Don't forget that the windows have to be very well fastened into the surrounding hull.

We have had a couple of very severe storms, and been knocked down until the deckhouse was submerged, but our hull and deck-house windows have done well. (A few squirts got through, but they were not particularly noticeable in the ensuing disorder.) The ⅜ inch toughened glass in the deckhouse windows measures 37 x 19 inches, while that in the biggest hull window is 17 x 12. It is possible to build the boat like an armoured submarine: the best thing for the nervous is to have removable deadlights of ¼ inch aluminium plate, and enjoy the pleasure of good windows during 99 per cent of the time.

Though it may be very nice to contemplate a cooling breeze coming down a skylight or ventilator just over your bunk, do not do it. Sooner or later the breeze will come with water. It takes just one second to get your bedding wet; it takes ages at sea to get it even tolerably dry. One can tell the boats with this design fault as they arrive in Barbados or the Azores: their drying mattresses are slung across the main boom, and the telltale banners of their shame fly in the rigging. Surprising how often these boats have been well reviewed in the magazines.

> 'The *Beak-head* is . . . of great use as well for the grace and countenance of the ship, as a place for men to ease themselves in' [This is the derivation of the sailor's term *head*.]

Two heads are better than one, for sooner or later one will become a blocked head, usually while guests are on board. This is not always due to items being put down without being eaten first (watch out for people who eat their cherry stones), though that is often the trigger. The underlying cause is usually scaling-up owing to the salinity of the water. It is necessary to dismantle the flexible tubing every six months or so and beat it against the quay, preferably when there are few people about. An alternative method is to flush the loo a few times with a 10 percent solution of hydrochloric acid, which can be bought over the counter in most Med countries for just this purpose. It is not a way endorsed by the manufacturers.

We changed the heads on board to Lavac because this loo has a separate pump above the basin. We carry a spare pump so if a loo pump becomes blocked it is a comparatively simple task to fit the spare, leaving the unpleasant servicing job to a more convenient time. We originally fitted a holding tank head because it looked as if everywhere was going ecology-mad, but well-meaning attempts to control yacht heads have generally ended in an administrative shambles, as in the USA where, except for waterways with locks, the legislation is now discreetly ignored.

If the electrical situation will stand it, it is worth having some sort of washing machine. There is a simple, small plastic one on the market in France for about £80, and many liveaboards have one, making a point of an occasional day in a marina in order to do the washing. Laundromats are almost nonexistent in the Med. Smaller boats do the washing on the quayside, but in the larger boats, where the machine is usually plumbed in, take care that the whole system has some sort of drip tray, for almost all machines spill water to some extent and even if your hull will not rust, the gungy soapy mush will soon expand like the Quatermass experiment and fight you for possession of your ship.

Most authorities recommend that sullage tanks, to take drainage from sinks, showers and washbasins below the waterline, should be enclosed. Our experience is the opposite. We have an open sump in the keel in which is a submersible pump, and an automatic switch operated by air pressure as the water level in the sump rises. (Float switches are unreliable.) Received opinion is that this is supposed to be smelly and nasty. It is situated in the engineroom, which is well ventilated, and it does not seem to smell at all, or at least not as much as the engine, and it has the big advantage that any gunge can be easily observed and readily dealt with.

One sees a lot of boats with miniature electric fans. We have an exhaust fan above the galley stove, but no other, and I am not inclined to add one, though I must confess that visitors fresh from the coolth of an English summer sometimes talk about the heat. When in a big ship I have had to sleep with two fans directed onto my uncovered body, but this should be unnecessary in a well ventilated and insulated yacht.

If at all possible, have all machinery in one compartment that you can get into. It is no joke having a diesel engine in pieces all over the living room floor, and it ought not to be necessary except perhaps in the smallest yachts. Nor should the machinery be fitted in like a three-dimensional jigsaw puzzle for this is a poor inducement to do maintenance. Ideally one should not have to remove A to work on B or vice versa. The engine space should be very well ventilated for hot climates. We once had a fair amount of water down the engineroom ventilator when laid well over in a storm, but it was an exception. Even so it is as well to have flaps on the ventilators, and unlike me, remember to close them at the right time.

A practical navigatorium with good shelf space for both large and small books. Because the shelves are athwartships shockcord is adequate for retaining books, and enables them to be withdrawn and replaced onehanded.

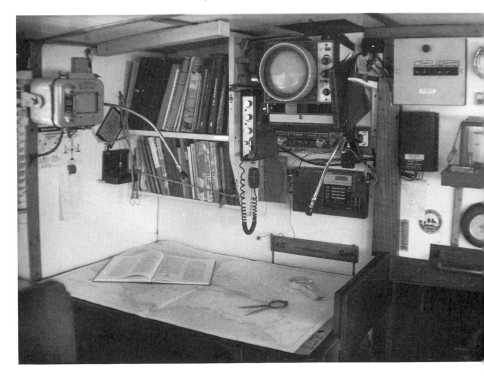

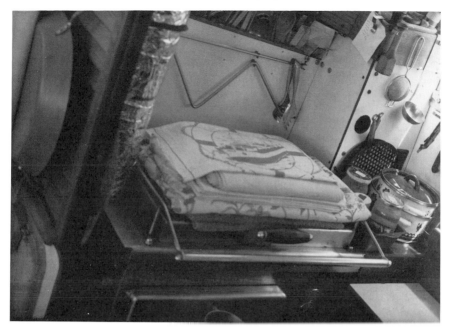

The Perkins diesel stove, showing how the ironing is done. Note also the fiddles stowed in clips, the stout crash bar and pull-out extra work space at bottom right, stowage for large paella pan (top left) and pastry board (bottom left). Everything here stays put even in very rough weather.

Some yachts equip themselves with guest cabins in the hope that they can do the occasional charter to help pay their way. I am in two minds about this. It seems to me that chartering is getting ever more professional and customers are demanding more and more facilities. In these conditions agencies are not too keen on the casual charter, which in any event is never so lucrative as the professional. They can also be hard to find just when the owner wants them. The alternative is to devote that space to more comfortable living. Of course when friends come to visit they have no super cabin, but our friends are the sort who would holiday with us in a 5-tonner, and we can accommodate them better than that. However it does not solve any financial problems for the owner.

Double bunks are now accepted but it is as well to have a method of dividing them, even for non-marital reasons. Part of our padded headboard can be lifted out and slotted fore and aft to make two very comfortable sea berths.

All in all, do not concentrate too much thought on the boat as a boat. Think of her as living room for a good deal of the time. If you can do so before buying or finishing her, sit aboard and use your imagination. Surprising what you might come up with.

117

How to Compare Cruising Boats

'Considerations for a Sea Captain in the choise of his ship'

It is comparatively easy to contemplate a yacht which one is going to use for a purpose which is already thoroughly familiar. However, not many people will be familiar with the complete dedication to the way of life required of a confirmed liveaboard, long-distance cruiser. If they are, then they are unlikely to need any help choosing a boat, but for those who would like to consider another person's outlook, I have devised the following rough assessment system. I do not expect it to stand rigorously when applied to any and every boat, but if it is used to give an idea of whether a yacht is a genuine or suitable design for long-term cruising, one can then eliminate a lot of the rubbish and end up by choosing on one's personal tastes and that feeling of attraction to a craft that is the foundation of a true boat marriage.

Before making a final choice, if you plan to go offshore read *The Ocean Cruising Yacht* by Don Street. Don is an opinionated eccentric, but he is a seaman. Many of the people who criticise his book do so not because there is anything wrong with it but because they have in some way fallen foul of the author's abrasive manner. For my part, I like someone to say something is lousy if there is good reason for saying so. You could probably say it about this evaluation scheme: I know it's not perfect, it is just something of a contribution to the debate.

Don's book is laid out to comment on fittings and features in some detail. Ignore his enthusiasm for the yawl; he owns one and is clearly in love with it and unable to see its faults. (I think it is a half-baked compromise between a ketch and a sloop, with the useful features of neither, but then, I've never had one.) But do pay some attention: go counter to 20 per cent of his advice and you could still have a sound and serviceable boat to cruise in; go counter to the lot and you would be a fool.

COOPER'S YACHT EVALUATOR

Take a piece of paper and a pen. Draw two columns, head one *Sea* and the other *Comfort*. The questions are arranged so that an affirmative answer will score as indicated in one column or the other (sometimes in both), while a negative answer will not score. Where a question is complicated there will probably be a few words of clarification immediately following. Part One is divided into two parts, for monohulls and multihulls; obviously each yacht can be considered under only one of these headings.

PART ONE

	Sea	Comfort
Monohull section		
(1) Length overall of ship: is it under 30ft	0	−2
30−35ft	1	1
35−40ft	2	3
40−50ft	2	4
over 50ft	1	4
(2) Draught: is it under 6ft	0	4
6−6½ft	2	2
6½−7ft	2	0
over 7ft	2	−4
(3) Is the length of the keel bottom more than half the waterline length?	2	0
(4) Is the after lower tip of the rudder less than 1/5 of the length overall from the stern?	−3	−1.
(5) Is there a retroussé transom?	−2	−2
(6) Is the keel bottom horizontal, or nearly so?	1	0
Multihull Section		
(7) Length overall under 26ft	−1	0
26−33ft	0	1
33−40ft	1	3
over 40ft	1	4
(8) Is there an automatic sheet-release gear?	2	0
Combined, all types		
(9) Is there clear standing headroom throughout at least 50% of the accommodation?	0	3
(10) Is there a wheelhouse? Or if not, is the conning position well protected?	1	4
	2	1
(11) Deck integrity. Is the area of cockpit (including seats) that is below the level of the main watertight deck: nil	5	0
less than 24sqft	3	0
between 24 and 40sqft	0	0
over 40sqft	−4	1
(12) For each hatch or skylight score	−1	1
(13) For each Dorade type ventilator over 4in dia. score		1
(14) For each hatch or skylight over a bunk	0	−4
(15) Is the mast(s) in tabernacle(s)?	0	1
(16) Is there a triatic stay?	−1	0
(17) Is there room for a bicycle on deck?	0	1
(18) Can a rigid tender be carried aboard?	1	2
(19) Is it easy to get aboard from the water?	1	1
(20) Easy access from shore by either bow or stern?	0	2

(21) Are there more than four openings below waterline?	−2	0
(22) Add together the breaking strain of all standing rigging that reaches the deck (see table at end). If the total is greater than		
7 × displacement in tons	10	0
6 ×	7	0
5 ×	4	0
less than 5 ×	0	0
less than 4 ×	−6	0
(23) Mast compression:		
if greater than 2 × dispacement in tons	10	0
if greater than 1.5 ×	5	0
if less than 1.5 ×	−10	0

Calculation of compression strain is somewhat complex; there are yacht designers who have never heard of Euler's formula. If you can find out from a mast maker, well and good; or you could try the approximation given in Skene's *Elements of Yacht Design*; or omit this question.

(24) We define the foretriangle as the distance from the foot of the forestay to the foreside of the mast at deck *times* half the height of the mast as far as the highest foresail halyard sheave.		
If this is greater than 40% of area of all plain sail	−4	−2
if greater than 50%	−6	−3
(25) Are there running backstays?	−2	0
(26) Is there a permanent gallows for the main boom?	1	1
(27) Are there internal halyards?	−2	0
(28) Is there roller reefing/furling on head-sail?	4	3
(29) Is there roller gear on main (and mizzen)?	2	2
(30) For each sail over 400 sq ft deduct	−3	0
(31) For a yacht over 10 tons displ. are there two or more *geared* sheet winches?	2	0

Anchors etc

(35) Is the bower (main) anchor self-stowing?	2	1
(36) If the bower is over 40lbs, is there a power windlass?	1	3
(37) Bower anchor cable. Is it chain,		
more than 150ft?	4	0
less than 150ft?	1	0
all nylon?	−1	−1

(38)   Bower anchor size. Calculate frontal area of craft: multiply mast height from waterline by beam of hull, both in feet. (I know the boat is not that wide at the top of the mast, but the wind is a lot stronger up there and this is a good approximation.) Divide this area by 8. This gives desirable anchor weight in pounds, and applies to Danforth, CQR and Bruce anchors. Anchors of other types score nothing, and that includes imitations of above.

If no anchor of above size	−5	0
If one anchor of above size	4	0
If two	6	0
If three	7	0

(One might reasonably have one or two additional anchors at about three-quarters this size for use as a kedge or lunch-hook.) Q 38 applies only to conventional sailing yachts.

(39)   Chain cable size. Diameter of link in 16ths of an inch. Datum size is $\frac{1}{12}$ the anchor weight in pounds plus $\frac{1}{16}$. Minimum $\frac{1}{4}$in.

If chain over or equal to above size	4	0
If chain smaller	−4	0
(40) Is the engine petrol (gasoline)?	−2	−3
(41) Does fuel tankage in gallons exceed 3 × engine hp?	1	1
(42) Is there a second means of generating electricity?	0	3
(43) Are deck and hull skin well insulated?	0	4
(44) Are there two separate batteries?	1	2
(45) Water tanks. Are there at least two, with total capacity (Imp.gal.) more than 10 × displacement in tons?	0	4
Two tanks but more than 6 ×	0	0
One tank only (ignore rubber tanks)	−1	−6
(46) Can you actually sit down on all four sides of the engine?	0	2
(47) Do you have access to the engine without dismantling half the accommodation?	0	1
(48) Is the heating system independent of electricity?	0	2
(49) Is cooking by either diesel oil, paraffin or bottled gas?	0	1
(50) Is the cooker either gimballed or fully fiddled?	0	1
(51) Is there a fiddled draining board or putting-down space?	0	1

(52) Is there a fridge?	0	2
(53) Does total dry locker space for clothes exceed 6 cu ft per permanent bunk?	0	2
(54) Number of permanent berths. Divide displacement in tons by number of berths:		
if over 5	0	6
under 5 but over 4	0	3
under 4 but over 3	0	1
under 2	0	−5
(55) Is there separate saloon and sleeping accommodation?	0	3
(56) Is there a wc compartment with shower?	0	2
(57) Non-clothing lockerage, above the cabin sole: is there more than 1.5 cu ft per ton displacement?	0	2
(58) Is there a good clear area of deck for lounging?	0	1
(59) Is there an autopilot?	2	4
(60) If no autopilot, is there a windvane?	2	2
(61) Is an echosounder fitted?	1	0
(62) Are there at least two deck cleats, eyes or bitts, each capable of taking a lateral pull of half the weight of the boat without pulling out?	4	0

(How to tell? Well, it's a bit difficult to provide a complete answer: such a fitting will probably look too big, but won't be. If in any doubt, it's not big enough.)

Table of Approximate Breakloads for 1 × 19 stainless steel wire, for use with the above Questionnaire

Circumference	Approx. diam.	Breakload
5⁄8 inches	4 mm	4,700 lbs
3⁄4	6	8,000
1	8	12,000
1¼	10	17,500
1½	12	30,000
1¾	14	46,000

Now add the scores of each column separately. The *Sea* column is meant to give some estimate of whether the yacht is fit to go to sea at all as a cruising boat. Do not expect the score to be conclusive; I am quite sure that there could well be exceptions, but most really worthwhile cruising boats should score well over 50 points. The *Comfort* column has a broad coverage of those factors which affect one's standard of living; the idea is not to provide sybarism to the Onassis standard but to try to achieve a living above the 'grotty squalor' level, the sort of compromise between comfortable existence at sea and

The Refleks diesel oil heater, which being fanless is quiet. Later models are a bit more elegant.

relaxed life in port. A good score in the Comfort column would be 60, but 50 might be treated as a minimum. We have inevitably leaned heavily on our own preferences and opinions but have tried to allow for other points of view. If you have a strong opinion on some factor that differs from ours, then give it your own weighting; the important thing is to use common criteria for all vessels surveyed.

For interest, we reckon *Fare Well* scores 58 + 65. Bearing in mind that all boats are something of a compromise between sea-keeping and comfort, it might be as well, after first making sure that there is an adequate score under each heading, to compare totals.

A problem with this 'evaluator' is that it takes quite a time to assess each yacht; it is a very detailed examination giving a weighting of some sort to most things worthwhile in a liveaboard yacht. To save time one should have a means of discarding unsuitable craft by drawing up a shortlist. Keep the two broad criteria, seaworthiness and comfort. I suggest the following are seriously on the debit side in assessing seaworthiness in the context of this book:

Deep, short, fin keel which tends to directional instability.
Rudder hung right aft, which is vulnerable to damage, and also becomes inefficient when pitching in a following sea.

123

Large foretriangle with Bermudan rig is tough on small crews.
Main shroud chainplates well inside deck edge: leads to higher tension in shrouds and greater compression in mast.
Anchors not self-stowing, hard on weaklings like me.
Running backstays are a pain in the transom.
Bendy masts often bend too far, right over perhaps.
Two or more sails over 400 sq ft. Tough on small crews.
Steeply cambered decks are a poor foothold. In theory OK on one side when heeled. In practice, at sea one is never at a constant angle.
Guardrails less than 30 inches high are tripwires.
Cockpit that is not self-drained, and adequately so.
All things are a compromise, but I think I would not like to trust my life in a yacht with more than five of the above debit points.

Items that detract seriously from the joy of living in a yacht are more idiosyncratic. Make your own list, but consider:

Lack of good shelter at the steering position.
Lack of separate sleeping/daytime accommodation.
Cockpit that is uncomfortable to lounge about in.
Lack of a simple heating system.
Insufficient fresh water (less than 200 gals)
Poor hanging lockers.
Poor ventilation.
Engine access in living space.
Pokey little galley, ill-lit or ill-ventilated.
Less than 20 feet of bookshelves.

I would not be very comfortable in a yacht with many of these points. Set your own limit: five perhaps.

In the end, whether you are looking at the short assessment or the more detailed, you have to face the fact that logic often plays second fiddle to love in the choice of both spouses and boats. Did you really go through all this sort of thing before choosing your wife? Minus three for a long nose, plus two for good puddings? Of course you didn't (I hope). And you probably won't choose your yacht this way either, but you might have fun looking at a few.

Naming your Boat.

When we came to registering our new home we had to face up to the problem of naming her. We would have liked to keep her existing Dutch name, *De Tijd zal 'tLeren IV*, which means 'Time will teach you', but we do not like names which have numbers after them, and we had found it impossible to cope with the Dutch name outside Holland. Almost unpronounceable to the English, it would be completely so to the French, Italians and Greeks, it promised us a lifetime devoted to spelling it out in full, and having radio messages garbled out of recognition.

Hosanna she became. It is a word that is reasonably common to all languages, it is cheerful, and it doesn't tread on anyone's toes. Things which have to be thought of, or should be, if one is off to foreign cruising grounds. Also it is one of the traditional Lowestoft fishing boat names; names with a ring to them like Kipling's trawler-minesweepers;

'Call up Unity, Clarabell, Assyrian,
Stormcock and Golden Gain'

If you are intending long-distance cruising it is as well not to give your boat names like *Cough-drop of Loughborough*, or *Pwllhelly Phyllis*. Make up your own little list of impossibles. We once came across an Italian yacht called *Titty*. And off the coast of the USA we overheard a distress call from a boat called *Sexy Lady*. It was very difficult to take it seriously.

In the West Indies, where all the local traders keep watch on VHF, we heard a very aristocratic English voice calling 'Scuba Shop, this is Darling Two'. Eventually a deep bass Paul Robeson answered 'Hallooo Darling!'

Even our old *Fare Well*, which you might have thought was straight-forward enough, was written down sometimes as 'Fairly Well,' or 'Fairy Well,' and on one never to be forgotten document in Turkey as 'Fart Well'. Take care.

CHAPTER SEVEN

People, Pets and Pests

'There are so many young Captaines and those that desire to be Captaines, who know very little, or nothing at all to any purpose' ...'

A great many preconceived notions can be left on the quay on departure, along with the cardboard boxes, empty beer crates, broken gadgets bought at the Boat Show and other cruising detritus. Among these could be stereotypes long overdue for discard, such as: old ladies cannot be expected to climb on board boats, girls can't row, children are not useful, and pets are a nuisance at sea.

You now enter a world where many a nippy Grannie leaps lightly into a dinghy and trims it without being asked as others follow. She has probably steered a yacht in a gale on an Atlantic crossing. Yon lovely girl, so slim and ethereal, can probably get the starboard jib-sheet to the winch and hove in while you are still thinking about it, let alone row you a mile ashore. The rope you have just thrown to a likely-looking native, who is standing there looking perplexed while the wind carries you rapidly away from the quay, is apt to be seized by a tow-headed eight-year-old, who makes a bowline in the wink of an eye, drops it over the upwind bollard and disappears down the companionway of that little Dutch sloop. As for pets, my crew would never be complete without a cat.

Without too much prejudice, then, let us look at who can do what on board, and how to avoid unnecessary conflict.

It is no longer true that 'Captain' equals 'male'. Many girls and women are Skippers these days, so when I speak of Captains please believe that they are not exclusively masculine. I am more familiar with a male Skipper, and being told what to do as regards navigation and ship-handling. Other areas are my concern: the feeding, health and welfare of the crew are in my charge. In case of bodily accidents, I take over — not because I know more than Bill, but because *in that situation* I have a cool head and don't mind the blood. Much. Also, Bill still has to sail the boat. (Ah! you say: but what if the Skipper has the accident? We'll come to these things in Chapter 11.) I am also in charge of victualling and storing for long voyages, which is as it should be since I am usually also the shopper and cook.

How to be Captain

'The Captaine's charge is to command all.'

Our good Captain Smith once again says it all in a nutshell. The one person who need not worry about his status is the Captain: it is never in doubt. No company president, managing director, or even eminent surgeon on his rounds tailed by milling underlings, can know the power of being Master under God (as the Lloyds policy puts it) of a ship, however small. The rest of us, according to another well known source, are a little lower than the angels, which presumably puts the captain slightly above them. This gives him a natural authority instantly recognized by landsmen, which is not surprising. What *is* perhaps surprising is that the quiet authority of a good Captain is recognized even when he is in bare feet and ragged shorts, and by his/her spouse.

No ship can ever run satisfactorily as a commune: the job of a Captain is to be Captain. I have never been Captain (except for a few hours entering the Turkish port of Datça, when Bill had a bad attack of Saladin's Revenge), so of course I have every right to comment on the subject, especially from the point of view of the crew. I use the word 'Capting' to signify Bossiness without leadership, so if I answer my spouse, 'Yes, Capting,' he knows I consider he is merely throwing his weight about and not giving sensible orders. He does not do it often.

A good Captain explains a manoeuvre in advance, and thus does not need to shout complicated instructions at a bewildered crew at the last minute.

His orders are clear and unambiguous, thus he does not need to repeat them with rising hysteria and ever-increasing decibels.

If his crew make a mess of it, he wastes no time cursing. He says 'All right, folks: we go round and do it again.' (He is allowed to grit his teeth, however.)

If he makes an error of judgement he accepts it without fuss and does not blame his crew for it.

He does not get too excited if the anchor chain comes in slowly, when it always *does* come in slowly.

He shouts when ambient noise at the crew's end makes it necessary. Having said that:

Captains are the ultimate authority on everything connected with the ship and crew. Wise mates and knowledgeable crew may help him to make the decisions, but he is the arbiter.

He should make sure all on board know his policy on certain important mishaps and events, such as fire, shipwreck and man-overboard.

He should be able to delegate many tasks, but it must be clear whose responsibility they are, and he should be prepared to back up his delegate with authority. It is important that he should be loyal to his crew, as they are to him.

A good Captain is recognizable not by his autocracy and didacticism, but by the respect in which he is held by his crew. It is not necessary for him to be the best qualified one on board, since it is possible for highly qualified people to be bad Captains. This is not to say that experience and knowledge are not to be acquired wherever possible; but courses of instruction should be carefully selected by recommendation rather than picked with a pin from alluring ads in the Yachting Press: thus you will avoid those courses run by old and bold military men who are nutty about semaphore, and condescend to your wife: 'This the little woman?' they roar, 'Soon make a good cabin boy out of you, eh?'

The Yachtmaster's Certificate, for example, is all useful knowledge and updated at intervals; but to have gained it is not the be-all and end-all, nor is the Coast Guard Captain's Licence in the USA. Both these admirable qualifications tend to be oriented towards local waters and conditions, and should be regarded as forming merely a sound basis for a great deal of further experience: there will be much to learn about sailing in more distant parts.

A good Captain conducts an orchestra in which he may not play the bassoon too well, but he knows its function as part of the whole and all the players look to him for direction. Or to her, since both conductors and Captains may well be women these days. This causes no bother to most people, as she is usually in this position because her crew feel comfortable about her being there. It is again a question of respect. If certain bigoted and reactionary people find it intolerable to take orders from a woman, they should leave, and find a bigoted and reactionary Captain who will suit them better.

Every Captain will make mistakes, and sometimes they will be serious. Apportioning blame may be balm to the wounded spirit, but it is unproductive. After disasters, start from NOW. He may find himself in dire straits through no fault of his own, or indeed anyone's, and he will still blame himself. We left Bermuda with an excellent weather forecast, heading north with the expectation of leaving the West Indies well before the hurricane season: June, the rhyme goes, is too soon (for the hurricanes to come). On the eighteenth of June, two days out, we got warning of a tropical storm which had rapidly deepened into Hurricane Alberto. After the vortex had passed us, with no great damage, we were struck by a violent squall and a flash of lightning, early in the morning. Bill's only crime was being on watch when it happened, but the shock of it, and the despair at seeing our sails in ribbons, laid him very low for a while. We were three on board. The watch below, Nora and I, were precipitated up on deck by the noise and the knockdown. Even if richly deserved, recriminations are unaffordable luxuries at such times, and this squall had been far too sudden for any action to have been effective. Nora and I made comforting and reassuring noises to our stricken Captain, and as soon as I could get the stove going we fed him on quantities of scrambled egg, since we were in no immediate danger and all had headaches from the

ORTE DE PÊCHE
AULIEU, FRANCE

lightning strike. Then we took a deep breath, and under his direction began to restore the ship to order. We were still 400 miles from land and it was going to be a slow and uncomfortable voyage, but it had to be faced. Neither Master nor crew can say at some point 'I don't want to play any more.'

What if the Captain and crew really don't get on at all? Suppose your Skipper, at the Yacht Club bar so smooth and full of salty tales of successful voyages and dangers overcome, turns out to be sufficiently bogus to be a menace to both his ship and crew?

Suppose he retires to his bunk at times of stress, abdicating to his crew decisions which he should make, and for which he will later blame them? (This is a true story, and happened to a friend of ours who is a very experienced crew. She continued to the end of the voyage, and even though the ship reached Europe some 600 miles north of the position the cataleptic skipper thought he was in, no hurt or damage occurred, probably due to a good crew on the watch for trouble.)

Suppose the athletic girl taken on for crossing the Atlantic screams when the boat heels, or is afraid of the dark and won't keep night watches? Or the strong lad turns out to be impossible to live with?

Most incompatibilities of this kind can be avoided by a shakedown cruise, with no commitment on either side. Living aboard is about long-term tolerance, so a series of weekends or holidays afloat are not really the answer, though they may reveal intolerably irritating habits or personality aspects. You need to fight your way through a few situations to find out how you are going to get on under stress. To be able to duck out of trouble too easily, as you mostly can on weekend and holiday cruising, negates the point of the exercise. Most of all, you need time to work together and evolve an everyday smoothness of running, so that routine tasks become second nature, and there is more time and energy to cope with unexpected surprises. Thus, while no one is perfect, you will not set off on a long cruise with someone who rubs you up the wrong way. I have said elsewhere that marriages may not survive the strains imposed on them by the cruising life (this goes for friendships and Captain/crew relationships too), but marital breakdown, mutiny and mid-Atlantic mayhem are outside the scope of this book.

As you will have noticed, a great many observations that can be made about Captains are inextricably entangled with those about Crew, since they are two sides of the same coin. Should a short-handed Captain take on a 'pierhead jump' (an unknown crew who joins at the last moment)? It is a desperate measure, fraught with risk and uncertainty. Only the Captain can weigh need against risk. In the West Indies such a crew must possess an air ticket outward before being allowed to sign off the crew list of any vessel. It is the Captain's responsibility to ensure that such a ticket exists, or he risks being landed with the person indefinitely. We have sometimes taken on someone at short notice: they were all a great success, but they came with recommendations from people we knew and trusted. Many couples we know have had a very different experience, however, even resulting in vowing never to take crew again however short-handed they were. The sins of the said crew varied from drug abuse, smuggling, theft and laziness, to actually taking command of the yacht in mid-Atlantic, from a rather elderly couple who were powerless to stop them. The only time we took a crew who had not been personally recommended by someone *who had actually sailed with them,* but only by a man they had done some boatwork for, we regretted it all the way from Gibraltar to the Azores.

You must also be aware that if drugs are found on your boat it is liable to confiscation, even if you were unaware of their existence. It is not necessarily the hippier looking people who take drugs. Which takes us back to reliable references, living with prospective crew for a few days, and discovering their attitudes and habits. At close quarters one has a better chance of finding out before it is too late. We come, inevitably, to:

How to be Crew

'The saylors are the elder men, for hoising the sailes, haling the bowlings, and stearing the shippe.'

There is no task in a boat that is sexually exclusive. Some jobs require brawn, and there are women who can do them and have enough breath left to whistle at the same time. Others of us are rather less muscular, but perhaps good at fiddly jobs requiring great patience. Apart from being helpful, tolerant, humorous at the right moment and tactful, it helps to have a little knowledge.

For ABSOLUTE BEGINNERS and a few others we could name, we have included a 'Starter Pack' at the end of the book on the Bowline, and one or two other essentials. While unlikely to prove the definitive work on the subject (indeed, this book is not about seamanship), NO-ONE WHO HAS TAKEN IN THE FULL IMPORT OF THAT SECTION IS USELESS. Anyone who can make a bowline, and has learnt the intelligent use of fenders without bumping into the rest of the crew is already of considerable help; I particularly address myself to those windblown lovelies who are so disrespectfully called 'crew's comforts' by their companions.

With even this small amount of knowledge you would not be unwelcome on most yachts. Better still (as Noel Coward said) if you don't bump into the furniture. Such happy beginners are more use than theoretical know-alls who will devise you a spendid new lead for the jibsheet which carries away the starboard rail when tested.

Nevertheless, to be of real use as a trusted watchkeeper a crew member should know:
— where everything is kept, and what it is called

— how to switch on the engine and use it
— what the normal reading should be for all dials and meters
— how to lower and row the dinghy
— the Rule of the Road at Sea
— enough coastal navigation to put a fix on the chart
— basic sail and shiphandling
— how to steer a compass course
— the first steps to take in several various emergencies
— and how to use the VHF or other radio

(The RYA publish annually a booklet called *Practical Cruising Courses* which lists recognized sailing schools, with details and prices of the courses run. Go on one.)

We now have to recall that the crew and Captain are likely to be members of one family, or friends (long may they be so), and there is a lot to be said for *everyone* learning *everything*. In *Freya*, whom we met in the Chesapeake and the Bahamas, the family, with two young daughters, changed tasks daily so they all had their turn at engine bleeding, navigating, cooking and so on. This system might suit you very well. Diffident crew members also appreciate being given an area of personal concern, and time to research and study it. Such areas could be meteorology, cooking and victualling, radio, engines or first aid. The Captain does not have to be the navigator.

Bill and I use the 'specialist and backup' system. He is such a good navigator that it is hard for me to compete; but it would be obviously stupid for me not to know my coastal navigation, or how to take a sun sight and work it out, however slowly and painfully. Conversely, I am a far better cook so I do most of it, but we would not starve if he had to do it for awhile. When Bill is upside-down in the engineroom on a rough day I am guiltily aware that I would far rather be steering, cooking, sail trimming and piloting (all at once) *plus* handing him his tools, tissues and tea, and receiving in exchange bad language, bad temper and blame. The 'dirty bits' of the boat are not for me, unless I am required to wriggle into some small corner that Bill is too big to get into.

We are well aware that most cruising crews consist of one man and one woman, most of the time. It behoves both of you to be capable. Running a yacht properly requires teamwork of operating theatre calibre.

Whether your crew is large or small, we will suppose that they have been chosen after a shakedown cruise, and you have weeded out (or selected, according to preference) smokers, vegetarians, flat-earthers and bridge fiends. Even when the crew has been tailored, as it were, to fit, irritating habits should be curbed. In a small space the utmost tact and tolerance is essential. Snoring, nail clippings, washing (either too much or too little), black hole filing systems and food fads are all annoying; make your own nasty little list.

Good netting protects these French youngsters. It is quite effective for parents too.

If the crew is the basic man/woman one, there is room for you to sulk (as we do) at opposite ends of the boat till tempers are recovered. At sea, this is hardly necessary, since the days are busy, and we hardly meet at night except to hand over the watch and are usually pleased to see each other by breakfast time.

We have a little rhyme that describes the sort of crew we do not want to take with us. It goes:

> No no-hopers, no topers,
> No one round the bend,
> No no-soapers, no gropers,
> No windbags (either end).

Children and Babies

The children we meet who live aboard yachts are almost invariably courteous, at home in any company, pleasant to talk to, willing and reliable. They are integrated with their family in a way that is fast being forgotten when children no longer work alongside their parents at any demanding task; especially against time and the elements. They now do not help with the harvest, mend the nets, help launch the lifeboat, or dig for victory as used to be the case; and so do not share

133

the satisfaction of a difficult job well done. A sea voyage, however, is something that is achieved by the whole family; and the pride in it shines out of the childrens' eyes.

A single child often misses the company of other children, and plenty of opportunity should be found for mixing, since it is too easy in an adult environment where responsibility is the watchword, for the child to forget how to be a child, and to find difficulty in relating to his own age group when the time comes.

If the child or children accompanying you are of school age, you have to face their education. Whether you do this alone or with help from their teachers, or by correspondence course, you are in for a tough time. In Australia, France and the USA correspondence courses are quite usual. Ten-year-old Ben Lucas on *Tientos* was working on an Australian course, which needed assistance from his mother Pat. The parents of Grant Dawson on *Iolanthe* had tried both the Calvert system (USA) and the British PNEU course. They preferred the latter as being more of a challenge, though the Calvert system needed no assistance from parents since everything was provided down to the last pencil and rubber and the child could be left to tackle it alone. Most parents prefer to be more actively involved, however, though it costs many hours of work.

One couple we met had had remarkable co-operation from the school that their child had attended: a stack of about twenty books was provided and a syllabus of work covering the next two years — which must have taken some dedicated teacher a lot of time and trouble to prepare.

However you go about it, it is no joke having to cope with lessons when you would rather be swimming; and this is as hard for the supervising parent as it is for the child; if you are temporarily in a yottie community it can help to run 'the school' on one boat, in rotation: the children benefit from interaction and competition even if they are doing different courses, and only one parent need supervise the gang. Mornings are best for the heavy work, while the minds are fresh (you will notice that a good school timetable puts the maths and Latin before the first break if they can), leaving the more pleasurable side of things till later.

Thank goodness, there *is* the other side of the coin. Great delight and interest can be found in visits ashore, studying people and places, the local museums, the customs and culture of many lands; and some of the language does not come amiss either. There is also a wealth of sea and shore life: fish, birds, plants, dwellers in rock pools and in sand holes, shells, trees and flowers. Recognition books for all these things should be part of the 'school library'. A scrapbook will find a place for exotic bus tickets, postcards, programmes, labels and so on.

A well kept log by each child combines many disciplines: writing, drawing, recording things seen, self-expression and observation are only a few of them. A rough book would help to lay out an attractive page. Since such a log will one day be a treasured reminder of the voyage, it would be worth presenting the child with a really important-looking hardcover book, such as are now available with unlined pages and attractive leather-type bindings, to encourage best efforts and the production of something to be immensely proud of.

Small babies pose few problems at sea. My six-month old required feeding, a change of nappies and a safe place to sleep; nothing else. She did not seem to be at all worried by even quite violent motion, and was certainly not seasick: this seems to come with the toddler stage. At times of stress (ours, not hers) we put her in a carry-cot wedged between the two forward bunks where, to our amazement, she learnt to stand up — briefly, before sitting down suddenly when we hit a wave.

As for feeding, battling with baby bottles on a stormy night is a very good way to get scalded, as I discovered. Bottled milk is not nearly so convenient as draught, especially at sea: I have yet to hear of any one coming to any grief through breastfeeding. You certainly don't get scalded. Nowadays I should probably use a cold-water method such as Milton for sterilization of the bottles, and think of a foolproof way of warming the milk.

Baby food, in jars or tins, is widely available in the western Mediterranean, the States and the bigger West Indian islands, but stock up if you are venturing farther.

When my mother took me sailing at six weeks old (a daring thing to do in those days) she put me in a box of bran with a muslin square under me, and tossed out the damp bran as necessary. I have heard of sawdust, sand and seaweed being used in the same way. Kitty Litter is feasible, but a little lumpy. It is great for adults when the loo gets blocked, but is not available in the wilds. Nowadays we have disposable napkins (diapers to the Cousins) and you would think that washing nappies was a thing of the past. So it is, in many parts of Europe and the USA where disposables are readily available. If you are going to remote places, however, they will be expensive and hard to find. They are too bulky to store many on board. You may have to revert to the terrycloth or muslin squares of Grandma's day.

Mark and Felicity on *Scout* used a mixture of disposables and terry nappies for young Teresa. They were given a preliminary cleaning by towing astern, a watch being kept for dolphins who enjoy stealing them to play with! They needed a thorough final rinse in fresh water, or terrible chafing and soreness would result.

At eighteen months, Teresa loves the shipboard life. She is used to being dunked in the water (many yottie babies can swim at six months) so she has no fear of going under water, but she cannot quite swim yet without her inflatable armbands.

Yachts with small children on board usually reinforce the guardrails with netting, to fill in the gap down to the toerail that a small child might slip through. We have netting on the foredeck as after all it is just as well to stop adults and sails falling through.

It has to be remembered that toddlers are all little Paganinis: great fiddlers. I watched recently, fascinated but unable to intervene, as three year old Suzanne on the neighbouring boat unpegged her mother's bikini from the guardrail and, chuckling, dropped it over the far side. We lent them our net, always handy for such events. Teresa loses tools and other objects by posting them into the rubbish bin. Sea mothers need even sharper eyes than their shore counterparts, since there are so many knobs, switches, buttons and hand pumps on a yacht; and they cannot all be put out of the reach of an active and curious toddler. I have seen a variety of ingenious devices to protect vital switches — shockcord, wedges, Perspex lids over a whole bank of them: necessity is the mother of invention.

In times of activity or crisis, babies are plonked in a safe place. This is essential for parents to get any peace at all. It takes the form of a playpen, or a well wedged carry-cot or 'padded cell'. The best idea, which I have seen many variations of, is the pilot berth transformed into a miniature nursery, well cushioned, with a strong net that snaps in place over the front. The baby comes to consider this as 'his', it is comfortable, full of his soft toys and comfort blankets or pillows, and he seldom objects to being put there for a spell. And even if he wimps a bit, you know he's safe and can be ignored till the rush is over or you have had your siesta.

Children are people too, and while their skills are yet few they can be aided to feel valuable. They should join in all the activities they are capable of, and be taught the right way to do them. They should be given definite jobs to do, such as care of the fishing gear. On long passages they can be asked to read the log at intervals and record the result. It can be their job to identify and record birds, fish and sea creatures seen. The tasks must be seen to be genuinely useful or rewarding, and take them to the limit of their capabilities, so that they are not shrugged off when they are not in the mood: responsibility starts early at sea. It all helps to prevent boredom. (Yes, long passages can be very boring.)

How to be Navigator

'The Master is to see to the conning of the shippe.'

Traditionally a man's task, this is changing fast. There is no foundation for believing that women are less numerate than men: many of us were very badly taught. We can, however, learn. A female navigator is a threat only to very old-fashioned Captains who have forgotten that centuries ago no Captain would have been able to 'see to the conning of the shippe' since that was a well protected mystery known only to the Master, and the wealth of published pilot books, tables and charts that we now have did not exist. Only much later did the job of the Shippe man and the Captain merge, when it was realized that a practical seaman made a better Captain than the aristocrat who knew nothing.

Navigation is a practical skill. The theoretical side can be learned at school (see the yachting press for ads) and there are also evening classes, usually associated with various Certificates. To acquire the practical knowledge, there is no substitute for doing it. Like driving, it is a skill that is probably NOT best imparted by one's spouse if peace is to reign. The courses at the National Sailing School at Cowes were excellent, what a pity they no longer exist. Similar courses are widely available and ensure that you do not remain an eternal student, without confidence in your convictions, but return with a self-assurance born of knowledge, coupled with a respectful wariness from having done it yourself.

A good navigator is always aware of his ship's position in space, and he is always checking the instruments which tell him where he is. He checks his compass daily: in coastal waters against known transits, at sea against the rising or setting of the sun or moon. If something puzzles him or does not add up, he will not rest until he has solved the problem. He pays regard to a strong feeling that something is wrong. He is rigid about keeping his DR (deduced reckoning) going, and expects you to do the same when it is your watch. He will be very unhappy if you fib about the course and speed, whether because you nodded off and did not pay attention, or because you would prefer your performance to seem rather better than it was. He checks his sextant for index error in case someone has fiddled with it. He is the one that notices what time the electronic log failed, and remembers to allow for the half hour you spent going round in circles when the jib furling gear jammed.

He never leaves anything to chance. You do not hear him say 'Yes, I *think* that's Cape Krio, we can alter course now.' He checks till he *knows* that it is Cape Krio. Otherwise you end up like the honeymoon couple we met in the West Indies, who mistook the radio mast on Union Island for that on Mayreau Island, and instead of (as they thought) entering harbour ran on the reef off Carriacou.

Harmony can be maintained at the chart table by not getting ink, cocoa rings, gravy, chewing gum, setting lotion etc on the charts. Pencils should not be allowed to drop or the lead breaks at half-inch intervals all the way through, causing terrible anguish as pencils are always sharpened when the Master doesn't know where he is, and the irritation effect is cumulative. Practice with a cheap plastic sextant, and you won't be worrying about damaging that gorgeous brass and varnish antique that your spouse is so dotty about.

Avoid using the Navigating notebook for shopping lists, and the dividers for opening tins, and perhaps the Cook's wooden spoon might not get used for stirring bilge paint.

How to be the Weather-man

'It overcasts. We shall have winde, foule weather.'

I don't think it is chauvinistic to say that women are (by my observation) much better at languages than men. It may be that we are more willing to try. Perhaps it is to do with having to make sense of what the very young and very old are saying to us: we seem to have a greatly enhanced aural perception. That is to say, we can listen to a toothless old biddy in the marketplace speaking a thick dialect in a language we don't understand; then turn to our astonished menfolk and say, 'It's four and a half Filas for a Katlo, and please will we bring the container back.'

This leads to the women getting the job of listening to foreign language weather forecasts, which at times of bad reception sound far worse than the market lady and there are no nods, gestures and mime to assist comprehension. Thus, we get to be the meteorologist, too.

If you have previously studied nothing more weighty than your corns, it is time to find out why you can't break Buys Ballot's Law, why weather systems have fronts but no backs, and why:

> When in port you choose to stay
> The Goddam gale will go away,
> But when to sea you choose to go,
> The Goddam wind comes on to blow.

Courses in Meteorology for Yachtsmen are run mostly in conjunction with the Yachtmaster's Certificate, in the UK. They are another subject that can be taken as evening classes (see your local Education Authority list, which usually comes out in August for classes beginning in September) or as practical weeks or weekends as part of a Cruising School, such as the 'Weather under Sail' course run by the Island Cruising Club in conjunction with the Royal Meteorological Society. Courses can be of various lengths, with emphasis on met and practical forecasting according to students' needs — as well as the usual navigation, seamanship etc.

Since most weather forecasts are read at normal speed, you need a shorthand of some kind. While there are international symbols for weather phenomena, they are not adequate; and you will need to supplement them with your own. Do not believe the RYA booklet *Weather Forecasts* when it blithely tells you that the international symbols 'will enable you to appreciate at a glance the information which is contained on any weather map which you may see displayed in Clubs or Ports of call.' This applies (as do most RYA statements) only to Great Britain. Elsewhere in Europe, the Mediterranean, the West Indies and America (except for some huge and expensive marinas which rarely concern the cruising yottie) the weather reports are in words, on teleprinter or standard form, in the local language and often the local handwriting. A very few Port Captains are beginning to have grey-on-grey Weatherfax reproductions, which are so appallingly smudgy and hard to read that they always put the plain words teleprint form up as well. Even in a foreign language it is easier to read.

Both the RYA handbook and *Reed's Almanac* have a weather vocabulary (three languages in *Reed's* and six in the RYA booklet) and these are very useful, though they contain identical mistakes in Spanish and Italian. *Weather for Sailing* and *Meteorology at Sea* (by Ray Sanderson pub. Stanford Maritime) explains weather symbols and how to take down broadcast information, link it to your own observations, and construct and understand weather maps. If you can get the radio broadcast report down on tape, you can worry it out at leisure. You will get used to the orderly progression of it, and the sound of the words, and soon be able to take it down direct.

Italy gets the Gold Sou'wester for the best TV weather report in the Med, on RAI (Radiotelevisione Italiana) Channel 1. France has a good one. Most of the radio reports are good, and Greece translates into English after their morning bulletin.

In America you can buy a tiny transistor radio which keeps you informed of the weather round the clock, from the National Weather Service. The reports are broadcast on WX1, WX2 or WX3 twenty-four hours a day and updated as necessary. The radio costs very little, and most people find it well worth having for coastal and offshore use.

The only weather services which reach right across the Atlantic in either direction are in Morse. The Admiralty List of Radio Signals, Vol 3 is certainly the most comprehensive book of weather broadcasts in the world, both voice and CW (Morse), but it is usually out of date by the time it is published and is laid out like a Chinese puzzle.

If you do not know Morse, big ships have radio operators on board, most of whom are happy to pass the time of day with you and give you a weather forecast: they get bored on long passages too. Do not expect to see more than two or three ships, big or small, on your entire crossing, though, and do not try calling up US warships, as we did in mid-Atlantic. At first they would not even admit that they were there at all, reminding me of a large Newfoundland puppy trying to hide in a daisy patch. Then they seemed to think that the weather forecast was a classified piece of information. After much delay and seeking of permission they gave us a cautious description of the weather we were actually experiencing at the time. The Russian 'trawler' shadowing them was much more helpful.

The cruising yacht is very much on its own and must be self-sufficient. We act at all times as if there were no such thing as rescue services, which indeed is the case in mid-ocean. We are proud of our ten years of sailing and cruising with no calls for assistance: if we were in trouble we coped with our own resources. Judging what the weather was going to do next if you could get no forecast is an important and normal part of that resource.

Finally, if you ever need detailed weather forecasting, if you are looking for a weather 'window' to start a particular voyage for example; you can get expert forecasts tailor-made for your boat, your crew and your voyage, over the period of a month, from the British Meteorological Office at very modest cost.

How to be Cook

'The cooke is to dresse and deliver out the victual.'

It is a poor cook who is not also a psychologist. This comes fairly easily to most women, who knowing how to cook on shore have a head start at sea, and therefore get landed (not the most apt word here) with the job. Notwithstanding centuries of professional contempt thrown at the historical sea cook, and the extensive list of rude names for his dishes and his person, his contribution was vital and his lack of it often lethal. It is a job of immeasurable importance. Preserving morale in bad weather or other adverse conditions may rest heavily on the cook. 'Fate cannot harm me, I have dined today' said Sidney Smith. There is something unbelievably heartening about hot food and drink, and anyone who can rustle up an appetising one-pan dish in hell-and-high-water conditions is more to be prized than a Cordon Bleu. I've not noticed that men are any better at this than women: I have a strong feeling that it depends sometimes on who is hungriest. But the young male still tends to give cooking a low priority, and will stuff himself with anything that costs him no trouble rather than remembering the welfare of others, as a true cook should.

Practical help on cooking and victualling will be found in Chapter Nine, but before you embark be sure to take a few books to help you cope with the odder products of nature. You may not actually have to eviscerate a duck-billed platypus, or lightly kill an armour-plated turtle that is looking you straight in the eye; but you can see the way my mind is working. You may be leaving the fish fingers and pre-packed drumsticks far behind, and encountering unfamiliar fruits and vegetables as well.

Be sure you learn to make bread, in all its varieties. Fresh hot bread is as good for the spirits as the sight of land after a long voyage.

How to Steer and Keep a Night Watch

'Steer steady and keep your course so you go well'

Steering looks so easy. To some people, it is: they fall into the way of it immediately. Others find it hard. They wrestle and wrench the wheel;

they oversteer and the ship hunts this way and that like a dog after truffles. The compass confuses them and the watch below groan as the ship's motion deteriorates. They chase the spinning compass card till they are dizzy, and seem to have no tenderness or coaxing in them, to sense the ship's needs. Fortunately, most of us learn to be at least adequate helmsmen. In bad weather half an hour may be quite enough at the wheel or tiller. It is hard work; you are likely to be steering because it has become more than the autopilot can cope with, however excellently (better than most of us, rot it) it can perform in calmer seas, and your concentration quickly tires. A certain mad exhilaration can set in with a force 7 behind you; you think you are doing very well indeed, like a drunken driver. It took quite a bit of persuasion to pry me loose from the wheel on one such occasion when it could be seen that I was tired, losing control of the ship, and likely to gybe all standing. I was soaking wet, singing loudly, drunk on the weather and indignant when firmly removed. They led me, babbling, below and quelled me with porridge.

Steering is more than just fooling about with the wheel. Unless told otherwise, the helmsman 'has the con'. This means that he is currently in charge. As well as steering the correct course, he should have an eye to the following:

Are the sails flapping, or setting correctly?

Has the wind or weather changed?

If the engine is in use, are the revs, the fuel guage, the oil pressure and temperature all reading normal?

Other ships in the vicinity, the lights they carry, their probable course, speed and distance away.

The sea. is it getting rougher, or a swell developing?

Is the visibility getting worse?

Can you see any shore lights or lighthouses?

Odd noises or smells often require investigation.

If the log fails, the time and reading should be logged at once, and thereafter you must estimate the speed as best you can. You will also have to be honest about the course you actually succeeded in steering, however reluctant you might be to admit less than perfection, since the DR depends upon it.

Finally, the ideal watchkeeper will know when to call the Captain for something he really needs to know, and when he can be left to sleep.

All this probably seems a lot to pay attention to. It is just as well that it seldom happens all at once, and that a night watch can be a period of great peace or even paralysing boredom. If there is a moon and stars, and enough wind to carry you gently along: that is dreamstuff, and often enough happens. If you are in a nasty sea left by the last storm and slatting about with no wind, it can be exasperating. To pass the time some mentally write books, some listen to the Walkman (what a boon this is: no more do the loud-music freaks, whether adherants of Bach or Bacharach, Delius or Duran Duran, disturb the sleep of the watch below). Bill invents things, plans coups d'etat and generally puts the world to rights. I have imaginary conversations with the Great, write poems and songs, which I sing (quietly).

It can be a long night.

How to be a Deckhand

'The younkers, or common saylors, for furling the sayles, bousing or trising, and taking their turn at the helm.'

If you are a team of two, it pays to do nothing in a hurry. Whether changing sails, or berthing, or any other bit of seamanship, take a little time to think. If you are entering a new harbour, the crew should check through the binoculars where any other yachts are; whether the mooring is likely to be stern-to or alongside, and whether the quay is provided with bollards or rings; or (as sometimes happens in remote Greek islands) a park bench and a lamp post. It is also important to note where the ferry berths, and if there is an irate little harbour official blowing a whistle and waving you off your chosen spot because that big freighter that you have only just noticed is coming in there and you are badly in the way. Having avoided these things, and the shallow end where all the little fishing boats are, you now get out what mooring lines you need and place your fenders where they will do some good. If there are bollards, it is often a good idea to put a good sized bowline in your line before you even throw it, especially if there are no obvious sailors on the quay. Wait till everything is ready, and untangled. There is TIME.

This avoids the panicky hurling of tangled ropes at the last minute, which inevitably fall short; we see this happen countless times every summer. Since there is so often a rapt audience, it is nice to do these things well. It is sad to see a headrope thrown towards the shore too soon, so that it stops short and falls in the water. Skippers should not expect a 40 foot line to reach across a 50 foot gap just because they say 'Now!', and deckhands would do well to practice (on a quiet quay out of sight of mockers) coiling and throwing a line that is at least 30 feet long. A good able seaman can throw an unweighted line 60 feet on the level.

A few good practice heaves will kill two birds with one stone (perhaps literally if you use that nasty ferryboat trick of having a weighted monkey's fist at the rope's end). One, you learn to heave the line with your whole arm; and two, you learn to judge the distance. Thus you avoid throwing too soon, and having the line snake out beautifully to its end, only to fall short into the sea; or that movement akin to closing a chest-high filing cabinet which gives the same result, the rope slithers into the (inevitably) oily water and heads like a homing pigeon for the screw. There should be no need, given the necessary forethought, to go through that rib-tickling performance that has all the other yachts in stitches: the last-minute disinterment of what seems to be a doormat knitted in 1½ inch nylon, heaved despairingly ashore for the dock committee to wipe its feet on, before the entire mat is dragged back into the water by the rapidly receding yacht attached to its other end. To bring the house down, the line has only to catch in the prop as the yacht circles.

Anchoring also stands a bit of secret practice before your public debut. You will still occasionally drop your anchor neatly into the dinghy (thoughtfully brought to the bow as you knew you were going stern-to, and subsequently forgotten) or get the chain caught in the hawse pipe, or fetch up a snarl which jams in the fairlead. But you will get it right nine times out of ten, and avoid the really calamitous things like failing to make fast the end or, as I did once, pulling an extra metre of chain up through the navel pipe, absentmindedly allowing it to slip off the gypsy that controls the links and onto the smooth warping drum. Since there was no longer anything to stop it, I watched aghast as with a thunderous roar the entire 45 fathoms of cable ran out into deep water. Right to the bitter end. Which was properly made fast and fetched *Fare Well* up with the sort of jerk you give the lead when your puppy is about to eat something disgusting. Bill achieved new heights, both in jumping up and down and creative language, while we slowly got it all back in again.

Pets and Pests

'Hale the Cat!' — Captain John Smith

Of course he does not mean cat like our Nelson. Our egregious Captain, from whom we quote so much, lists the following on a man-o-war in 1627: the Cat, the Hounds, the Falcon (a kind of cannon) the Crab (a launching device), the Crow's nest, the Crow's feet, the Fish block, a Goosewing, Hogsheads, Marlin, Ratlines, Monkey, Sheeps' feet, Sheepshanks and Whelps.

Apart from these, many and various are the birds and animals we have met at sea. Their company is comforting, not only to single-handers (who can otherwise end a three-week voyage talking non-stop for hours to the first person they meet) but to any crew who are not averse to animals. People will put up with a lot to have their pets with them; we have known a tiny yacht weighed nose-down with two enormous and beloved dogs, stowed forward like a couple of bower anchors. They had to be rowed ashore every few hours. Their owners got a bigger boat the next year. We met a Dane in Spain who swore he had rowed his dog ashore twice a day all the way from Denmark.

We have met parrots, large and small. Nelson is very fond of birds. So are we, but not to eat. The first parrot we met was a huge scarlet Macaw which came up our gangway on its owner's shoulder. On

143

confronting Nelson — black, alert, chops a-slaver — it squawked and committed an indignity on its owner's shirt, and had to be shut in the car in hysterics. That was the start of a great friendship.

Moored next to us in Aegina, near Athens, a young circumnavigating family in *Active Light* had a tiny green parrot. Nelson was not hungry, but even a sleepy cat was enough to frighten poor Birdie across the street and onto the awning of the Taverna opposite, where she had to be coaxed and climbed for. We met them again in Grenada in the West Indies, where we were all at anchor, and were able to exchange pleasant visits with bird and cat safely apart.

While birds are easy to look after, dogs are a horse of another colour, to mix metaphors. If you are doggy-minded you will take your dog with you and care for it like an extra child — which it will be, not being as self-sufficient as a cat or with the simple needs of a bird. A dog produces large turds which (unlike the cat) it does not know what to do with. It is theoretically possible to get your dog to use the scuppers, or to home in on a short length of tree attached to a stanchion, or a square of artificial grass. We have heard of all these being tried, with or without tempting bottles of 'Do it here, Doggy' perfume. In the cold real world, however, we observe that all dog owners have to use a shovel and hose the deck down pretty frequently; or row the culprit ashore at intervals which interfere with one's beer-time.

Dogs do not like being left. It takes only two of them, howling because their Dad and Mum have gone ashore, to turn a quiet anchorage into Banshee night in the Wolf forest. On the other hand they are a good deterrent for thieves (though our Nelson could be a bit frightening, with the eldritch shriek she used to fend off unwanted toms, and the moonlight glancing off her one eye, an emerald as large as a saucer). At least dogs are Faithful Pals. Cats are anybody's: if you upset them (by hoovering or varnishing, for instance) they go and live with someone else for a few hours, whereas a dog will grin miserably and put up with it. Cats are better in rough weather, it seems to me. They seem to be like humans as regards seasickness: some are and some are not. We know of one kitten that had to be found a shore home because it was very seasick, but we also know a very large number of contented ship's cats.

I have heard that Keeshonds (Dutch barge dogs) were trained to leap ashore with a headrope in their teeth and drop a bight over a bollard. We never managed to get ours to do this in the days when we took children, dog and all, out for the Sunday cruiser race. Ours was a good dog in a boat, so breeding helps a bit; he kept out of the way and did not moan, and when we were tacking up the narrow rivers of the Broads he would leap ashore on one tack, use a tree, wait until we tacked back again, usually having made only a few yards in two tacks, and jump back on board. He was so much a part of our racing crew that if we crossed the finishing line without him we were threatened with disqualification.

Nelson stands by to repel boarders with her one sharp eye. We have never had rats on board. (photo Tom Goedicke)

For long-term cruising, however, cats take a lot of beating. They are neat in their habits, and when you run out of Kitty Litter they tolerate sand or pebbles. (This once led to a misunderstanding when a young pebble-trained cat, who was my guest while his people went home for a week or two, decided that my Christmas bowl of walnuts was The Right Place.) They are philosophical about bad weather; an example to humans, in fact. They find the warmest, driest spot on board (on your lap under your oilskin for example) and hole up for as long as possible. When it's all over they emerge, all smiles and hungry. Nelson could suspend all bodily functions for about 36 hours when necessary: if only we humans could too. If she *had* to go and her tray was awash, she would come and tell you so, complaining indignantly until you put it right. Braced, intent and swaying with the ship's motion while producing her own, she then did her housework rather more rapidly than usual, skipping with relief back into her chosen hideout. Sometimes this was her box behind the compass (cats are not magnetic) but sometimes she liked to wriggle well down into some folded canvas; a bundled-up staysail became such a haven for her when on a transatlantic passage that we let it be until we reached the Azores.

It is a difficult task to get your cat or dog vaccinated against rabies in England. At first I was told that it was impossible, but with a little persistence I got a bit higher up the chain of command and asked how, as we were going to sea, to get Nelson vaccinated. 'Oh, a Ship's cat' said the man. 'That's all right.' So Nelson became a ship's cat and was duly vaccinated. The vaccine is not normally used in Britain because at present the country is rabies-free and tests at once reveal an infected animal. These tests are much more equivocal on vaccinated ones and uncertainty would set in. When the inevitable happens and someone smuggles in a rabid cat or dog, or quite likely brings in a horse (yes, horse: they are allowed to enter and leave the country freely to go to race meetings, with no rabies quarantine restrictions) — when, as I say, the inevitable happens and rabies comes to Britain, the rules will change and vaccination will become normal. In the meantime the veterinary headquarters of your county should be able to assist you. Make sure you say it's a ship's cat as this cuts through a lot of red tape.

I carried the resulting documents with me for the next nine years. No authority in any country ever asked me for them. In Gibraltar she was vaccinated willy nilly; British rules then prevailed about bringing in animals, a bit odd considering that any squirrel or fox can trot over the border with Spain when it feels like it. Cats and dogs were confined to the yacht. Gibraltar has recently relaxed this rule: now if you are a resident of Europe visiting Gibraltar and your pet has a valid certificate of rabies vaccination dated not less than 28 days before your arrival, and providing you do not arrive from North Africa, it will be allowed ashore.

Malta still has the British regulations. Being an island, it makes sense. However, they have no quarantine facilities and do not allow your animal even to be confined to the yacht. They employ the draconian solution of shooting them. This leads to a high rate of pet smuggling in Malta, which defeats the aim of the regulations. I recall a lady who gave both her small dogs sleeping pills to get them into Malta in her yacht. One woke up too soon and was duly destroyed, but she succeeded in smuggling in the other. She was not British, but Brits are not all blameless in this matter either.

Cats eat mice and kill rats. Until you have had one of these pests on board you have no idea what a good thing cats are. We met a yacht in Corfu in a state of siege after one month of Spanish Rat: they could buy only enough food for one day, which had to be kept in the oven: the only rat-proof place they had, as it had eaten through clothes, flags, Tupperware, and even teak lockers. They were ready to sell their lovely little yacht for a song, rat and all, but they acquired a small cat and had no further trouble: they had already tried traps and poison.

In some parts of the world you are still required to sign a document concerning the health of any shipboard rats, in case you are carrying the plague. We found one of these in St Thomas's in the Virgin Islands, but rather piquantly rephrased: they wished to know 'if there was any unusual morality among the rates on board' (sic).

Mice are almost as destructive, it just takes them a little longer to chew through your Tupperware. They are also fond of other varieties of plastics. We once had the saloon lights fused by a mouse that bit through the electric cable. It was one of Nelson's failures: she went through a phase of posting lizards and beetles down the forward ventilator into the roof space. Once, when she wasn't hungry, she posted a live mouse. It couldn't get out again and the roof space was only an inch or so high: too small to feed the cat into it.

Calling Nelson many dreadful and unpopular names, we removed a panel and tried some Italian Mouse Glue, a fearful substance that you spread on a piece of card which you then lay in the mouse's path. You then sit back and wait, hoping that the mouse is stupid enough to walk across it and stick, like Brer Fox to the Tar Baby.

I must confess that I was not anxious to deal with the pathetic results that seemed bound to ensue. I need not have worried, the mouse was not that stupid. After some days the stuff slumped off the card and began to drip down the cabin wall. The regular scrotch, scrotch, of chewing mouse went on. We took the panel off again and threw the card, now dusty and ineffective, away. The drips down the wall remained sticky for weeks and appeared to have no solvent known to man.

I was relieved when the mouse, tiring of polyfoam, decided to try a change of diet, bit through the electric cable and fried itself.

This one shameful incident apart, however, Nelson was all that one could hope for: she never allowed a wharf rat on board. In Mahon, in Minorca, she ratted diligently. After snoozing all the warm day, come Cat-time, that darker than twilight time when cats and shadows blend, she would yawn, stretch, test her claws on the rope doormat and slink down the gangplank to vanish instantly. Other cats would appear from the waste land and derelict warehouses; a whisker here, a flash of white sock there; but Nelson, black as ebony, invisible, was marked only by an occasional sharp rustle, followed by twitters and squeaks as she pounced and bit swiftly through the neckbone. Rats were serious business, and she did not play with them as she did with lizards and mice.

Some people, especially in the States, have neat-looking metal rat-guards on all their mooring lines, usually an aluminium disc about a foot across. Sorry, but to circumvent a determined rat, and there is no other kind, they should be at least a metre in diameter. It is hard to find stowage for four or five of those. I prefer a rat-guard that purrs. The purr of a cat is also a great tranquilliser, and has no side-effects.

Sooner or later you will have **insect trouble**; flies in the galley or midges round the barbecue. In a few places the mosquitoes are large enough to make life a misery. You will know where, because you will notice the screened verandahs, and the eerie blue light of the electric bug frier. A very promising party of ours in Calabria broke up in disorder when, at dusk, swarms of mosquitoes drove us below decks. An hour later they were all gone, and we were able to reassemble.

Laurel

On entering the Intra-Coastal Waterway in America we asked the advice of a weathered waterman about mosquito screens. 'Well,' he drawled, 'ya might put one on yo door there; but our mosquitoes are too big for yo windas.' As we did the trip in winter and spring, we had no trouble.

Where mosquitoes abound we have tried anti-mosquito candles, and nearly burnt the boat. We have tried Off and Autan and Oil of Lemongrass; Boots' Jungle Formula has been highly recommended. The bugs don't come near you but nor do your friends. A vicious little breed of mosquito is found in the Eastern Mediterranean. We went

148

FISHERMEN'S COTTAGES
CORFU

ashore to have a barbecue and noticed what appeared to be a shepherd's bed in the branch of a tree, about 6 feet off the ground. While our supper cooked we made many jokes about savage beasts that couldn't climb trees (we couldn't think of many), and became more and more uneasy as the sun set. Then, in the space of about one minute, we learnt the reason for the tree bed: we were set upon by millions of tiny but savage little beasts, kinky about ankles, none attacking above the knee. After the quickest clean-up and evacuation ever, we rowed back out to *Fare Well*, our tingling ankles peppered with bites as close together as the dots on a smocking transfer.

One gadget that seems to work in a small space is the mini hotplate on which venomous pastilles are warmed till they give off fumes. These are available in Italy. The warmer did not suit our electrical system, so Bill contrived one in a Kit-e-Kat tin which worked well. Then *White Whisper* told us of their simple and effective solution: put the pastille on some copper gauze above the oil lamp. Turned down to the absolute minimum, it makes the pastille fume nicely.

There is a pocket battery device which is said to scare bugs away with ultra-sound. I know what I'd think about people who carry vibrating objects in their pockets.

If you are in an area where malaria is rife, then take no chances and sleep under a net. This at least does not smell, cause fires, or make your friends look at you oddly.

Inevitably we come to **cockroaches**. When we built the boat we wrote to Shell asking them to recommend a long-term insecticide. We sprayed two coats of it on the foam that covered the interior of the steel hull, on top of the fire-retarding paint and inside the linings. Since no one was likely to touch it, it could be lethal and it obviously was, as it kept *Fare Well* insect-free for six years. Not until we were coming back from the West Indies did we finally 'catch' cockroaches: not (luckily) the 'Mahogany Mice' of the Caribbean but a smaller breed. However, like illegitimate babies, even little ones count. We took steps. Nelson ate some (they were crunchy). I took out the loose Formica linings from the galley drawers and sprayed them with Baygon (the Greek anti-katsarida kind which bears very little relation to the lily-livered stuff of the same name which is all they will allow you to have in the Western Med).

As a precaution, I had bought in the USA a trap called a Roach Motel, and I dug it out for use. It was well named: it seemed to invite them in for a hamburger and a·night's sleep, and then let them go with me picking up the bill for their entertainment, which was not cheap as I had bought two of them. I found only one cockroach in it, and that was slightly bent as if Nelson had chewed it a bit first and it had gone in there to have a martini and recover. When we came to the conversion of *Hosanna* we found that it was now very difficult to get a long-term insecticide. Some of them have been completely banned, and the use of the remainder is restricted to industry, who are supposed to be more responsible about the use of such dangerous substances than we poor mortals with our cats and our children to think about. It requires great persistence to get any.

We tried a secret mixture imparted to us by the German skipper of a charter yacht, alongside whom we had berthed is St Lucia. 'Haf you cockroaches?' he asked us. 'No,' we said proudly. 'Now you vil haf,' he said, and gave us his recipe, Jorge's revenge: sweetened condensed milk and powdered boric acid. (Now wash your hands please.) The cockroaches yaffle the mixture, and the boric acid concretes up their insides till it's like treading on plum stones. (No, don't try it as a remedy for the runs. It is cumulative and dangerous, so prevent the puss from eating doctored cockroaches.) I found that Jorge's mixture dried solid and was ineffective after a few days, so I mixed icing sugar with it instead. Hal Roth in *After 50,000 Miles* quotes entomologists at the University of California as saying that any additives to the boric acid are unnecessary and countereffective. Well, my mixture, put in a flat tin and wedged where children and cats couldn't get at it, must have got up the cockroaches' noses and choked them. Something worked, we have no cockroaches at present.

It must be the size and obviousness of cockroaches which upset people and cause a disproportionate amount of hysteria, since in fact they are quite harmless and not known to be the carriers of any disease.

Flies are infinitely more dangerous, but do not cause the same reaction. A fly alighting on the table to lick up a beer spill elicits a halfhearted wave of the hand, instead of the panic and recourse to major artillery in the shape of slippers, pilot books and even winch handles that characterizes the appearance of a cockroach. And yet, friends:

> The fly that on your bread has wiped its feet,
> Has also been and wiped them on the meat.
> But worse than that, this morning (for a treat)
> It trod in something nasty in the street.

Whether buzzing round the galley, or groggily dive-bombing your nose in the bunk, they have got to go. I keep the galley noticeably cleaner in warm weather to discourage them, covering any exposed food or fruit and leaving no water in the sink (flies too have to drink). We have a fly-swat, disgusting but non-pollutant. We also have a fly-shooter, which gives visitors endless harmless amusement and even kills a few flies. If desperate, we use an aerosol spray. No need to gun down individual flies: this is total war. Shut the windows, spray the area and go up on deck for a while. Then come back when it's all over, like the politicians. Of course you empty the rubbish as often as you can.

In Greece, every household keeps a pot of basil to keep the flies away. This is the little-leaved basil, not the one with large leaves grown in Italy to go with tomatoes. The Greeks tuck a sprig behind one ear or carry some in their hands; you will see the pots on their caiques and yachts as well. I have tried many times to grow my own pot of basil but it quickly succumbs to salt-blast, or else goes over-board in a choppy sea (this happens to all my on-board gardening), so I cannot say if it works. Since Greece is one of the few places where you can still buy old-fashioned flypapers it may be a triumph of hope over experience.

In September the **wasps** arrive, unless you are well out to sea and stay there. This leads to breaks in the conversation while you or your guests perform Kung Fu, ending with a wham on the table that makes the glasses rattle. Eating on the poop becomes a little less than perfect, and bare feet are inadvisable as wasps are dying all over the deck.

You can rig up a diversion in the shape of a tin containing enough soda pop, Sprite, or 7-Up for them to drown in: they seem very fond of it, but there will still be a few left to zzzz round the salad. After one especially efficient attack with the fly-swat we watched the stretcher-bearers arrive in the shape of hornets, come to carry away the dead. One tried to carry two corpses at once and ditched slowly into the sea, like a crippled Lancaster with two bombs slung under it. It made nearly as much noise, too. The less ambitious hornets cleared our decks of dead and dying wasps in no time at all.

Worms. In the early days of 'abroad', when we were in our 'teens, both Bill and I caught roundworms, Bill from a Spanish paella and I in Morocco from heaven knows what. This caused a lot of excitement; passing a creature about 9 inches long and quite firm in texture is a startling event. My doctor reverted to alchemy and prescribed extract of male fernseed. It was not surprising, therefore, that I tried to find some remedies to take with me before we left on the Great Cruise.

When the chemist came out of his little white stillroom to find out what hophead was buying twelve packets each of Stugeron and Kwells, and decided that maybe this little sailing lady was not hooked on seasick pills, I began to ask him about worms. He backed off and disclaimed all knowledge. Fortunately, in ten years of cruising, not all of it in civilized places, we have not had occasion to use any remedy.

All the baby books mention threadworms, but not the round or tape variety, which in Britain seem to only attack dogs and cats. It is very easy to get multi-worm tablets for your pets, and you should take some as it is easy for them to pick up infestations on shore. Round-worm eggs are carried on fruit and vegetables, and tapeworms in undercooked meat. The eggs are not visible to the eye, but heat kills both types. Since we do not like to forego our salads and raw fruit we wash them well, in a little potassium permanganate (a few crystals in the water will be enough) just before eating them.

There is no great cause for panic if you do acquire an internal guest, as those mentioned are more upsetting than harmful, unlike hook-worm. If you are interested in herbal remedies, try 3—6 grains of fresh garlic bulb, or ½—1 fluid dram of juice. Or, to eliminate round and threadworms, and paralyse tapeworms: steep shredded pomegranate bark in a tightly closed container, reduce by half, and take 4 oz followed by a purgative. Better to use modern remedies such as Pripsen, which do not require purgatives afterwards.

We knew a yacht that took on board a pathetic little Greek kitten, only to find that it was infested with pathetic little Greek **ticks**. Their bedding burst forth from below like spinnakers on the downwind run, and clothing bloomed in the rigging, scented with pyrethrum. I've seldom seen a gayer sight, even at Carnival. Frying ticks with a cigarette-end is nauseating but effective. You can also use ether on cotton wool (but mind you don't chloroform the cat or dog).

Pests that come into the boat on fruit and vegetables, apart from those already dealt with above, can be reduced by discarding all cardboard boxes on the quay. Salt in the washing water deals with slugs and caterpillars (always make the fussiest person on board responsible for this chore), so you might as well use clean sea water with a little permanganate of potash to pinken it.

Weevils are rarely come across in well packaged goods these days, but they will occur in the West Indies and the Eastern Mediterranean, when buying pulses, cereals or rice from the sack or in paper bags. If you can put the stuff in somebody's deep freeze for twenty-four hours, in a plastic bag, this will kill any eggs, and you can then transfer it to beetle-proof containers. Watch things like instant mashed potato and dry dog and cat food, which are very prone to attack. If you find a few beetles in something, you need not throw it out as they are not in themselves harmful; but never add coarsely ground black pepper to your risotto until you are sure there are no weevils in the rice. If there are more than a few it becomes psychologically unappetising and is better thrown away.

A word about monkeys. We were berthed close to a rather theatrical family in a small yacht in Sicily. They had two young children, and two monkeys that were bad-tempered, noisy and ill-disciplined. (The children, however, were charming.) The parents paraded up and down the quay with the monkeys on a lead, getting lots of attention. Nelson watched from her top-of-the-gangway sentry post, with distaste. Next day the parents were bored with their pets and sent the children to walk the monkeys. They got a little too far from their boat and were cut off by a large friendly dog, who barked at them playfully. The monkeys' reaction was instantaneous: with shrieks they shot up to the childrens' heads, where they loosed their bowels ready for further flight. For the next hour the dock committee watched with suppressed glee as the parents, tight-lipped and grim of mien, scrubbed their hapless children under the dockside hose with magnums of shampoo.

Other people's unwanted pets, whether roaming toms after your maiden moggie's virtue or those rangy pooches who seem to be able to pee for half an hour on your freshly washed mooring ropes, are discouraged by the handgun in the form of a water pistol, or (the heavier artillery) a Squeezy bottle of water, if possible iced, directed at the active member.

I'm told that goldfish get seasick.

CHAPTER EIGHT

Maintenance and Repairs

'... Decayed by weeds or Barnacles ... which will eat thorow all the planks if she be not sheathed.'

There is a class of yachtsman who says 'Get it fixed', it is fixed, and he signs a cheque. He is usually one of the racing fleet, or he keeps his boat in luxury style. He is unlikely to be a dedicated liveaboard for these are fairly firmly in the do-it-yourself class; though at either end of the economic scale there are those who occasionally employ a little casual help, or who actually provide that help. In any case they are all watching pennies, and tend to spend their winters or refit periods where moorings and living are cheap.

Sadly, it is in just those areas that spare parts are hard to find, that local labour, while cheaper, is not up to the latest techniques, and that communications with the industrialized world are a bit tenuous. Which is why those places are so attractive. It is important, therefore, that all maintenance and minor repair work be able to be performed using on-board resources, ar at worst using comparatively primitive facilities.

It is not a function of this book to instruct in elementary nautical maintenance, so I will refrain from travelling too far down that path, though I think I will find myself wandering a bit now and then. Rather, I want to consider how the live-aboard can minimise his inevitable problems by appropriate action before starting out.

Engines

There are some companies whose diesels may or may not be the best, but whose engines are found world-wide and whose service is first class. In my view, chief among these is Perkins, whose engines in one form or another are found everywhere in tractors, combine harvesters, trucks, buses and fishing boats. I have come across sheds in Rural Calabria (there is an Italian saying: 'si trova niente in Calabria' (one finds nothing in Calabria) and it's not true) and huts in Africa piled high with every conceivable Perkins part. At every depot I have visited it has been 'Yes, how many do you need?', and I have not found any other make of any other thing anywhere near this standard. If you add to this that our Perkins 4236 engine has done over 5000 hours without any major attention, you will understand my feelings. Apart from the prime movers on our generator, I have no intimate knowledge of other makes, so I have canvassed among my friends.

In the bigger boats, General Motors and Caterpillar diesels do well, and service seems to be good. Gardner still hold the best reputation for sheer reliability. Ford suffer because there are so many differing marine conversions not all of which are well done, and though spares for the engine itself are not too bad the problems attaching to service of the marinizing parts are great. Fiat and Renault fail by reason of poor service away from their home ground. BMC reports are patchy. Mercedes have a good reputation, which seems not always to be borne out in practice; parts availability seems to depend on nearness to centres of prosperity.

In the smaller ranges, Volvo have lost a lot of their one-time popularity because of poor spares availability which is getting steadily worse, and I have heard two complaints where spare parts turned out to be sub-standard. In 1990 the situation seems to be improving. Yanmar seem to be going to the top of the league table; though their spares availability is not yet first class, they are improving. Farymann and Petter, whose engines are in use on so many agricultural pumps and farm generators, ought to have a good spares service for their marine versions, like Perkins, but they do not. Spares are hard to find anywhere for both engines, and even their local agents complain; one of them showed me his almost empty racks. He had been waiting months for valve springs. Also engines of this type have been converted for marine use and not done well. In Petter's case the combination of aluminium cylinder head with raw water cooling and a world-wide scarcity of the anodes essential for marine use, is a perfect plan for trouble.

There are of course other diesel engines suitable for yachts: Lister, Westerbeke, DAF, among others. I have no personal experience of these engines, and have been unable to consult anyone who has, so I must refrain from comment. I refuse to discuss petrol engines at all in the context of yachts.

Beware of Gardner engines that have been reconditioned by backyard firms using poor parts. Also beware when a good company is taken over by a bad one and the whole standard starts to fall.

If there is an engine already fitted in a yacht you are thinking of buying, then in addition to the broad views I have given, view with suspicion any product of a small company that is the wholly-owned subsidiary of a major conglomerate holding company. The small company's managers may be competent and conscientious (though not necessarily) but they are completely at the mercy of the management of their parent company, whose decisions will pay little attention to the interests of customers at the far end of an attenuated chain and affect such matters as spares availability and their overseas distribution.

Might I please appeal for someone to produce a range of marine diesels with all adjustments, controls and service points on one side and the top? It's not impossible. A German company called Fisher have a small diesel generator with everything brought to the front, but it has raw water cooling, and for me, once bitten, twice shy.

One reads a lot about diesel fuel in backward places often being contaminated. I have never found it so, and suspect that water in the fuel so often written about comes from on-board sources, as it did on the only occasion when we suffered from this problem. But supply pipes should have very good water trap type filters, preferably mounted in parallel, and each separated by cocks so that one can change one filter while the engine is running on the other. Other filters are needed in line, of course, preferably two. Carry a fair stock of filter elements, but change them frequently and in rotation, because they all have metal in them somewhere and this is liable to rust while in storage, thus rendering the filter element useless.

Make sure the fuel tank has a draw-off point above and clear of a sump. It should have an access big enough for a clenched fist, to enable the sump to be easily cleaned out.

Obtain from your engine's makers a world-wide list of equivalent filter elements and lubricating oils. Manufacturers who will not supply such a list and parrot cry that only their products are good enough for their engines should be given an early cold shoulder: they are living in a dream world: it is impossible to obtain the well known brands in many places.

Be cautious about devices containing Jabsco pumps, and fit pumps with rigid impellers if possible. Jabsco agents are found in many places, but there are so many different impellers that few retailers have more than a small number, which never includes the one you want. In addition the company plays amusing games and changes the numbers every now and then, presumably to baffle their own representatives, which they do very well. Any company which does that sort of thing and does not supply retailers with a list of equivalents cannot be said to care much about its customers. In 1990 it was difficult to get Jabsco impellers in France.

Outboard motor (and all two-stroke) service is of a very variable standard. I think all companies appoint agents who are little more than salesmen, and mechanical competence varies from 0 to 100. The best I ever came across worked round behind Barclays Bank in Bequia, in the Grenadines. He was the only man who ever got our Evinrude working satisfactorily, and, sadly, he was getting on in years.

Spars, Sail and Rigging

First, a story. We met a modern yacht that had been dismasted off the Canary Islands. They were still there ten months after their mishap, waiting for a replacement aluminium spar. By contrast, an old schooner discovered rot in the heel of the foremast while cruising Turkish waters. A new heel was scarphed in in ten days, the labour cost then being around one pound per hour.

Now, new masts are not needed that often and one may well cruise a lifetime without the necessity, but those stories illustrate a general rather than a particular point. Sooner or later repairs will be necessary to something, and if those repairs can be effected from local resources then one gets sailing again cheaper and sooner. The lesson applies, though with less force, even when cruising to sophisticated countries where certain basic standards differ. For example, electrical replacements following our lightning strike in the USA were more difficult and expensive to obtain because our equipment is 24 volt, which is not common over there.

A good solid spar can be got almost anywhere trees grow. I have heard of an impecunious French owner who stole a telegraph pole for the purpose; though this displays initiative it is not likely to enhance the reputation of yachtsmen. Nevertheless it makes a point.

Going with a wooden mast will probably be a lower sail plan, cheaper galvanized wire rigging and cheaper sails. Some people chop and change their sailmaker, looking for an advantage here, or a bargain there. My family have used Jeckells for a long time, and though we might get a sail that is less than perfect on rare occasions, I do get excellent service, and I think anyone else would — a thought that would apply to a regular customer of any other old firm such as Cranfields. As an example, following loss of an old but reasonable mainsail in June, we had a replacement arrive in the USA within nine days, at a cost of approximately half the lowest quotation there, and that was when there were over $2 to the pound. The old sail, blown out in Hurricane Alberto, had lasted eight years; it is still serviceable as a spare. A good cruising sail, if protected from the sun when not in use, should last a good ten years.

That does not apply so surely to roller jibs, which somehow seem to get more unfair wear. Sacrificial strips along leech and foot are a nuisance. I designed our replacement genoa to be mitre cut with the cloths parallel to leech and foot, and with the outer cloths of stronger material. I have always found cloth to be stronger lengthwise, and old smacksmen knew this too, for it is the way they cut their 'tow foresails', which were the forerunners of the modern genoas. If the leech or foot deteriorates in the sun, it is comparatively easy to replace the affected parts. Do not leave jibs rolled up when out of use for a long time or over winter. This is a common practice to be observed in marinas and a temptation with roller headsail gear.

Generally, sail and rigging maintenance is a continual process, mainly because it is one of the more pleasant chores. But once a year at least all sail seams should be checked, because they are the weak points. We have an ordinary Singer sewing machine capable of zig-

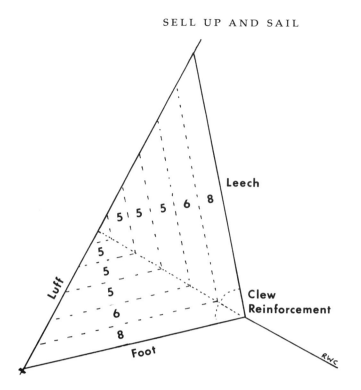

Roller reefing jib with heavier canvas in the outer cloths, for better strength and longevity. Ample clew reinforcement is also necessary.

zag stitching, but it will not sew several layers of heavy cloth very well. Neither will our friend's Reads, which is sold as a sailmaking machine. I have a deep feeling that an old-fashioned second-hand Singer would be best, and sew one's homeward-bounders in straight stitches.

Paint and Protection

If one is living aboard and cruising continuously it is sometimes easy to overlook passing time and the need for annual checks. In the Med these are done over the winter, but even then one has to allow for quite a bit of bad weather when work is impossible or inconvenient. In Corfu it rains a lot, at Bodrum, we had gales and even snow, and last winter at Rome we had snow on several occasions and even ice on the deck. Painting in these conditions is not really a good idea.

Painting is important in a yacht. I have a feeling that a lot of fibreglass boats could have done with it from time to time, but for wood or steel it becomes essential. We try to keep a little paint in a small glass jar to touch up instantly any damage, and some is bound to happen. This way the annual chore, for that is what it is, is eased. GRP boats should keep two-part filler and gelcoat.

The big paint job is so purgatorial that it has to be carefully planned. Part of it will be on the slip or hard, but upperworks can be done afloat. The chief purgatory is the preparation: whether sanding, wire-brushing, descaling or whatever, bits fly and a door left open soon leads to marital disharmony. With sand-blasting the situation is even worse.

I am going to interject a word on behalf of the mate here. It is necessary to work hard and long at this chore to get it over sooner, and if 'sir' expects 'madam' also to do a full ten-hour day with sander or brush, then it is unfair to expect her to cook the evening meal afterwards. We regard as an essential part of the cost of the exercise having baths and a dinner at a local hostelry each evening. Every time we look at the bill, we work a little harder.

Talking of sand-blasting, it is possible to buy portable equipment from a firm in Reading. In a large steel boat this might well be worthwhile, though a compressor is needed too.

Preparation, somehow or other, is the key. I have been concerned with painting steel ships for a lot of my life and have become disenchanted with paint companies. Apart from doing the job under laboratory conditions, the paint industry has made no real advance in protecting steel at sea since the First World War. The chipping hammer, red lead and oil paint routine I knew when I first went to sea lasted just as well as the latest advice and products of the industry. Here, for amusement, is a parody of a paint company's specification: Steel should be sand-blasted to North Korean standard X24. This must be done with relative humidity below 10%, and in total darkness. All loose dust must be removed, and the steel should be coated with 5 microns of our No.7 priming solution within ten minutes of sandblasting. Because this primer is part-cured by moisture in the air, this must be done with relative humidity above 70%. The primer should be covered by alternating coats of our 303 super-effective barrier, and our 404 semi-permeable undercoat until a thickness of 25 microns is built up. Overcoating time of the 303 and the 404 is between 12 and 13 hours, but the latter should only be applied in bright sunlight combined with rising humidity. Failure to meet these conditions invalidates any warranty.

What I really want to emphasize is that paint companies make paint for use only in ideal conditions, and write their specifications sitting in an office. All too often conditions at the sharp end of life face a worsening weather forecast, with an obligation to be off the slip by the day after tomorrow, inevitably leading to the decision to slap it on and hope for the best. Is there a paint company producing a product for us?

Varnish is not compatible with our existence, at least not on the upper deck. Beautiful Italian yachts gleam from the attentions of vast crews of nautical charwomen: sometimes one has pangs of envy and this leads to a token bit of varnish in the cockpit, but it is not really a practical affair in hot sun.

Antifouling becomes a problem as one moves from one area to another. Do not fall for International Paint's sales pitch that their paints are available world-wide. While I think their paints sold in Britain are about the best available, and paints with the International label are found elsewhere, they are not to the same specification in every country and one can come badly unstuck (and so can the paint). In the USA they print a full analysis of the paint on the tin, and this is very helpful. One wonders why they make no effort to state the same valuable information in other countries.

Since the banning of Tri-butyl-tin (TBT) anti-foulings for pleasure craft has become virtually worldwide, owners of steel boats are in a fix. Paint companies are advising us to use products they previously said were unsuitable! We do not have an answer. Considering how few steel and aluminium boats there are, we could have been exempted if the RYA had been better organised.

Hauling Out

The place where you haul out needs selecting with some care. In general, the more primitive the equipment the more it costs, an example where sophistication seems to have its benefits for the yottie. The western Med, which is littered with more marinas than it seems there are boats to fill them, each with its own boatyard, is in need of business so competition keeps the price down; while the equipment, generally a Travelift or similar, is fairly new and reasonably well operated. It is in these places that a yacht of whatever type can be dealt with.

Further east in the Med the number of marinas decreases, and with it the number of Travelifts and their standard of maintenance. And the prices rise; it has never been properly explained why it should cost six times as much in Greece to haul a yacht as it does in Spain.

Yachts with a long straight keel can be hauled out on the old-fashioned ways, or on a proper marine railway. We have been out on the municipal slip at Barcelona, and at the de Gasperi yard at Porto Santo Stefano (surely one of the best yards in the world). At both of these the care and competence were of the very highest. We came out on an old cradle over a shingle beach at Erol Ayan's yard near Bodrum, one of the high experiences of our lives; a wonderful place, but the whole thing was hair-raising and not at all cheap.

In the Western Hemisphere, we hauled out at Hazzard's slipway in Georgetown, South Carolina, a lovely family boatyard and cheaper than Greece or Turkey. We had planned to haul again, but found that the high cost of antifouling paint made it pay to wait until we got to Spain. I found the lift operators at the Club Nautico in Palma and also at Trehard's in Antibes to be good, and at both places the charges were reasonable.

Facilities are not good in the West Indies. There is a slip at Grenada and another at English Harbour; there may well be others, but I did not see them. There is, however, a 3 foot tide in some parts and it is possible to do something of a job between tides. The big problem there is the long grass-like weed that grows close to the waterline, but it is no great chore to drop over the side and remove it every few weeks. I found a home-made tool like a butter pat made out of ¼ inch ply very effective.

In the USA Travelifts are frequent, though as most Americans own boats of a similar size to those in northern Europe, most lifts have a maximum load of 20 tons (bigger ones do exist). Some American yards tolerate do-it-yourself, though most of them demand that you buy paint through them. In most of the Mediterranean DIY is considered the normal course of events. In Turkey, labour was so cheap that I employed jobbing painters who worked very hard but used about 30 per cent more paint than I did. Conditions are changing in Turkey; the marina at Kus Adasi has a Travelift, and one is planned for Bodrum when harbour works have made the place safer.

Keep a few photographs of the yacht's underwater profile and section to help lift and slipway operators. They cannot always read lines drawings, though in a good yard these are a help when slipping. Clearly mark the strength bulkheads on the hull with chalk, say, so props and shores are wedged into the right places. It is a good thing to mark the gunwale permanently with the positions of the the log impeller and any other sensitive device or projection. There is no reason why a steel boat cannot have lifting eyes welded to the gunwales, so dispensing with slings which often scrape off quite a lot of the paint that you have laboured so hard to put on.

Repairs and Failures

Quality of repairs varies enormously from place to place. The more primitive the place the more ready are the local craftsmen to undertake anything, usually with tolerable results. You do not buy spare parts, you have them made at half the price. It is only when one rediscovers the village blacksmith that one sees what Western sophistication has lost — the Mr Fixit, par excellence. In the West Indies, however, the development and education of the local people is such that there are very few local craftsmen. Exceptions occur: there are some good wooden boatbuilders at Bequia, and they get some good wood up from South America.

Let us stop to consider the skills that are likely to be found in all but the most primitive places. I suggest:

Diesel mechanics of some sort. Most places now have diesel engines in trucks, tractors and fishing boats. It is rare to find somewhere without some diesel ability, though it might be a bit haphazard.

LEFT
With a long, moderate depth keel it is possible to haul out with primitive equipment, if used skilfully. A deep fin-keeler would be helpless in the more primitive parts of the world. This shows Fare Well *coming out over the beach at Erol Ayan's yard near Bodrum in Turkey.*

RIGHT
The fixed lift at Sibari, Southern Italy. This type of lift is very useful for sailing craft, but it has proven somewhat inflexible, and I understand it is being replaced.

Simple welding and brazing.

Elementary woodwork, carpentry rather than joinery. Often there is shipwright ability, particularly in planking and caulking, the latter being competent owing to the roughness of the former.

Metal turning, and casting of small parts, but seldom enough to turn up a new shaft for instance.

A sewing machine, usually old enough to be strong enough to stitch anything bendable.

Hydraulic knowledge. This may surprise you, but it is becoming a common feature in agriculture and trucking.

What is rarely to be found outside yachting centres?

Aluminium welding.

Stainless steel welding (sometimes at basic level, but almost never with the right rods).

Electronic capability and spares.

Electric capability above household or car level.

Swaging or Talurit wire fittings.

Sand-blasting, except unintentionally in strong winds.

Facilities for hauling out fin-keel boats.

Fibreglass repairs. Spray painting.

Spare parts for nautical equipment.

Unless one is going to confine one's cruising to the coasts of Britain, the Riviera or the USA, it is worth pondering the two lists. To take to

the out-islands a boat built of exotic materials, with state-of-the-art rig and electronics and the current racing hull form, is to run a big risk of having pleasure spoiled by non-functioning, non-repairable, sophisticated gear, and a lesser but definite risk of disaster due to the inability of both local craftsmen and yourself to service or repair even quite minor damage.

Insurance underwriters might well take more note of the repairability of the craft they insure, bearing in mind that the majority of claims are for damage rather than total loss.

If one tried, one could have a very pleasant boat that would reduce or cut out a lot of the payments the owner has to make to others. She would have shoal draught, a reinforced cutaway stem and a powerful stream anchor. She would avoid marinas; just drop anchor and put her bows to the beach. Rig the passarella over the bows. Have four 10 ton screw jacks vertically in tubes through the hull next to the bulkheads and at refit time just jack her up clear of the water. I would not think they would cost more than a couple of haulouts, and from then it's paying for itself.

Simple strong masts, simple strong rigging. No electronics, and basic electrics only. (Electric navigation lights are essential: no others are remotely adequate. Electric engine starting is also desirable.)

Rigging and sail maintenance is not difficult, just absorbing. One will need, for sail repairs, a more substantial kit than those typically sold to the dilettante in Cowes. A yard or two of various weights of cloth to suit sails and awnings, and different weights of seaming thread on commercial size reels. Twine for whipping, roping, grommetting and serving. Each of the crew to have their own palm to fit, and practice how to use it. I have not found stay-put sail-repair tape effective for even temporary repairs, possibly because it had been in the locker a long time before being used, though round-the-world racers have access to much better products. We find that it is best to fix sail repairs of seams with strong parcel tape and then to sew over the taped seams. This makes the job much easier and the stitching perforates the tape, making it simple to rip off afferwards. We have also had success with a temporary repair by glueing a patch on both sides with Evostik contact adhesive.

If travelling far afield, take spare cordage. Not only is it a consumable item that must be replaced, but it is also an attractive commodity in less prosperous communities; the theft of all of a yacht's running rigging is by no means unknown and one should be able to replace the more vital items at least. If your standing rigging is highly tuned, so that tension is critical, it is important to have some matching steel wire. Stainless steel wire is unobtainable in many places, and even when it is you cannot be sure exactly what you are getting: these steels differ quite a bit, and some are unsuitable for a salty environment.

Always use anhydrous lanolin for greasing shackles, rigging screws and other deck fittings. It is not only more waterproof than grease, it does not wash off, and it is cheaper and less messy. Never use graphite grease in a steel or aluminium ship or fittings because it can produce local galvanic corrosion problems.

As a logbook we use an A3 page-to-a-day diary and this becomes also a maintenance reminder. Put items that are time-critical on their expected days. Normally it will be highly inconvenient to do that job when that day comes round, and when the page is turned the job gets forgotten. This likelihood can be reduced (though not eliminated) by having a bookmark. When an item crops up which cannot be done at once it is added to the list on the bookmark, eventually to be crossed off when done. I have a very large bookmark.

If you have no engine hour meter, then whenever you use engine or generator note the time run in the log and keep a cumulative total. I record it only to the nearest half-hour, trying to be consistent about rounding up or down as appropriate. Even in the tropics, use antifreeze in the cooling water because it has good corrosion inhibiting properties though it can be understandably hard to find.

Do not forget to keep your sextant lightly oiled, and attend to compass gimbals. Swing the compass yourself once a year to check for alterations in the deviation. If it is only a degree or so different just make a note on the card, but if there are some large differences, or if the differences are clustered in the same quadrant, then check to see if you have left anything magnetic about or have moved or fitted something significant. If there is no simple explanation get a professional adjustment done. Note that after passing through a violent thunderstorm or if the ship is on a cardinal heading for a long period, the magnetic characteristics of a steel vessel can be altered quite a bit. Take an early opportunity of checking, but you should do that daily in any event. Such changes are normally not permanent.

Repair problems are best avoided by keeping things simple. What you cannot repair yourself with on-board materials and facilities is probably going to cause trouble sometime. Things do go wrong; even well designed, well made items break or fail for no apparent reason. Murphy's Law being certain in its effect, you can bet your life things will fail just when you need them. Here are a few examples of pre-planned jury-rigs that can be used to manage temporarily. We call them 'homeward-bounders'.

Bulldog clips for rigging, or better still, double throat wire grips (Davey & Co. cat. no. 1626) which do not cripple the wire. Keep quite a lot of the right sizes stowed in lanolin to keep them usable, and a few lengths of wire rope or short chain to bridge a gap. If a wire parts and you have no spare wire, make eyes with the clips and close the gap with a lot of turns of small cordage, which is better than one or two of larger.

Carry a little impeller pump of the sort that can be used on an electric drill. I have used one when the cooling water pump on the generator failed, and for other less important jobs.

Holes in rubber exhaust hose need a short length (an inch or two is enough) of the right size steel pipe. Cut the hose, insert pipe and secure with hose clips. Holes in a rigid exhaust are best closed by a hose clip over a soft leather patch (if wet exhaust), or over an asbestos pad (if dry). On wet exhausts, heavy cloth and rubber are usable. Hose clips have a variety of unofficial uses — they do not merely stay round, they can be used to bind all sorts of things together.

Various advisory or regulatory bodies approve copper tube for diesel fuel lines. I think this is dangerous in a boat that is well used, for copper not only work-hardens by having its shape changed repeatedly, but also time-hardens when liquid is flowing through it. In either case it becomes brittle and breaks when it will cause most trouble. Bronze pipe would be fine, but I prefer the flexible woven metal type, which are not overly expensive. Metal-clad plastic will only protect against accidental physical damage, but it does not proof the tube against fire. But when your copper (approved) tube breaks, and it certainly will before the plastic, that can lead to fire, too. For this eventuality (the break, that is) keep some strong plastic tube and clips.

A frequent failure spot is a metal elbow in a wet exhaust system. Spares are very heavy, and the darn things go so often that one can get caught. Look around lorry agencies for rubber cooling water elbows, which can be the right size. Indeed, they might be cheaper, lighter and better fitted from the kick-off.

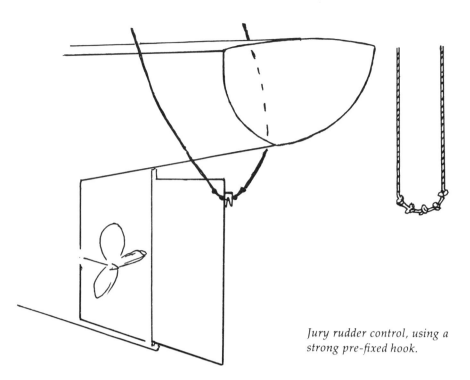

Jury rudder control, using a strong pre-fixed hook.

Steering gear fails from time to time, mostly solvable by using an emergency tiller. It is not unknown for the rudder shaft itself to break, leaving the rudder intact but swinging freely. As a precautionary insurance against this horrible event, arrange a small V-shaped notch (open downwards) near the top after edge of the rudder. It is easy to lower over the stern a bight of rope with a few overhand knots in it. With one end either side of the boat, pull gently up and the knots can be jammed into the V, thus getting the rudder under some sort of control without having to go over to do it.

Spares and Tools

Finally, here is a list of the spare parts I have needed over the past ten years, which must indicate something. The tool list is somewhat longer than for normal cruising. If you become able to use all of these tools competently before you start you will be better off than I was at that point, for a lot of these have had to be added to my original outfit.

Do not let the chores spoil the sailing.

Spares used in Fare Well

These were used in more than ten years of continuous cruising. The number in parentheses is the number used where this is more than one.

166

On Deck

Oil seals renewed on SL521 windlass (2).

Shockcord, various sizes, over 50 yards.

Cordage for sheets and lashings.

Shackles. I mostly use galvanized, and replace them when they rust. But stainless ones do fail, and of course the pins I lose never match the bows I drop at other times.

SL hatch stays (3). Canpa hatch handle.

Various hinges with brass pins (not strong enough).

Canpa hatch sealing round the acrylic.

Winch handle. Deck caulking.

Rotator for towing log (dropped overboard).

In the Engineroom

Submersible bilge pumps (3); float switches (7) and air-pressure switches (1) for same.

Water Puppy washdown pump (2).

Godwin freshwater pump shaft seal and bearing.

Sight-glass plastic tubing on FW tanks.

Fuel-oil tubing, olives, cocks, bits and pieces.

Exhaust rubber tubing, exhaust elbows (steel) (3)

Dozens of hoseclips.

Water pump on refrigerator (2)

On the main engine:

Flexible lube oil pipe, set of cooling water hoses, numerous filters, shaft gland packing.

On the generator prime mover:

The Farymann needed: injector, water pumps (2), set of flexible mountings, fuel pipes, valves and valve gear.

The Petter needed: new cylinder heads (2), valve springs (7), new lube oil piping, water pumps (2), water pump impellers (3), set of flexible mountings, bleed screw on injection pump, injector, corrosion inhibiting anodes (22). A lot of blasphemy.

Electrical

Lucas AC5A alternator (3).

Lucas 440 regulator (6).

Lucas indicator bulb for above circuit (2).

Auto voltage control for G&M 3kVA 230V alternator.

Transformer (1), rheostat, and bridge rectifiers (2) for G&M alternator.

Brushes for all motors.

Diodes in SL Shorepower rectifier (5)

Main batteries (2)

Battery isolating switches (3)

Japanese battery changeover switches (2)

A large-scale rewiring following lightning strike.

Diodes for Sharp Autopilot (2)

Solenoid spool valve in Cetrek hydraulic pump.
Ammeter
Many switches, sockets and plugs of all types.
Fuses.
Dry batteries by the dozen.
New torches.
Fluorescent tubes 24V (3); there are 10 fitted.
Bulbs — dozens, but especially the 24V 6W.

Navigating Instruments
Impeller assemblies for Walker Trident Mk 3 log (14!), and major
    repairs (3).
Wind instrument complete due to lightning strike. Photo-transistor in
    anemometer. Vane blown off wind direction instrument — twice.
Rotator and flywheel for Walker Cherub log.
Echosounders: various small repairs, 1 new instrument and 1 trans-
    ducer (Seafarer) and one co-ax plug.
Radio receivers (2). Pencil sharpener.
Magnets for compass correction; they rusted away in time.

Domestic
Weights for pressure-cooker valve, and seal.
Sewing machine driving belt. Tap washers.
Photo-electric cell for Perkins Mate cooker. Sealing strip for hob of
    cooker. Fire-cement for cooker furnace.
Lavac WC: spare seat seals (2), flap valves (2), joker valves (5). Tubing
    for WC installation. Lavac WC bowl: the aluminium casting dis-
    integrated.
Fire extinguishers (3) — routine replacement.
Some Tupperware. Thermos flask.

A Spares List for Consideration

For (each) engine
Water hoses
Pump impellers
Any flexible pipe
Complete exhaust run
Filters
Pipe couplings and olives
Gaskets and seals
Mountings, if flexible
Valve springs
Plastic fuel pipe and clips
Hose clips, dozens
HP fuel pipes (from pump to injectors)
Spare belts

Duplicate flanges for hoses
Coupling bolts

Electrical
Terminal strip
Crimp terminals
Alternator regulator warning lamps
Circuit breakers, fuses
Switches, sockets, plugs, light bulbs
Assorted resistors, capacitors, diodes, transistors — you may not be
    able to use them, but someone else might on your behalf.
Lucar connectors
Cable of all sizes
Windlass relay
Motor brushes

Other
Spares kit for all pumps
Rubber sheet (2mm)
Paint, brushes etc
Soft aluminium sheet (3mm), or copper in wooden boat.
Threaded rod, nuts
Bits of plywood, timber
Sealing compound
Caulking
Stainless sheet (about 1.5mm)

On deck
Drive belt for windlass
Bolts, nuts for spreader roots
Shackles, thimbles etc
Canvas and thread
Cordage
Bulldog clips
Lanolin
Oar for dinghy (plus oarlocks, if of the loose type).
Flags and ensigns
Eyebolts
Clevis and cotter pins
Whipping twine
Shockcord and terminals
20ft of largest wire
20ft of smallest wire
Winch handle
Wooden plugs, assorted
Sail battens (if foolish enough to have them)

Tool List

I did not start out with all these. A lot have had to be added on the way, which tells one something.

Saws a general-purpose, medium tooth
large hack and small hack
coping (if jigsaw not carried)
spare blades

Hammers large ball-peen
claw
chipping

Screwdrivers for no. 4, 6, 8, slot-screws
dumpy for no. 8 slot-screws
small and large crosshead
dumpy crosshead
very large slot
angled slot and crosshead, preferably ratchet
percussion

Chisels ¼ and ¾in. firmer. Hard chisels

Files small triangular, round and half-round
large round and half-round
half-round wood rasp (the wood-butcher's *vade mecum*)
thread-restoring files

Clamps assorted, including adjustable opening
Vice, or a Black & Decker Jobber or Workmate
Bradawl
Bevel guage
Square
Small smoothing plane, rebating plane
Pliers: large, small pointed, and circlip
Spanners: ring or open tube according to choice
Socket set. Large and small adjustable. Pipe wrench.
Large and small Mole wrench or Visegrip
Nut splitter
Stud removers
Taps and dies
Hand drill
Steel rule, calipers
Allen keys
Punches, drifts
Sheet metal shears
Oilstone, rough and smooth each side
Dentist's probe
Long angled, surgeon's forceps (the best dropped-item recovery tool)
Funnels

A corner on the quay can be very useful for painting a bowsprit, and for ranging anchors and cables so that all links can be checked.

Electric tools, and tools for electrical work
Two-speed drill up to 10mm
Jigsaw
Orbital sander
Small angle grinder (steel boats)
Soldering iron
Wire clippers and strippers
Insulated screwdrivers (lots)
Pointed-nose small pliers
Multi-test meter to read 0−25V DC, 0−250V AC, 0−10 ohms, 0−100 ohms, and 0−1000 ohms
Crimping tool
Long jump leads (lorry type, say about 20ft)
Short jump leads
Plenty of screws, bolts, nuts, washers, friction washers, self-taps, tacks, panel pins and nails to choice

171

CHAPTER NINE

Victualling

'Many suppose anything is good enough to serve men at sea.'

The Galley

Apart from the heads, nothing will get more use on your boat than the galley. If you wish life aboard to be the peaceful and enjoyable experience we all hope for, it repays much thought and planning. You will never get it completely right, but your first cruise will show up any design faults and mistakes in emphasis. *These should be rectified.* Even small inconveniences can become very irritating if encountered several times a day, and are intolerable in bad weather.

> 'The Cooke roome where they dresse the victual may bee placed in diverse parts of the shippe'

Think of the following things:
Does the galley work at an angle of (say) 40° on both tacks? Will the lockers or cupboards open without depositing their contents on the floor? Is everything strong enough for the cook to hang on to, or fall against? Are the things that you need in bad weather easily and conveniently stowed? If the pan you need is at the bottom of a pile of seven, Murphy's Law makes it certain that the 45° roll will come just as you have them all out on the floor to reach the one you want. Items in constant use should have prime space, closely followed by the mugs, bowls and stores needed in bad weather. Separate the pans (especially if they are non-stick) with cardboard picnic plates to prevent noise and scratches. Drawers in the galley sometimes make more sense than cupboards or shelves, especially if they open fore and aft. In any case they need strong catches of some sort: mine have a vertical retaining bar.

The kind of stove you choose to cook with needs some thought. Bill mentioned the different fuel options in Chapter Six 'Below Decks' in some detail; I need not repeat them here. Top-of-the-stove cooking is fine for holidays, but for living aboard you will want to cook as you did on shore which means an oven and grill is desirable. So are good saucepans, which should be tall and have well-fitting lids. They should not deform if dropped, and have well insulated handles. I have never regretted the stainless steel pans I bought for *Fare Well* which after fourteen years of constant misuse are as good as new. Remember that your stove (and you) may have to cook at a sharp angle, or even crashing up and down (I have the dubious satisfaction of knowing that my diesel stove will function at a 60° angle: we were in this position for several hours, so it was quite important at the time). You will therefore need well designed, high fiddles to keep your pans in position on the stove in a seaway. In addition, check that water cascading down a hatch will not put out the stove and prevent its use in a storm, as has happened on some racing yachts. At a time when hot food is most needed, you will be glad that you positioned your stove in a safe dry spot.

My stove has the added advantage that the stainless steel bolster that covers it will take a folded sheet. This means that if I fold the washing carefully and place it, still a little damp, on the warm bolster, I can walk away and let the ironing do itself. The stove is not gimbal-led, but is mounted athwartships. (Its fiddles have always prevented a serious loss of soup.) It heats the water too, and has a strong crash bar.

Gas stoves have the great advantage of instant heat and adjustability.

Both my diesel stove and the coal stoves still to be found in older boats are hot to use in the tropics—cold lunches become the order of the day. Many boats nowadays are thinking about Microwave ovens. Their advantages are short cooking times, and therefore less power consumed, they do not heat up the galley in the tropics, and they fit into a small space. Though their output is measured as 600 watts, they will draw between 1000 and 1500 watts, and would need an adequate AC generator. A drop-down door model is best on a boat. There exist small all-purpose oven-grills with a hotplate on top. They are very convenient where space is limited, but their power consumption is as much or more than a full-sized electric oven, and at nearly 3000 watts is more than small inexpensive generators can cope with.

Whatever you choose to cook on, have another method of cooking, just in case. An all-electric galley is no good if the power fails, and it is possible to run out of gas. In *Hosanna* I have a split hob, with two gas burners and two electric plates (these hobs are now easily obtainable). The saloon is heated by a wood stove, on which we cooked our lunch while in the boatyard, using an upturned biscuit tin on a trivet as a Dutch oven, if it wasn't stew. (My lamented diesel cooker on *Fare Well* became much too expensive; for *Hosanna* we were able to buy the hob, a regular small oven, and the generator to run them for the same money.) A small charcoal barbeque could be a back-up, useful in good weather; or that old standby the single-burner Primus (the self-pricking one) or a small Camping Gaz stove in case of dire need.

The sink, as Bill has said, is best with natural drainage. This has been a help to us on some occasions of emergency, such as bailing out the engine room. Since both are in the centre of the boat, it is a fairly easy matter, with two of us, to bail straight into the sink. When we were fighting an engineroom fire it was possible to get water to it with a good deal of control, for the same reason. As regards one sink or two, while Don Street swears by a double sink, even if they are too small to wash large pans in (it does make an extra catchall while working), I prefer one bigger one: if only because it drained one bucket of bilge water before the next one arrived. Don is right to point out that small sinks save water, but this is achieved at sea by placing a smaller plastic bowl in the larger sink, which has the added advantage of cushioning against breakages.

Equipment

Avoid the temptation to clutter precious workspace with domestic appliances that will not work without shore power. Go back to the mechanical aids our grandmothers used, and if you want them handy create storage space for them. I would prefer to take such things as hand mincers and coffee grinders (rather than an electric mixer or food processor which are too bulky for most galleys), a well-engineered hand beater and a wall tin opener that will not rust in a few days. You will not, as on holiday, be either camping or eating out all the time, so be sure your equipment suits your style of cooking. If you are a dab hand at cakes, take your cake tins. I use the non-stick Skyline loaf tins, which I keep cushioned from scratches with paper towels or picnic plates and are still rust-free after several years' use at sea. If you are good at patés or potted tongue, take the containers you know to be the right size, and the piece of wood to weight them with. Take an elegant dish for your speciality: sometimes one wants to splash out, joining the neighbouring boat for a combined dinner; and a little style is a welcome change. Not that the salad does not taste just as good from the plastic washbowl — take several, they have many uses.

Spend time looking for your favourite tools in stainless steel. It took me years to find a pair of stainless tongs, without which I cannot even boil an egg, that fitted nicely to the hand. Chromium plate soon loses its shine when subjected to the chafe and roll of a boat, and then rusts disgustingly. Strong plastic can be a good alternative: sieves, ladles, potato mashers come to mind.

As well as my tongs, the things I would not be without are: a pressure cooker; a wall-mounted can-opener, invaluable when fast sea stew is needed; a small spatula or butter spreader; a hamburger press (mine is plastic). Plus my only electrical kitchen gadget, which is the neatest handheld mincer and beater I have ever come across, called the Bamix Magic Wand. It consumes 100 watts on 240 V AC and used with a tall jar or jug will purée soup, beat cakes or chop vegetables. It was designed for the blind and is very easy to clean.

Apart from the pans already mentioned, you will need frying pans and lidded casseroles (good quality enamel seems to last well, but the

174

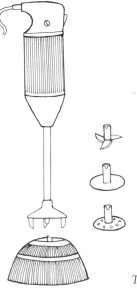

The Bamix 'Magic Wand'

cheap ones chip too quickly). Stainless or aluminium dishes of various shapes and sizes are handy, as they have many uses either for cold food or in the oven. Be sure to measure the space available in your oven and get ovenware that fits well: it saves spills if the pans don't skid from side to side. Most yacht ovens are too wide, imitating those on shore. I use the brown ovenware that you can buy in Spain; used on calm days or in harbour we have broken only one in ten years. Mine are mostly oblong and the largest one fits the oven exactly and will do lasagne for ten or bake a huge fish.

On Don Street's *Iolaire* a very large pan is carried in case of lobsters. He says you can coil your dock ropes in it when not in use. We have one, but keep it in an inaccessible place with the large bowls that are required on such occasions inside it, since it is also useful for large quantities of rice and spaghetti.

A board that fits over the sink for extra workspace is commonplace now, but was not when we built *Fare Well*. We invented our own, wood on one side and Formica on the other. When not in use it slots into a specially made groove alongside the stove. This board is for bread or pastry. A separate one, smaller but thicker, is carried as a chopping block as meat and fish often come in their original state, and a cleaver goes with it. A minute timer, preferably the four-hour kind with not too loud a tick, can be invaluable not just for cooking but reminding you of watch changes, weather forecasts and even the noon sight. Fasten it firmly to a dry bulkhead, as landing in the washing-up bowl is not good for it.

Consider your gadgets from this point of view:

Do I use it a lot?

If it is electric, is there a mechanical substitute?

Is it robustly made, of a rust-free material?

Is it reasonably resistant to going wrong, breaking or getting trodden on?

Is there a simpler way of achieving the same result?

Having said that, I would be the last person to discourage you from taking any beloved device that you would be unhappy without. Be sure that it has a safe stowage, and try and protect it from the salt air.

Before we leave the galley, let me remind you to find space for the indispensible roll of paper towels, and for the teatowel and handtowel which otherwise are always on the floor among the spilt sugar, rice and onion skins. There should of course be a better place than the floor for such things, which brings us to:

Rubbish, garbage, trash and hygeine

Some larger galleys have a free-standing bin just as you might find ashore, but this roams about in bad weather, and in smaller spaces it is probably better to have the kind that is fastened behind a door. The most convenient bin I have ever had either ashore or at sea is my present one. It is fixed behind the door under the draining board to my left, the door drops forward on a chain just long enough to allow the bin-lid to open, and it is easy to reach from the sink. The galley floor is best kept clear and *clean*, since your dinner will occasionally land on it.

> Always clean your galley floors:
> The portion dropped there may be yours.

You don't want to slip on a greasy floor, either, so choose your flooring with care to be both non-slip and nice looking. It's hard to know if a soup-coloured floor is clean.

We have a rule that engineroom dirt is not to be washed off in the galley sink. Bill disobeys it constantly, so I have to provide a sludge-and-rust coloured towel which he carefully avoids using. So any diesel puddings are his fault.

When you are hundreds of miles from shore, rubbish has to be tossed overboard. Paper and food waste will disappear very quickly, into the maws of fish. Tins if punctured will sink and rapidly disintegrate, two miles down. Bottles are filled with sea water and sunk. We try not to throw plastic overboard *anywhere*. In harbour or near beaches and seashore, keep your rubbish and land it when you can, putting it in the appropriate containers if available. (It may, alas, yet end up in the sea, dumped over a cliff by the local authority.)

If you have ever been woken at dawn by the relentless clonk of floating bottles along your hull; maddeningly loud and arhythmic to screaming point (you are waiting not just for the proverbial second shoe to drop, but for the next ten bottles), you will not, after a party, drop your bottles over the side to perform their *musique concrete* through the anchorage, waking more people than a change of wind among a ten-yacht raft-up. Perhaps the only legitimate use for firearms on board is for potting these offending bottles and sinking them.

While I am ordinarily rather a slob at washing up, tending to leave it till I feel like it, I get more diligent if there are flies or wasps about. If there is nothing to attract them in the way of sticky surfaces and leftover food, there is nothing for them to wipe their filthy feet on. Sometimes they even go away.

> In fifty years there may be no more green
> The beach be hideous with oil and trash
> The air unbreathable, the sea unclean,
> And yet, I bet, appearing through the ash
> A yacht survives amid the polythene
> And in the rigging is a nappy wash.

Keeping your cool: Refrigerators and ice boxes

Fewer and fewer long-distance yachts nowadays travel with no means at all of cooling food. A refrigerator is both a boon and a tyranny; it makes a lot of difference to one's life, but it eats power. (See Chapter six for comments on fuels.) Top-opening fridges make sense on a boat, but most of them have poky openings which make both access and cleaning difficult. Our fridge can be defrosted in about ten minutes as it drains into the engineroom sump. We had hamster baskets made to fit it, four at the top and four at the bottom. If we care to use the extra power, the bottom will take frozen food. Defrosting and cleaning is done as a combined operation, both of us working fast: remove the eight baskets, hose down with fresh water, dry off and replace baskets. If the bottom is not full of frozen food, we put in a half-gallon container of sea water, frozen if possible, to act as an extra cool bank. This also helps in case of a power failure. In this dire event, do not open the cabinet, and try to increase the insulation by covering it with a sleeping bag or deck cushions while the failure lasts. After more than about 24 hours (given a tightly packed, well frozen and well insulated mass) you may have to decide if a big cook-up is going to be necessary to save the food.

Iceboxes of the type that take a large block from the fishhouse are found in many yachts, and the ice lasts a surprisingly long time: ten to twelve days in the Tropics and three to four weeks in cooler waters. Keep the ice as dry as possible by draining off any standing water. You should have no trouble finding ice, either in the Mediterranean or the West Indies, but it is heavy. Anywhere there is a fish market, there will be ice. If you can get half-gallon containers of sea water frozen for you, as is sometimes possible in the specialist freezer shops in the Med and the States, you can pack your box with these and obtain a drier cold. In the Pacific however, ice is harder to come by. I can do no better than refer you also to the excellent chapter on refrigeration in Don Street's book *The Ocean Sailing Yacht:* I have never read a more helpful or practical account.

To end with: *ice cubes* are worth a mention. The usual flat trays are of little use on a boat; they spill when you heel. For years I searched for a top-opening untippable ice cube maker. When the answer appeared it was, like all the best ideas, astonishingly simple, a compartmented disposable plastic bag, filled from the top and then tied off, which will fit good humouredly into odd corners of the freezer. My present packet of these is French, and contains ten sachets of eighteen ice 'cushions'. This excellent idea is now available everywhere.

With no refrigerator or icebox we are back to Grandmother's meat safe, a wooden box with fly screen panels which was placed somewhere dry and airy, and if possible cool. An insulated polythene cool box in a dry bilge can be effective. Other cooling methods you will have are the sea water, which is often no cooler than the air, and the evaporation principle, used by the earthenware butter and milk coolers. A cloth or muslin dipped in fresh water causes rapid cooling as the wind passes over it, as does the Osokool type of porous box with a well for cooling water. (This water should be fresh, as salt will clog the pores, but little is needed.)

Marketing

This should be a pleasant experience, spiked occasionally with culture shock, and cushioned with coffee and cold drinks.

Those of our American friends who are used to the brown paper bags that go straight from the supermarket into the boot (trunk) of their car, will do well to acquire a capacious shopping bag, several in fact. The ubiquitous string or nylon net bag of Europe comes to mind, which is great for stowage on board but less good for bringing home the bacon, since sharp items protrude and bite the calves of the hapless marketer. The best sort of bag is something waterproof and rather shapeless, perhaps with a drawstring top, that will subside into the inevitable pool of water in the bottom of the dinghy without disintegrating or the contents taking harm. Such a bag can also be carried on the head, which is much better for your spine than hanging off-balance at the end of one arm. I often see Yotties with rucksacks, another way to carry quite a heavy load safely. Europeans shopping in America, *per contra*, will soon realize that the paper bags, while ecologically sound, will not survive a soggy dinghy ride, and will take their own shopping bags with them to America where they can be difficult to find.

Entering a 'supermarket' on a Greek island, you will find a dim cave, smelling of wine, olives and sheep cheese. The shutters are closed to keep it cool. It is dark, the floor is uneven and the clutter is unbelievable. Only the owner knows where the lamp oil is, or what lies buried under the empty fruit crates, or how long he has had that dusty pile of rubber knickers for a previous generation of babies. (For today's babies he has a rather less dusty pile of Pampers.)

Be careful how you step back or you will be caught behind the knees by the weighing machine that stands on the floor and end up sitting in an open sack of rice. The bolts of cloth on the shelf are brown, brown and black; there are innumerable battered boxes of coloured thread and large hanks of natural wool for weaving the local rugs. Wine is from the barrel, olives from the vat and lamp oil from a drum: bring your own bottle. As it is several days since the last ferry, the vegetables are not what they were and the last of the fruit went this morning, but then you should have bought your produce on the day of the ferry, as everyone else does. However, there is wine, feta cheese and olives, and the bread that comes fresh every day, hot and redolent of the wood oven it was baked in.

Compared with this, the supermarket in the Virgin Islands really *was* a supermarket. The packets and tins were on self-service shelves and showed signs of having been wiped over fairly recently. There was a great deal of strip lighting though only a quarter of it was working. There were trolleys, some with a full complement of wheels, and there were a few baskets that did not snag your clothes with broken wires. Almost everything available in the States was available here — tins a little bent and packets a bit battered by the long journey, and rather expensive; but here were your hominy grits, your canned chicken-and-dumplings, your Hershey bars and Betty Crocker cake mixes. (Was that a beetle in the cornflakes?) Local produce was tucked away at the back in coarse grey paper bags: the dried beans, cornmeal, black-eyed peas and delicious transparent tubes of split pea soup mix, like a miniature barber's pole of orange, yellow and green. Here too were the bottles of Hot Pepper Sauce, and a cold box for the sows' ears, pig's tails and chicken gizzards. Were there beetles? Yes, some, but at least they would not be resistant to every known bug destroyer.

I find it all intensely interesting from one extreme to the other. I love to know what people eat, and how they cook it, and where better to find out than the shady covered markets of Europe or the Western world, where a cool breeze wafts through with scents of fruit and spices, where the cries of the vendors are accompanied by the country tattle of chickens, goats and donkeys and good food is to be had at low prices.

I get my heavy shopping over early: it's cooler. (In Yugoslavia you may find everything sold by nine o'clock.) My 'donkey', who is only too anxious to leave, takes the load back to the boat, leaving me to the leisurely delights of tasting, chatting, balancing price with quality and

179

discovering new things. No-one in a supermarket has time to chat as the market ladies have. They will tell you how to prepare and cook unfamiliar things, that if you wait a week the peaches will be cheaper, that the market will be closed tomorrow for a Fiesta, that the broad beans are new and tiny enough to be eaten raw with cheese. I discover treasures in obscure corners, I observe how things are bought and by what name, and what is in the cupboards at the back of the stall. With a bit of luck I come home with something cheap and delicious for lunch, which is well deserved since everything has to be logged in and stowed somewhere first, a time-consuming chore.

Having done it, though, you can then go off to quiet bays and not worry about shopping for a while; only about trying the new recipe one of the market ladies gave you. The language of cooks and those who are interested in cooking is surprisingly easy to follow: if you don't know the word a little mime helps. Before I learnt the Greek for eggs I had to act the hen admiring her product, which used to cause great merriment; perhaps life is less fun now that I know more words.

Stowage

'How the Ordnance should bee placed, and the goods stowed on a ship.'

Stowage is a fine art. There are three requirements. One: your goods should be safe from bending, breakage, beetles and bilge water. Two: they should be accessible. Three: you should be able to find what you want easily.

To take the last point first, I recall how Clement Freud, taken on to cook magnificent dishes for a long yacht race, prepared a splendid scheme of labelled lockers and a detailed inventory of every bit of food he had in them. Alas, they had to leave immediately the stuff was delivered on the quay. It was bundled in anywhere it would fit by the frantic crew and he lost all track of it, getting occasional nasty surprises during the trip.

Whether you keep an alphabetical 'where to find it' notebook, or a list of the contents of every locker and drawer taped just inside it, or have a phenomenal memory, it matters not as long as you can find what you want. A filing system by which everything beginning with, say, S goes in the same place sounds alluring, but has practical drawbacks. One is that you get incompatible substances oddly mixed together, like soup, sandals and seizing wire; and the other is that of nomenclature: B for butterscotch, or S for sweets? B for bandaid or P for plasters?

The Set Theory works well: stow like things together. It is logical, which helps other people to find things. Thus your paint locker is also the logical place for solvents, brushes and sandpaper; as the Bosun's locker is for all sorts of nautical bits and pieces which do not fit into the come-in-handy box, which all cruisers know and love if not by that name.

We start with the heavy things, which ought to go near the bottom of the boat. That means the dry part of the bilge.

Tins: you will read many an account, in books about world-girdling or Southern Ocean racing, of the tedious task of varnishing all the tins and painting on some sort of shorthand to indicate the contents. (This lead to a friend of ours saving a tin of 'goose' for his birthday, only to find on opening it that it was gooseberries.) We do not do anything to our tins, other than group them by kind in plastic bags. We then put them in the bilge, meat aft, fish forward and vegetables amidships. A dry bilge should be the norm for cruising; if you have reason to believe that your labels will soak off, change to a drier boat. The plastic bags are merely to help separate a batch of tinned soups from the sort of tinned meat that goes with salad. There is also a bag with party delicacies in it, for birthdays and such. (The portion of the bilge which contains the sump, bilge pump and/or strum box must be kept free of anything which could clog the pump if the worst should happen, so it is a good place to put hard objects with no extraneous bits to float off, such as drums of antifouling or gallon jars of detergent, well wedged in against chafe.) If you have room, large flower pots and square plastic buckets make good separators, and the latter are always handy: we find we lose one plastic bucket per storm overboard, on average. Beer crates are also good, but too large for many boats.

Bottles: the bulk of these can stow in the bilge, too. If you get your duty frees there may be quite a lot of them. We used to pack ours carefully with corrugated paper, but when we ran out of it we found that jamming them in head to tail was just as effective: breakages are almost unknown, though a beer bottle popped its crown cap due to excessive fizz.

Those bottles that you want handy can be stored in cradles, on their sides as in a cellar, or behind a retaining bar, in circles cut to fit or an arrangement of pegs. All these restraints need to be at least 3 inches tall if you want to prevent clinkage when rolling.

Glasses go with bottles. They can go in similar circles, or be slotted into a holder if they are stemmed, or be packed fairly tightly into a drawer. The cheap French glasses will stack, but sometimes jam together unless separated by a leather tag or paper. It is also possible to fit a bracket rather like a toothmug holder for glasses, and it's very good policy to have one to hold the helmsman's glass or mug in reach. We find these holders very good for pencils and have them everywhere, with a circle of rubber or foam plastic at the bottom to prevent rattles.

Plastic containers should be of flexible polythene rather than the hard transparent acrylic, which breaks too easily. The lids should fit well

(Tupperware has been a boon to yachtsmen) to keep out beetles and dampness. A determined mouse can chew through them and a rat will be through in two bites. (Keep a cat.) Nevertheless they are indispensible for dry stores such as flour, cereals, pasta, rice and all the things that cannot be left in their original paper or plastic bags. (The heavy polythene used for five-pound bags of rice seems to be beetle proof, provided you protect them from chafe.) I have seen very impressive galley drawers built to fit their containers, all top-labelled and awesomely neat. My herb drawer is less orderly, as the jars and bottles are all different sizes and shapes; I've never known a serious cook who was able to stick with one brand of herbs and spices, ranged neatly in racks to fit as in the glossy magazines: we are not to be regimented like that. At least mine are all top-labelled and easy to find. A combination of square and round shapes also means that you can get a jar out when you want it. This was not the case with a drawer I once saw packed tightly with square containers of the same height: you could not get a finger in to lift one out. I find the plastic storage baskets now on sale useful for things that are not used every day. All the curry and Chinese ingredients go in one, to be got out when needed, all cake and pudding things go in another, and so on.

A ready-use shelf near your stove should hold all the things that everyone needs constant access to, such as tea, coffee, cocoa, salt and sugar; it should also hold half a dozen tins of bad weather food (see Bad Weather Cooking).

In Spain, it is possible to buy strong polythene milk containers with a double-sealed screw-on lid. I found these ideal for large quantities of wholemeal flour and the like, the 3½ and 5 litre sizes suited me best. Being cylindrical, they stowed in the bilge and did not chafe as the squarish ones containing soft drinks or detergents did. We had supposed that the latter would stow beautifully in the bilge, and so they did, but after six months or so in close contact with their bedfellows they began to chafe and crack at the corners, and the resulting foam was astonishingly hard to mop up. We still use such containers, but are more careful about protecting them from chafe.

Remember that foil packets of instant mashed potato and dried soups and vegetables are irresistible to weevils, which can eat through them with ease: put all your packets into a lidded box. Cardboard boxes and packets are also not beetle proof, put contents into:

Glass coffee jars are heavy, but they seem very strong and we have not broken one yet. Take extra lids though: they *do* break. Cut out any instructions from the packet and tape them to the jar.

Oblong bins often sold for cleaning materials can be screwed in suitable places such as the engineroom. A shelf or bracket for them to stand on prevents them breaking away from the screws if they are used for heavy items. Ingenious use can also be made of flowerpot holders and deep sink tidies; for the brushes and scourers by the sink and in the heads or shower for organizing everyone's toilet gear.

Stainless steel and plastic tool clips have many uses, from preventing the washing-up liquid falling in the sink to actually holding tools. We wish the stainless ones were to be found in a wider range of sizes.

Nets are good for fruit and vegetables, since they are airy, and if strung horizontally help to minimize bruising. Net bags, hung from hooks so as to occupy those almost unusable spaces, can be used for a variety of awkward objects.

Cardboard boxes are not recommended. Some yachts will not even allow them on board long enough to unpack the groceries, but unload on the quay because they are believed to harbour cockroaches. While the cockroach, according to one of my authorities, is an innocent little creature and one of the few to whom no blame can be attached for carrying any disease, it breeds fast, is aesthetically unpleasing and crunchy underfoot. The Pests chapter will help you to deal with it.

Other almost unusable spaces, such as behind linings, I have seen used to make little shelves for cassettes, hidey-holes for insecticides and rat bait where the cat and the children can't get at them, or once where there was a rather larger space holes were cut in the lining and various brushes stuck through them, with their heads on the inside and the handles in the space behind.

Large shelves can be made more practical by the use of plastic baskets; you can even colour-code them. They are good for sewing materials, the bulkier items of first aid (bandages, rolls of adhesive tape) and personal gear.

Short-term Victualling

At the end of the book you will find detailed lists, country by country, of what to buy where, what is hard to find and what to store up with. Here I shall merely suggest a general campaign.

Some people prefer to do all the shopping at once, and hire a taxi or donkey to get it back to the ship. On the Intra-Coastal Waterway in the States you can often borrow a 'courtesy car' to do this. In Europe, stores will sometimes deliver to the quay; it's worth asking. If the heavy shopping is done a day or so early there is plenty of time to stow things properly and choose your fruit and vegetables with care. If you then get them back to the boat without bruising and stow gently, they should last well.

Most Mediterranean bread is meant to be eaten the same day. If the baker takes the trouble to bake every day, he reasons that you should pay his bread the respect it deserves by buying it daily. Wrapped bread is looked upon with scorn and is only available in the larger centres. You can give your daily loaf a longer life, after you have enjoyed its first crusty day, by keeping it in a clean polythene bag, and thereafter placing a hunk of it for immediate eating in a lidded casserole in a moderate oven for awhile. This needs a certain amount of judgement as you want the result to be close to fresh bread, not a dried-up rusk. A damp tissue in the casserole helps. When this has all gone, you will need crispbread or crackers. I have not seen in Europe the long-keeping 'half-baked' loaves available in England and America.

Meat for a week is easy if you have a fridge. With the possible exception of France, Mediterranean butchers do not hang their meat and it benefits enormously from a sojourn in your fridge of at least four days, especially lamb or beef.

If you have no fridge or icebox and the weather is hot, take raw meat for one day (perhaps two if you have a cool spot for it), cooked meat for one more day, and cook up a double batch of meat in the pressure cooker *which you then do not open*. With the valve shut it is hermetically sealed and will keep three or four days. Once you have opened the seal, treat as cooked meat. Thereafter you will have to rely on tins, and dried and preserved forms such as salami in its infinite variety; a boon to yachtsmen as it should hang in the air anyway. How long will it keep? In 1944 we returned to the house we had left in 1939. In the deserted larder we found, hanging lonely under a shelf, a forgotten salami, given to us by a grateful Czech at the outbreak of war. In that drear time of rationing we seized it with glee. It was used, slice by precious slice, in all kinds of ways; the smallest dice giving an exotic flavour, a bit chewy after all those years but delicious.

Eggs and butter all keep well enough for a short cruise. Salt butter keeps better in normal conditions, but if you want to keep it in the freezer use unsalted butter. You will need a keeping kind of milk: condensed, powdered or UHT (Long Life); the same goes for cream if it is wanted.

Even for a week, put biscuits, crackers or cookies in an airtight container. There is something horribly demoralizing about soggy biscuits.

Long-distance Victualling

'Gammons of bacon, dried neat's tongues, Beefe packed up in vinegar . . .'

Long-distance means long enough to cross an ocean, though the same considerations apply to a long cruise among the more backward or isolated communities where supplies may be difficult to get. A month to six weeks should encompass most ocean passages if one takes the more practical routes between ports.

Not enough attention is paid, I believe, to food for long passages. The lad who airily assured me in Barbados that he and his all-male crew had crossed the Atlantic on beer and cornflakes was pulling my leg (I hope), but there is more than a grain of truth in what he said. I've seen the least experienced youngster sent off at the last minute to victual the ship with a hastily compiled list in which liquor had clearly been discussed at length, but which was vague as to kinds and quantities of other items. I have sometimes been spotted as a yachtlady and asked for advice right there in the market a couple of hours before departure. If you are starting from England, explain to the manager of your local Cash and Carry Store that you need bulk stores for a long voyage, and you will usually be allowed to shop there on a one-time-only basis. Lipton's in Gibraltar give a discount to long-distance cruisers if they spend more than a certain sum.

Where do you start? Where do you begin when planning food for a long voyage? Some swear by Frederick M. Gardner (see below); I went by multiplying a head count times meals times portions. On our Transatlantic crossing to the West Indies I was glad of the surplus remaining, as tinned and bottled stores were expensive and sometimes hard to find in the Windward Islands.

While we try to live on local produce where we can, to do so in the West Indies would have caused deprivation to the carnivorous males among the crew, despite the omnipresence of fried chicken; as steak dinners ashore were largely beyond our means.

I suggest that you start by reading the previous section on short-distance victualling, as much that I have written there is also relevant to long distances. I then have merely to underline and expand, without repeating myself.

How much do you need to take?

Carry food and water for twice the normal expected passage time, plus emergency provisions and water for a further ten days. You do not want to end up 'down to the last tin of corned beef and licking the dew off the deck', as one of our singlehanded friends described his landfall. Mr Gardner's famous list 'The care and feeding of a Yachtsman', lists items by weight and calls for 5½lb of food per man per day, of which 14½ oz was meat. To that he added a gallon of liquid per head per day for drinking. So he expects four people for 40 days to consume over a ton of food. It takes a bit of organizing. I studied this list with great interest before our first long ocean passage and came to the conclusion that three men and two very tiny women would consume rather less than that. No way can I eat nearly a pound of meat a day. So I decided to think in terms of the number of meals per day and the portions required, and allow a bit extra each time in case of extreme hunger. My deliberations will be found at the back of this book, and are easily modified for larger or smaller appetites.

What should you take?

Tins You will need plenty of tins of meat. These should be solidly packed protein, not the kind that is full of gravy where you find only two walnut-sized lumps of gristle with difficulty by using a magni-

The bicycle that carries bulky gear ashore for repair can also save a long hike back from the market. This folding bike has a solid, simple frame and 3-speed gears that are useful on shore excursions; it has also survived immersion. (photo Mark Brackenbury)

fying glass. Good tinned meat and fish is expensive, but is worth the money especially if you have no fridge. Good buys are corned beef, chopped pork, sausages, stewed steak, luncheon meat, ham and tongue, and for special occasions steak and kidney pie or pudding, pheasant or grouse if you can run to it. Fray Bentos make an excellent range of pie fillings: steak and onion, steak and mushroom, and steak and kidney, which were extremely popular with the crew. So was the stewing steak from Ireland brand-named Casserole, and Libby's Beef Stew. Newforge's Irish Stew tasted very good, but we had to add a lot more meat to it. Campbell's Meatballs which I thought would be great with spaghetti, turned out to be pasty and flavourless. I washed the gravy off them and replaced it with a good strong Italian *ragu* (spaghetti sauce) full of onion, tomato and basil, which made them a bit more interesting. If you get tired of tinned hamburgers you can make meatballs from them, too.

Tinned chicken is always a disappointment; it is too soft in texture and the flavour is changed. The best we found was the chicken and dumplings of the Southern US. However I carried a few small tins of chicken in jelly, to add variety and extra protein to bad-weather soups and risottos.

186

Vegetables that survive canning best are *petit pois* (tiny peas) haricot beans (get some of them au naturel rather than in tomato sauce, for a wider variety of uses), *garbanzos* (chick peas), spinach, sweet corn, beetroot, celery (the texture is wrong but the flavour is good), tomatoes (very useful), lentils, green beans, broad beans and mushrooms (but dried mushrooms have better flavour).

In Spain, tinned cauliflower and brussel sprouts are available; we found them rather soft, but the cauliflower made quite good 'Crème du Barry' soup, and the sprouts, fried with onions, made a change. Carrots are useful for a touch of colour, but fresh ones kept so well that I hardly ever needed the tinned variety. We carried assorted tinned Chinese vegetables, but missed the crunchiness of the real thing.

Tinned fish are very handy in all varieties. Octopus and squid survive canning well, mussels taste tinny. Tinned kippers and salmon make good paté or kedgeree. Paella mixture (a small tin of mussels, squid and octopus available in Spain) can make a good fishermen's risotto as well. Pilchard-and-potato pie is good. Sardines make a delicious 'spaghetti con le sarde', while anchovies make a good spaghetti sauce when mixed with garlic, chilis and olive oil. Tuna is good for everything.

Take a little tinned fruit; your fresh supplies ought to last well, but something like pineapple or raspberries can make a treat.

Other tinned goods that I found valuable were the small tins or jars of spaghetti sauce available in Italy in four flavours, or the less good and rather sweeter ones available in the US, to which more meat, fish or mushrooms could be added to make a very satisfying meal, especially with wholemeal spaghetti.

Many of these tins can, of course, be used for cold lunches, perhaps accompanied by a cup of hot soup if the weather is cool or a salad if it is hot.

Dried food, cereals, grains, pulses and flour

These keep almost indefinitely in damp-proof containers. Fresh water is necessary to reconstitute and cook them. They add texture and crunch to tinned food and have a fresher taste. Dried haricot beans, split peas, lentils and chick peas are all good in spite of the jokes. Rice is essential in my cooking, both white and brown, but the brown takes longer to cook (soak it for 24 hours first). Pasta of all kinds keeps splendidly as long as beetles are kept away — they love it too. Wholemeal pasta is available and makes a better food. Burghul (bulgar or cracked wheat) makes interesting pilaf as a change from rice.

Protein-rich cereals On long voyages among remote islands, such as the Antipodes-Red Sea run or across the Pacific, you can find your diet short of meat and fish. The same can apply if you cannot afford large quantities of tinned meat.

It is worth studying the following facts with care and in more detail than I have space to give here. (The *Small Planet* books listed in the appendix will tell you more.) Certain grains and legumes, *eaten together*, increase those proteins usable by the body to more than the sum of their parts, which explains why the poorer nations thrive on rice with lentils, cornmeal and kidney beans, bulgar and chick peas, and perhaps even baked beans on (wholemeal) toast. (Not the tinned sort, though.) So take with you dried haricot beans, lentils (all colours), split peas, soya beans and soya flour, chick peas, butter beans, peanut butter, and powdered milk; and combine them with brown rice, bulgar (called burgul or burgoo by sailors), wholemeal grains and pasta, for nourishing pilafs and spaghetti dishes; add small pieces of meat or fish if you have them, and plenty of spice and flavour. These can be excellent dishes and extremely varied and tasty. Recipes will be found in Middle East and Indian cookbooks, so do not be lulled into substituting tins of baked beans in tomato sauce, which make everything taste of ketchup. The pressure cooker will make short work of the dried vegetables, which can be cooked in stock or soup to add different flavours to suit whatever meaty morsels you have.

Muesli and similar mixtures keep much better than the crisp breakfast cereals (like cornflakes, which sog very quickly and take up much more room). You will need bread flour, white and wholemeal, and ordinary flour, but you can take a tin of baking powder to make your own self-raising flour. Wholemeal bread mix is worth its space. Cake mixes can be useful when time is short, but they keep less well than the individual ingredients because of the fat content.

White and wholemeal flours if kept dry and beetle-free are good after a year, but the same cannot be said of shortcrust, scone or cake mixes. Bread mixes keep better than cake mixes, but you should carry some Fermipan patent dried yeast, such as 'Harvest Gold', to ginger it up when it gets elderly.

Bread   There are times when a loaf of really solid high-protein bread is worth a whole trayful of bridge rolls. Try this one: it makes a dark, delicious and satisfying loaf.

HIGH PROTEIN BREAD

1 packet (10oz, 280 grams) wholemeal breadmix.
(Grannie Smith, McDougal's, etc.)

Follow the instructions on the packet, adding to the dry mix:

1/3 cup wheatgerm (a generous $\frac{1}{2}$oz)
1/3 cup soya flour
1/3 cup instant powdered milk
1/2 teasp Fermipan (dried yeast)

Stir into the hot water you will use to mix the dough a tablespoon of molasses or dark honey, add to the dry ingredients and knead for five minutes. You won't need a bread tin if you then shape it into a bunloaf.

188

Put it on a greased baking tray; place it, tray and all, inside a large roasting bag (take with you several of the turkey roasting size), secure the bag with a wire tie and leave in a warm place to rise for an hour. Bake as instructed on the packet, and eat with enormous pleasure.

You will notice in the list of ingredients on the breadmix packet Ascorbic acid, vitamin C. This is not to do you good, but to cut out one of the rises. If you make your bread from scratch, you can do the same, by adding one crushed 50 gram Vitamin C tablet per pound of flour.

AFD (air freeze-dried) foods are made in quite a few varieties now. Apart from the well known dried soups you can get beef, chicken and shrimp curries, farmhouse stew, savoury mince and beef Stroganoff. They need fresh water to prepare and take time to cook. Their texture tends to be rather monotonous, but they have their place especially for bulking out leftovers. It's worth reminding you that the average ship-board beetle gnashes its way through foil packets with disturbing ease, so keep them in a metal or plastic box, and be conscientious about the lid. In Italy you can get an excellent freeze-dried mixture of about ten diced vegetables, intended for minestrone. There's an English equivalent, too. A handful of this in any soup or stew is good: you can also use the whole packet with a little salt pork or bacon, and pasta, for a dish you can stand the spoon up in.

Dried fish is always heavily salted. Throughout the Mediterranean and in parts of the West Indies you will see boxes of rough-looking sheets of cardboard, vaguely fish-shaped, light on one side and dark on the other. It is, in fact, fish; called *bacalao, baccala,* stockfish or salt cod. It keeps forever and is very good when properly processed, but even if you get a preliminary amount of salt out by soaking it in sea water and then fresh, it still needs rivers of fresh water washing over it for 24 hours before it is edible.

Dried mushrooms are a splendid idea: they have much more flavour than tinned ones. The French and the Chinese have very good ones.

Dried egg I have mixed feelings about. It's probably all right in cakes; otherwise use it to eke out the breakfast scramble or omelette. To make scrambled eggs entirely with dried eggs brings back too many wartime memories, but today's kids might like it, knowing that there are plenty of other things to eat and bacon or Bacon Grill (tinned) to go with it. (Address in Appendix.)

Dried and salt meat is another matter. Salami has already been mentioned. If you have no fridge or icebox, a piece of smoked bacon will hang in a cool place, dusted with black pepper to keep the flies away. Hams are trickier, since the cut section dries a bit, but a leg of mountain ham we bought in Yugoslavia lasted all of a Mediterranean summer. It was heavily smoked and we kept it in a net inside grease-proof paper which was changed regularly. Similar hams are to be had in Spain, Italy and France.

Boil-in-the-bag and foil dinners Some are very good indeed, though

BOLULU
RAFET USTANIN
YEMEKLERI

BODRUM MARKET

ERİŞ TECİMEVİ

KONFORLU

BERBER

they are expensive and the portions are small. They have an inestimable value for no-fridge voyagers, as they have a long shelf life. They make good party food. Stowed so they do not chafe through they last almost indefinitely. Chicken and duck in these packs are infinitely better than tinned.

In Italy a boiling sausage known as Cotechino or Zampone is put up in the same way. It can be boiled in the bag, and is excellent hearty food sliced and eaten with lentils, mushy peas and mashed potatoes. Other sausages such as garlic and liver sausage to be eaten cold are appearing in the U.K. in long-life foil packs too; no need to refrigerate these either. All these sealed packs *can* be boiled in sea water.

Do not take just one kind of food, even on a short trip. I heard recently of a crew almost succumbing to despair; they had been furnished with boil-in-the-bag meals, but the alcohol cooker that should have heated them was ruined by salt water in a storm and a single Sterno burner was all that remained to cook for ten people. Freeze-dried food is useless without the fresh water to mix it with, and tins need an opener (carry two or three). As a last resort in storms you could take a few of the self-heating cans now available. They are expensive, but in dire need you might feel a hot meal was worth it.

Other ways of preserving

Vacuum-packed bacon and cold meats keep very well in a fridge or icebox, as does paté. Even if you have no fridge there is a great deal of choice. Paté will keep for a month, potted in jars under a layer of butter to seal it. You can keep a brine crock (I use Tupperware with a well fitting lid) and salt down pieces of pork, hocks, trotters, slabs of belly or tongues. If you leave them in the crock for three days they are mild enough to cook in the pressure cooker without previous soaking, and will then keep for two weeks or more in a cool dry spot, though my guess is that it will get eaten fairly rapidly. Not for nothing were the sailors of yore called 'salt horses': a little practice in the ancient art of salting and pickling may stand you in very good stead if you wish to cruise in the wilder parts of the globe, even in the Eastern Med and the north coast of Africa where the Muslim culture makes pork and *charcuterie* hard to find.

Bill and I became genuine Salt Horses earlier last year. I was looking for a tongue to salt before cruising eastwards, and in an Italian market allowed eagerness to overcome caution when I found one after a long search. I bore it back to the corner of the market where my 'donkey' was waiting with the heavy stuff. Beaming, I showed him my prize. He sighed, and pointed out the stall where I had bought it, where I could now plainly see the horse's head that adorned the sign. I had bought horse tongue. I pickled and cooked it just the same — it was excellent: we ate every bit with relish.

In the Dordogne they pot down goose and duck in the autumn; the meat is cooked gently in goose or duck fat, potted and covered completely with the fat in stoneware jars. It keeps for a year in a cool larder. My food bug authority worries about this, so if you want to experiment make sure you get an authentic recipe and follow the instructions carefully. The dish is known as *confit d'oie* (goose) or *confit de canard* (duck). I made some to take with us when we left England: we ate it and survived.

What to put in the freezer

If you are fortunate enough to have a freezer, and still more fortunate to have one that works, pack it with the solidest meat available. It is a waste of space and energy to fill it with bone, gristle and other bulky inedibles. Choose cuts with a minimum of bone or none, and reduce chickens to legs (or thighs and drumsticks) and boned breasts. Put them into packs of the number of portions needed for a meal. Do the same with chunks of stewing beef or lamb: you will be very glad at sea that you took the trouble to remove all the fat and gristle and pack it in convenient meal-sized portions. Shrimps are good packed in small amounts to add to fish soup, paella or risotto; even a hundred grams is handy sometimes. Chunks of cod or haddock make a change if the fishing is not going well. Keep a careful record of what is in the freezer, where it is approximately (baskets help), and cross it off the list as consumed.

I would grudge freezer space for prepared dishes, vegetables and junk food, but you might not agree. Morale is a funny thing — if you feel that frozen doughnuts might at some point do the trick, don't let me dissuade you!

Perishable foods

Salt butter keeps better than fresh sweet butter but it is harder to get in the Med and more expensive as it is usually imported. Margarine keeps longer than butter. Both are available tinned. Cooking oil keeps extremely well; merely choose one which suits your pocket and your taste.

Long Life milk (UHT) and cream keeps for five months, and we think it is nearer to fresh milk than either powdered or condensed; it is a matter of opinion. (We were amused to find that it arrived in the States while we were there: hailed, of course, as 'new'!) Long Life cream tastes better on tinned fruit than tinned cream, and is fine for cooking. Nothing beats fresh milk for cornflakes or just drinking, but I have yet to meet a cruising boat with a cow on board. Or even, come to that, a hen. Which brings us to:

Eggs

Fresh eggs need no refrigeration: indeed Common Market regulations make the chilling of eggs illegal. Buy your eggs from a hen personally known to you, along with her assurance that they are new laid, i.e. this morning's or at a pinch yesterday's. *Do Not wash them.* It is not an old wive's tale that eggs should not be washed: it is illegal in the Common Market for eggs to be washed before packing. The reasons are: a new-laid egg is protected by a film thoughtfully provided by the hen for the purpose; this film is removed by washing. Also, a dry egg is impermeable to bacteria but this impermeability breaks down if the shell becomes moist, and while the egg is wet germs can pass through the shell and set up premature spoilage. (In the US eggs are washed and dried at the packing stations under strictly monitored conditions.) In Europe, if you are fussy, you may gently brush off loose dirt and feathers, but leave any washing until just before you cook the egg.

It will now be clear to you why an egg that has been chilled should be avoided: on removal from the fridge condensation occurs, the shell becomes moist and bacteria can enter: shortening the life of the egg.

Keep your eggs carefully packed (we found fibre trays cut to fit square buckets which we kept in the bilge were perfect) at a temperature of about 10°C/50°F; a cool dry bilge for example, and they will keep for a month with no further attention. On the average Transatlantic crossing in either direction you should have no trouble.

How to deal with a bad egg As this is now a rare event in Europe and the USA, I revive some forgotten tips. After four weeks, start to test your eggs in a glass of fresh water. If they sink they are fine. If they float with a bit of the shell above the water, have ready a clean yoghurt pot or other disposable container: avert the nose and break the egg into the pot. If it is bad, you will know at once. *Do not* pour it down the sink: unless you have a salt water pump at the sink you will waste too much water flushing away the smell. Just deep-six it over the side, pot and all. If you are doubtful, you did use a clean pot so it will be OK for well-flavoured omelettes or ginger cakes. If your egg is undecided whether to sink or float it is probably not young enough to be a breakfast soft-boiled egg, and the whites may refuse to whip, but it will still be usable for most purposes. A flattened-out runny yolk or white means the egg is old, but not necessarily bad.

No, you cannot test them in salt water because they would all float.

A new-laid egg (up to three days old) is very hard to peel when hard-boiled, and takes longest to cook, but you won't have that problem for long. If your journey is going to last longer than a month or five weeks, some of your eggs will need to be preserved. This is done by sealing the shell, either with waterglass (a solution of sodium silicate obtainable these days only from very old-fashioned chemists) or petroleum jelly (Vaseline.) Make sure you get the odourless kind: eggs absorb smells and tastes very easily. In waterglass, eggs keep for a year. After six to nine months you cannot count on unbroken yolks, but otherwise they are great.

The Care and Treatment of Sick Vegetables

There is no reason why you cannot eat fresh vegetables from the Canaries to Barbados, or the West Indies back to Europe. Oddly enough, this will be more difficult coming east from the Americas or going across the Pacific, for it has little to do with the length of the journey.

It has *everything* to do with whether your fruit and vegetables have been wounded in the chill-room of the supermarket, or killed in the gas chambers of the commercial fruit merchants. If they have, then for keeping purposes they are not worth a damn. You have only to compare the potato clamp at the frosty field's edge, the onions drying from hooks in the barn, the apples laid neatly on the attic floor to keep all winter (and what a memorable smell that was for the children!), the pumpkins stacked on the outhouse roof in bright orange rows, and the pomegranates and persimmons left on the tree to burn like lanterns in the autumn night, as used to be common and still is where life is simple, and then think of the expected life of the produce you bought this morning at the Supermarket. If you don't put that cucumber in the fridge at once it will dissolve into a pint of greenish water by morning. The lettuce has suffered already in the car. The cabbage and oranges may last till the weekend. Not much else will.

Chilling kills fruit and vegetables They die of hypothermia. Buy them straight off the tree, out of the ground or off the vine, from the farm or market (but *never* from the Supermarket of the western world). Choose them with the care you would give to selecting your next child from the orphanage, carry them gently without bruising them, and cradle them like babies in a cool and airy spot. If you wash them at all (to rid them of slugs or beetle eggs) dry them with great care and thoroughness to prevent mould. Unlike babies, you go through the whole lot daily and throw any doubtful ones overboard. We kept our main stock of fruit and vegetables in the dinghy under a canvas cover raised over the oars to give a through-draught; it was easy to check them over.

Fruit and vegetables

East-to-west Atlantic crossings, November to March: you will be buying your stores in a Mediterranean climate, in the markets of Spain or Portugal, the Canaries or Madeira. Quality and variety are excellent and prices are low.

Will last six months: pumpkin (if you do not pierce the skin). Potatoes, onions, lemons wrapped in foil; and carrots, Jerusalem artichokes and parsnips buried in earth or sand.

Will last a month or more: citrus fruits, tomatoes if you choose them hard and all shades of green and wrap them separately in paper towels or newspaper (but not foil because the acid in tomatoes eats through it), and put in a cool dark place. Check daily, eat the reddest and throw out any squashy ones.

Will last about three weeks: cucumber, marrow (do not pierce it), avocado pears, apples.

Two weeks: cabbage, carrots (kept loose), green peppers, melons.

Ten days: aubergine, globe artichokes, pineapple, courgettes. The latter benefit from wrapping as for tomatoes, and careful watching. If the flower has not dried off the end they are particularly subject to mould.

One week: lettuces (check for slugs, etc): be sure they are dry and wrap firmly in Clingfilm. The big Romaine lettuces and the Iceberg keep especially well. Soft fruit, figs, grapes, cauliflower, green runner beans and celery.

Eat first and fast: spinach, cabbage greens or spring greens, watercress, Dutch lettuce.

If you like chilled salad, and you have a fridge or icebox it is of course permissible to chill all these things just before serving. After all, you have to kill a chicken before eating it.

West-to-east crossing, in May to August: you will be buying your produce in the West Indies, North America or Bermuda. For the US or Bermuda the notes on European shopping apply, with some alterations for the change in season. You will have to 'think seasonal' to avoid chilled produce. Remember: get it out of the ground or off the tree (or from under the hen).

Bermuda is a special case; you will find it harder to follow the rule that a chilled vegetable is a dead vegetable, because a large proportion of green stuff and fruit is chilled and imported from the US for immediate consumption. At great expense, I might add. Never mind, it's only 18 days to the Azores. Actually, there are a few market gardens in Bermuda, but they require some hunting down.

The West Indies have some unfamiliar edibles worth describing. The large variety of roots (yams, eddoes, tannia, dasheen) keep well for months in a dry place. Yams and sweet potatoes are big enough to have doubtful pieces excised: use the mutilated ones first. Sweet cassava can be kept buried the same way as carrots and artichokes. (It is the Bitter Cassava from which the poisonous juice must be extracted; it is mostly used for laundry starch.) Pawpaw should be bought green, when it can be used as a vegetable until it turns golden, then it is eaten as a fruit after a week to ten days. Coconuts have a long life: while they come to no harm from a bump or two, it is worth stowing them securely or they crash around the boat like cannonballs.

Mangoes keep about a week. The huge bananas known as plantains are only for cooking; as they are very starchy you can treat them like potato. Breadfruit has the same function and keeps well. It grows on one of the most beautiful trees in the Caribbean.

Christophene, in appearance like a pale green knobbly pear but a better keeper, cooks like a crisp marrow. Aubergine is often called melongene or eggplant.

The bunch of bananas that is the badge of all long-distance cruisers in the West Indies, hanging somewhere in the rigging, is something else. Even if you put a few 'hands' in the dark and cool to slow the ripening, you will still have to eat them fast when their time comes. You will need recipes for banana bread, banana curry, banana milkshake, banana cake, banana pudding, fried bananas and rum-buttered bananas, just for a start. They will cost you about a penny each, if you shop right.

Other items

The best way to remember every item you will need is to imagine your way through a day, from the moment you rise till the time you go to bed, and write down every thing you eat or use. Thus you will not forget the toilet roll, can-openers, washing-up brush, tartar sauce or salt. Then do it again going through events that crop up only weekly or monthly. (Yes, ladies, don't forget those; or your Pills either.) As Captain John Smith reminds us, at sea '... there is neither Ale house, Taverne, nor Inne to burne a faggot in, neither Grocer, Poulterie, Apothecary nor Butcher's shop.'

Deep-Sea Cooking

SONG OF A SEA COOK
I think what pleasant thoughts I can
  While bending o'er the frying pan
But truth to tell, I'm ill at ease:
  It's hard to cook in seas like these.
      But break the eggs and stir the pot
      And try to be what you are not:
      A cook with stomach not upset
      Who hasn't lost her breakfast yet.

Why do they always ask for more
  When half the stew is on the floor?
How can they eat so heartily
  When I can't even drink my tea?
      But peel the spuds and cook some duff
      (Three pounds of flour should be enough)
      They'll eat like the proverbial horse
      Even if served with Diesel sauce.

Cooking in bad weather

'... give every messe a quarter can of beere and a basket of
bread to stay their stomacks til the kettle be boyled ...'

If you are the sort of cook that most of us are, fine on deck but subject
to sickness down below unless horizontal, you have to develop a
method if you are not to starve yourself while feeding the crew.

One method is to bring all the ingredients up on deck, in one or
more washing-up bowls, and do the preparation up in the fresh air.
This is suitable for put-together meals like salad and sandwiches.
Enlist help and it will be done fast.

A variation of this is the do-it-yourself buffet. Again washing-up
bowls are used, to avoid everything landing on the floor of the cockpit.
You cannot, of course, lay things out nicely on a plate, so recourse is
made to smaller bowls and boxes with lids. Larger ones can contain
potato or tomato salad, smaller ones sliced meat and salami, or tuna
transferred from the tin. This is where I would use paper plates on the
wicker plate-holders available in the States, which save washing up.

At some point in the day, however, you will have to serve something hot, since that is what is really popular in bad weather: a
steaming pot of something rib-sticking such as soup, stew or risotto.

For this I have a second method based on one-minute dashes to the
galley, interspersed with fresh air up on deck until it is time for the
next dash. (An extractor fan in the galley also helps.) There is no need
for gourmet cooking under these conditions. Your crew will be more
than grateful for that simple dish known to all sailors under various
names such as lobscouse, slumgullion, potmess: in fact, Sea Stew.

FORCE 8 STEW Choose a moment when you are feeling particularly
strong, and make your first dash. Bad-weather stores should be handy
in the galley, so if you also have a wall tin-opener it will take you no
time at all to put in a large deep pan: one tin of meat, one tin of
vegetables, one tin of soup and one tin of drained potatoes. (It does
not seem to matter what kind these are, the result is invariably
excellent, though some mixtures you may discover to be more favourite than others.) Light the stove and put the pan on, with lid. A
pressure cooker is deep and works well—even without the lid. This
mixture is very thick, and at intervals further dashes will be required
to prevent it burning and to turn the whole mass over with a wooden
spoon. When the entire contents are gently bubbling, serve in large
mugs to three people.

This is the most delicious food you ever had if you are cold, wet and
hungry. Starch seems to be needed for queasy stomachs to work on, so
risottos and spaghettis are also good, but they are more time-consuming
to cook. Force 6 Stew, by the way, is made with fresh vegetables and
potatoes instead of tinned ones, as the cook should be feeling stronger.
Veg cleaning and preparation can be done on deck, using helpers, but
watch your knives don't get chucked overboard with the peelings.

Anyone who is too sick to eat Sea Stew should be encouraged to eat at least some wholemeal crackers, and if you boil a kettle for a hot drink try them with bouillon or Bovril, whch may go down better than tea or coffee. It is good to give the stomach something to work on: we find porridge and brown sugar very heartening too.

During Hurricane Alberto we had hot food the first day (eggs for breakfast with oatcakes and coffee, soup for lunch with fruit cake, and sea stew for supper); then water got into the batteries and for the only time in ten years the stove would not light and we had cold food that day. The following day Bill got some of the batteries going again, and as the huge seas were beginning to subside we celebrated with an enormous lunch of T-bone steaks and raspberries and cream. Gosh, it was good.

Once the alarms of the first day of the hurricane were over we drank a lot of coffee, some of it laced with brandy.

On the 'cold' day we had rum punch, which boosted morale without confusing the brain too much, and ate apples and chocolate and fruit cake, with the occasional ham sandwich.

It is noticeable that people who normally spurn puddings and cakes and sugary drinks, such as all three of us, turned in a time of worry and crisis to sweeter food and drinks. We were also immensely hungry, perhaps partly because it was hard to sleep through the noise and violent motion.

This brings us to:

Other useful ways to cope with bad weather when cooking:

Use a damp sponge cloth or dish towel on the table or worktop to anchor plates and mugs.

Pour drinks out fore and aft, not athwartships: who holds, also pours.

Don't fill saucepans or mugs too full.

Hand things up to the cockpit, either singly or in a wicker breadbasket for each person. This will take a mug of stew, bread, implements, and an apple or tomato.

Mugs are better than bowls, which are better than plates.

There should be somewhere the helmsman can put a drink safely, without it ending up on the deck.

The high-friction Dycem plastic, which we call 'Sticky blue', can be cut to fit any surface. It has been so successful that we have been able to dispense with fiddles except on the cooking stove. (Address in Appendix.)

Used and empty utensils should be put straight into the sink ready to wash up, so they do not roll underfoot.

Night watch food

Night watches consume a lot of energy and except in pilotage waters they can also be very boring. The night watch will lose all sense of morality and burrow like alley cats in a dustbin through the cook's precious stores. If you do not want your menus totally disarranged, and large desserts intended for tomorrow to disappear without trace, you must provide a tempting and adequate night box. A large Tupperware bread bin might just be big enough.

It should contain both sweet and savoury items, such as dried fruit and nuts, cheese (wrapped portions are handiest), wholemeal crackers, chocolate and boiled sweets, granola bars (a sort of solid muesli), fruit cake and biscuits. If you are on a long passage where fresh fruit is limited, make it crystal clear whether fruit is allowed as an extra or counts as part of the daily ration, since it is impossible to satisfy a three-apple-a-watch man with the stores carried on a small boat. Some yachts fill Thermoses with soup and coffee for the night watch, others (if the autopilot is working well) find that the watchman gets a welcome break by making his own hot drink.

Food for morale

'And after a storme, when poor men are all wet, few
of those but wil tell you a little Sacke or Aqua Vitae is much
better to keepe them in health than a little small beere or cold
water, although it be sweet.'

When morale is low, break out some treat or delicacy: a tin of Dundee cake or shortbread, tins of Boeuf Bourguignon or smoked salmon pate. If the weather is fine and spirits need to be raised, pancakes, drop scones or new rolls with honey do wonders.

Find an excuse for a party: celebrate (or commiserate) something — the best day's run or the worst, 500 miles, 1000 miles, the day we saw the whale — and get everyone to help with a splendid dinner. Give a prize for the most inventive costume or headgear, or the best limerick.

I always keep a bag of small presents on board. Whenever I see anything small and attractive ashore, I add it to the bag. Thus one can always cope with an unexpected birthday or find a suitable prize. You can also run a sweepstake on the noon-to-noon run.

Water

Skip will not let me wash my hair
Nor yet my grubby underwear;
'The water's getting low,' he shrieks,
'We've just enough for ten more weeks.'

Water, the lack of it, and where to get it, occupies the mind of cruising people a great deal. The habit of being mean with it *must* become second nature.

If you run to the luxury of hot water, you cannot allow the tap to run hot without saving the cold water that comes out first. On our boat this is done by having a jug of the right capacity kept in the *head*:

when the jug is full, the water will be hot and the jug of cold can (and must) be used elsewhere, in the kettle for instance.

'. . . a little pumpe made of a Cane, a little peece of hollow wood . . . to pumpe the Beere or water out of the Caske, for at sea wee use no taps'

Small toddlers love pumping water and turning on taps. Make sure that the water is not frittered away without your knowledge; a press-and-release tap would help, being harder for a toddler or guest to use than a Whale pump or a foot-button.

Have plenty of buckets. One cannot have too many, as one always seems to lose one (plus a doormat) in every storm. Then when it tips it down in the West Indies or the Pacific, you can fill your buckets and have a water frolic. Some people can plug their cockpit drains and turn it into a huge bath.

If you are really short of water it is possible, indeed desirable, to use fresh water twice. First, where hygiene is essential, such as washing oneself or the dishes. Having done that, the resulting water, according to its state, may then be used for the galley floor, or engineroom overalls. Hair needs a lot of rinsing, but the water used is usually still clean enough to wash clothes in. Judgement has to be used here. To shore people who have water to wash cars with, this must seem rather revolting. (We did say that the life is not all paté and champagne.) I can assure you that Bill, coming up from the engineroom with filthy hands, is quite glad of leftover washing-up water to get the worst off. All galleys should have a salt water tap, if only for fire-fighting!

A very refreshing gambit that takes a minimum amount of fresh water goes like this: heat a cupful of water to boiling and put it in the bottom of a warmed jug. Hold your face over the jug, under a towel as if you were inhaling balsam. Your face will be nicely steamed. Wipe off the grime and salt with a tissue and hand the jug to the next person in the queue, reheating the water as necessary.

Water that has been used to boil potatoes or pasta can be used for soups or freeze-dried food, but go easy on the salt. Water drained from tinned vegetables can be used for the same purposes or to boil potatoes.

To illustrate an important point: once in Yugoslavia we went on a Club Mediterranee sailing barbecue, which was going to be done in style with rice and spaghetti cooked on the spot. Everyone helped. Well, nearly everyone. Some of the men went off to taste the wine at the local tavern three kilometers away, and returned disgusted. 'One has drunk a wine of the most execrable,' said a tired Frenchman, 'and one has spat all the way home.' He began to wash his mouth out with wine from the huge jars we had brought with us. 'Where is the water to cook the rice?' I asked, looking towards the jars. 'That's all wine,' said the organizer, 'we will use sea water.' 'Have you done this before?' I enquired with some doubt. He brushed my worries aside with superb confidence: what do the English know about cooking? So we duly cooked rice and pasta for forty people in sea water. Both were totally inedible, and I have since found that the same thing happens with potatoes. You cannot cook vegetables in pure sea water.

I have done some tests, and find that 5% of sea water is enough to make it quite salty enough. That is 1 part in 20, or 1 fl oz of sea water to 1 Imp pint of fresh. You would have to be pretty desperate for that to make any difference.

Washing at sea

Washing machines are not often carried by the long-distance cruiser. There is a small plastic washing machine that I have seen on live-aboard yachts, which seems to please its owners being light but solidly made. As they don't heat the water they don't use much power; but they *do* use a lot of water, which is probably why I have seen them in use only in marinas or close to a dockside tap.

When water is pretty short, as it always is on long-distance cruises, the time comes when the Skipper's shorts are sufficiently redolent to be capable of independent movement and will come when you whistle; with the embarassing affection of an elderly and appallingly smelly dog. Now is the time to consider washing in salt water. Any strong liquid detergent will wash satisfactorily. If it is choppy, put the clothes in a tub and let them slop around with the motion of the boat doing much of the work for you. You can get some of the salt out by a last rinse in fresh water; otherwise your clothes will be stiff, the salt will attract moisture so that they never fully dry, and you could end up with a painful skin rash caused by chafe, particularly with jeans — or worse, 'gunnel bum' (salt water sores).

In places where it rains, such as an east-to-west Atlantic crossing, it pays to see a shower coming and get out the clothes and buckets to benefit by it. To get oneself and the clothes one is wearing thoroughly soaked in fresh water can be very refreshing, and is usually an occasion for much hilarity and splashing about. The west-to-east crossing is considerably colder and normally contra-indicates such skylarks, but it would depend on the degree of desperation.

Acquire an old-fashioned washboard and that useful article known as a dolly or posher. Washboards are still found anywhere there are no washing machines, such as the Greek Islands and the West Indies. The dolly is rarer, but it is not hard to make one of the milking stool variety illustrated. If you were used, on shore, to a washing machine and a tumble-dryer, you will be surprised and pleased at how much longer your clothes last when you wash by hand, provided of course you don't lose them overboard when you've pegged them out to dry.

Before I learnt the art of clothes-pegging I lost overboard two good towels, a pillowcase and a woollen jersey. All sank to the bottom with extraordinary rapidity before we could seize the net. Spring-clip pegs are not strong enough.

Washday ancient and modern. Greek washboard, a copper and a wooden 'milking stool' dolly, all-plastic clothes peg.

A ¾in. in circumference (6mm) rope makes a good washing line. Lead it across the wind if possible. Pegs that have no metal parts to rust are best: the old-fashioned Gypsy peg or all-plastic ones. Turn the clothes inside out (the strong sun will fade them quickly otherwise) and peg them firmly in such a way that they parachute across the wind. Lead the line through arms, legs or felt loops if you can. They will dry in no time. Bring them in while still a little damp, fold carefully and stack in a warm place. As they finish drying, they will 'iron' themselves with no further attention.

Some practical hints for Boatwives and ships' husbands

The WC and Shower Compartment   Seawater used for flushing the loo causes scale to form. Putting some vinegar in the bowl from time to time, especially if you are leaving the boat for a few days, helps to minimize this.

The second most important habit to acquire (the first being not to waste water) is to put nothing down the loo that could lead to a blockage. It helps everyone to remember this if there is a seperate lidded bin for hairballs, cigarette ends, matchsticks, dental floss and even more unmentionable items. If your taste is for waggish notices on brass plates, now is your chance to let rip. Otherwise a simple green cross painted on the lid will indicate its use to most people. It will not stop children from poking about in there to see what it contains, but that all comes under the heading of a broad education. My children learnt a lot that way.

The Accommodation is what the Yacht Brokers call your living space. We find we need safe places for spectacles these days. Pockets for them — and indeed for anything that needs to be readily to hand, such as seasick pills, sunscreen cream, finger plasters, bottle openers and so on — can be made from felt, leather, fabric or any suitable material, and screwed or stuck to the linings or cockpit in strategic places. Double-sided sticky pads can be used to fix not only these but digital clocks, perpetual calendars, navigating gimmicks, and even pictures and photographs if they are not too heavy. Fewer screwholes keep up the Resale Value!

You might doubt that magnetic racks would be of any use. We have one for kitchen knives and one for small tools. Only the big carving knife and the heavy ratchet screwdriver get jerked loose by a choppy sea: they are fine for smaller items. Don't site magnetic racks near a compass, it goes without saying.

Stow seaboots upside-down on dowels of suitable length. This not only helps them to dry but prevents them from filling up with rubbish and dead wasps.

Keep plastic foam offcuts to stifle any clinks and bumps that can disturb your sleep in choppy seas: cassettes, bottles and glasses are the worst offenders.

A cylinder type vacuum cleaner has many uses apart from the obvious one. Ours helped us to build the boat. It was second-hand even then and has swallowed everything from wood shavings through nails and screws to lumps of rubbery caulking compound, drilling swarf, rust chippings and grinding dust. Put together backwards it can be used as a heavy duty blow-dryer for newly painted areas, or even damp bilges if you should be so unlucky. We are thinking of coarse bilge painting, naturally. (We would not blow dust and flies on the sort of paint and varnish where dogs must not sneeze and cats must not tread.)

Few cottons and canvases can stand up to seawater and hot sun, but lining your curtains with heavy cotton prolongs their lives. Cockpit and deck cushions are usually vinyl covered, which lasts well but sticks to hot bare skin. Most people make loose cotton covers for them and accept that they will need replacing frequently. It's worth it not to find your thighs securely stuck to the cushions in hot weather.

CHAPTER TEN

Cruising Grounds

'One to the top to look out for lande.'

In discussing the type of yacht and her gear there has inevitably been some emphasis on voyaging and bad conditions. Your typical boat dweller is not out to score miles or win trophies, or even to get unnecessarily wet and tired; it is simply sensible to consider the worst, so that in the vast majority of cases the cruiser is well within tolerable limits of safety and comfort. In looking at cruising grounds the emphasis must be on the pleasant side of life afloat, although everywhere has its share of bad points which I will have to mention. Once again, there is a lot of subjectivity.

Ocean crossing for the likes of us is not a case of long-lasting heroics. I am confining this to consideration of the more congenial places which can be reached without taking dubious risks, or by extreme physical effort. Thus our ocean crossings are confined to the nicer parts of the Atlantic, and I will discuss routeing later on in Chapter Fifteen.

Most people contemplating this life have a palm tree in the vision somewhere, so I will start with the West Indies. For our purpose, these start at Trinidad, close to the South American shore, and include the Windward Islands, the Leewards, Dominican Republic, Haiti, Puerto Rico, Cuba, Jamaica and a few smaller units. Most have a mixed colonial history, and the main population is of African descent from slaves, or in some cases of Spanish origin. There are many ethnic Indians in Trinidad. Some islands are very poor with unstable or uncertain economies, others have become more prosperous by exploiting tourism. It is a sad reflection that the islands in worst shape are almost entirely those that were British possessions: the realization hits one with shaming force.

To nautical tourists such as ourselves, there is an inevitable pull towards the Windward Islands (the Grenadines, St Vincent, St Lucia, and Martinique) afterwards to the more diffuse Leewards; Dominica round to the Virgins. At this time, the parts farther west, Puerto Rico to Cuba, are less attractive, mostly for political reasons, while the Central American isthmus is a part of the world one might well avoid.

It may be a long time before things improve there. There are also the islands off the coast of South America from Trinidad to Curaçao, the smaller of which are becoming more popular; though being downwind of the main group they are not so readily convenient to cruise.

The major fly in the ointment for the private cruising yacht in this whole area is the large fleet of bare-boat charter yachts. Some are essentially private craft let out on the occasional charter and these are no problem: the difficulties arise from what I will call industrial chartering. The boats are almost always badly equipped, badly maintained and often badly sailed. The usual customers are Americans. Now, the USA probably has more private cruising yachts than the rest of the world put together, and probably more competent yachtsmen to sail them. In the same proportions she has also more boorish idiots, and it seems that most of them holiday in a bare-boat in the Caribbean. Search and rescue facilities in this area are scant (there are exceptions, notably Barbados), and these charterers, used at home to nannying by the very efficient Coast Guard, put out a scandalous number of distress calls, many for trivial reasons and others for want of elementary prudence. British registered vessels are bound by law to answer distress calls. Sadly, the professional, crewed charter yachts, many of which are British flag even if only of a debased kind, have been driven to ignoring these calls.

In addition, the bare-boat fleets have established bases which reserve for their exclusive use facilities which were once available to all. People on a three-week holiday from a very prosperous country can outbid longer term visitors for the scarce resources, and exert pressure for shallow sophistication and high prices, the main benefits of which go to external investors and do not reach the local people.

But the pleasures of the area outweigh the minor irritations. There are wonderful anchorages and beaches, and the sailing between is excellent. We found, almost without exception, the local people friendly, extrovert and cheerful, the officials good humoured and courteous. Generally the poorer the community the nicer the people and officials, and it was in the more prosperous Virgin Islands that we found the only examples of rudeness, and even those were not too bad.

Formalities are generally not irksome. Almost every island is a separate sovereign state, so that a lot of clearing and entering has to be done and a lot of expensive courtesy ensigns carried. Most islands make a moderate entry charge, and some yachtsmen resent this because harbours tend to be open anchorages with few port facilities; but considering that the islands are poor, such a charge is hard to find unreasonable.

The cost of living in the islands is based on the US dollar (apart from the French islands, which are heavily subsidized by France). Much of the foodstuff is imported from the USA, often by air, so that these items are expensive except the ubiquitous frozen chicken. Apart from the wealthier, more developed islands, up-market foods are hard to find. Yacht chandlery is virtually non-existent except in Antigua and St Thomas and there it is expensive. Repairs can be undertaken at Antigua and Grenada, where there are boatyards with reasonable craftsmen, slipways, and berths with electricity for a self-refit.

Mail from Britain or the US to the islands is generally quite good, the telephone service not. Public telex is often under the dead hand of the Cable & Wireless Co. who put unique and incomprehensible restrictions on its use. Air communications are very good and air freight is recommended for parcels. European flights go regularly to Antigua, Barbados, Trinidad and the French islands; and the smaller inter-island services are very busy and really quite efficient, if sometimes a little hair-raising. Landing on Union Island or St Bart's is not for the faint-hearted.

Diesel fuel is only conveniently obtained at a few places, but as the wind is so reliable, pleasant and free, diesel does not loom large in most people's minds. The most convenient points that I found were at Grenada (St George's), Martinique, English Harbour and St Thomas. If a really large amount of fuel is needed, a trip to Venezuela might be worthwhile.

The weather is very pleasant during the European winter. The temperatures are moderated by the tradewind, which is usually about force 4 but does rise occasionally especially in certain channels. The most I recorded in one winter was force 6 off Kick 'em Jenny, near Grenada, where the seas were also unusually disturbed. It rains every few days, usually a sharp shower which should be used for topping-up tanks for fresh water is not easy to get in quantity. During this season hurricanes hardly hever happen.

In summmer the weather is not so pleasant, but to compensate there are fewer tourists. The weather is hotter, wetter, a bit more capricious, and hurricanes do happen though they are not by any means an everyday event. The old rhyme tells you when they start: 'June too soon, July by and by, August you must, September remember, October it's over.' Do not rely too much on this doggerel: we were damaged in Hurricane Alberto on June 18, 1982 though that was farther north, off Bermuda. If you are in the Caribbean there is a wealth of local knowledge, hurricane holes in which to get secure and precautions to take. These matters are out of the scope of this book; my hurricane experiences (two) have both been well offshore and it is quite another thing close to land.

Charts and navigational publications are hard to get. A chandler's shop in English Harbour had a few in 1982, but all were out of date and over-priced. The only reliable source of charts throughout the Caribbean as a whole is at St John's, Antigua (Marine and General Services, St Mary's St), but even here do not expect a stock of charts of distant waters.

For electronic or technical repairs, I found English Harbour the only worthwhile centre. There is also a specialist spare part finder who proved very efficient. All these people could be contacted on VHF. In fact, in the West Indies, almost everyone can be contacted on VHF — Sam Taxi, the Scuba Shop, the Red Snapper Restaurant, and Teeny Weeny Sweeny (the hairdresser). Some restaurants make a general call on Channel 16 to inform all stations that their menu for tonight, and reservations, are on channel 68. The radio is seldom silent, but on the whole the system functions very well: it is because everyone uses the radio that one finds it useful in a way not possible in over-regulated Europe or the USA. The radio discipline is better than on Long Island Sound on a weekend.

As one goes farther west the cruising gets less congenial. Big money dominates the Virgin Islands scene, and prices rise, marinas are found and sophistication starts to shriek. By St Thomas one is in an American city and the supermarkets are well stocked, but the people lack the manners of the poorer islands. The welcome is often still good, but there is something missing.

The US Navy make a nuisance of themselves (quite unnecessarily) exercising north of Puerto Rico, while the coast of Cuba has to be suspected of being unfriendly, and many insurers specifically except it. I have not been to Jamaica recently, but have conflicting reports as to whether it is currently advisable.

One reads a lot of alarmist articles in magazines about piracy, violence and robbery, and I will discuss our views on this later, in Chapter Eleven.

If one required to leave a boat, say for an emergency visit home, the marina in St George's, Grenada has good security; alternatively there are facilities in English Harbour. Up-market marinas, at up-market prices, exist in Antigua, Tortola and St Thomas.

The Bahamas

Moving northwestwards from the Caribbean Islands, one comes to the Bahamas, another independent ex-British colony. It was peopled largely by loyalists from the revolting American colonies about 1778 and these white people with their black slaves were the forebears of many of the present inhabitants. In the north, the Abacos, much of the populace are so firmly Nonconformist that you might imagine you were in Scotland. You might, but it would be difficult, for the weather and scenery are very different. The Bahamas are flat, palm-clad, sandy islands set on a series of broad shallow banks penetrated by the odd deep-water tongue of ocean. The local industries are tourism and drug dealing, but the latter is a closed shop and the participation of amateurs from outside is much resented and dangerous.

The southern islands are more remote and less densely populated, with scope for some very quiet cruising though provisions have to be looked for. The northern islands are close to Florida and have large numbers of shorter term visitors. There is a bay called No Name Bay south of Miami which I selected as a good dawn jumping-off place for a day sail to the Bahamas: so did half a hundred others. The Florida Channel between that state and the Bahamas is one of the busiest waterways in the world, with some very long multi-barge tows using it, and it merits some care when crossing, especially at night.

The Bahamas are islands where souvenirs are few and an artist/ craftsman could earn a bit, but the cost of living, being so dependent on nearby Florida, is high. The country ought to be prosperous. The currency is at par with the US dollar, but there are local notes in circulation, as well as American ones. The officials are pleasant, courteous, but not noticeably industrious or efficient. Communications are good with Florida, and then from Miami are excellent. Mail and telephone services seemed to be good. The banking system, where it is of British or Canadian origin, is above average.

The other sort of banks, the coral ones, require care. Paradoxically, the old British charts are the best. One of these, no. 1496, was engraved in 1844 with the last new edition in 1907 and its detail is first class. I occupied myself for some time with checking several of the areas of the banks, and though there were some differences I would say that if used with a little prudence and common sense this chart is infinitely preferably to the US chart of recent publication. But any chart cannot cope unaided. The latest supplement to the British Pilots should be carried, but even better are some of the recently published yachtsmen's guides. The Chart Kits published in Needham, Massachusetts by the Better Boating Association are a good investment and based on US government charts.

There are several places to leave a yacht in the Bahamas, but none of them are ideal and many are over-expensive. Unless one's departure is very urgent (in which case Marsh Harbour suggests itself), it would be better to head for Florida, a short trip away. There one finds every possible facility.

The East Coast of the USA

There are many people who spend their lives cruising the Intra-Coastal Waterway with its two ends, Chesapeake Bay and the Florida Keys. The Chesapeake is a bay of great size, which can get very rough on occasions but has many delightful places to visit: Washington, which has been largely rebuilt by the industrious natives since my ancestors burnt it; Annapolis, the home of the US Naval Academy; Jamestown, St Michael's, Oxford and Cambridge. The Florida Keys are a string of islands connected by a causeway, extending round into the Gulf of Mexico.

The Intra-Coastal does extend north of the Chesapeake, as far as New York (where one can moor in the middle of Manhattan for less than the price of a hotel room), but the depths are not sufficient for most sea-going sailing craft.

It is superfluous to say much about the USA. The natives are friendly: however terrifying they may be as tourists, on their home ground they are charming, hospitable hosts, generous and efficient, with a vast appetite for apparently tasteless food. But in fact the country changes. The west shore of the Chesapeake, close to Washington, is rich, sophisticated and comparatively crowded. Progressing southward through the backwoods (literally) of South Carolina or Georgia, one finds people of less material wealth, and many of those at the supermarket checkouts are paying in welfare food stamps.

The waterway country is very evocative of the Norfolk Broads on a vast scale, with trees, reeds, herons, bitterns, flat country, estuaries and rather a similar state of mind among the local people. It is sometimes a long way between settlements; there are remote, lovely quiet anchorages, oysters for the gathering, strong tides and many bridges which open very efficiently; the fixed ones have a minimum High Water clearance of 65 feet (except for one at Miami, which can be avoided by a short hop at sea).

There is only one lock; at Great Bridge in Virginia. The water is spread very wide, but it is shallow. A draught of 6¼ feet is about the maximum recommendable, and one must expect to touch bottom occasionally, especially near the southernmost inlets.

Provisioning is often difficult as in most US communities all the stores are now in out-of-town shopping malls. For this reason some isolated marinas have a (sometimes rather battered) 'courtesy car' which one may borrow free for local use.

The bigger centres are crowded and made hideous by speeding water-hogs in fast power boats; one cannot consider the southern part of Florida as attractive any more. But there are plenty of good marinas where one can leave a boat to do some touring, and good facilities everywhere for hauling out and refitting.

American marinas are very different from those we have become accustomed to in Europe. The mega-marina does exist, of course, and is very much better run than its European counterpart, but the typical US marina is a comparatively small family affair, often with only 30 to 50 berths, sometimes a little scruffy but almost always with a real, friendly welcome.

The climate is surprising. In winter southern Florida is pleasant, but from St Augustine northward expect some very cold spells. It can be bitterly cold in North Carolina. In summer, the whole area is very hot and humid and has the world's biggest and hungriest mosquitoes. Spring and autumn are delightful.

US officials vary. We found Customs officers everywhere to be courteous, helpful and on the ball. The Immigration people were appalling and aggressive. Visas are no longer necessary for British citizens.

US Customs will give the yacht a Cruising Permit on arrival, valid for six months, and though some states will renew this or extend it, others will not (South Carolina is one). Only yachts registered in countries with some mysterious reciprocal arrangement will be granted this permit, and it is difficult to get a definitive list. Britain is on it, so is France, but apparently Belgium is not. Yachts without a Cruising Permit have the chore of entering and clearing outwards in every state. With a permit, the obligation is to report by telephone every time one moors at an accessible place. In some states the Customs have a toll-free number for this purpose which is very considerate for the US public phones are bad.

In view of all the publicity for the Bell Company, that last statement calls for justification. The telephone service is geared entirely for the resident. Once you have a telephone and thus an account with Ma Bell (as the company is known), then the service is quite astonishingly good with facilities that are unknown in other countries. But as a stranger with no account, you do not exist. Pay (coin) phones are rare and very, very expensive. And in spite of the US being a signatory to International Maritime Communications Agreements, one is not per-mitted to make a ship-to-shore radio telephone call without a US phone number to charge it to. I have even heard of a transfer-charge call being refused from a foreign ship. The situation is a public scandal.

Do not fall into the trap of regarding US Customs or the Coast Guard as merely benevolent nannies. There is massive drug smug-gling through the creeks and inlets of the Intra-Coastal, and the Water-way is well patrolled. The Coast Guard, though apparently staffed entirely by teenagers, is very much on the alert. They run the rescue service, maintain navigation marks, and keep watch on Channel 16 and also on 22A, which foreign vessels do not have and about which the Coast Guard seem to be permanently confused. Note that several VHF channels have different user designations in the USA.

Buoyage is different, adhering to IALA System B.

The electricity supplied from shore in most marinas is another oddity. Voltage is 110V and is apparently unique in using alternating current of 60 cycles instead of 50.

The regulations against pollution are strict, and in the case of yacht heads and holding tanks are so draconian as to be unenforcable. There being no pump-out stations, ordinary marine heads may be used at sea. I understand the whole situation is under review, when some of the ecological over-enthusiasm may be tempered with real-ism. On the Great Lakes, and in the canals and lakes north of New York where there is little outlet of water to the sea, the situation is different and the laws are enforced with vigour. There, marine heads may not be discharged overboard.

A brief word about the north, though these waters are not really our province as the season is so short. Cruising the New England coast is really delightful, though it does require alertness and good navigation because of the strong tidal streams, especially farther north, and the frequency of fog. Navigation marks are good and facilities are excellent. In fact the whole of the US coast is good cruising, and the people badly need to meet a few foreigners.

The Mediterranean Sea

The Med is a wholly different cruising ground to those we have discussed, for history and scenic beauty rather than the quality of the sailing is the chief attraction. Generally navigation in small craft is not advisable in December to March, and should be indulged with caution in November and April. It is around the equinoxes that conditions become especially capricious, and quite like British weather. Depressions that come in from the Alantic are deflected at the last minute, and forecasts become unreliable. In high summer the weather is usually dry and stable. Winds over much of the Med are characteristically light and variable then though there are places where usable winds are good.

The Strait of Bonifacio, and the Sicilian Channel particularly close to Cape Bon, have predominatly west winds and east-going currents. In the Aegean, the summer (Etesian) wind, often called by its Turkish name Meltemi, can blow for three or four months from between northwest and northeast, sometimes reaching gale force, when ferry and even air services are interrupted. A particularly troublesome bit of sea, winter or summer, is the Gulf of Lions. It is not so much the wind strength that causes problems to the small-craft navigator in the Med; there is often a very short and steep sea going with it, and it is this which does the damage and causes acute discomfort.

Spain

The country welcomes yachtsmen. There is a rule limiting one's stay to six months in any twelve, but it is often not rigorously enforced for yachtsmen who are clearly behaving themselves and regrettably not all do so. The big centre for yachting is Palma, Mallorca, where there are expensive marinas and yacht clubs and where it is possible to haul out quite cheaply. The cost of living in Spain is no longer as low as it was, but berthing in the public ports is cheap; the variety and quality of food is generally good, and many services are first class.

The Balearic Islands become very crowded in summer, and though it is possible to find a little peace in Menorca, the most easterly of the islands, the numbers rise there each year.

There are innumerable good places to leave a yacht unattended, and some good places for wintering including Palma and Alicante, though in both the cheaper or better berths are dominated by deadbeat semi-derelicts that do not appear ever to leave moorings. Communications are good from Mallorca, even in winter, though the other islands are less well served. On the mainland they are generally good. The south coast attracts its wintering fraternity, including rich Arabs and pop stars on flying visits, though this is hardly a recommendation. We were surprised at the end of 1989 to find a steady stream of yachts quitting Spain, all saying that marina prices had risen to a ridiculous level.

France

The French Mediterrenean coast sometimes seems to be one long marina stretching from Spain to Italy. There are thousands of berths, so yachts are often not particularly welcome in the ordinary ports. Consequently cruising is poor, unless you like going from one marina to its twin along the coast. Wintering is on the expensive side but is convenient, though the winter weather west of Cannes can be cold; to the eastward the coast is sheltered by the Alpes Maritimes from the worst of the cold winds, and temperatures (and prices) are higher.

One should consider France as a country with everything one is likely to need. The food is excellent and the prices are not as high as, for example, Italy or England. Communications are very good, though public telephones are operated by special card, and are frequently vandalised. In 1988/9 the Post Office was being affected by industrial unrest.

French Customs officers have always been very helpful to me, correct and courteous. One may keep one's yacht there for six months in any twelve: longer stays involve payment of VAT (unless papers are handed in and the yacht not used), but longer stays are not part of the cruising life we are discussing, which pre-supposes a process of moving on.

Corsica has much the same organization as mainland France, but there have been reports of officious Customs officers in Ajaccio. There is unfortunately a certain amount of sporadic terrorist activity still going on (1990) but it does not seem to be directed at the casual visitor. Nonetheless, a Corsican courtesy ensign has become traditional and I would not buck the trend.

France, in common with most Mediterranean countries, is very strict about enforcing cabotage laws, which restrict chartering to own-flag vessels. Foreign-flag yachts may not charter or take passengers for reward, and the penalties are heavy. In this context cost-sharing, or even a contribution towards expenses, has been held to be evidence of a charter. So far as I know, only Britain and Holland believe in the freedom of the sea; all other countries, the USA included, have very restrictive laws, so BEWARE.

A major disdvantage of the French system of mooring in marinas is that the visitor never knows the condition of the submerged chain. Here is a mooring chain in a marina that charged £16 per day for its use. Beware!

Italy

For a country partly dependent on tourism, Italy does very little to encourage the yachting visitor. It taxes him for a start*, whereas the motorist is given subsidized petrol and motorway tolls. True, the tax is meant to replace harbour dues in public ports, which are otherwise free, but it has to be paid whether or not one is in a public port. And because Italy is par excellence a state of chaos, it is often very inconvenient, not to say virtually impossible, actually to pay the money over.

Nonetheless, Italy has many good points. Food is generally good and hardware is obtainable. Apart from the mail service, which is appalling, communications are not too bad, but parcels from abroad can take several weeks creeping through the Customs: air freight is best. Railway travel is particularly cheap.

Officialdom is generally polite and courteous, but they often work in rotten surroundings and the bureaucracy is intolerable. One has to acquire a document called a Costituto which is issued by the Capitano di Porto at your port of entry. It is like a yacht passport and is likely to be demanded at each port visited.

Disadvantages: one is that the country is almost unbelievably dirty and litter-strewn. We joke that it is impossible to run aground on the shores of Italy because one would be brought to a halt by floating plastic bags long before getting into shallow water. (Apart from Italy,

* In mid 1990 reports say this tax has been abolished.

we have found little obvious evidence of sea pollution anywhere else in the Med.) There are innumerable strikes, sometimes including Customs officers or lighthouse keepers. Radio beacons are unreliable. Thieving is common, but not in truly rural areas, with the exception of southern Sicily where it seems to be part of the religion. The main disadvantage of Italy in 1990 was expense; I think their currency is grossly over-valued vis-à-vis other European ones. For Italy read also Sardinia. In Sicily, especially on the south coast, one can be plagued by urchins, on whose honesty it is impossible to rely.

Marinas are to be found close to the French border and at intervals along the Riviera. Others are spotted down the west coast, and there is a further cluster in the north Adriatic catering largely for the Germans who, each summer weekend, pour over the Brenner Pass in their Mercedes like the hordes of Genghis Khan. On the whole, service in an Italian marina is not at all bad though often not cheap. Places to winter on board are numerous though none of them are particularly popular, those in the north Adriatic because of the severe winter climate, various others because of the security problems: if the place is insecure it is not worth the risk, and if it is secure it is like living in a beseiged fortress. An exception which is convenient to the Eastern Mediterranean is at Sibari in the Gulf of Taranto. This is a well run marina in an honest rural area, but it is so isolated that it would mainly be of interest to someone wishing to leave a boat unattended.

Yugoslavia

This is a communist country earning a great part of its foreign exchange from capitalist tourists. Tourism expanded rapidly after Tito, who was no fool, allowed limited private enterprise in the tourist industry. Tolerable restaurants appeared almost overnight, where before there had been only culinary disaster areas.

Officials vary. One I met who had been rescued by the Royal Navy at some time in the past kissed me on both cheeks and formalities were over in seconds, after which a bottle was produced to celebrate old times while some poor Germans were kept waiting. At Dubrovnik I found them unfriendly, formal, though nevertheless correct. I had cleared outwards for a passage to Italy and on my way back to the yacht had followed my customary practice of spending my last few dinars, when I was given the bum's rush and told that after I had cleared I should do no further business and was to leave forthwith. Our sternropes were cast off for us even before I could start the engine. The officer may have been technically correct, but it is a correctness I have never otherwise experienced and it does nothing to encourage one to return.

I think another reason why I like Yugoslavia less than some other countries is that I have virtually no Serbo-Croat, the most widely used of the several national languages. The people, if they speak a foreign language at all and it is not very common, generally speak German, which country provides most of their tourists, although in those parts that were once part of Italy the older folk speak some Italian. This inevitably puts me at a distance, and probably accounts for my view that the Yugoslav is the least friendly of all the Mediterranean folk.

Communications are poor, our mail experience was mixed, telephones proved impossible. Telex can be found, and sometimes it works.

The cost of living is cheap, but except in the major tourist centres this may be because there are very limited goods on sale. It is the only country I have ever visited where there were queues for bread and other staples. Markets for fruit and vegetables are good but sometimes very early in the morning. Spare parts or technical services are few and far between though I got a very good and prompt hydraulic repair at Mali Losinj.

Marinas exist in the north and near Dubrovnik, but I have no personal knowledge of them. My chief pleasure in cruising this coast lies in the lovely island anchorages, peaceful beyond measure.

There is now an 'entry tax' for cruising Yugoslavia, but it does not seem to be at all unbearable.

Tunisia

This is an Arab country, formerly a French colony, and is heavily dependent on tourism and exports to the Common Market. Its coasts are ideal for a short cruise, preferably in spring or autumn as it is extremely hot in high summer.

Officials are courteous and pleasant, but display that Arab tendency to ask for gifts, though compared with their close neighbours in Libya they are paragons of virtue. No harrassment or impediments are otherwise put in the way of the visiting yachtsman.

Communications are not bad. I found the telephones in the city of Tunis usable for foreign calls, and mail was prompt. Flights connect well, the cost of living is moderate though some items are hard to find, fuel oil is very cheap. The people on the whole are friendly.

Marinas exist although services are sketchy. I know of yachts who have wintered here happily, the climate making up for any practical problems or deficiencies in luxuries.

Greece

This is a very popular country for cruising and deservedly so, but it could do better if it tried. The islands are beautiful, and varied in their beauty; the scenery is outstanding, history abounds, the ordinary person is very hospitable, the weather in summer is good, the tavernas are cheap. Well, what more do you want — good wine? Well, sorry about the wine!

Tourism in the Greek islands started with yachting, and to facilitate it the Greeks were the first to introduce a document there called the Transit Log. It was a big hack through a rather Levantine bureaucracy, and it made life a lot easier. Recently, with the expansion of general tourism the Greek government has forgotten the debt it owes to the foreign yachtsman, and things are not quite as easy as they once were. But they are by no means bad. Regulations are somewhat difficult to interpret because one is told different things at different places, and by different officials. The regulations also seem to change much too often for comfort, and are seldom publicized in the yachting press. At the moment it seems that one can stay up to twelve months without any problems, but after that a tax of 15 US dollars per foot of overall length is levied, although it is pursued with differing degrees of determination from place to place. Authorities differ on the length of interval between successive terms of twelve months; no one, it seems, will put anything in writing in case they make a mistake.

On arrival, a Transit Log is obtained at a port of entry. It lists crew, also all removable dutiable articles on board, and gives some details of the yacht. Generally its issue entails payment, which is another new development. (Note that should any article on this list be lost or stolen, you will be charged import duty on it.) After issue, when you cruise the Transit Log has to be produced to port officials on demand, and sometimes a modest sum is demanded which goes to the local council. If one stays away from suspicion of illegal chartering there are few problems, but the authorities are so paranoid about the subject that it crops up from time to time, especially if one is in a yacht of over 10 tons or so.

It is not illegal for you to embark crew or friends who have flown out to you for a holiday, but if they make any contribution to your expenses, however small, this is held to be a charter. Your friends might also have difficulty with their return charter flight if, during your cruise, you call at another country and then return to Greece, owing to an obscure IATA regulation that no one else enforces. In Greek law the offence is declared by the Coastguard officer, the fine imposed without trial, and any redress is by appeal. Fortunately Greek courts are fair and justice will usually be done in the end, but the hassle can be long and expensive.

Nonetheless, Greece is worthwhile and one of our favourite cruising grounds. It is still very much less crowded than the western Mediterranean; there are still a lot of deserted anchorages to be found, and the proliferation of flotilla companies, a few of whose flotillas are not always well managed or tactfully led, has not spoiled the social life ashore except in very few places. Sadly we cannot say the same of certain 'holiday clubs' for younger people. These can, and sometimes do, upset everyone (including local people) by loutish and gross behaviour.

Cost of living is cheap, especially in the remoter parts where luxuries are unobtainable. Retsina is a cheap wine to drink; it contains

AGHIOS STEFANOS, CORFU

pine resin and is an acquired taste, but worth acquiring if you plan to stay a while. Laurel likes it at mid-day mixed with lemonade. Tavernas and restaurants are price controlled, except for the luxury category, and very good value.

Customs duties on imports are very high, and in practice it is difficult to import spare parts for a yacht. The only places with any supply are Corfu, Pireaus and Rhodes; good craftsmen can be found there though they are often not noted for their speediness.

The telephone service to foreign countries is very good, mail is tolerable, but avoid poste restante to small towns owing to the difficulties some Greeks have in reading western script, which leads to letters being misfiled. Ferry services, both air and sea, among the islands are

Laurel

excellent and inexpensive, but all radiate from Athens, a sprawling, ugly city to be avoided except for its monuments.

Ruins and historic sites abound in the country, and a big cultural effort is made with interesting plays and concerts in appropriate historic settings. The Greek language is not nearly such a problem as one would think, because, unlike the Slavonic tongue, it has something in common with our own.

For wintering there are several marinas, though services in them are far from good. Gouvia in Corfu is barely half finished, but can be used. The island has a very wet winter and the marina tends to become rather a sad sea of mud. People do leave their boats there unattended, but from my own observations during a winter I would not do so. Some people like to winter at Rhodes, but there is some doubt about Mandraki harbour being well sheltered. The marinas round Athens are very expensive for poor facilities; that at Alimos, for example, suffering from theft.

Hauling out is difficult throughout the whole Eastern Mediterranean. The open beach boatyards at Mandouki, in Corfu, are not recommended. Levkas and Nidri are better propositions, and both are good places to leave a boat unattended.

If summer cruising in Greece, it is wise to start in the north. In both the seas this is the dominating summer wind. That in the Aegean can sometimes be very strong.

A diversion

Before going on to write about Turkey it is appropriate to divert onto Graeco-Turkish relations, which tend to have some impact on sailing in the Aegean.

Greece was for about six centuries part of the Turkish Empire, ruled by the Sultan of Turkey, as was most of southeast Europe. This was not a very pleasant experience. Actually it was not a very pleasant experience for the majority of Turks either. The Greeks made a few attempts at rebellion, but they were unco-ordinated and were put down with the cruelty which was the norm for that period.

Eventually the Turkish Empire weakened, as all empires do, and with the help of the Russian, French and British navies the Turks were thrown out of Greece, and after a brief period of chaos the Greek kingdom was established under an imported King in 1830.

Greek hatred and fear of the Turks continues to this day. In 1919 the Greeks, encouraged (to our undying shame) by most of the wartime Allies, invaded Turkey, which had just had a revolution deposing the Sultan. The new leader Kemal Ataturk (the Father of the Turks) repulsed the invasion very vigorously and ruthlessly, precipitating a mass exodus of people of Greek extraction from Turkey in 1922 (among which was the young Issigonis, designer of the Mini), which was so very movingly reported by a young newspaperman called Hemingway.

To this day, in Greece there is no movement towards reconciliation, and children are subjected to ridiculous horror stories. In Turkey there has been considerable softening of attitude, and I believe that animosity to Greece has diminished considerably. There is no trust, however.

It is because of this mutual mistrust and the one-sided hatred that cruising between Greece and Turkey can be subject to problems. In Greece there is resentment that the foreign yachtsman should want to go to Turkey at all, and though they are getting used to it they still resent it. There is a lot of irritation with what is called 'zig-zagging', i.e. going down the coast alternating between Greek and Turkish ports, which would be a very nice way to cruise the coast.

There are comparatively few niggles for the foreign yachtsman in Turkey, and as the Greek government became less sympathetic to yachting tourism the Turks put out the welcome mat and have creamed off a good deal of the trade.

Turkey

The Turks have their own version of the Transit Log, though it is still not fully understood at some of the less frequented ports. Unfortunately some of the old regulations did not change. One can still be pursued by Biblical looking gentlemen demanding Light Dues for virtually non-existent lights, and there is still a requirement for a yacht to leave and re-enter every three months.

During our winter's stay in Bodrum I had the misfortune to injure myself so that it was obvious that we would be unable to leave at the expiry of three months. With an interpreter I sought the advice of the local Customs Director. I was told not to worry, but to come back when I eventually wanted to go. I could get nothing in writing, but was reassured by my interpreter that all would be well.

After five months, at leaving time, I called on the lady Customs Director again, taking a box of English chocolates as the ritual token gift. All supplicants wait in the office and each case is subject to general discussion, and so was mine, agreement being reached with much nodding of heads and smiling. I had disgracefully over-stayed the permitted time and for this serious offence I would be fined two pounds. The lady explained that had we made an official application for an extension it would have required several affidavits, all costing fees, and we would not have received an answer for months or even years. The Turks are expert at coping with the deficiencies of their extensive bureaucracy. Let them get on with it.

It must be realized that Turkey is a Muslim country, though in practical terms the majority are Muslim in much the same way as the majority of Britons are members of the Church of England. There are thus some basic differences in style of living. For example, pork is rare, though drink is common enough; in fact there is more drunkenness in Turkey than in most Mediterranean countries, and it seems that the more restrictions are imposed on the drinker the more he gets drunk. Festivals are different, too.

November 11th, when we had just got into our winter berth, was Bayram, meaning festival. The streets were virtually awash with blood as every family slaughtered a ram to commemorate the ram in the thicket found by Isaac. Tradition has it that part of the sacrifice should be given to the poor, who are not so very numerous in Bodrum, so local townsfolk took pity on the poor infidel yachtsmen and all of us received plastic bags containing dripping pieces of mutton. There were so many that we got together under the guidance of a French professional chef (himself a liveaboard) and hung the meat. We borrowed a restaurant that had closed for the winter and had a big barbecue for all our benefactors. It was a good party and started the winter's social life very well.

Spare parts are difficult to get in Turkey so there is a flourishing industry producing one-offs, often better made than the originals and far cheaper. Craftsmanship is generally good, labour is cheap, and they are prepared to tackle almost anything.

The cost of living is low, the vegetable markets are superb, though the meat and fish, as so often in the Med, is disappointing. Turks themselves tend towards a predominantly vegetarian diet. Restaurants are good, the cooking is better than in Greece and the presentation more soigné.

Communications are not so good, particularly away from cities. The main road south from Izmir is now paved and the bus journey is no longer the wild-west adventure it once was. The bus services between towns are excellent and cheap, but the air services do not inspire much confidence. The mail is outstandingly good; mail from the UK to Bodrum, even before the road was paved, consistently arrived faster than anywhere else in Europe. Gossip had it that there were so many unemployed that the government made them all postmen and there was thus one man per letter.

Banking services are also good, though a bit long-winded, everything being cross-checked several times. The language has a confusing grammar but is easy to manage in basic form as spelling and pronunciation are both simple. In fact most educated Turks are multi-lingual, the result of effective secondary education. Medical services are not good, diagnostic facilities are often almost non-existent.

Kus Adasi has become a major wintering port for long-cruising folk. Sadly, Bodrum marina, which I prefer, has closed in the winter when the odd southerly buster gives trouble, but the breakwater has been extended, so perhaps it will soon be the best winter port again. Other marinas are under construction, and if plans are fulfilled there will be some reasonable facilities for haulout and repair. Oddly enough, I expect the plans to be fulfilled.

Since we first wrote in 1985, Turkey has enjoyed a dramatic increase in tourism, and many places have changed character to some extent. Some of the lonely anchorages, like Ölu Deniz on the south coast, are either out of bounds to yachts or are no longer lonely, and some of the interesting Turkish cuisine has given way to 'western' cooking. This happens everywhere; by going there in numbers we spoil what attracts us in the first place.

Cyprus

We have not been to Cyprus for nearly 30 years, so I can only distil the comments of friends. Cyprus is not a cruising ground, but it contains a major wintering port. Larnaca marina has all facilities, and most report it is a very enjoyable spot for the winter, though like some Spanish ports it has apparently collected its quota of immovable deadbeat boats. When a marina gets this it tends to develop a cliquey atmosphere and some of the open social life of the winter is lost, but not everyone (by any means) mentions this feature. In fact adverse comment from those who have actually wintered there is really quite rare. Another marina is nearing completion at Limassol.

Communications with Cyprus are very good, and the authorities are co-operative about the import of spare parts. There are good English speaking schools and medical services are good.

The place is overhung by the intractable problem of the Graeco-Turkish quarrel, but this has little daily effect on the visitor though yachts which have been to the Turkish part of Cyprus are not welcome in the Greek part. Slightly more surprising is that they are not welcome in Greece either. The quarrel, once violent, is now being fought out at the petty niggle level.

Cruising farther east than Cyprus is now outside the terms of a normal Lloyds insurance cover, and no wonder. It is a pity, for Beirut used to be a good port of call for a yacht, and once Haifa was a good place to winter.

Malta

This island was once a favourite wintering place, but fell out of favour when an anti-Western government introduced some spiteful legislation. The government has changed again, and they are making efforts to get back their former reputation for hospitality. Latest reports (1989) suggest they have still quite a long way to go. But really, to be a good wintering port, it will be necessary to improve the shelter in Marsamuscetto Harbour. A bad Gregale (a gale from the north east) does not occur every winter, but oh my! when it does ...

Other Mediterranean countries

There remain Morocco, Algeria, Libya, Egypt, Albania and the Black Sea.

There are comparatively few ports in Morocco, and the ones I have visited have been generally uncongenial — in each case I have been ill and so have some of the crew. I am therefore completely biased. Tangier is certainly no longer the fun centre it once was and the British consulate has closed.

Algeria I have not visited, though a friend tells me that he was politely received and hospitably entertained. One can ask for little more. Libya is now really beyond the pale of consideration, as is Albania.

Egypt has a lovely winter climate and I feel that Alexandria, which has a cosmopolitan population, could be a good place to winter, but I know of no one who has done it. Those (Irving Johnson is one) who have shoal-draught yachts can, with a certain amount of persistence, get into the River Nile and go up to the head of navigation, which would be quite a trip.

The best comment I can make on these countries is that Africa is Africa, even though these are the more civilized parts.

The Black Sea is little cruised. Generally the north wind is strong, making the coast of Turkey an uncomfortable lee shore and these Turkish ports are not as congenial as their Mediterranean counterparts. The communist countries that make up the rest of the littoral are not noticeably friendly. Yachts do visit Bulgaria, though I have not. It is very cold in winter and plagued by mosquitos in summer, the delta of the Danube being marshy. Although I am the holder of a Russian Medal, I was refused a visa to cruise their waters.

There are reputed to be minefields off Libya and Albania. That off Libya would have been recently sown, but that off Albania has probably been there since it was laid by Yugoslavia at the end of the World War, when two British destroyers *Volage* and *Saumarez* struck. But the fact that the mines are old makes them even more dangerous; not only

For wintering one can sometimes find a marina under construction where a reduced price can be negotiated. This is a view of Sibari in Calabria with only three yotties in residence.

may some of them now be out of position, but the detonators and primers become unstable and anything can happen. Anyone but a lunatic would stay out of the prohibited areas, but as small sailing boats can be blown off course give the fields a very wide berth.

In 1976 the Canadian yacht *Arbaleste*, the home of Mark and Nora de Goutiere, was blown off course by a northwest gale and lost track of her position. They were arrested by an Albanian patrol vessel and in harbour were repeatedly questioned about both their navigation and their politics. They were, however, also offered any provisions or stores that they needed. Finally they were obliged to sign a confession in Albanian and were released. As it was still blowing hard, a naval officer said they could remain another 24 hours, but the whole experience had been so unsettling that they left, escorted to the edge of the 15 mile limit.

The lesson has to be drawn that communist states are likely to be scrupulously correct to any craft making a visit to their shores, but the experience is not likely to be a joyous one. It should be pointed out that though ships may call at ports and request certain facilities, this does not impose an obligation on the country to permit any of the crew to land. It can also be noted that there is a history of Soviet ships being most obliging and courteous to yachts met on the high seas.

Documentation

We have been taken to task by some readers of the first edition who had not yet set off deep cruising, for not saying anything about this subject, and several people at the symposiums were clearly troubled by it.

There is a simple reason why we said nothing about it. The subject has never given us the least bother and we didn't think it worth mentioning.

There is no point in going minutely into it country by country because the detailed rules are constantly changing. Please let us reassure readers who are planning their voyages: *Do not worry.* But be sensible all the same.

The requirements are different in virtually every country, and often in different ports within the same country. *Do not worry.* I assume the boat is properly registered in your own name, because boats registered in the name of companies in Panama, Guernsey, Gibraltar, etc. can get into difficulties, this being occasionally a signal of someone up to no good. If the boat is in your name the formalities pertaining to the craft will give no trouble. They may take a long time, but time is not of the essence.

You can save time if you make out copies (several) of your crew list. (Very often the words 'Crew list' are the only English words a Greek Port Captain knows.) These lists should not only have the names in full of everyone on board but also Passport numbers, dates and places of birth, maiden names (and once we were asked for names, dates and places of birth of our parents too). Do not worry. Stay calm.

We know of a Frenchman who cruised his yacht with the old British registration certificate of a yacht that had been scrapped. He had renamed his boat to match. He never had any trouble. You, being honest, are not going to have any either. No one has so far ever checked the number carved on our main beam.

I assume you have proper passports that are in date. I assume you have taken the precaution of getting a visa for those countries who are scared to let you in without one. I assume you have found out if any vaccinations or inoculations are required and that you have the appropriate certificates. It's all tedious on occasions, but really quite simple. Do not worry.

If planning to go to both Israel and Arab countries, or if you wish to go to Northern (Turkish occupied) Cyprus and also want to go to Greece, then you can get in advance a second passport if you tell the passport office what you want to do. Don't mix the passports up, keep one for the sheep and the other for the goats.

Be careful about giving passage to persons of countries that are regarded as 'difficult' in the country you are heading for. Even this is not as bad as it sounds.

Stories:

We arrived in Antigua with two South Africans on board in the days when the famous Sergeant King was in charge of immigration there. Our friends wished to disembark and fly home. Within a short time, thanks to a friendly approach, our friends went ashore with the scourge of the Caribbean helping them with their baggage.

People, even officials, are fundamentally nice people.

Some friends of ours embarked the young Greek boy-friend of their daughter for a short cruise and headed for Turkey without thinking. Their guest, when he discovered which harbour they were entering, was petrified. He expected to be decapitated or worse. The Turkish immigration officer told the quaking youngster he ought to have got a visa, then threw his arms round the boy's neck, kissed him and said 'Welcome to Turkey'.

There is an indication that Turkey may demand visas for Britons in retaliation for something they imagine Mrs Thatcher has, or has not, done to someone. Check up. These brou-ha-has usually die down before long.

But do not worry.

Some countries are beginning to demand evidence of third-party insurance cover. Not many. Italy is, I think, the only country to do it nationwide (get a certificate in Italian from your insurers), but some marinas are now demanding it as a condition of entry, not to the country, but to their marina. (Suppose you set the boat in the berth next to you on fire?) France and Greece are the only places which we know to be affected.

In all our cruising we have never been asked for documents issued by the port we have left, nor have we ever been asked for de-ratting certificates, though once we were asked to produce evidence of good health. Any evidence. We wrote out our own certificate and stamped it with the ship's own 'official' stamp, which we put over the top of some left-over British postage stamps. It did the trick. Do not worry. *Check:*

(a) Passports—in date—visas—not an unpopular country.

(b) Boat registration.

(c) Boat insurance if applicable.

(d) Inoculations.

Remember that people do arrive in the most awkward countries improperly documented and still have a good time, provided they are not aggressive or nasty. *So do not worry.*

CHAPTER ELEVEN

Misadventures

'. . . some accident that requires the help of all hands . . . which in most voyages doth happen.'

Crime

There are two sorts of relevant crime; those committed by yachtsmen and those against yachtsmen, with the occasional merger of the two.

One of the features of long-cruising is its suitability as a way of life for the criminal who is either retired or resting. It is sad that in recent years the professional criminal has become aware of this: sad because inevitably the processes of identifying, tracking and arresting them will impinge on the freedoms of the cruising yottie.

When only a small number of retired criminals were involved the forces of international law and order did little, for attempts to track individuals would have been inordinately expensive. The occasional cigarette smuggler was arrested, but there was no great international co-operation for one country was not over-concerned about another's smuggling problems. But the alarming increase of narcotic abuse has brought yachtsmen into notice.

Drug smuggling is of two broad types: the highly professional operations of organized crime, and the more casual, small-scale activities of individuals. The 'casual' smuggler is of any nationality and can operate anywhere, though there is much activity close to the USA. The American authorities try hard, but they have a very difficult problem because of their closeness to some very anarchistic small states. Yachtsmen on the spot become aware that Mr A, who was paid crew on the charter boat XYZ in 1983, appears in 1984 as the owner of a Swan 65. No-one checks on his sudden wealth; his boat is registered behind nominees in a British colony, and he is all set for a life of comfort. And a major contribution to his ability to enjoy the fruits of his dirty enterprise is made by the British government through its laws on colonial banking, company registration and ship registration. These laws become a major factor in the activities of organized crime, and not only in its drug smuggling mode. Most of the hard-drug traffic in the Mediterranean and Caribbean happens under the Red Ensign and there is no doubt that it is falling into disrepute, to the inevitable disadvantage of British yachtsmen in general.

Ownership of these yachts is vested in companies set up in Jersey, Guernsey or Gibraltar; the shares are held in the names of nominees, often living in Sark; the yachts are registered not only in these places but also in Southampton or London. Laundering the proceeds takes place in many ways, but one is by buying and selling these yachts through certain brokers in the South of France, the transactions passing through banks in all the financially rotten parts of the world i.e. Switzerland, Lichtenstein, Luxembourg and the Channel Islands. A significant blow could be struck against organized crime by closing the secrecy loophole of company and ship registration in the Channel Islands and other British colonies. And our national ensign would enjoy a better respect.

That apart, most crime perpetrated by yachtsmen is petty, and typically against their fellows. French yachtsmen in the Caribbean have a rotten reputation. This is hard on those pleasant, honest froggies who wish to enjoy civilized cruising, and in the Med, for example, these are more typical. What seems to have happened in the Caribbean was that, with the great expansion of yachting in France and the national hero-worship of such excellent seamen as Moitessier and Tabarly, many young Frenchmen set out to build cheap steel yachts for themselves. Armed with a hundred kilos of pasta, a load of salami and *vin de table*, they sailed for the palm trees with stars in their eyes and nearly empty pockets.

And then the money ran out. Jobs were not to be had. To return costs money, to go on to the South Seas costs money, and in a bind it becomes too easy to cut the painter on someone's Zodiac — and these are substantially untraceable. Though this activity is largely laid at the door of the French, others including the local people are not above a little of it. Given the fragmentation of the islands into dozens of tin-pot little states, there is very little that can be done; the criminal can keep on the move.

So far as crime against the yottie is concerned, the wanderer is somewhat at the mercy of the petty pilferer. It is impossible to live in tropical heat and turn one's boat into a fortress: the open air is an essential ingredient. Fortunately there are few places where pilfering is a serious problem, for the more primitive the culture (assuming there is some culture), the more likely the inhabitant will have strong conceptions of hospitality and a lack of covetousness. Most of us try to steer clear of big cities.

From the experiences of ourselves and friends, I think it unwise to leave a boat unwatched, even for short periods, in open harbours in big cities. By open harbours I mean those where there are no dock gates with police or Customs men controlling entry by the public. Typical among open harbours where care is needed are Barcelona, Baltimore (USA), Brindisi, Marseilles and Palermo, but there are many others. Most yacht marinas in or near a city are prime targets for thieves, and this particularly applies where the marinas are open to public access, such as Antibes and many others along the Riviera. This leads to a lot of boats in these marinas being fitted with intruder alarms, and given the intrinsic unreliability of marine electronics it means sleepless nights for all crews living aboard when these things go off semi-continuously. In fact, the intruder alarm when fitted to small craft goes off in error so often that no-one pays any attention.

In some countries, notably Italy where dishonesty is part of the culture, there is a very fierce desire to protect the property which a person has, even if he stole it from someone else in the first place. Marinas in Italy tend to have a more positive security system, sometimes leading to a sort of prison camp mentality. One, near Rome, was surrounded by a double chain-link fence, with vicious dogs running unleashed between them. There was only one gate, double locked, and a scrutiny before entry that stopped just short of body-searching. There was a conscientious night patrol, but in spite of all this, thieves arrived by water one night and stripped several boats of their electronics. This marina, unlike some, welcomed liveaboards as reliable watchmen who actually paid the marina, not vice versa, for the privilege of keeping watch.

If you are frequently leaving your boat unwatched in any marina or large port, locking up becomes necessary. Doors and hatches in sea-going craft are generally stoutly made and good locks can be fitted. But these are not necessarily the whole answer because thieves are often adept at undoing them. It is worthwhile devising a complex door or hatch opening system that is apparently contrary to logic. We know of one case where such an entrance to a boat was attacked and battered without the raiders gaining entry, even though it had not been locked.

For our own part, we have lost very little to the pilferer, which indicates that too much worry probably attaches to the question. The total over the years was a teak-handled knife, a tape recorder that we left on deck while we were ashore, and two fenders which might have been badly made fast. Our total financial loss is probably less than the cost of a good lock. But note that we steer clear of cities.

Nowhere illustrates the tendency of cities to corrupt their own populations better than Greece. In the Greek islands or the countryside, the traveller's property and person are virtually sacrosanct: one need not lock or even close doors for short or long absences. The refreshment of experiencing such open honesty is most invigorating to the soul. But at Alimos Marina in Athens, there is both petty and systematic stealing.

One point to watch in regard to petty theft: it does not pay to report it. Your chances of getting your property back are virtually nil, but to report it is to involve oneself with officialdom, sometimes to have one's freedom of movement restrained and, final indignity, in almost all countries the local Customs will assess you, the loser, as having imported the item and charge you duty on it, effectively multiplying your loss. This last unfair and unreasonable insult is the clincher.

The most common stolen artifact is an inflatable dinghy, with or without outboard motor. There seems to be a worldwide market for these items, and I am surprised the *Financial Times* does not list them under 'Commodities' with the day's range of buying and selling prices: 'The Zodiac market moved narrowly today with a fair supply from St Lucia which found ready buyers. Avons were in steady demand and gained £4. Metzeler lost ground in early trading with a large batch of nearly new from Palermo, but recovered later to close the day £2 lower.'

Normally inflatables are cut adrift from the parent yacht during the night. Old West Indies hands hoist their dinghies in at night, or else fit wire painters, but these are difficult to make really secure to an inflatable. The ease with which they can be stolen and then hidden for later disposal is a very important factor in the choice of which type of tender to carry.

Liferafts are occasionally taken, for their cost is substantial, but as they are more easily traced they do not find such a ready market.

Running rigging and on-deck gear is occasionally stripped from a yacht. In Brindisi this can be done by real experts while the crew are sleeping peacefully below. Brindisi is a bad port both from the point of view of real theft and pilfering, the latter being done both by local urchins and by the swarms of hitch-hikers waiting to embark on the ferries for Greece. The fact that Corfu suffers from thieves is due not to Greek dishonesty but almost entirely to the young tourists. But it is in Italy that thieves have real chutzpah. At Palermo, thieves who had been locating the dinghy they wanted found to their dismay that the owners had chained it to the stern davits. They stole the davits too.

There is also an active market in whole yachts, mostly confined to those in quantity production, which are less easily distinguished one from another. The liability of having a particular type of yacht stolen is in direct proportion to its ready resale: so it does not necessarily pay to buy yachts with high resale values, which can anyway change.

In Antibes the yacht next to us, a German-owned Amal, was visited for several days by an overalled young man in a battered van, who did certain work aboard, and this aroused no suspicions. Nor was anyone alerted when the yacht sailed. It was by chance that a friend of the owner (who was at that time home in Germany) saw the yacht in Palma and went to greet his chum. He was an alert man, suspected something was wrong, phoned his friend and brought in the police. The thief was arrested, and it subsequently transpired that he had selected the yacht some time before and had negotiated a series of West Indian charters for her before actually committing the theft.

Many people contemplating long-cruising are concerned about piracy, which is the taking of a vessel or the robbery of crew, cargo or equipment on the high seas, i.e. away from harbour. This crime has been much played up by the press, particularly in USA, to the level of mild paranoia.

In the chandlery at Bahia Mar, Fort Lauderdale, I waited to be served while an American bought a rifle, a sub-machine gun, and two pistols for about $1200. While they were being wrapped I enquired where he was bound with such an arsenal and was told the Virgin Islands. I could not help observing that he would be better off without them, which led to a frosty attitude on the part of the shop-keeper, who furnished, in season, many such armouries.

From which, you may gather, we are not armed. In my experience firearms are a positive liability; or to put it another way, the pro-weapon yotties have more problems from carrying weapons than the unarmed get by not.

For consider the question of how to use these weapons. 'To be a good gunner, you must learn it by practice.' Guns are killing weapons. It is no use having one unless you are prepared, instantly and without stopping to think, to point it at someone and fire to kill. The typical handgun is a very inaccurate weapon, and cannot be used to wound without seriously hurting. It is only possible to pump bullets in the general direction of the target and hope one of them will do sufficient damage to stop an assailant, if it is in fact an assailant. A rifle is not a close-quarters weapon (unless it has a bayonet — God help us) and is designed for comparatively accurate longer-range work. Anyone with any experience of naval gunnery will know of the great problems attaching to sighting from a platform moving randomly in three dimensions. Skilled naval gunners with complex control gear hardly ever hit anything: what chance has an excited amateur?

All these weapons must be kept clean, lightly oiled, and ready for instant use if they are to be effective. In many ports they must be declared, probably landed under police control and collected again before sailing. There are heavy penalties for transgressions of firearm laws, which differ from place to place so that one is never sure what they will be.

In real life one is also faced with the problem of identifying an assailant as such. An American yachtsman (it is almost always Americans who get into trouble with guns) panicked and shot dead one of the crew of a Spanish trawler near Alboran. The trawler was approaching to swop fish for foreign cigarettes, a common practice at that time. That trigger-happy yachtsman became a sadder jailbird.

So how do you tell if the boat approaching is friendly or vicious? Do you shoot anyway? Hardly. And do you think that if they are real pirates they will be unprepared for your rather limited self-defence? They'll be ready, and they'll blast the hell out of you at the first shot, or ram you. The only people you will discourage by arms will be friendly ones.

We once went into Agios Andreas Bay at the southern end of Ithaca to find an American ketch the sole occupant. No doubt he was irritated at having his solitude spoiled, but the situation hardly called for his appearance on deck with a shotgun, telling us to get out of the bay as

BOUZOUKI SHOP,
CHIOS

Laurel

233

it was only big enough for one. It is the impulsive exploitation of the enhancement of power given by a weapon that is so dangerous in the hands of a person who is temporarily, or even partially, unstable. What did we do in Ithaca? We told him to grow up, we anchored. He became quite friendly later. This story, which we have related from time to time, recently came back to us as having happened to someone else. I hope there are not really two gun-toting nuts around the Ionian Sea.

I believe that the very ownership of a weapon fosters paranoia. If already of that tendency, it becomes more accentuated and even dangerous.

What about attacks in harbour? These do happen. Whereas we have no personal knowledge of any authentic example of piracy, we do know of people who have suffered personal injury in harbour. It is necessary to consider whether these incidents would have been prevented with firearms. They all concerned intruders boarding a yacht. At least one of the yachts carried arms but had no chance of using them. Two of the three cases were murders, in St Vincent and in Port of Spain, Trinidad. That in Friendship Bay, Bequia was almost murder. Two of the yachts were American, one was British. It is impossible to be sure, but I believe that the mere possession of firearms would not have altered the outcome of any of these cases, where the murderers had been able to get to close quarters before being observed.

Do not make too much of these very regrettable events. They are regrettable and deplorable, but are not really as common as all that. Sadly, the St Vincent government do not appear to investigate or prosecute crime against foreigners with any energy whatsoever. Trinidad did produce and sentence a culprit.

The whole thing is a question of prudence once again. Nothing will eliminate robbery and/or violence. But in places where it is known to occur, then some vigilance will reduce both its probability and its impact. Port of Spain is a big commercial port and not a noticeably congenial place for a yacht. But in Bequia one would be visited by a lot of native people, very friendly for the most part, some begging, some selling, but fundamentally law-abiding.

Do not display ostentatious wealth. Even modest possessions by North American or European standards are wealth beyond dreams for many of these people. If you have any doubts about a place, you have the means of leaving or you can take precautions. There is no call for paranoia, just observe a little, ask a little, get to know the local feeling.

What precautions? Do not leave dinghies in the water, or leave boarding ladders down, or ropes and fenders overside. If you are very seriously worried about a place do not sleep on deck, and fasten hatches and large openings in a half-closed position that will allow ventilation but not admit a person. Take reasonable care, but do not reduce yourself to a fortress mentality all the time.

Places where theft is virtually unknown are the rural areas of Greece and Turkey. The more isolated and rural areas of southern Italy away from tourist centres, the Canary Islands away from tourist centres, the Azores except for Punta Delgada, the out-islands in the Bahamas and the rural parts of Yugoslavia. In all other areas it pays to take at least elementary precautions against petty theft.

Theft of all types is endemic in the French and Italian Rivieras, and in or near any Italian town of more than 20,000 inhabitants or a Spanish one of more than 50,000. In Athens, in Egypt, and to a lesser extent Tunisia. In Morocco. In the touristy parts of Portugal.

Accidents

'Master, let us breathe and refresh a little, and sling a man overboard to stop the leakes.'

Not all damage to boat or person is caused by a criminal. Mishaps happen. In our experience most accidents between craft are trivial, most are clearly defined as to fault, and in most cases the defaulter makes amends instantly and without quibble. Three times we have suffered minor damage while made fast. Once in Boulogne from a member of the Royal Motor Yacht Club, who departed shouting 'Sorry, old man' and who did not answer our letter. Twice by Italians who volunteered compensation and paid in full.

The problem is that chasing compensation in foreign countries, in foreign languages and via post is a most unrewarding and frustrating pastime. Better to do a modest deal on the spot while the other fellow's conscience is still troubling him, than to hold out for full and complete indemnity. Most yachtsmen are decent types, thank God, and long may it last.

Major damage is a different matter. Here insurance is a very definite help, for even if the perpetrators cannot be traced or brought to book, underwriters can be expected to settle in the terms of the policy, or even a little more in some cases.

If you commit the damage yourself, to another vessel or a person, then you will probably appreciate being insured. This is a mischance all the more likely as yachting centres get more crowded and increasing numbers of novices take to the sea with certificates obtained at evening classes, fondly believing they are competent. To sail without good third party cover is foolhardy and anti-social, especially as more and more people new to the sport bring a motor-car mentality to sea with them. One must also remember the fortune that many modern yachts represent in money terms, and the high cost of even cosmetic repairs.

Personal Accidents

Minor damage to the person is discussed in Chapter Fifteen, which is about treatment that is totally within on-board resources. But one can have major accidents or mishaps that require surgery or hospital treatment, and though this cannot be considered a minor matter it will have to go in that Chapter too, together with some comments on health insurance.

Not all accidents to the person happen on board, or even to your own crew. Everyman's mishap diminisheth me, to bastardize a good quotation. We once had a difficult time helping fellow British yotties coping with the problems involved when a singlehanded yachtsman was killed in a motor accident in Italy. The British Consul at Florence was not merely unhelpful, he was positively discourteous.

Laurel and I frequently travel about together in little excursions from *Fare Well*, and it is always a possibility that an accident to one would involve the other too. Such accidents do not have to be fatal to be bothersome to strangers. And the problems ensuing, if temporary neighbours whom you have only met the day before, or local officials, have to trace your relatives or whatever, are so very great that some small precaution should be taken.

Each shorthanded cruising yacht should have displayed close to the main hatch a small, semi-permanent notice saying, 'In case of urgency or difficulty, contact . . .'. One should also leave a will in a place of safety, and in the case of couples (because the likelihood of both dying at the same time is greater than for shore-dwellers) consult a lawyer about whether special clauses should cover this aspect. If so, draw up compatible wills.

On a less gloomy note, it is a good idea to have a square foot or so of surface, close to the main hatch, painted in blackboard paint. We leave messages on it in chalk, or at appropriate moments write up announcements of pure joy.

Accidents at Sea: the Legal Position

I have mentioned already the obligation to go to the assistance of a vessel in distress. This is detailed in Section 6 of the [British] Maritime Conventions Act of 1911, the terms of which will have been enacted by all nations signatory to the Convention. We are obliged, so far as we can without danger to our own vessel, to render assistance to every person (even if such a person be a subject of a foreign State at war with Her Majesty) who is found at sea in danger of being lost. Failure to do so is a misdemeanour. This is further amplified by the Merchant Shipping (Safety Convention) Act 1949, which should be read. (It is too long and detailed to include here: copies can be had from Her Majesty's Stationery Office.)

The procedure for dealing with casualties on board is in Section 73 of the Merchant Shipping Act 1970. Casualties (and note that the ship herself can be a casualty) must be reported to the Department of Transport as soon as possible, and in any case not later than 24 hours after arrival at the next port. The report should contain a description of the incident, give details of injuries to personnel and damage to the ship, the name and official number of the ship, her position, next port of call and ETA, and should go to any DTp Marine Office, or to the Marine Directorate at Sunley House, 90 High Holborn, London WC1V 6LP.

Also coming under 'accidents' we have Births, Deaths and Marriages at sea. The law covering deaths is given in the Merchant Shipping (Returns of Births and Deaths) Regulations 1979. A master is required to make a return of births in a ship, or of deaths in or from a ship. It should be made as soon as practicable (but within six months) to either a Marine Superintendent in the UK, a British Consular Office in foreign countries, or the equivalent of a Marine Superintendent in a Commonwealth country. There will also be local procedures if a body is landed at a port (the Regulations warn), but the UK regulations apply whether or not the body is landed, buried at sea or not recovered.

The official record of a birth or death is in the register entry made by the Registrar following the receipt of such a return from a Master. Marriages on board have a legal basis only when conducted by an authorized person, and when the ship is in the territory covered by that person's authority, and the official record would be held under the law of that territory. A British shipmaster is not, and never has been, an authorized person, and there is no UK machinery for recording marriages at sea. An entry in a log book is not, of itself, legal evidence of a marriage.

There is no legal obligation to recover a body sighted at sea, because of the dangers of capsizing, disease etc, but sightings should be reported to the nearest authorities. Do so by radio, if possible. If reporting by person, the report in a foreign country should be made to the British Consul in the hope of avoiding local problems. That is the official position; there must always be a strong incentive not to sight bodies at sea.

If wrecked, the yachtsman is normally not entitled to be treated as a shipwrecked mariner for the purpose of repatriation, and any in this unfortunate difficulty would be treated by a Consul as a normal distressed British subject. And God help them if my experience of British Consuls is anything to go by.

It is worth noting that while on the high seas a British registered ship is considered an extension of British Law, but once she enters the territorial waters of another state the situation is not so clear, particularly if citizens of that state or their property are affected.

Loss of Skipper

A particular disaster that worries a lot of wives, mates and less experienced members of a crew of two, is the loss of the skipper, whether permanently overboard or temporarily through injury or sickness while at sea. It is such a real worry to some that it justifies a word or two.

The crew must be able to handle the craft, even if only under power or with reduced sail. Even for a novice this is not so impossible as it might seem, especially when needs must. Some people are afraid to discuss this, particularly wives with their husbands, but it is worth making the effort because the conclusions will never be forgotten.

In any event there are a few simple precautions to be taken. In big ships it is normal for the radio room to be given the ship's position every watch so that in emergency they have an approximate position always at hand. In a yacht I always plot the position at least once every four hours, whether by fix or DR. I always have in the ready drawer charts for diversionary ports to which I might have to go for some emergency, and my plan for the voyage lists some of them. Because Laurel is the Met Officer she is always aware of wind patterns and the weather; because she often works out a sight alongside me, she knows how to do it; because I insist she uses the VHF from time to time she is not nervous on the radio (and a lot of people are). She is not so hot on engineering but she can start, stop and use the engine.

Loss of anyone aboard is a terrible disaster. Its effect and the awful fear of it can be mitigated by a discussion and decisions of what to do if the disaster happens. That is probably enough to make sure it never does.

Internal Damage to the Yacht

Even with good care and maintenance, things do go wrong in ways that are dangerous. I once had a shaft coupling disintegrate off Ushant. It had been badly machined by someone I was entitled to expect to do it well, and the chatter of the bad fit destroyed the metal. The shaft dropped back leaving a 2-inch diameter hole. One of my crew on that occasion was a professional cabinet maker: I have never seen a wooden plug made so fast, but it took a lot of getting in against the water pressure. It could not be put in the outer end. The lesson I drew from this was to have ready-made plugs for all the openings in the hull.

But perhaps the most frightening possibility is fire, particularly at sea. We had one and I was fortunate in having been trained in ship fire-fighting. The experience is instructive. I had fitted a ventilating fan above the batteries, and the exhaust side had Tannoy brand ducting secured by clips supplied by the manufacturers. The ducting consisted of a wire spiral thinly covered by plastic. In the compartment there was a deckhead-mounted Noxfire automatic extinguisher.

At about 0330 when somewhere northwest of Corsica (we always have a bad time round there), sailing in a very rough sea at the tail end of a gale, Laurel, who was on watch, called me to say there was a smell of burning. I opened the hatch to the engineroom and found the whole space full of flame and smoke. I shut the hatch; the fire was clearly beyond the capacity of extinguishers and I naturally thought that the automatic one had gone off but had failed to cope. In fact, it never did go off.

After some time I managed to get the fire under control using a very fine spray of sea water. As the smoke cleared I saw the cause. The ducting had fallen out of the clips, which were clearly not adequate for the extra strains of violent motion in bad weather (a feature that is distressingly common in items designed by wizz-kids who have never had a wet shirt). The ducting had dropped on to the battery terminals, rolled about and soon worn away its thin plastic coating; the wire had shorted across the terminals, igniting everything nearby, helped by the contents of a plastic can of paraffin that I had been idiot enough to stow there.

Lessons learnt (some of them I knew already, but needed a reminder):

Cheap and flimsy fastenings just will not cope with the violent movement of a small boat in bad seas.

Contrary to popular advice, it is a good precaution to cover batteries, but the covers must permit the passage of gases. A strong plastic mesh is effective.

Paraffin and any cans of any fuel, particularly in plastic containers, should be on deck.

Automatic extinguishers, even when in date, cannot be relied on and are therefore not worth the money.

Butyl insulated wiring, specified by Lloyds as being fire resistant, burns as merrily as other, less expensive plastics but is more difficult to extinguish.

Our thick-walled plastic diesel fuel lines did not ignite or melt, even though damaged. This may be because the engine was running and the tubing was cooled by the flow of oil in it.

The sort of fire extinguishers that can be carried in a small craft, while adequate for a minor outbreak in the early stages, cannot cope with a serious blaze. Crew cruising a lot need to have actual experience of putting out electrical (the most frequent cause) and fuel fires using only a water spray. Not a jet, but a *spray* of as fine droplets as you can get. It is cheap and effective, but it is a definite skill which the long-cruising yachtsman should acquire.

Boiled batteries do not work.

The mess from a fire is horrible.

We were in more physical danger from the fumes of burning plastic (battery cases, wiring insulation etc) than we were from heat and flames.

Other mishaps to the yacht involve the loss of mast, and canvas. We carry enough spare or alternate sails to get by, perhaps less efficiently but nevertheless practically, if some are blown out.

Loss of a mast is more serious, and is best dealt with by getting them strong enough at the start. The extra cost will probably be less than the excess on one's insurance policy. Cruising boats should not go around with the bendy fishing rods sported by the racing folk. It helps to have a two-masted rig too, but only if there is no triatic stay. (I am not sure triatic stays contribute very much anyway.)

What to do if you lose a mast is very well covered in salty books on seamanship. Racing yachtsmen write about it frequently in magazines, but mostly they have large crews of gorillas to heft spars about. All the more reason for the cruising man to consider his double-strength masts and rigging, and then double again to be on the safe side.

Lightning

During the various talks we have given we have been surprised at the interest shown in lightning at sea. *Fare Well* was struck once, and Bill was struck once before in a small warship; it is one of those very rare sea-going experiences which seems to fascinate everyone.

Quite a long while ago *Yachting Monthly* had a correspondence on what policy to adopt when entering a violent thunderstorm, and one writer advocated donning rubber gloves and boots. Bill, being rather a rude sort of sailor, wrote in, suggesting that someone had forgotten to include a condom. The then Editor, Des Sleightholme, doyen of yachting wits, wrote back that he felt the comment a little ripe for the readership, and finished with the following:

> The lightning flashed, the thunder crashed,
> The mate of the watch turned pale,
> For St Elmo's fire struck his rubber attire
> The moment he touched the rail.

It is St Elmo's fire that one is more likely to encounter, especially in a steel boat. In a GRP boat or a wooden one, there is a lot to be said for having a bond between the sea water and the top of the mast. Of course the standing rigging does this if the mast is not metal, the only link required being between the chain plates and the water. The reason for such a bond is to keep the electric current flow on the outside of the boat.

Thunderstorms in the tropics, and also in the Med, can be very much more violent than we in temperate zones are used to. We once counted 42 lightning flashes within one random minute. In these circumstances it is obvious that there is a huge potential difference between the atmosphere and the sea.

It is only when this difference is unable to disperse peacefully that it runs riot and strikes. During a night thunderstorm one will often see St

Elmo's fire (a brilliant display from the masthead looking like a 'sparkler' type of firework). This discharge is helping to prevent the violently damaging strike.

I was on deck both times when struck, and it was difficult to assess exactly what was happening. Both times there was an enormous display of St Elmo's fire at the masthead, in both cases the sparking seemed to extend several feet, and it went on some time. In *Fare Well* (then in the Gulf Stream) the sparking increased rapidly in intensity as I watched. I felt the sensation usually described as one's 'hair standing on end', even though I was wearing a cap. It was an extraordinarily strong sensation. It developed into a feeling of being lifted off the ground a few inches, of stopping breathing, of being held by the back of the neck, of being absolutely unable to move at all. Those below felt nothing.

During this time I was aware that the sparking at the masthead had turned into a brilliant ball of light about twenty feet in diameter, and that the rigging was glowing white.

Suddenly, as if by throwing a switch, it all turned off. I fell to the deck in a state of shock, and all the fire and sparks at the masthead disappeared. Notice that I have given no time-scale for these events. I was not aware of any sensation of time passing. It is possible the whole sequence took place in a second, it might have taken ten or twenty; I have no idea.

What was the damage to a steel boat?

To me personally, nothing that a good breakfast could not put right. There are few things that do not yield to a good breakfast.

The problem was: no breakfast yet. The only interior part of the boat affected was the wiring, which suggests to me that the current flowed in the skin of the boat and set up a strong magnetic field that induced current into some, but not all, of the wiring. It must have done so at great speed, for in some cases the wire had melted before the fuse had blown. Generally wires melted or insulation blew open at sharp corners, and the damage took the form of a directional blast along the wire. It was as if the current had a linear momentum and could not negotiate the tight bend, mounted the banking and left the track like a racing car.

Some physicists I have discussed this with deny that such an effect is possible, but I have seen it, and I have found one scientist who says there is some evidence that very violent flashes of current have what he called a 'plasma effect'. Well now.

Question: Was that a strike or a very bad attack of St Elmo? Answer: Who knows? Next question: What can one do about it? Answer: nothing more than I said above.

If it was just very bad St Elmo, then in the thunderstorm going on at that time, it suggests to me that a good electrical path up to the top of the mast, together with a good area of conductor in the water (we had recently had a spectacular grounding in coral which had taken a lot of paint off our keel), inhibits a strike by organising a very effective discharge.

If it was a proper strike, then compared with the devastated condition of both wooden and GRP boats that have been struck (all I have seen have taken fire), I cannot help feeling that a boat built of a good conducting material has advantages for the tropics.

What else was damaged? All the electronic fittings on the mainmast were blown apart, but to my amazement I found that some of the instruments themselves (those which had been switched off) survived the blow. All the electronics on the mizzen mast, including the Decca radar, survived. Our radio sets all survived (they were switched off, and their aerial plugs removed: my practice in storms). Several electric motors did not. The stator coils in the generator had to be re-energised.

As for the standing rigging, it appeared to be undamaged, possibly because the current was flowing over the surface rather than inside the wire, and of course the wire was soaking wet in the heavy rain, which may have cooled it. Anyway it survived several more years of use and abuse.

There was one other important effect which does not go under the heading of damage. The whole ship became highly magnetised and the compass was wildly in error. Fortunately we had logged the direction of the swell a couple of hours before the storm, so we had an angular reference. Without that, in completely overcast conditions and 400 miles from land, we would have had absolutely no idea of which way to go.

It turned out the compass deviation was about 90° to start with, but within an hour this had fallen to 35°. A week later it was about 15°, but it took three months to fall below 5°. It never did return to its former state; after about six months we adjusted the magnets to remove the last couple of degrees.

It wasn't much fun clearing up the mess, but it was a fascinating intellectual exercise trying to sort it all out.

All in all I feel there is not enough objective evidence in existence to justify any heavy expenditure on this problem. One can, however, take the simple precautions I outlined at the start. At least they won't do any harm. And doesn't it pay to keep the log up to date?

Emergencies Outside the Boat

These are emergencies which can lead to the abandonment of the enterprise, its interruption or a temporary trip home for one of the crew. Illness of a close relative, for example. It really is impossible to give advice to cover so many different problems in so many possible places, and at widely varying times. We have only had to make one emergency trip home in ten years, and that from a Greek island.

I would counsel maintaining a contingency fund of cash on board to cover both fares and additional costs that will be entailed in such an event, if there is any chance of it occurring. It is possible that a real family emergency while cruising the South Pacific could be ruinous. (See Finance chapter.)

Some Brief Comments on Fighting Fires in Small Craft

'Captain, we are fowle on each other and the shippe is on fire.'

The nature of fire

To start, a fire needs three essential elements: fuel, oxygen and a source of heat. I think that for our purpose we can ignore some of the more esoteric chemical fires which the full-time fireman may have to deal with, and consider the more simple ones. In a yacht there are fuels galore for a fire: diesel oil, plastic linings, foam upholstery, the resin in fibreglass, paints, wood, cooking fat and gas to name the more obvious ones.

Heat is necessary in two ways: the fuel has to be raised to its ignition temperature, below which it will not burn. This varies with the material, and for some is remarkably low. In addition a source of heat has to be applied (even if momentarily) at a temperature known as the flash point and this triggers the flame. This also varies with the material and again can be quite a low temperature.

To extinguish a fire, break the triangle of fuel, oxygen and heat. One can remove the fuel, cut off the supply of oxygen or lower the temperature of whatever is burning — or preferably do a combination of these. Even if the flames are put out, if the temperature of the fuel is not lowered below its ignition temperature the fire can re-start.

We remove the fuel by, for example, throwing it overboard. Very effective, but sometimes not practicable. We can remove the oxygen by smothering the fire, with a fire blanket or foam, for instance. We can cool the fuel with water or certain chemicals.

Fire extinguishers

These are essentially for first aid. They are useful and necessary to provide a very quick means of dealing with minor outbreaks which have been detected in the early stages. Of course they are also helpful even with major fires, for in these circumstances every little helps.

Given that their chief effectiveness is against small fires, one should choose extinguishers that do not themselves cause a great deal of damage, inconvenience or mess. In every case that I have seen a dry powder extinguisher used on a small fire, it has caused more mess and damage than the fire. This experience cannot be extrapolated indefinitely because the fire, if unchecked, would obviously have gone on to cause a great deal of damage, but it does contain a lesson.

One should also get an extinguisher that is easy to use. Instructions to beat the top on the floor, shake for a minute, then point away from the fire for five seconds are too complex to remember, and far too difficult to absorb if on the edge of panic.

Extinguishers with certain chemicals are dangerous to the user. Carbon tetrachloride (Pyrene) is a close and poisonous relative of chloroform, and must not be inhaled for any length of time, especially if there is any alcohol in the body. A supposedly safe chemical is BCF, but given its constituent halogens I have my doubts. It is supposed to be very effective, but it is no good if the propellent which is supposed to get the chemical to the fire has leaked away gradually, which has happened to all of this type that I have experienced. In all cases the makers offered to replace them free, but that is not a lot of good when one is far away; one has to have something to rely on, and should not need to check it every few weeks.

Carbon dioxide is a good material in a boat. It is a very heavy gas and does no damage. Because of its weight it does not leak away from the boat, as it would do in a caravan, for example. It is very effective against fat fires in the galley. It is possible to use some of the contents on a small fire and still have the remainder usable if you are unlucky enough to have another; a very important point at sea where replacements are unobtainable. It works on all oil fires, but it does not cool the fuel, so after putting out the flames that has to be done. Its failure to cool means that it is not good for dealing with fires in carbonaceous or solid materials. It replaces oxygen so you need to watch out you can go on breathing.

Foam extinguishers are really only for oil and petrol fires. They make a horrible mess and do not cool effectively. They need a certain skill to be fully effective and are probably not really suitable for small yachts.

Automatic extinguishers usually work by having a fusible plug which melts in heat, or by having an electronic actuator which senses smoke. I have known the former go off by accident, and also to fail to go off, but I have never heard of a case on a boat where they went off as promised. In my view they are a snare and a delusion and are best avoided. I have no field experience of the other type in action, but I mistrust electronics in small craft. I have rather more faith in my wife's nose.

So, what sort do I have? I have three BCF. I would have preferred carbon dioxide, but could not get any when ours were already overdue for up-dating. Now, after one year, one of the BCFs is down. One must be sure to renew extinguishers according to the makers' recommendations.

Any other firefighting materials? Yes, a fire blanket is worth keeping, both to smother a small fire or to use as a means of removing burning material. It's cheap and has nothing to go wrong. But remember a blanket does not cool the fuel — this must still be done, and very quickly.

Sprinkler systems, which ought really to be called spray systems, are worth installing in large yachts, especially in machinery spaces when it may not always be possible to get in to fight a fire. They give off a spray of very fine droplets of water, usually sea water. As their effect is not carefully aimed they do a fair amount of devastation, particularly to furnishings, so in my view are not recommended for automatic use, when they could be expected eventually to go off unasked. For an automatic system in the engineroom I would prefer carbon dioxide, but remember that engines cannot run on it. If the access is down a hatch, do not go leaping gaily down when the fire is out — there will be no oxygen for you to breathe, and maybe toxic smoke as well. Again the burning material will not be cooled, and could therefore re-ignite if the CO_2 is dispersed.

Big fires

In this context we define this as a fire beyond the capacity of your hand-held extinguishers. It may not be very large, but perhaps it is very intense and very soon could be large. In a yacht there is only one firefighting material available in sufficient quantities: water. You are surrounded by it, but to succeed you must use it skilfully. Water can be used against almost any type of fire if used well.

Fire Brigades are occasionally called to deal with ship fires in port. Very soon there are dozens of 3 inch hoses snaking aboard, and before long the weight of water in the vessel either sinks her or destroys her hydrostatic stability by creating free surface which capsizes her in her berth. The Liverpool brigade used to be very good at this; they hit the jackpot in 1953 with the *Empress of Canada*. It certainly puts the fire out, which enables the firemen to call it a success. It usually writes off the ship, puts a busy berth out of action, and may cause more financial damage than letting the fire burn itself out.

At sea one is rather more concerned with preserving his ship, so he makes sure every bit of water let into her will be used to the maximum advantage. The jet of water used so often and so dramatically on fires in buildings has a point in enabling firemen to get water to the seat of a blaze they could not otherwise reach. It also blasts apart solid material and cools it. In its place, it is the right way of doing things. In a ship, and especially in a small ship, it is very seldom the right way. Notice I do not say 'never' or 'always': there is no such conception in fire-fighting.

Water serves the important purpose of cooling. Its most effective way of doing this is not by conducting heat away but by evaporating, which uses up a very large amount of heat energy. In most circumstances, therefore, it pays to deliver the water in an ideal form for instant evaporation: this is as a very fine spray.

A fine spray also acts as a sort of curtain. As the fire uses oxygen, it draws in more air and feeds itself. The spray curtain, though not a complete screen, reduces the flow of air to the fire. As the water droplets evaporate efficiently they turn almost instantly to steam which, because it has many times the volume of the water it came from, helps to create a quite effective barrier to air.

Jets of sea water conduct electricity well. A *perfect* spray of fine droplets, because the droplets are separate from each other, will not conduct. In practice, of course, a spray is never perfect, but I have taken part in experiments showing that a fine spray of sea water can approach to 30 inches away from a high-voltage source without the nozzle giving more than a mild tingle to a person holding it with bare, wet hands. It is not for repetition with backyard lash-ups: it is potentially a very dangerous thing to do and the experiments were very carefully controlled, but it demonstrates that in the presence of low-powered electrics it is acceptable as a fire-fighting method.

The conclusion I draw from these last three paragraphs is that a fine spray can be used effectively against any likely fire aboard a yacht. Ideally the spray should be under some pressure: it can be pumped by hand using a galley pump. If enough pressure is obtainable the Jet-Spray hose 'gun' used aboard many boats for washing down decks and paintwork is good. If pressure is low, then a shower fitting is better than nothing. A rose from a watering can is good, but something of a rarity aboard a yacht. Rather than chuck buckets of water over a small fire (which can actually help it spread) I have found that dribbling water from a sponge can be more effective.

How do you use a spray?

The spray's weakest effect is against solid materials. In this case use it to drench the burning items and to keep wet the adjacent area. Even when the flames are out, continue cooling until the surfaces stay wet. If in doubt remove charred matter with a knife or coarse rasp and cool again because it might still be very hot inside.

Galley fires

Of course CO_2 or the fire blanket are best used first. One must also cut off the supply of fuel to the stove. A lot depends on the state of a fat fire. If it is entirely inside a saucepan (and one should endeavour always to use deep cooking utensils in a boat) put a lid on it and cool the pot down. Don't let any water get in the fat or it will spatter explosively. If the fat has spilled and spread, then we have an oil fire.

Electrical fires

There is not really any such thing: electricity provides the initiating heat and flash point and it is other matter that burns. The problem is usually that the electricity goes on supplying a source of great heat, which hinders attempts to extinguish the fire and also constitutes a hazard.

Usually the trigger of the fire is a short-circuit, which may or may not be arcing and therefore may not be easy to see. Try to identify the problem point and cut off the power to it. Smoke can prevent one from being able to see, so this is not always by any means easy. It is possible to use a spray curtain to contain the smoke to some extent, enabling one to see the seat of the fire. Apart from the regenerative potential of a continuing short-circuit, this type of fire usually turns into one of the others. A particular problem is that when plastic electrical insulation burns it gives off poisonous fumes.

Oil fires

If the area of oil that is burning is large, use the fine spray curtain as if one was holding an umbrella against a very strong wind, and slowly sweep the surface of the oil to try to reduce the burning area and to 'gather' the burning part into an ever-decreasing area. Do not leave any burning patches behind; go back and sweep again, slowly. You are both cooling it and reducing the oxygen supply. You will not succeed quickly. Try not to use more water than the fire is evaporating. If the oil is sloshing about in a moving boat this can be helpful because it is assisting cooling somewhat, but it does make containment with the spray more difficult. If there is a lot of oil (and water) in the bilge try to pump it out; ecology comes a poor second just now. The oil, even if hot, is unlikely to cause problems in the pump. It is important to cut off as soon as possible any supply of fresh oil to the fire, so it may be necessary to concentrate on cooling the site where the isolating cocks are before tackling the main blaze, if more oil is actually leaking into it.

Smoke

It is a sad thing that many of the comforts of modern life produce toxic smoke when they burn, for example fabrics, upholstery and mattresses, plastic linings. Others produce carboniferous smoke which is not necessarily poisonous but which stops us breathing. Incomplete combustion can produce Carbon Monoxide which *is* poisonous. Sea water mixed with battery acid gives off chlorine, which is deadly as well as choking.

Some of these toxic gases are lighter than air, and in fire conditions, when they are hot, they can be expected to rise. Under most conditions it pays to approach fires giving off a lot of smoke by keeping as near the deck as possible. Wet cloth over mouth and nostrils will filter particles, but will not stop most toxic gases. It hardly seems worth lumbering up a boat with breathing apparatus, but if necessary, it may be possible to improvise with a diving face mask and some tubing.

Of course all these are easy at a fire-fighting school. The important thing about actual fire-fighting, when every fire is different, is to be aware of the principles, to know the methods (and if possible to have exercised their use) and then to use your intelligence. The tradition of rushing to a fire is a very good one, but on arrival do not go mad and waste your resources. A few seconds to determine the nature of the fire and to plan the battle will be amply repaid.

The point at which you call for outside help depends on what help is available, what means you have to call it, and the relationship of the fire to your resources. If in doubt about your ability to cope and help *is* available, take a moment to call it.

Most port authorities insist on a Fire Brigade being called, because they have an obligation to protect other vessels. They usually have power to tow away a burning ship to a safe berth and similar draconian rights. In these circumstances, i.e. in port, you must summon help, but unless the fire is beyond your control remember you are still in command of the ship.

IN CASE OF FIRE
Call the whole crew.
Get to the fire quickly, but calmly.
Determine the generative centre of the fire.
Assess the dangers of toxic gases and take precautions.
Cut off any outside supply of fuel, or potential fuel.
Select your fire-fighting apparatus.
Attack the generative centre if it can be reached.
If not, determine your route to it.
Keep on until flames are out.
Thoroughly cool the previously burning material.
Check at frequent intervals afterwards that you have not overlooked
  any hot spots that are smouldering.

'The fire is out, God be thanked.'

The Panic Bag

Having advised that a good rigid dinghy is in many respects better than an inflatable liferaft, I have to remind you that the latter does have a survival pack of sorts on board. Therefore if you use a rigid dinghy as a lifeboat, you should have a pack to help you survive. We call ours the panic bag. Some people object to the use of the word panic in this context, saying that it is the last thing one should be aware of in this circumstance, but I disagree. Actually using the word reminds one of the danger of panic, and inhibits its formation.

Ours actually consists of two bags: the First Panic Bag, which is kept in the dinghy on passage, and the Second which is kept reasonably handy for grabbing if there is time. For those with an inflatable liferaft, it might be worth comparing my lists with the contents of the provided survival kit, and making up a bag to contain the difference. (You cannot check the raft's pre-packed supplies: they aren't always as promised.)

Our lists are based on consultation with a survivor friend, and also my own 600 ocean miles in an open boat.

THE FIRST PANIC BAG
4 × 8 pint water in opaque plastic bottles
2 strong drinking cups (Melaware)
4 red flares, 4 orange smoke day markers
Torch, spare bulb, spare batteries
200 multivitamin pills in plastic jar
100 Horlicks tablets
1lb boiled sweets
Swiss Army knife, dinner knife, spoon
Tweezers
Small compass, mirror
Needles and thread
Cotton wool
Small bottle TCP antiseptic
Tube of Aureomycin antibiotic cream
100 tablets Tetracyclin
Tube of sun screen ointment
Seasick pills
Sponge (Bailer is already in dinghy)
2 small hand towels
2 'space blankets'
300ft codline
Fishing line, spoons, hooks
Greek style foul-hooks for fishing
Greek 7-pronged harpoon head (a barbed miniature Poseidon's fork)
Gaff for fishing
Set of small chartlets in a plastic bag
Survival type solar still (RAF surplus type)

THE SECOND PANIC BAG
2 inflatable cushions
2 single blankets
2 wool sweaters
3sq yds 4oz canvas
Some fresh lemons in foil
2 parachute flares
Small funnel
Candles, matches in screw-top jar
Araldite (epoxy glue)

More boiled sweets
4 more pints water
More sunscreen ointment
8 assorted tins of food
Can-opener
2 pairs sunglasses
Bucket

CHAPTER TWELVE

Navigation

'If you don't know where you are going you will probably end up
somewhere else.' — Peter and Hull, *The Peter Principle*

Being a professional Navigator, I cannot help putting in my two
pennyworth on the subject, especially as all those who can row a boat
seem nowadays to set themselves up as experts. Many people I have
talked to who are contemplating the long-cruising life but have so far
cruised only local waters, have expressed nervousness about their
navigation. They should not.

This is not a navigation primer. I intend to add a little to what can
be found in any good book on navigation; and it involves points that
have particular relevance to long-cruising.

Navigation has in common with medicine that the experienced
practitioners have set up an elaborate mystique to defend their monopoly, and frighten off would-be amateur interlopers. In medicine the
process seems to be strengthening itself, but I am glad to say that
among navigators there is now a much healthier attitude. You do not
need a First MB to put a couple of stitches in a cut, and you certainly
do not need a Maths degree to get an astronomical position line.

I am now going to pay homage to a lady, the Blessed Mary Blewitt,
whom I consider the first person to write for the layman about navigation succinctly, sensibly and very well. And for choosing to include in
her book *Navigation for Yachtsmen* an Appendix on compass adjusting,
by another expert, that is a lesson in clarity.

Types of navigator

But to return to the problems of the far-ranging navigator. First decide
what type of navigator you are: there are two broad types, those who
shit when they can see land, and those who shit when they can't. It is
rare to find anyone fitting neither category, and usually such a person
is too unintelligent to recognize danger. There are a few who fit both
categories and usually stay at home.

The first type tends to favour navigational aids that reassure them of
perils comparatively close to; i.e. radar and echo-sounder, while not
bothering much about accuracy when they are over a hundred miles

from the nearest danger. The second type, however, are nervous without frequent fixes, and end up with so many electronic aids that their masts look like Christmas trees.

How Much do you have to Spend?

With navigational equipment (i.e. hardware), decide how much money you wish to dispose of. It is possible to spend a fortune and to be no safer than the fellow with his money still in the bank. I have tried hard to check myself for signs of becoming an entrenched, conservative 'antient Mariner', but still advise the novice to avoid electronics. In the offshore yacht these gadgets largely benefit the trade.

The failure rate of electronics in a yacht is so high that all cruisers should make themselves able to navigate by the old horse-drawn methods before pouring money into the hole marked 'gadgets'. A particular problem with electronic failure is that some equipment gives no indication when it is not working accurately. Some have 'down' indicators for this purpose, but nothing to say when the down indicator is itself down. In remoter parts of the world there are no repair facilities, and it is generally impossible to send things back to the makers: in these circumstances guarantees and warranties are not worth the paper they are written on, nor is the Sale of Goods Act. (When buying something in Britain and being told 'there is a five year guarantee', I reply 'how much discount without the guarantee?' If the dealer will not give one, it implies the guarantee is worthless.)

Radio Direction Finding (DF), with which most home sailors are very familiar, is of little use overseas where radio beacons are sometimes scarce, or even more probably not working properly. In a steel boat DF needs expensive installation to give adequate results, and the ship must be swung, as for a compass, to tabulate relative direction errors.

The only electronics I would wholeheartedly recommend are inside the Seafarer Echo-sounder. It is simple, cheap, robust, and the makers give good service and provide circuit diagrams. Its weak point is the transducer, so fit two. (A third one aft of the screw, to be used when backing in towards a quay, also makes sense.) I also have a transducer in the dinghy, where it is very convenient for sounding out an uncharted anchorage. Even so I carry a complete spare set, wrapped in plastic with silica gel to keep it dry.

Electronic logs are worse than useless. All of them. I tried a considerable number before I had enough sense to realize this. For long passages use a towing log — the Walker Cherub is a bit of fine old-fashioned 'Made in Birmingham' British engineering. The impeller is big enough not to be taken by other than the largest sea monsters. For the measurement of speed I mourn the passing of the Smith's Pitot log, obviously too simple, cheap, effective and reliable to have been kept on the market. A do-it-yourself Pitot log is straight forward to make (see diagram). It will have to be calibrated, but that should present no problem.

Anemometers and wind direction indicators are more reliable than logs, but they are really a bit of an unnecessary luxury. If the wind feels strong then it is as strong as it feels. If it blows the tea out of the cup you should have a reef down, if it blows the cup out of your hand, try two reefs and pray.

Radar can be a blessing, but for most of the time it is dead weight aloft. Fog is not unknown in the more congenial parts of the world: it is common off the Ionian coast, for example. But do not spend money on a radar set without some serious study on how to use it, and for a yacht, get one of the simpler sets with a good pedigree; servicing radar can be a financial nightmare. Decca sets are generally more reliable than those of any other make I have experienced and I hear good reports of the Furuno, but no consistently good reports of any others. Remember that radar uses a lot of power, too much for continuous use while sailing. Do not waste money on sets which advertise low power consumption. Adequate range in bad conditions uses power, and if you are going to rely on radar then do not rely on toys. An internal tuning system is important; if switching on at sea it is no use having to tune the set on a 'target' if none apparently exists, for one would not know if the set were tuned.

Position-fixing systems

Omega, though world-wide, is expensive, not very accurate and needs special charts. Loran C is localized, very good indeed in US coastal waters, less good in the Caribbean; it is quite good in parts of the Med, but it becomes unreliable to a dangerous degree, while still giving the appearance of accuracy, in some of the contiguous waters. Satnav under the present (1986) system is not nearly up to the extravagant claims of those smooth salesmen at boat shows. I recall an occasion when two yachts were discussing their differing satnav positions in an anchorage in the reefs. As it was near noon two equal altitudes established that neither was right. Such is the faith of humans in machines on which they have unwisely spent a lot of money, that they were unbelieving and had to be convinced by a later star sight. But note that the two sets of the same make differed by about three-quarters of a mile. In its presentation of position and in its dead reckoning, Satnav is also a prime example of the danger of spurious accuracy in navigation, which I will refer to again. Decca is no use in the areas under discussion, and Consol no longer enters the picture.

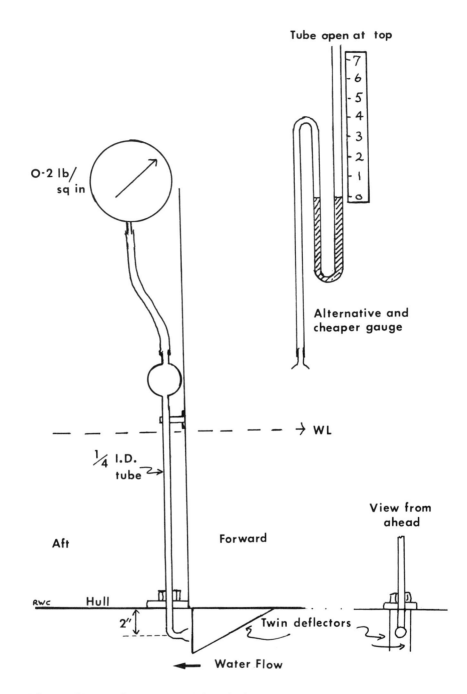

A log working on the Pitot principle, which one can make. A ¼″ ID metal tube extends 2″ below the hull, and has an expansion chamber and pressure gauge above the waterline. The detail sketch shows the twin weed deflectors in relation to the tube opening.

The Broader Aspects

A problem for the long-cruise navigator is that many of the techniques he will, or ought to, use are not those dealt with in most courses in Britain or the USA. In Britain the chief aim of most courses is to fit the student for the Yachtmaster's Certificate in one or other of its forms. These naturally have a home waters emphasis, and this applies to some extent to the Offshore syllabus too. There are problems associated with waters that are inadequately surveyed, ill-provided with marks and lights, with meagre tidal data, and where the expected, conventional and prudent arrangements for keeping up to date are not available. I regret to say that although the Hydrographer of the Navy is beginning to consider the requirements of his yachting customers (who in some parts of the globe constitute the majority of users), this consideration applies so far only to home waters; he is still publishing new charts of overseas areas that are, from a small craft point of view, very much worse than the old ones. For example BA1703 (Majorca and Minorca) is a poor job compared with 1317 which it replaced, and not only because the scale was reduced from 193,000 to 300,000. The whole field of books of navigational data is an ergonomic nightmare: it was never planned, it just grew piecemeal, and is badly in need of a complete review. The trouble is that the professionals are so familiar with the present chaos that they will resist change.

Navigational Publications

It is very necessary to do a lot of planning before leaving home waters, because charts and other works are not readily available or are very much higher priced overseas. I do not infer that you have to stick to an itinerary; it is possible to cover a lot of variations in one's planning, and this is desirable because one does not get to know a lot of the good things about an area until you get there.

It might be thought than Britain and the USA, which are the only countries maintaining effective world coverage of navigational data and both have advanced business outlooks, would have devised an effective marketing and/or distribution system for their wares. Brilliant surveyors these gentlemen are, businessmen they evidently are not, though that does have some advantages. It is virtually impossible to buy US Defence Mapping Agency or National Oceanographic and Atmospheric Administration charts or publications outside the USA, and even there the ordering system (computerised, of course) is so ludicrous that it should be turned into a party game.

The typical DMA chart gives the appearance of having been drawn by a long-sighted computer that has forgotten its reading glasses. It uses bottom contours extensively and, for example on the Bahamas Banks, shows large blank areas between shallow contours when the variations in the bottom between these limits are many, various and of the highest value to small craft. That this type of inshore data is not without military value was demonstrated in the Falkland Islands.

British charts and publications have a slightly better availability, but suffer from a random system of numbering that leads to mistakes when ordering large numbers of charts. Even at major stock-holding agents it is possible to find charts out of stock far too frequently, and some neighboring agents have a friendly and sensible reciprocal arrangement to help out customers when the Hydrographic Department have let them down. The charts themselves vary from work-of-art standard to virtually useless outline diagrams, but though the basic surveys are sometimes very old, I find that British charts, on the day of purchase, are more up-to-date than American ones.

Sadly, Admiralty charts are published in a hodge-podge of metric and natural units. (Each individual chart is consistent within itself.) To be totally metric, or totally natural would be quite indifferent to me, but the present confusion is irritating and dangerous. The interim changeover period has gone on far too long. The whole unnecessary exercise must have been a major cause of the quite indecent rise in the price of British charts, which are now among the most expensive. Though there are individual bad ones in the Admiralty catalogue, as a general collection of small-craft charts they are a lot better than any others. They have the advantage of being printed on strong paper, but why are they not printed on both sides to save both cost and storage space? Quite a good feature of British charts is that they are almost entirely of a standard and very convenient size.

In certain areas it pays to buy locally produced large-scale charts of the coastal waters, and this is a policy approved by the Hydrographer. Some countries have very good hydrographic services. I have found Turkish and French charts clear, reliable and easy to use. Italian charts are more confused and their boundaries are not well planned. Greek charts, though otherwise quite good, suffer from an inability to convey information to foreigners due to their alphabet and the oddities of the language. Unfortunately British charts transliterate Greek grammatical constructions (particularly the genitive case in its three genders) and thus proliferate the confusion of Greek place names.

The law, and other considerations

Notice to Mariners no. 18 of each year lists those publications that all British registered ships over 12 metres in length *are obliged to carry*. These requirements would astonish many yachtsmen, as well as leading to the serious overloading of a typical yacht of 12 metres overall. Common sense has to prevail. I have used the International Code of Signals (one of the obligatory volumes, and a large one too) on only one occasion in the last ten years, and that was to find an appropriate flag hoist for Christmas Day in Bequia. (We hoisted MOX meaning 'a child has been born' and about 150 other craft had to ask us what it meant.) Merchant shipping notices are not really appropriate to a cruising yacht, and the Mariner's Handbook is something to read before going, unless you plan to navigate in ice. It is a fairly slim volume at least.

The Nautical Almanac and Navigation Tables are essential, even if you prefer milliamps and computers for everyday use. The Lists of Radio Signals are very bulky and mostly irrelevant to a yacht, particularly those with no radio transmitter. Too often the details of radio-beacons are out of date on publication even if Her Majesty's Sationery Office is not on strike, and the whole publication lags behind commercial almanacs such as Reed's. Lists of Lights, tide tables and atlases are necessary, but again the commercial publications are better where the coverage is available.

Charts carried must be of appropriate scale to identify hazards and marks and they must be up to date, which leads to the next requirement. Notices to Mariners must be carried. This is an example of a regulation drafted by well-meaning blue-suited gentlemen in comfortable offices in London. Just try getting Notices to Mariners in the Bongo Bongo Archipelago. Better still, just try getting them anywhere: I called in at Potters in London and found only a meagre selection. Notice to Mariners no. 14 in each year (if you can get it: I succeed one year in three) has a list of places where Notices may be consulted, and I nominate this list for the Trask prize for romantic fiction. I have made a particular point over the years of visiting these places when in the vicinity, and in the vast majority no Notices were available. Even when they were one was not permitted to take away a copy, and you cannot correct charts on your knees while seated in a windy Consulate hallway. The fact is that Consuls do not give a damn. The volumes are so heavy that having them sent airmail is out of the question, and seamail never catches up with a cruising yacht. The whole system of chart correction, based on the facilities of a world-wide empire and on a plenitude of labour which no longer exist, is badly in need of redesign.

Correcting an outfit of charts is a big job. Warships carry a specially trained rating to do this, which with 500 charts is a full-time occupation. Something has to give in a yacht with a crew of two, and having fallen behind when I had only some 200 charts I never managed to catch up, so I gave up. Here is how I try to keep as up to date as I can, in the special circumstances of our cruising life. It is not ideal, it is merely a practical partial solution to an otherwise insoluble problem.

First, I make the reasonable assumption that only a small proportion of Notices affect a yacht. Whenever I return to England or Gibraltar I get every Notice I can, and throw away those sections that do not deal with areas in which I navigate. I then cut out those Notices that might affect a yacht, ignoring for example the instruction to insert a sounding of 250 metres somewhere, and divide these into batches according

Laurel

to which Admiralty Pilot is involved. When on board I pencil in the Pilot, on the appropriate page, either a precis of the chart correction or a reference. I can then throw away a lot more paper. I never use a chart for pilotage (i.e. for coastal navigation) without also using the Pilot book *with its latest Supplement*. Taking care, and keeping fully aware of the limitations of the system, I think it is the best way of coping with a large folio of charts in a small yacht. The Admiralty Pilots (Sailing Directions, to give them their proper title) are a very good investment.

They are in the process of changing size, which I do not like, but one must give credit for the fact that the newer editions are much better written and do contain a lot of matter relevant to small craft. I have no doubt that they would contain even more if the Hydrographer were to be informed of points of interest.

I would also counsel carrying the List of Lights. This can be a great help, though a penance to correct.

A significant entry for the electronically minded is that all operating and maintenance manuals for any Navaid carried must be on board. Try getting a proper maintenance manual from some of the cowboy manufacturers about in the industry.

Chart agents

Buying charts abroad, as already mentioned, is fraught with difficulties. Notice no. 2 in each year, as well as the catalogue, gives a full list of agents and is again a bit of a humourless frolic. Most of these agents have only a very few local charts in stock, mostly aged and dog-eared, uncorrected, and at outrageous prices. (The record price so far was £11.55 in 1981.) It is little wonder so many yachts are navigating on photocopies of other people's charts. This is unavoidable, being preferable to going chartless; I have done it and I hated it.

The Admiralty Chart Depot at Gibraltar has now closed, but a good selection of charts is available there from commercial sources.

The commercial department of the Admiralty needs to get itself into the twentieth century, before the twenty-first overtakes it.

The best source of British charts in the Med is from Cdr Mike Healy, 10 Rue Jean Bracco, 06310 Beaulieu-sur-Mer. He also stocks a large range of English Language nautical books including this one (I hope).

Pilotage

Now a little on coastal navigation, particularly in poorly charted waters. It is big-ship practice to try to fix the ship at least every twenty minutes when inshore, and more often than that if going fast. In a yacht one does not change position enough to make such a frequency appropriate except in conditions of very strong tides or when very close to the shore, where even so a different method of navigating is desirable.

It is unfortunate that on many ill-charted or ill-marked coasts there exist offshore dangers that are also unmarked, so that although fixing may not be practical, one cannot relax attention. In any case there may not be sufficient identifiable marks on which to fix. Even if you have Loran C or Satnav, the inaccuracy of the system, coupled with possible geographic errors in an old survey, would make reliance on such a method foolhardy.

Clearing bearings

The best way of sailing such waters is to keep a network of clearing bearings. I write them on a blackboard by the compass, and though my mate will lean against it I can usually make them out if I cannot remember them. Using clearing bearings, one may not always know where one is but one does know very well where one is not.

A clearing bearing is a compass bearing of a fixed object such that, provided you stay to the appropriate side of that bearing, you cannot strike a danger situated closer to you than the fixed object (see diagram). Some of my charts are inked in with clearing bearings ready for use. They are also marked with transits (objects in line with each other, called 'ranges' by our American cousins) which are very useful for giving a position line proof against any compass error, and also for checking the compass (which should be done frequently, if possible once a day at least). It is far too easy in the relaxed atmosphere of a cruising yacht's cockpit for someone to leave something magnetic close to the compass.

Navigating by clearing bearings is particularly appropriate to short-handed sailing, when it is difficult to leave the cockpit to do detailed chartwork.

In a steel craft a handbearing compass is useless because it cannot be compensated properly. It is best to get a main compass with a bearing sight, such as the Sestrel Moore, and mount it so that one has all-round vision across it. Alternatives are to have a transmitting compass away from the ship's magnetism, perhaps up the mast, with

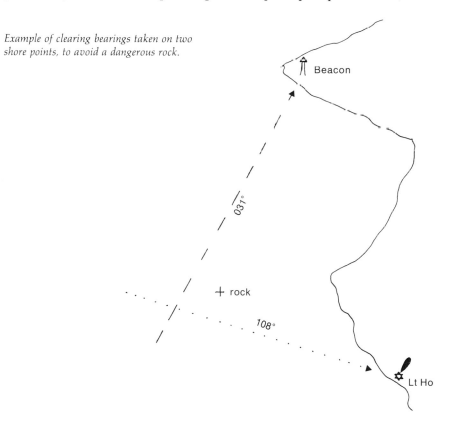

Example of clearing bearings taken on two shore points, to avoid a dangerous rock.

Beacon

031°

+ rock

108°

Lt Ho

convenient repeaters for steering and taking bearings; or to use mounted alidades which take relative bearings, which can be related to the ship's head at the moment of sighting (and not to the course) to give the compass bearing of the object.

True bearings

Note that most charts and pilot books give bearings in their true form, and these must be converted to magnetic and compass form by corrections of variation and deviation. This system has grown because variation due to the earth's magnetism varies from year to year, and because each vessel has to correct for its own deviation anyway; most navigators like to do both corrections together as a sort of ritual. Did you know that the earth is overdue for a complete reversal of polarity: the North magnetic pole will move to the southern hemisphere, and vice versa, and that the move will be comparatively sudden? A mere hundred years or so? It does not look as if it has started yet, so this little snippet is for amusement only.

An exception to the rule about true bearings occurs on charts in Imray, Laurie, Norie & Wilson's West Indies series, edited by that arch-eccentric liveaboard Don Street, who is probably the only man living as opinionated as I am. Don gives all his bearings in magnetic (not compass) form — we argued about this for quite a time, but I was unable to get him to see sense. In spite of this, these charts are very good for yachting use and probably the best in many areas.

A few more words on the reliability of charts, which should never be assumed to have oracular authority and which are not claimed by their most devoted surveyors to be more than aids to navigation. Look at the date of survey in the legend (title), or on newer charts the data source diagram. This will give some idea of the methods of survey used, and in the older charts the number of soundings printed will give some idea of the comprehensiveness of the survey. As the British Hydrographer is also moving towards (less useful) bottom contours, this indicator is no longer valid for new editions. In very old surveys, which were often made under very hard conditions, straits and channels were usually surveyed one side at a time, and the correspondence between the two sides may not always be exact: it is better to fix using marks from one side or the other, but not both, if it can be avoided.

Outward Bound

Now let us go deep-sea, that is out of the danger of hitting land. There is an old saying, 'Outward bound, don't run aground'. This means that if you are going to be at sea on a 20 day passage it is not worth cutting across a dangerous sandbank when leaving harbour, just to save ten minutes. But people do it! A yacht inside us at Ramsgate got us up at 0400 in order to sail for the Caribbean. When we sailed on a similar voyage four hours later we found him stuck on a sandbank just off the pierhead, and though tempted did not have the heart to leave him there.

Sights

Forget about star sights. The only star sights I have taken since retiring have been for amusement or practice, or in order to fix the geographical position of somewhere when I suspect the chart to be in error. (It very seldom is.) To cross the ocean in a sailing craft at an average speed of 5 knots, the sun will suffice. The moon can be useful but is by no means essential.

Do not worry about the theory of astronomy unless you wish to get pleasure from knowing more than the minimum required. Sunsights can be taken entirely by rule of thumb and my form (see Appendix).

It is desirable to take a morning sight, a noon meridian passage and an afternoon sight in each day. The times will vary according to how high the sun is when it crosses the meridian (your north-south line), but in general one does not want to take the sun when it is too low down, say below 30° from the horizon, because of refraction errors in the atmosphere which cannot be predicted with complete reliability; nor when its altitude is very high, for then it becomes difficult to bring the sun down to the horizon, and to get it to sit comfortably right beneath itself, especially if the ship is rolling. This problem has to be faced at the meridian passage, when the sun is at its height, but there is no need to look for trouble. The compass bearings (azimuths) of the sun at the morning and afternoon sights should ideally be 60° or more from the meridian, but do not worry if cloud or breakfast hold you up. Perfectly good results are obtainable with angles down to about 30°. Likewise, do not fret if you take too long over your afternoon inspection of the inner surface of your eyelids. Even if the sun does get a bit low, it is still observable; though the position line should be treated with a little caution, it is still worth having.

Strictly speaking it is not necessary to take sights as often as this in good weather at the start of a voyage, but it does become important towards the end when making a landfall, when conscientious daily sight-taking will have you so expert and confident that you stand a good chance of making the right harbour without getting emotional and having to swear at your wife.

Spurious accuracy

There is such a thing as excessive, unnecessary or spurious accuracy. A sextant reading to a tenth of a minute of arc is overkill when used with the Air Navigation Tables (AP 3270), even supposing one has the manual skill to get that accuracy from a sight of a body at high altitudes from a small boat in a seaway. The Ebbco plastic sextant, the better quality version for preference, is quite adequate aboard a yacht.

Nevertheless, do not get too careless. Even most pros take three or more shots for each sight and check that the differences of both altitude and time are consistent. A convenient way of doing this is to set the sextant for fixed intervals of either 3 minutes of arc or 4, and then to record the times as the sun kisses the horizon. With equal intervals of altitude, it is easy to check that the intervals of time are about right. You would be very skilled indeed if the intervals, or differences, were all exactly right; such fine accuracy is virtually unobtainable.

However, accuracy over time is important. Near the Equator 4 seconds of time can mean about 1 nautical mile when translated into a position line. But a chronometer is hardly required any more. Even quite cheap quartz watches will maintain sufficient accuracy for a 30 day passage, and with a shortwave radio receiver one can get frequent time checks. (I would not be without means of getting the BBC Overseas Service news from time to time: just think of arriving at Grenada in the middle of an invasion by gung-ho US Marines).

When plotting a sunsight it is not normally satisfactory to use an ocean chart for the scale is too small; it is likely the whole day's run will fit into an inch or so. Navigation textbooks say that one should use a plotting sheet, which has a compass rose in the centre and a latitude scale without any numbers on it. After inserting degrees of latitude to choice, one is then faced with constructing a longitude scale because this will vary with latitude.

Well, all this is good to keep idle navigators busy. I find it simpler to use a large-scale chart of the same latitude as I am in, but for a different part of the world. I then have only to change the numbers on the longitude scale to suit my position and I can do my plotting on that, later transferring the position to the ocean chart. In fact it is hard to make an error as one is keeping a daily check on progress, and on transferring the position any boob would be immediately apparent. One has to get used to the idea of plotting a position line in the middle of a desert, but the idea rather amuses me. Navigation schools and shore-bound experts may scream with dismay, but I have used this method for thousands of sights for over 35 years without mishap.

Even in sight of land the sextant can be a lot of use if you are familiar and easy in its use. I use mine for vertical danger angles or for obtaining the ranges of mountains using Lecky's Tables. It is a very fast method and much less trouble than switching on radar, but the tables are virtually unique and out of print.

In bad weather, when maybe you or the crew are feeling unwell, take especial care. One French destroyer I served in had notices plastered round the ship saying *Valeur et Discipline*. Whether such notices achieve anything depends, I suppose, on those to whom they are addressed, but if you are the sort that responds to exhortation then stick them up. If you are not sure of your position, then, however miserable you may feel, DO NOT PUT THE SHIP ON A COURSE THAT COULD BE DANGEROUS, as you would be that much less able to cope with an emergency should one arise. Even if it means standing off in acute discomfort, that is better than the Shipwrecked Mariners' Hostel, supposing one exists. Do not cry for help because you are miserable — get out to sea where you will be safe as long as the ship remains seaworthy.

If you get Lost

This is particularly relevant to making a landfall, and is a branch of navigation that is insufficiently treated in textbooks, perhaps because professionals either do not get lost so do not know how to cope, or more likely do not wish their fellows to know that they have been lost. Well, there have been several occasions when I have not known where I was, so here goes.

First, remember that if any navigator happens to be exactly where he thinks he is, it is purely accidental. This is true. Navigation is not an exact science, it is a craft in which judgement plays a very important part. All systems and aids contain the possibility of errors and all human beings make them. What makes one a professional is being aware of the possible or likely errors in the method he uses, and subconsciously being completely aware of the degree of reliability of his position. In theory, this is complex mathematics, but there are plenty of practical wrinkles. It is impossible to give complete, generalized counsel as to what to do in any or all cases of being lost — there are too many variables. One thing to do before getting into this mess is to keep charts and pilot books up to date; that can make it a lot easier to get out of it.

If you are clearly well offshore you do not have an urgent problem. You have a problem, it is true, but it is too early to start worrying. Provided weather conditions are reasonable and the shore is not a lee to a very strong wind, approach it. The problem may even solve itself. I will not discuss nighttime. My advice with a doubtful position close to land by night or in bad visibility is to b***** off out to sea and wait until conditions improve.

If, having raised the shore, you cannot identify any feature or find your chosen haven, then you have a problem. If it is a question of visibility, wait and stand off. But if the weather is fair, and if the coast is not a dead lee with known or suspected offlying unmarked dangers, then approach it cautiously at an angle. I, personally, would go down-wind in such a situation, but know of competent friends who would do the opposite. It may be something to do with whether you describe a bottle as half full or half empty: I always believe things will improve.

One good reason I have for approaching downwind is that if one does come across a danger one has more scope for hauling clear very quickly. To do so going upwind puts limits on one's manoeuvrability without tacking, which is not always the work of a minute when shorthanded. Another reason is that one changes one's position faster. If landmarks are not distinguishable in one place, then get somewhere else as soon as reasonably possible. Still another reason is that the motion will be less, making observation and chartwork easier.

Where aren't you?

In this process there is the advisability of changing one's outlook. You do not know where you are, but there are plenty of places where you know you are not. Start eliminating: huge areas go at once. The length of time since your last known position should give you a radius of possibility, and even if you had lost your compass, for example, I am sure you would have been able to have found an approximate direction. It is probable that the unknown area that you occupy is less than 100 miles along the coast; it is almost certainly less than 200.

Inspect all the relevant large-scale charts and the pilot books for any features in this sort of distance. There may be reference to a chimney or radio mast. Unless you are very unlucky and they have just been demolished, you can cross off those bits of coast within their visibility distance. And so on. Things will narrow down. Is part of the coast hilly, or swampy with offlying banks? Are there soundings? Are there ships in sight? Are they on courses that might converge at a point? If so, they are almost certainly going to or from a port; that is a position line of sorts, and I once found Colombo that way, though this is the first time I have ever confessed it.

Don't forget the simple things

Is there a river estuary? This often brings discoloured water as well as a lot of floating rubbish. (If approaching Italy you will see many floating plastic bags, and you can recover a few to see the address of the shops printed on them; known in the trade as 'bag of buns navigation'.)

This problem does not always follow ocean crossings. We once headed for Majorca after being hove-to for a time. Approaching at right angles to a coast with many similar features is almost as bad as approaching a coast without any at all. This was a virtual cliff of high-rise buildings. After studying the chart, 'I think we're either off Cape X or Cape Y', I called up to Laurel, who was on watch. 'It's Cape X,' she said, looking through binoculars. 'How . . .?' 'Well, that hotel with the red balconies is the Cape X Hotel. There's a sign that says so.'

I once drifted in the little yacht *Phoenix* which had no engine, for two full days in the Malta Channel, completely blanketed by thick fog.

At the end of this I had only a vague idea where I was, but as the fog began to clear one evening I saw over the horizon the signs of fireworks. Someone had given me a Roman Catholic calender which had the Saints' Days on it. It took only a moment to identify which parish church was busy beating the hell out of the Devil, and then I had quite a reasonable position line.

Once at night well off a coast I saw what appeared to be the loom of a lighthouse where none should be. (The loom of a light is the beam in the sky when the light itself is out of sight below the horizon.) It was oddly irregular. In fact it was a busy main road with a sharp rising bend and the beams were the headlights of cars going round it. Jokes about navigating by road maps are out of place: not all valuable information is published by the Hydrographer. For another example: nautical charts do not show the flight paths of aircraft. With a low fog it is very useful to be able to pinpoint where aircraft turn for a final approach; this is helpful off the mouths of the Tiber, near Fiumicino Airport, among many other places.

Ferry timetables can be of value. Apart from being a rare potential fixing aid, the ABC shipping guide helps one to avoid these tracks, for ferries are notorious for being inconsiderately driven.

Hydrographers Again

Another word or two about the Hydrographer in charge of BA charts. I am very critical of the organization, occasionally of the design or printing of charts, but the standard of surveying is generally excellent and has been so, given the instruments available, for a very long time. There are very few serious errors on charts, and I am very sceptical when I hear someone say (and it happens quite frequently) that they ran aground because the chart was wrong. Mostly they were not where they thought they were. But things do change, and at an alarmingly increasing rate, while the Hydrographer cannot keep survey ships up every little by-water. If you do come across a change, or an error which you are sure *is* an error, then drop a line to the Hydrographer. It is called an H note, and a blank form is found at the back of all Supplements to Admiralty Pilot Books. This form should be used if you can, for it is a reminder of the background details that H would like to know. You may be a novice, but if you are off the beaten track you may be the first to report something that may save a ship; you are keeping up the standard of charting and helping to keep down costs.

Remember that navigating is not a mystery any more. There are many techniques that will come with experience, but the cautious novice, exercising common sense and using intelligently the little knowledge he already has, will get by and gently learn more. It is an old axiom that there are old navigators and bold navigators, but no old and bold navigators. PRUDENCE is the word.

267

CHAPTER THIRTEEN

Social Life and Entertainment

'. . . then all the rest may do what they will til midnight.'

Entertainment might seem an odd subject for those to whom sailing itself is an entertainment, but when the navigation of a vessel from one place to another is the prime motive, some forms of diversion are needed.

Reading is the most obvious. People used to books cannot easily manage without. There are no libraries available to the wanderer, so one has to have reference volumes to taste. Most yachts carry a paperback library comprised of those loved books which one keeps to read over and over again, and also those less loved books that are enjoyable once and are then swapped with other yachts for similar works.

Swapping paperbacks is a continuing process. It is sad that British and American paperback publishers now use a form of unsewn binding that falls apart before long. To bind reference books in this way is little short of fraud, and they are certainly unfit for the purpose for which they are sold. Many yachting centres have secondhand bookshops, where your nearly new paperbacks may be swapped for a fee.

If you are going where books in English are unobtainable or very expensive, it may be worth sending for the *Good Book Guide* (address in Appendix). This very well produced independent magazine comes out seven times a year, and not only gives excellent reviews of new books but will send you any book on their current list for the UK published price plus the postage, by airmail if you wish. There is no obligation to buy any book at all. If it is not on their list, they will get any book in print for a 50p surcharge: this can solve problems both with education and birthday presents, also gifts back home. You would need a good postal 'drop' however; Poste Restante would not be reliable enough.

Apart from reading, games are played rather more by the typical yottie than by his land-dwelling friends. A lot of chess is played. Some, including myself, indulge themselves with a chess computer, but it is not the same thing as playing with real live people. One soon learns the weaknesses of the programme, and finds after a time that one is not so much playing chess as outwitting a computer program.

One is drawn willy-nilly to a move sequence that one knows the computer cannot cope with, and it goes on failing because it is a totally obedient moron and will never learn. Real people spring surprises, and then one learns oneself.

Draughts (or checkers) and backgammon (or tavla) are played a lot. We are occasionally asked to play bridge, but as we do not play we are unaware of the extent to which it is enjoyed. I think not much, but then I always thought of it as a game for the residents of detached houses in Surrey.

A very popular game is Scrabble. There are certain difficulties playing it with Americans owing to their inability to spell. We solved the problem by using the *Shorter Oxford Dictionary* when aboard *Fare Well*, and Webster's when in their boat, but they had the worst of it because Webster's is kind enough to have both American and English spellings.

The Royal Cruising Club has a song book, and at a suitable time aboard their boats the skipper may hand them round like hymn books so that the anchorage resounds with song. The accompanying instrument for sailors' songs has traditionally been portable and easily stowed; a pipe, concertina or harmonica. Later a fiddle came in. Then, of all things, the yacht piano, which solved the ballast problem I suppose. Now we have electronic keyboards (where will it end?) and guitars. The traditional Spanish guitar, of thin wood put together with non-waterproof glue, has minimal aptitude for life in a yacht, but innumerable boats have one, occupying a lot of valuable space. We have the obligatory guitar. Someone should invent one, the inside of which can be used as a locker. Not content with the guitar, Laurel bought a dulcimer kit in the US and amused herself building it while coming back over the Atlantic. I hold my breath every time we see a double bass.

Hobbies

Sailors of old did not have a lot of spare time, but they had various diversions including decorative knotting (macramé), knitting, scrimshaw and some woodcarving. These are all enjoyable pastimes today, though real whales' teeth are getting as scarce as hens'. They all have the virtue of taking up little space, and when well done the products can be sold.

The problem is that many well practised shoreside hobbies do not translate to the sea-going life. Collecting is difficult because of space and the importance of protecting vulnerable and valuable items from sea damage. Postage stamps and books, for example. I have not heard of anyone actually having a model railway in a yacht, but I expect one exists somewhere. I sometimes wish I had an old-fashioned Meccano set.

If you have a skill, even a small area can make a workshop.

Almost any art or craft except possibly stained glass, fresco painting, mosaic and monumental masonry can be practised, and cloth crafts are particularly appropriate. Laurel once did a lot of patchwork; she says it is an occupation which can be done in any corner at any time and is easy to put down or take up. Let your imagination run along those lines and do as you will. Take any special tools with you, and spares too for they are sometimes unavailable or hard to trace.

One of the chief entertainments while cruising is the social life, meeting and getting to know other yotties or passers-by. One sometimes does not have a lot in common with the people in the next boat, except the sea and common experiences, but one can learn a lot from others.

When on board on our own the radio is valuable. It is wise to keep some track of world events; you do not want to arrive somewhere in the middle of a coup d'etat. The BBC World Service has a lot of news broadcasts, but its news seems to be mainly political in nature and it is always bleating away about the Third World as if the other two do not matter. Its entertainment is not so hot, but this is not its prime function.

The broadcast frequencies for any area vary during the day, and also from month to month as they have trouble from sunspots or human interference. A magazine *London Calling* is published which gives a lot of programme information, and there is a monthly sheet listing frequencies in use. Both these can be got from the BBC World Service, Bush House, Strand, London WC 1.

Other shortwave radio reception varies with locality and time, except for Moscow and Albania who always get through loud and clear with news about the workers' paradises.

Local national and provincial radio is heavily dependent on taste. In the West Indies one gets reggae morning, noon and night. In Europe all countries have an approximate equivalent to the BBC Home Services, and most countries have a programme with cultural leanings. France Musique is excellent, and has the great asset that its announcers have almost perfect diction which is a great help in learning the language. (How foreigners get on trying to learn English from the BBC I cannot imagine.)

Turkey and Greece both have cultural and music Third Programmes. The Greek one *was* excellent, but its former director is apparently out of favour politically. Now the service is only obtainable near Athens and is musically much less interesting, seeming to consist of interminable readings of avant-garde poetry. The Turkish programme put out a lot of trad jazz when I last heard it.

Radio in Italy is chaos. Everyone seems to start their own station, mostly to broadcast rock music and advertisements, and they are so unregulated that frequencies overlap. Some transmitters are so poorly modulated that the marine distress frequencies are affected, but no-one bothers. Near Rome there is Canale 5 which has non-stop classical music all day, and is very good when not subject to interference.

In the US the radio situation is a pale copy of the Italian; much the same in principle, but with some order superimposed, though not much is apparent to the outsider. For those with mental pretensions above the moronic there is Public Radio, which we thought good in quality and not only because they sometimes use BBC material.

A radio set worth looking at for carrying in a yacht is the Sony 2001. It covers FM, and both AM and SSB from 150 to 30,000kHz; it is compact, has push-button tuning and can be easily adapted to work off 12 volts DC.

We carry a JVC multi-system miniature television set, which works everywhere except France. I like to pretend it is for watching weather forecasts, which are often more easily absorbed if one can see a synoptic chart. The weather presentation on Italian RAI Uno is excellent: not only do the cameras focus on the charts instead of the face of the forecaster as is normal elsewhere, but the charts are well selected and well drawn. Often one has a moving sequence of satellite pictures, a 500mb chart, and both the latest actual synoptic chart and one as they expect to develop. Very, very good.

But television is also an effective language teacher. By watching children's programmes one gets talk in a simple vocabulary with simple grammar, usually spoken slowly and clearly. Advertisements can be in simple language, and repeat phrases over and over again, with pictures. This can be a great help.

There is not much entertainment from television abroad. One finds

271

an occasional piece of excellence that is relevant to us, the foreigners, but not often.

Yacht Clubs

Talk of social life leads us to consider clubs and associations of interest to the long-cruising yachtsman. There is a tendency not to belong to clubs. We are thus exceptions, though we question just what benefit we get from some. Loyalty dies hard.

We have to consider this mainly from a British point of view, as we know less about other countries' clubs than citizens of those countries. It is likely that the generalities we make about British clubs will apply to all.

Clubs (other than local ones) which set out to, or actually do, help the cruising yottie are:

The Royal Cruising Club, the most senior of them all. Its membership is limited in number, but that does not mean it is snobbish. Most of the members we have met have been good and friendly cruising people.

The Cruising Association. After being nearly asleep for some time it is now much more active. It has an excellent clubhouse in St Katherine's Dock, London with a lot of charts and information for consultation by those planning a voyage. We meet quite a lot of members.

The Little Ship Club has also been kissed by Prince Charming and is now wide awake, and extending its influence. For the long-cruiser it possesses the asset of having premises with comparatively cheap bunks right in the centre of London. When one has sold up, a base can come in handy.

The Royal Naval Sailing Association is a very active club (it organises the Whitbread Race for example), and has a fantastic spread of Hon Local Officers world-wide, almost all of whom are superior in every respect to those attached to imitating clubs. Though supposedly for serving or retired Navy, Reserves, and those associated with the Navy, these qualifications are so loose that virtually anyone can join, except servicemen's families.

The Ocean Cruising Club is a classless, and somewhat international club for those cruising the oceans. Qualification is a port-to-port voyage exceeding 1000 miles in a small yacht. It is run by people more interested in sailing than administration, which is good from some points of view and bad from others. At present it is overcoming a financial and administrative crisis. It does disseminate a lot of valuable information through its magazine, and constitutes the second largest batch of members that we meet in harbour and on the high seas.

The Seven Seas Cruising Association is run from the USA and is specifically for live-aboards. All members are Commodores and we find the sensation that all are chiefs without there being any indians rather eccentric. One ceases to be eligible if one moves ashore, even for short periods, and that is a good idea. The membership qualification is loose, so that one finds a high proportion of live-aboards are house-boat dwellers on the US east coast waterways. A very friendly lot.

It isn't all balmy breezes in the Med. Here in Ibiza a bad squall has an American and a South African yacht in trouble. Everyone turns out to help.

We were once in favour of a club for European live-aboards, but were nervous of initiating anything that would either fail because all the membership were so busy sailing that there was no administration, or alternatively it would, like so many clubs, end up by administering itself into the position of taking in its own expensive washing, thus achieving nothing at great expense.

I would still favour an association of live-aboards, but on the following basis: (A No-club club)

There are only three rules:

1. It shall be called the International Live-aboard Club, and anyone who lives aboard a cruising yacht outside the waters of his own country is eligible for membership.

2. The membership flag shall be flag F (for friendship) of the international code. There shall be no subscription, no flag officers, no regular general meetings, and no bullshit.

3. Any member encountering another member flying the flag shall extend aid and hospitality within reason, and that shall be the only contact between members.

Rule 3 is almost always observed by live-aboard yachtsmen anyway.

For many years I was a personal member of the Royal Yachting Association, but lately I got very disenchanted, especially when I discovered that many of their policies are actually detrimental to the interests of the long-term cruiser. The Secretary General told me that long-distance cruisers are a minority, but so are ocean racers, olympic helmsmen, and indeed most types of sailors when you classify them. I find that most long-term cruisers do not feel quite so strongly as I do about the RYA, possibly because they have not involved themselves. But general opinion is that the RYA has no relevance if you are out of British waters.

Magazines

No yachting publication specializes in matters of interest to long-cruising folk, though various journals have periods of temporary enthusiasm. The American *Cruising World* is probably the most consistent, but suffers a little from feminism. It is well produced, and is probably the nearest to a truly international yachting magazine. British magazines are generally inward looking (the charge of parochialism is again in mind) but there are some brilliant contributions from time to time.

The main problem with magazines is getting them. With their weight of advertising they cost the earth to post, and are little found in bookstalls overseas, even in established yachting centres.

Amateur Radio

Many liveaboards are radio amateurs or 'Hams'. There are regular 'nets' or times during which enthusiasts get in touch with one another. I will list these below as they are at the moment of writing, but they do change. Apart from the nets, it is possible in some countries to 'patch in' to the telephone network (officially) and call the folks back home (but not in Britain).

A problem lies in the nature and origins of amateur, non-VHF radio. Nowadays some countries actually like their people to use radio and get an interest in modern subjects like electronics. Grandma Britain, however, believes it will rot our teeth or send us blind, and it is made as difficult and expensive as possible to get examined for a license and stay legal, especially if one is a traveller or out of the country for some time each year.

This is a pity, for it is an ideal pastime for the cruising yottie. I asked the RYA to suggest to the licensing authority that there should be a special simplified, limited qualification for cruising yachtsmen to allow them to use only the established 'maritime mobile nets' and only when outside territorial waters. They were not interested, even though it would clearly be a major and inexpensive contribution to ocean sailing safety.

The inevitable outcome is that many yotties broadcast while unlicensed. They are deemed radio pirates and are liable to prosecution if caught, but with a modicum of prudence and cunning there is little likelihood of that. Licensed amateurs are prohibited from communicating with the 'pirates', but in practice have a hard job checking all of them because many pirates 'borrow' real call signs from someone of the same name.

If you are interested in this activity, and it can be fascinating, then it is much better to be licensed, but do try to get your license while still living ashore. Most places in Britain have amateur radio clubs whose members are usually delighted to help, and there are sometimes courses at evening classes.

Amateur Radio Nets of Interest to the Yachtsman

Believed to be correct at time of writing, but note that all nets change from time to time as frequencies come in or out of use.

GMT	Frequency	Description
0230	14,313	Seafarer's, Atlantic
0500	14,314	Pacific Maritime Mobile (MM)
0630	14,320	South Africa MM
0700	14,313	International MM
0715	3,820	Bay of Islands MM
0800	14,303	UK MM
0800	14,315	Pacific Inter-island
1130	14,320	South Africa MM
1130	3,815	Antilles Emergency Weather
1130	21,325	South Atlantic Round Table
1200	14,320	Southeast Asia Sea Net
1230	7,240	Caribbean MM
1300	7,268	Waterway Net
1600	14,313	Coastguard MM
1700	14,313	International MM
1800	14,303	UK MM
1900	7,288	Friendly Net (Hawaii)
2000	14,305	Confusion Net (South Pacific)
2330	7,190	Admirals' (!) Net (US West Coast)
2400	14,320	Sea MM

Well, that should keep you busy. Make sure you get time to cruise.

Flags and things

If there is one thing that the old guard keep banging on about, it is so-called flag etiquette. People who write for the RYA or pontificate in club journals on this subject seem never to have left Cowes, or else believe that no one else in the world goes sailing other than 'English gentlemen'. In the real live world, Britain now comes some way down the list of countries where yachting is popular: the amount of boats actually under way in some parts of the world greatly exceeds our own backyard fleets. We are no longer entitled to be the arbiters of taste in such a matter, because etiquette is, by definition, the generally accepted code of behaviour and these days the traditional British code is no longer the generally accepted one.

LEFT
A common Continental method of flying an ensign in a ketch. It is both practical and sensible. Sometimes the downhaul of the halyard is inside the tubular fitting.

RIGHT
Not often seen: the pilot jack in the bows, which is the approved jack for civilian vessels.

Now I am very fond of flags, but I have come to accept that the old traditional etiquette has had its day. Here is the situation as I see it, together with my own variations.

Legally, a British ship has only to show an ensign on entering or leaving a foreign port (Merchant Shipping Act 1894). The ensign she may use is also laid down, and the Royal Navy is supposed to, but no longer does, police this. In addition, a lot of countries expect to have their ensign displayed by visiting vessels, and in some cases, Turkey is one, the courtesy ensign is a legal requirement.

So, in *Fare Well* I show my ensign when it will be of use to others to identify my country of origin. As they cost quite a lot of money and I hate tatty flags, this means that I do haul it down by night, except that in many Mediterranean ports, when one is lying stern to the main town quay which is well lit, and on which the local population is taking their evening stroll, I like my flags to be seen and keep them so. I like to have the ensign on a good sized staff, so that I can dip it to warships (usually without getting any response, even from my old colleagues in the Royal Navy), and half-mast it as I did today for the funeral of the mother of the taverna keeper on the other side of the quay. If one half-masts an ensign, one also must half-mast the courtesy ensign, do not forget.

Courtesy ensigns by tradition were flown at the fore masthead. In yachts this was traditionally kept for the club burgee, but nowadays few cruising yachts belong to clubs, and if they do they usually fly the burgee at the port crosstrees. The starboard crosstrees are for the courtesy ensign. This is because mastheads are now often cluttered with Christmas tree decorations.

Many smaller yachts have their ensign tied to the standing backstay, where it stays until it rots. This is almost the current etiquette, so if you do the same no one is likely to notice. But it does add to the cost of living, and it seems to me desirable to have some sort of halyard so that when one remembers one can haul the flag down to prolong its active life.

International Code Flags are a waste of money, unless you wish to dress ship for a celebration. You will need flag Q on arrival in many countries, but apart from that most flags carried will be courtesy ensigns, which have become a bit of a nuisance since so many former colonies have become jealous little republics.

The best way of dealing with the problem of multiple courtesy ensigns, since they are so expensive, is to follow our previously given advice and carry a sewing machine and a couple of yards of material of each of the primary colours, plus some different coloured fabric marking crayons (Vogart is a trade name of a suitable brand) to do the intricate bits without which no modern flag seems to be complete. If possible arrive in a country with its courtesy ensign hoisted. Try not to be mean with size; flags are generally hoisted high and can look very tiny, which hardly seems a courtesy. In some places yachtsmen have been fined for having a tatty courtesy ensign; this raises several thoughts about what is a courtesy, and to whom. I do like to be punctilious about this; I have just been to have a look at the Greek ensign at our starboard yard, and I am ashamed to say the hem at the fly is coming apart.

All in all, present-day flag etiquette seems to have something in common with female fashion of the day: you can apparently wear what you like as long as it's decent. With flags, do as you think the situation requires, so long as you obey those bits that are laws.

Dressing ship

It is a present day nautical convention to hoist strings of decorative flags between mastheads and down to stem and stern in order to celebrate various occasions. Not many observe it, except a few British and Dutch with the odd American or German. We do it because I am a flag nut and think it looks good, but we do not do it for those rather formal occasions laid down by the Admiralty. The last time was at Meganisi in Greece where we were staying at the time of the Feast of Saint Bissarion, the local patron. It is an island of merchant navy men, and several called by to thank us for the courtesy. It all helps to make the yottie more welcome.

We once did it on Trafalgar Day while in France, and a French Naval Captain observed 'This is a good day for the France.' *'Comment?'* we replied, a little surprised. 'Well, we shot Nelson that day, and if we had not, we might well now be a British colony.' Everyone enjoys a sense of humour; we made another friend.

The usual form for dressing lines is to alternate the flags of the code with the pennants and substitutes. The order does not really matter — just make a colourful show.

Our dressing occasions are: the birthdays of crew, Trafalgar Day, St George's Day, Christmas Day, New Year's Day (when we also hoist a full string of courtesy ensigns for the past year), plus any special dates for the country or port we are visiting.

How to be a Popular Yottie

The considerations that apply to flag etiquette apply also to yacht etiquette — the arbiters are no longer those elderly blimps from Cowes or the New York Yacht Club who have for so long arrogantly imposed their values on Anglo-American yachting. The arbiters now are the people who actually sail, and they comprise many nationalities. The form nowadays can be summed up:
1.   Cause the minimum inconvenience to other yachts' crews.
2.   Help another yacht berthing close by you.
3.   Give assistance willingly, and without legal haggling, to anyone in difficulties.

These three tenets are obvious to most people who want to sail. In more detail certain usages have grown up around them, and I will give those I have noticed. If I have missed any, then I apologise to whomever I have offended.

Generators   Their use is growing, and it has to be faced that many yachts have them and need them. In general most confine generating to the forenoon. There is a growing tendency for a second run in the dog watches, between about 1600 and 1800, which is not so nice, but tolerable. In port you do *not* run generators before 0830, between 1230 and 1600, or after 1800 unless you want to incur the justifiable wrath of your neighbours. The major transgressors of this are Italian motor yachts; I recall one who persisted in running a generator all night in spite of protests. In the morning he found a rude word written in old engine oil on his teak deck, and no one had any sympathy. (Italian sailing yachtsmen are perfectly reasonable.) There are others who irrespective of nationality are boorish over this, but in the main the convention holds.

At anchor, when yachts are some distance apart, the convention is relaxed, particularly if it is windy, but in close anchorages such as Bequia or Union Island it is usually observed.

Dinghies In Europe, dinghies left ashore are inviolable. You should make yours fast on a long painter so that it can be shoved to one side to allow others to get alongside to land. In areas where Americans abound, and particularly where their racing circuses congregate, the unsolicited borrowing of dinghies is not uncommon. Americans seem to tolerate this noxious practice, which is generally anathema to our older civilization. Either take precautions or be surprised.

Anchors Be particularly careful when berthing bows or stern to a quay not to lay your anchor cable(s) across others. In many places it cannot be avoided, however. The first to arrive at Navpaktos, in the Gulf of Corinth, is obliged to be the last to leave; the centre of this tiny harbour resembles a diagram for a multi-part Matthew Walker knot, tied in cable. A great deal of tolerance is needed.

Untangling foul anchors is an example of the willingness of yotties to help each other. Usually anyone with a dinghy down will paddle out to do his stuff. Greek yachtsmen are particularly good about this. If you are moored stern or bows to with the usual taut cable, and someone fouls it when weighing, you have an obligation to respond to reasonable requests from the fouler, who is probably in the best position to know how he is foul. He will probably ask you to give him some slack, for a yacht without a power windlass is unlikely to be able to haul a tight chain to the surface so that he can unhook his anchor. Even if he has power, if he hauls up a tight cable he is likely to haul up your anchor with it, so some slack is usually desirable. If wind conditions are troublesome run your engine at modest revs to hold your stern off the quay. If you are the fouler, and haul out the anchor of a berthed boat, try to re-lay it as close to its original position as possible.

One does NOT buoy anchors in a busy port; the chaos if all did so can be imagined. If you are worried about foul anchors use a trip line taken back to your bow. In an open anchorage an anchor buoy can be of help to another yacht in avoiding anchoring too close. In a crowded anchorage it is a help to a newcomer shaping up near you to tell him how much cable you are lying to. It is the responsibility of the late-comer to keep clear of those already anchored, and this continues unless the first-comer changes the state by veering or shortening cable, or by letting go another anchor. The last to fiddle with the tackle has to watch out.

Berthing It is usual to help with the ropes of a yacht berthing next to you. In the Med, where harbours are often crowded, it is anti-social to berth alongside the quay. There are exceptions, such as Poros in the Aegean, or Khalkis, but for special reasons. Anyone berthing in this way has to be prepared for others to berth alongside them. In the Azores, Bermuda, Baltic and some Canaries harbours, yachts sometimes lie alongside six or more abreast. Outside yachts (other than tiddlers) must have breastropes to the quay, and springs to their neighbours. Utmost co-operation is needed, and is usually forthcoming to a measure that breeds friendships.

The old convention of always crossing over the foredeck of a neighbour is gone: many voyagers now have a proper sleeping cabin in the fore part of the yacht, and in warm climates often a wide-open hatch. It is proper to enquire (by day) how you should cross, and the responder should also pass on the information he has already got from yachts inside him.

Footwear The real seaman wears deck shoes because he knows that stubbed toes can be debilitating, and also that quaysides are often fouled by disease ridden dogs. Dilettante yachtsmen who spend more time polishing their yachts than sailing them have an elaborate ritual of donning or doffing shoes like a crowd of Japanese at a temple. But you cannot expect an outside crew to take off their boots just because you bagged the inside berth. Face the fact that if the deck of your yacht will not stand up to deck shoes it is not fit for its purpose. (A little small grit is very good for teak; it roughens it, improves its non-slip qualities.) On the other hand the shoe wearer has an obligation to see that his shoes are clean.

Smoking Do as you like in your own boat, but in harbour do not throw cigarette ends overboard. Many yachts put their dinghies down in harbour, and it's too easy to make a bad shot and get one.

Garbage The French and Italians tend to leave plastic bags of garbage on the quay, thereby encouraging rats, stray dogs and cats, and incurring the wrath and disrespect of others who mostly look for the garbage skip. This is often full, when there is nothing to be done except

Greek ladies washing using tubs and washboards. It's back to basics without a washing machine.

280

to leave the garbage alongside it. In the Caribbean and elsewhere, pay no heed to little boys who paddle out to your anchorage and offer to dispose of your garbage for a fee. They will rummage through it for anything of interest, and then leave the rest on that pretty little beach where you wanted to swim.

Quiet Quiet times vary from place to place. Some are still beating at 0300. A few miles away, at another port, the inhabitants will all be asleep by 2230. Local people may well welcome the income from tourism, but do not want to pay too high a price for it. Ascertain and respect the local convention.

Helping There is a tradition of helping others with navigation information. Where they are otherwise unobtainable, charts etc are loaned for photocopying. Linguists pass on the weather reports, and any yacht who has been in the port more than a few days should pass on the whereabouts of sources of essentials (water, or gas bottles) or even non-essentials that are particularly interesting.

It can all be summed up: Let's all have a good time, but not at the expense of others.

CHAPTER FOURTEEN

Routeing

'It is to be supposed by this time the ship is victualled and manned, the voiage determined . . . and all things else ready to set sail.'

This chapter is concerned with ways of getting between the various cruising grounds we have discussed in Chapter Ten. Some people will perhaps wish to remain in one area, but most who are seriously infected with the wanderbug will one day want to try somewhere else — it's what the business is all about. Sometimes one can make a sheltered passage from one area to another, but there are a few occasions where an ocean passage is necessary or should be considered as an option. Also, in this chapter, I am going to mention in very general terms some of the more distant parts. Even if one has no present intention of going that far, it is pleasant to know something of what may be.

For a Briton or European, the first problem to be faced is getting away from the country. If I say that a voyage direct to North America is contrary to the spirit of the casual wanderer, I think most readers will by now know what I mean. The trans-Atlantic racers, ardent disciples of the late Baron Masoch, tend to go this way, and that is argument enough. So we rule out 30 days of beating into the winds of a series of depressions. This means that, even if bound across the Atlantic, the first stage is a voyage south, not necessarily to Gibraltar but in that direction.

This is also the open-sea route to the Mediterranean. There are other ways of getting there, and they will be mentioned under inland water routes. For the moment, then, let us look at a passage to Gibraltar, or its vicinity.

The ideal departure for this passage is either Southern Ireland or Falmouth, because it is desirable to make some westing before crossing the Bay of Biscay. I advise keeping well outside the Ushant traffic separation scheme and special tanker channel; unless coming from the eastern part of the English Channel, it is better to be out of range of Ushant light. If you have come down-Channel and conditions are good, consider the Chenal du Four but not without proper pilotage information. Sailing vessels should always avoid passing close west of Ushant, even if the separation scheme were not in operation, because if bad weather comes the wind is more likely to be west than any other, and it will almost certainly be accompanied by a current pushing a vessel into the Bay. This is no laughing matter if bad weather persists. It is quite likely that a crossing of the Bay will have fine weather all the way in summer, but prudence is a valuable commodity. In the spring and autumn depressions are not only more frequent, but they become comparatively unpredictable in their movements. Prudence is then the more precious.

I would pass down the Portuguese coast well out to sea, out of sight of land, and only close the coast near Cape St Vincent. This headland has a traffic separation scheme round it, which is of doubtful necessity and a hazard of itself. Sailing vessels should round this cape very close to with an easterly wind, in which case they are obliged to foul the badly planned north-bound lane, though there is seldom very much traffic. With a northwesterly wind, which is the most likely, it is well to stay offshore out of the way of the north-bound traffic; keep a good offing if bound for Gibraltar in order to avoid the Banks, for though there is depth for a yacht the seas can be very unpleasant there.

The distance from Falmouth to Gibraltar is 1080 miles, and from Cork it is 1098 miles. Most cruising boats average between 100 and 130 miles per day. I had my best day's run ever in *Fare Well* south-bound some 30 miles off the Portuguese coast, logging 190 miles with only 370 square feet of canvas set. But we still took twelve days for the passage.

To do this journey in the reverse direction, that is north-bound, requires rather more determination. I would take a long leg out to the Azores, which are well worth a special visit in any case. The wind is predominantly northerly along the Portuguese coast and there is a lot of commercial traffic to have to watch out for. The very experienced Leslie and Kathy Downe in *Shintaro* were lost here, presumably run down.

Running down by a ship is more of a probability than it used to be. The standard of training and conscientiousness of some (but not all) ship's officers is poor, there are no longer cadets and spare hands to keep lookout, and radar is a poor substitute for the eyeball. Though the probability of a collision well offshore is still very small, it is remarkable how often one passes too close to some ship in mid-ocean, in circumstances where the slow-moving yacht cannot get out of the way even if she wished to. But in the shipping lanes the probability is by no means negligible, and these major trade routes should be avoided.

The Mediterranean

Within the Med, routeing is comparatively simple. There are a few caution-worthy spots. When crossing the Gulf of Lions check not only

the weather forecast but also that you know the bad weather signs (see Admiralty Pilot, Mediterranean Vol. II). Watch the Bonifacio Strait in rough weather for it seems to act like a funnel: the weather is always bad, and I always suffer damage to either myself or the yacht off Cape Corse. This last is, I think, a purely personal affair, but you never know.

There is often fog in the Sicilian Channel and in the Malta Channel, and the east-going current can be strong in both. They are both encumbered with shipping and fishing boats, and good watch-keeping is required.

The Straits of Messina is one of the few in the Mediterranean with a very strong tidal stream. I have personally measured 6 knots at springs. Consult the Admiralty Pilot and try to go through with a fair tide. Scylla and Charybdis, the whirlpools, may be seen, but since the earthquake around 1900 are no longer the menace they were once reputed to be, and one can sail right through the vortex even at springs with no ill effects other than being rotated a bit. But a small yacht should be a little cautious if there are strong wind-against-tide conditions.

Navigation of the Dardanelles is not difficult, though there is often a strong south-going current. It was necessary to call at Cannakale for Turkish clearance (1985).

West-bound across the Atlantic

Go south until the butter melts, then turn right: there is not much more to it. If leaving Gibraltar, it is better to wait for a Levanter (east wind), but that often brings poor weather generally. If coming from the north, it pays usually to keep well out and one can sometimes carry the Portuguese Trades almost down to the Canary Islands.

Most yachts call at the Canaries, and it can be quite a social scene there in November. The tradewind belt moves north in winter, and it is better to wait for it to establish itself up to 15°N or so, which can happen towards the end of November. Better time for the crossing is January: if going to the Caribbean for a long stay it might be worth spending a couple of months or more in the Canaries.

Only really freak weather should disturb the easy tedium of the passage. The occasional squall enables everyone to strip off and have a free shower, but make sure there is enough rain to wash the soap off before putting it on. Our cat, Nelson, enjoyed the voyage: she had never known fish to fly on board every night and surrender to her gargantuan appetite.

North-bound from the Caribbean

If bound for Florida it is better to go south of the Bahamas Islands, but give Cuba a good offing. There are some doubts about the surveys east of the Bahamas; ever since a flag officer of the Royal Cruising Club was wrecked there the charts have been assumed to be wrong.

Seriously, though, there have been quite a few yachts lost in those parts, and one should think very carefully before closing these low-lying banks. Whether the charts are wrong, or there are unrecorded strong currents, I do not know; nor, I suspect, does anyone else yet. It is not one of the most important bits of ocean.

If bound for the Bermudas, it is as well to start from east of Puerto Rico to be reasonably expectant of a reach. There are no problems. The Bermudas are well lit and clear of off-lying dangers to the south.

Heading to the USA from the Bermudas ought not to be difficult. I think I am in the running for the longest passage time — twelve days for the 630 miles. I know from bitter experience that this is a passage where one should take a lot of care about the weather. Excellent forecasts are broadcast from Portsmouth, Virginia by voice on SSB, and some of them are in English. The others are in what my American friend called 'Dixie', and I was left wondering how the Non-British might cope if we were to hire Glaswegians from the Gorbals to read our weather forecasts. For that matter, I wonder what *we* would do.

One of the important features of these forecasts is the relaying of the positions of the edges of the Gulf Stream. This ocean-going river flows at up to 3 knots in this part of the world and makes a lot of difference to a yacht's course made good. The edges are surprisingly well defined: the northern edge particularly can be recognized with some exactitude by observing the sea-water temperature, which will fall several degrees in a few hours when bound northwards out of the stream.

Because of the current flow, very nasty seas can build up when the wind is opposite this current. Gales from the northeast quadrant can be particularly dangerous. Only in the Pentland Firth off North Scotland have I ever seen such vicious short seas.

Watch out for fog in the colder waters approaching the New England coast. As soon as possible get the local weather forecasts from the special coastal VHF stations. Also beware of shipping bound to or from New York. There are off-lying dangers near the New England coast so do your homework first and carefully. Take note that by some administrative lunacy, the offshore buoys off Nantucket that would be so useful for a position check in bad weather all have the same light characteristic: flashing white, every 4 seconds.

If having left Bermuda you are tempted to return for any reason, then consider very carefully before doing so. The offlying reefs to the northwest of the islands are dangerous; and very dangerous in bad weather, being poorly lit and comparatively steep-to.

East-bound over the Atlantic

The most common route is via the Bermudas and the Azores, but a lot of yachts do go directly from New England and some miss the Azores. The passage to Bermuda poses few difficulties that we have not already discussed in the reverse direction. From Bermuda head northeast until the latitude of 40°N is reached, then steer along the parallel until a couple of days or so west of the Azores. The popular time for this voyage is May/June and then the weather will not be hot: often it is jersey weather all the way, and the winds can be variable and sometimes irritatingly light. There is always a chance of some strong winds, but most of the severe depressions should pass well to the north. (I do not guarantee that.)

Shipping is mostly light especially compared with the yacht traffic in May or June when something like 150 yachts arrive in the Azores each month from the west.

It is at this time that the US Fleet usually lays on a major fleet exercise right on the sailing-ship track. It seems they have no staff officers with any knowledge of the sea. The odd passing merchant ship can be diverted to keep clear of the flying operations, but yachts pottering along at 3 or 4 knots in the light breezes cannot be re-routed; the fleet has to suspend or alter operations for some time, at God knows what cost in terms of money and irritation. They take it out on the yachts by buzzing them at masthead height with jet aircraft, which is a puerile and dangerous business. Everyone gets cross and even the Russian shadowing ships don't like their routine being interrupted, though these are always more polite and helpful to yachtsmen than the US Navy. And all because staff officers are so ignorant that they organize exercises across busy sailing routes.

I should add that the Royal Navy is not without guilt in this. In 1983 some yachts taking part in the well publicized Azores and Back Race were harrassed and endangered by Her Majesty's Ships navigating without lights on the race route. They were also buzzed by helicopters, which is highly dangerous to small yachts. Perhaps the international problem is that the modern senior naval officer does not have enough sea experience to learn about other users of the sea.

But to get on to the Azores. They are an easy landfall, and a very impressive one after some 18 days at sea. Nevertheless they have been missed completely; I do not know how, but they have. The welcome is very good and the living is very cheap. From the Azores to Gibraltar, Portugal or the English Channel presents no special problems in the summer months.

Inland Passages

For passages through the French canals and rivers to the Mediterranean there are so many books giving detailed advice, and written by people with great knowledge of these waterways, that much comment here is not appropriate.

It is not a quick passage — there are very many locks, and navigation at night is not permitted — and in my view it should be a lingering cruise, not to be taken at the rush. The French canals are an experience in themselves. The quickest passage I know of is via the Marne, mast down to mast up 19 days, but how they must have sweated, and what delights they must have missed. The maximum length should not worry the type of cruising yacht that falls in our categories, but beam is limited to 5 metres, and draught to 1.8. The lowest bridge obstruction is 3.5 metres, and there are facilities for striking masts at both ends of the system.

Some yachts have sailed into the Bay of Biscay and passed to the Mediterranean via Bordeaux and the Canal du Midi, emerging at Sete. Not all yachts who do this originally intended to, it being sometimes difficult to get out of the Bay any other way. The Gironde estuary with its many banks can be very dangerous for small craft in strong westerly winds. One catamaran with the evocative name of *Cupid Stunts*, bound for Gibraltar in autumn, was carried to leeward by several days of bad weather and actually blown into the Gironde River willy-nilly. Her crew, who were mostly inexperienced, learned a lot, and enjoyed their passage through this marvellous canal.

The Canal du Midi was supposed to have its dimensions increased to the Freycinet standard which is common to most of the French canals, but this seems in 1990 to be indefinitely postponed. Also bear in mind that the Canal du Midi might be closed in times of drought, as in 1989.

The Rhine-Danube Canal, which should have been re-instated years ago, has been making slow progress for political reasons which are not

Celebrating the tenth anniversary of leaving England. Apart from the masthead dressing lines, the hoists from each upper spreader are the courtesy ensigns of all the countries we have visited, 23 in all. Note the precautionary use of two anchors, the prevailing wind in this harbour coming from the port beam.

the fault of the communist powers. It should open in 1992 but I will believe it when I see it. When open, vessels should be able to navigate across Germany, Austria and down to the Black Sea.

The USA Intra-Coastal Waterway

A brief description of this waterway is in Chapter Ten on Cruising Grounds. It is a very good way of going north or south along the US coast in spring or autumn, as it cuts off some difficult headlands like Cape Hatteras. There are enough inlets from the sea for yachts to make the odd outside passage if there is an occasional need to get a move on, otherwise it is a time to be enjoyed and not hurried over.

North from New York It is possible to go up the Hudson River, pass through some very beautiful country, and emerge either in the Saint Lawrence River or the Great Lakes via the New York State canal system. Masts musts come down and it is very strictly forbidden to discharge heads overboard.

The Saint Lawrence   A difficult river to go up because of the current, which when combined with an ebb tide can be very strong. Yachting on the Great Lakes is highly developed, but the visitor is well advised to consult locally about the weather, which can change quickly and raise very nasty seas in a short time. There are very strict anti-pollution laws, and a lot of problems with commercial shipping.

Elsewhere   The Panama Canal is a substantial undertaking for a yacht, and I have never done it. Some people have had uneventful passages; others have had events and damage. The Panama is not an expensive canal to pass through because the charge is tonnage based, but yachts without engines capable of 5 knots or more have to be towed.

The long passage across the Pacific does not appeal to me much, though it does not seem to cause many problems to the large numbers who have sailed it. But I have spent a lot of time in the Indian Ocean and thoroughly enjoyed it. Sadly, I have to say that political uncertainties in the area would detract from the pleasure today. There is nowadays quite a bit of yacht traffic from Australia via Galle in Ceylon and then into the Red Sea. A good alternative is the route via Christmas Island, the Cocos Keelings, Mauritius and Cape Town, though the last is beginning to get its share of political uncertainties. A practical problem is the Agulhas Current off the southeast coast of South Africa, where the seas in bad weather can cause difficulties even for big ships.

The main problem about the Suez Canal route to Europe (provided one is not daft enough to try to cross the ocean against the Monsoon) is getting up the Red Sea. In spite of the political complexion of the government yachtsmen are usually well received at Aden, but a similar welcome cannot be relied on at any Red Sea ports. This is a pity, for with the virtual certainty of head winds most will want to make a stop or two. Even Port Sudan, which was once quite popular, has to be approached with caution nowadays, and Saudi Arabia, for all its wealth and its religious teaching, and in spite of the millions of pounds worth of yachts owned by their citizens, has not learned yet how to give a civilized welcome to travellers.

The Suez Canal necessitates having an agent, unless one has unusual persistence, patience and a very cool head. The big trouble is that Egypt is not merely corrupt in every aspect of its business life, it is openly and unashamedly so. The actual cost of the transit is modest. However the agency fee can exceed the canal dues. It is obligatory to have a pilot, who will have little to do except watch the signal stations. You may be lucky and get a pleasant fellow for half the journey; you would be very lucky indeed if both pilots were congenial. The chances are that even the pilots will demand and expect 'gifts'.

The reverse voyage, down the Red Sea, presents few problems and is best done non-stop in the present world disorder.

I offer no advice on rounding Cape Horn. In my view it is a rotten part of the globe, and the only reason I can think of for going there is to prove something that one ought not to have to prove.

	Aden	Barbados	Bermuda	Brindisi	Chesapeake	Cork	Cristobal	Dover	Fayal	Genoa
Aden										
Barbados	6550									
Bermuda	6230	1220								
Brindisi	2320	4530	4210							
Chesapeake	6630	1680	640	4600						
Cork	4400	3400	2730	2380	3000					
Cristobal (Panama)	7630	1220	1640	5620	1750	4310				
Dover	4600	3710	3080	2580	3390	450	4660			
Fayal (Azores)	4430	2250	1800	2400	2220	1180	3260	1480		
Genoa	2810	4100	3770	750	4170	1950	5180	2140	1980	
Gibraltar	3300	3250	2930	1280	3330	1100	4340	1230	1130	850
Istanbul	2190	5050	4730	790	5140	2900	6150	3030	3000	1310
Madeira	3900	2630	2520	1900	2880	1250	3740	1400	670	1450
Malta	2330	4230	3910	360	4320	2080	5330	2220	2110	580
Marseilles	2900	3940	3620	840	4020	1790	5030	1920	1820	200
New York	6500	1830	700	4480	260	2820	1970	3250	2100	4050
Las Palmas (Canaries)	4000	2640	2560	1980	3060	1480	3800	1610	900	1550
Plymouth										
Port Said	1400	5150	4830	930	5240	3000	6240	3140	3040	1430
Ushant	4230	3420	2810	2200	3120	230	4380	310	1170	1770

	Gibraltar	Istanbul	Madeira	Malta	Marseilles	New York	Las Palmas	Port Said
Istanbul	1810							
Madeira	600	2420						
Malta	990	850	1590					
Marseilles	700	1390	1290	650				
New York	3200	5010	2770	4190	3900			
Las Palmas (Canaries)	710	2500	290	1680	1390	2930		
Port Said	1900	790	2500	940	1500	5100	2610	
Ushant	920	2720	1090	1910	1610	2990	1310	2830

CHAPTER FIFTEEN

Health and Welfare at Sea

'The Chirurgeon is to be exempted from all duty but to attend the sicke and cure the wounded; and good care would be had he have a certificate from the Barber-Chirurgeon's Halls of his sufficiency ... for which neglect hath beene the losse of many a man's life.'

Nowhere is it more obvious than on a long-distance cruise that sickness is more a state of mind than of body. Most cruising people find that as the pace of life slows to 5 knots on average and the world shrinks to the size of their boat, many bodily ills dwindle and disappear. On the other hand, you have a better chance of doing yourself an injury on a boat of cruising size than might be the case if you had stuck to golf and lawnmowers.

Consequently, while you need no longer exempt your Chirurgeon from all other duty, it would be well, as Capt. John Smith points out, that he have a certificate; nowadays from the Red Cross or St John's Ambulance Brigade, at least. It has to be said that the Red Cross and St John's courses are not enough for the long-distance cruiser. Even if we have access to advice by radio, we are likely to need practical skills such as giving injections, administering a drip, stitching wounds, and the control of pain and infection. Many doctors in the British Isles have a deep-seated mistrust of allowing any Tom, Dick or Harriet to acquire such paramedical skills or even read about them. In the US there is a crash course designed by a Doctor/sailor: the *Intensive Survey of Medical Emergency Care* (address in the Appendix).

In the first edition we wrote that there were no medical courses in UK for long-distance yachtsmen. They are still rarely run, and we think there is a need for more. It ought to be the RYA's pidgin to arrange such courses, but they have made clear their disinterest in long-distance cruising. Nautical colleges lay on the Ship Captain's Medical Course, which is not specifically intended for yachtsmen. Laurel attended the one at Lowestoft Nautical College, and reported:

The course is based on the *Ship Captain's Medical Guide* (known as The Book) which all British Merchant Ships are required to carry. We always had a copy on board for long cruises in *Fare Well* and latterly in *Hosanna*, and found it very useful in emergencies. Embarking on our travels again, I felt I wanted some practical knowledge to add to the drugs and equipment which we had carried on *Fare Well*. It was all very well having the stuff on board, but did I know how to use it all? No, I did not. Many people ask how we cope with sickness or accidents. The only response that we can make is: 'As best we can.' One knows that help is not within reach, and that the High Street surgery is 4,000 miles away. When the crunch comes you are your own barefoot doctor— you, with the worried look and the shaking hands. I ought, I felt, to be able to give an injection, and take a stitch-in-time with a suturing needle.

So I enrolled on the course, and began badly. I was ten minutes late, and I'd missed the whole of Preparing a Cabin for a Patient and half of Vital Signs.

There were six of us on the three-day course, four Merchant Navy Officers, and two yacht ladies: Caroline of *Heartsease* and me. We went at the pace of a motorcycle scramble. The breathless speed made us reel. We learned how to take blood pressure, record temperature, pulse and breathing, how to test urine and why. (Nurses in the old days used to taste it to find what was in it, said Rosie SRN, our Mentor, thank God we now use Labstix.)

We did Observation of Specimens, and Care of Bed Patients; we learned to face the enema, and to give rectal infusions (to fight the Demon Dehydration, the killer in many and varied diseases and conditions). We learned how to cope with Malaria, we saw a slide cassette on Heat Exhaustion and Heat Stroke.

Fortified by lunch, I then discovered more than I care to know about Sexually Transmitted Diseases. This lecture was beautifully sung by a Welsh doctor, who accompanied it with extraordinary slides. He began *pianissimo* with the diseases we'd all heard of, went into a fugue of oddities that were new to some of us, and ended up with a threnody on AIDS.

We then pelted through Poisons, including many gases that were relevant to the cargoes of Shipmasters, but not very likely on a yacht.

We roared past Resuscitation, hurtled through Haemorrhage, and halted for a while for Hypothermia (something that anyone who goes boating on the lake ought to know about, let alone long-distance cruisers).

We galloped past Gallstones, shot through Surgical Emergencies, were mesmerised by Mental Illness and Myocardial Infarction (which up to then we had called heart attack).

We were petrified by Palpation of the Abdomen, bemused by Bodies (disposal of) and bothered by Burial at Sea.

And all the time Caroline and I would ask: 'But suppose you haven't got room on your boat for all that apparatus/equipment/vast array of drugs?'

Improvisation can save your bacon, as I well know, and Rosie often assured us with examples.

I remembered once leaving Port Mahon (on a Friday of course) when

Bill was freeing the anchor from a heavy rope encrusted with barnacles, when a huge fish-hook caught deep in the pad of his middle finger. My first action had to be taking the strain off the rope, and therefore the finger. The second was to check that the boat was still safely anchored. The third was to sit down and think a bit.

'Push the hook through the skin (if no vital organ is endangered), nip off the barb, and withdraw', said the First Aid book. But they hadn't seen stainless steel Spanish fish hooks; they're more like something you find at the butcher's, with a whole ox hanging from it. Which was not far from the truth, as I pointed out to the Skipper at the time: he was not amused.

A brief effort to obey the First Aid book with the aid of bolt cutters was quickly abandoned for a Stanley knife, 'sterilised' with brandy.

Both patient and 'doctor' then drank some of the brandy (not recommended in The Book) and, shaking like leaves, cut out the hook, which was baited with something slithery that looked very evil. I wish I knew what, as the wound healed clean and with great rapidity, and we might have made a fortune selling it to a drug company. Observe that it never occurred to us to row ashore and find a doctor. One loses the habit.

I also recalled putting the Skipper's neck in traction with a handy billy and a seven kilo gas bottle over a pulley, and under 'Burns' you will find an ingenious use for the raingauge.

Back to the course. In two and a half crammed days we learned to stitch gaping wounds in surprisingly resistant foam rubber (very like the real thing, said Rosie) and *not* to put our finger on the knot. Knowledge of stitching I could have used on a couple of occasions for small wounds.

We learned to inject oranges. We learned to approach the plastic model of Resusci-Annie with confidence, despite her lying on the floor with her lungs exposed and a feral grin on her face. Her bared rubber teeth looked as if they could bite you if she didn't care for your technique, or your aftershave. I added the Brooke Airway to our list.

When it came to exam. time, we all regurgitated sufficient material (some of it only half digested) to pass; Caroline and I were the first women to do so at Lowestoft who were not Shipmasters.

What does all that make me? Certainly not the Doc. But next time something happens, I shall have a modicum of confidence to add to commonsense. I will hope to reassure my victim that my panicky search through 'The Book' will bring help and relief. Raising morale is my strong point. Even without the brandy. And I am more determined than ever to harp (to the point of boring my readers) on prevention of accidents and illness at sea.

If you are within reach of land, English speaking doctors who have been properly trained may be found worldwide by joining (for the cost of a donation) I A M A T, the International Association for Medical Assistance to Travellers whose address will also be found in the

Appendix. Otherwise advice *may* be available by radio: a call of 'Pan Pan Medico' should produce results if any doctor is monitoring, or any merchant ship or shore station picks up your call.

It is to be hoped that you will have gone to sea in a state of good health, as far as can be ascertained by checkups and dental work before you go. Cherish this happy state of affairs by thinking 'prevention' rather than 'cure'. Catch it before it happens. Eliminate the chances of sickness and bodily damage to your uttermost. Since this attitude goes hand in hand with the watchfulness that every good seaman cultivates, the quicker it becomes second nature to you the sooner, paradoxically, you can relax and enjoy your cruise. By 'looking for trouble' you are avoiding it!

A new scheme, MASTA, is a world-wide advisory health service for travellers. Approved by (and next door to) the London School of Hygiene and Tropical Medicine, they will tailor a Health Brief to your individual requirements, with details of all inoculations required, information and a list of medical items to take with you, and up-to-date 'health newsflashes' from all over the world, via their computer bank. Long-distance yachtsmen would need the more comprehensive service which could be very good value. Forms are available at branches of Boots, Chemists, or direct from the Bureau, address in the Appendix.

There follows, in alphabetical order, a list of preventive measures.

How to prevent
AIDS and STD's

It used to be sailors who spread Sexually Transmitted Diseases (STD's). Now that everyone travels, it is the tourists and the businessmen who spread the plague. Take the obvious precautions, remember that condoms have a limited shelf-life, and are hard to find in remote places. If you intend going to certain parts of Africa or South America, where AIDS is especially rife, it is worth asking your doctor for an AIDS kit, thus if you had to go ashore for any kind of treatment you would take with you your own syringes, needles, blood giving set, sterile swabs and plasma.

Appendicitis

This is the great bugaboo that frightens everyone. Many transatlantic yachtsmen have an 'elective appendectomy' in order to avoid any possibility of trouble. This would need to be discussed with your doctor. We feel that nowadays hospitals take away the disease you came in with and give you several new ones in exchange: this is even acknowledged by the medical profession in a fearsome Greek-derived term: Nokosogeneric (meaning arising in the hospital) disease. Stay out of hospital and stay healthy, we say.

However, it is a worry. We know of no-one who has died of peritonitis at sea since the sixties: it seems that modern antibiotics may be able to hold the situation until help is at hand.

Births

It is very difficult to get contraceptives in large areas of the world. To be safe, take a good supply with you, and have several different kinds in case you run out.

Lady, if you are seasick to the point of vomiting, or have even a short attack of diarrhoea, or vomiting, or both, the effectiveness of your Pill could be endangered. Talk to your doctor before you go about the possible effect on your sort of Pill: it might be necessary to use a supplementary method for the rest of the cycle.

Bodily damage

A yacht is made of hard substances that tend to be unyielding. If you collide with these substances, you bruise, concuss, crack ribs or break bones. The old Salts used to say: One hand for yourself, and one for the King. Learn the motion of your boat, when she may jerk or spin, as in a gybe all-standing or the wash of a big ship, or a sudden squall.

Expect the Captain to warn you if at all possible, that a big wave or jerk may be coming. Climbing the mast at sea should be attempted only in dire necessity.

The deck of a yacht is never smooth. It is dotted with cleats, rings, bitts, upstands, screwplates and deadeyes, all waiting to bite your feet. Wear good deck shoes to protect them from damage, as well as for traction. Bare feet are fine in harbour or at anchor, but get your shoes on for manoeuvres. Shipboard work often cannot wait while you hop around holding your toe and yelling.

A yacht big enough to go cruising in is under the sway of enormous forces. If something breaks or casts loose it can cause serious damage to people or boat. Part of seamanship, therefore, is learning how to approach and tame your tiger whether it be a flogging sail or twin boom; with the minimum of danger. Use preventers and guys to limit the swing of spars, and prevent gybing. Again prevention is better than cure, so check halyards for weaknesses, ropes for chafe, wire for kinks and broken strands (the latter are a constant source of lacerated fingers), replace bent shackle pins, and tape up protruding split-pins or enclose them neatly in plastic tube.

If the weather threatens shorten sail early, to lessen the forces you have to control. Even a handkerchief of canvas in a Force 8 can bat around like a tin roof in a hurricane, and a rope can assume the murderous quality of an iron bar wielded by a maniac.

Listen to the Flotilla. They believe that nothing can hurt them: after all, what could possibly happen on two weeks' holiday? 'I'm coming in a bit fast: stick your foot out and hold her off, will you, Harry?' The

This was posed to illustrate a very dangerous, but common practice. Never, never get feet or hands between the boat and the quay. Note the strong midship springing cleat — a rarity in production craft.

luckless Harry tries to stop 5 tons of fast-moving boat in zero seconds: oh dear, he's hurt his foot. But Dad is very busy at the other end: 'Maud, can you let a bit more anchor line out? What? No more? Well tie another rope to it then — be quick, I can't quite reach the quay. HOLD ON! What did you let go for? Stop crying, it's only a rope burn. Fred, take a line ashore will you. No I can't seem to get any nearer, we've run out of anchor line: can't you jump it?' Fred, challenged, jumps at the precise moment when the cleated anchor line brings the boat up short. He is lucky if he is precipitated into the water rather than onto the rough concrete quay, which will result in numerous cuts and abrasions if not worse. The same abrupt halt has probably thrown Mum against the cockpit coaming, a frequent cause of cracked ribs. All it needs now is for Sandra to stub her bare toe against a cleat, and on leaving, for Susan to jam her fingers in the anchor cable roller and Dad to get a hernia heaving up the anchor, unaware in all the excitement that the ferry has come in and laid several hundredweight of chain across it. All these things have happened, and a lot more, but not all to one boat, mercifully.

Even a simple thing like filling a bucket of water from the sea, if you are sailing at 5 knots, can almost dislocate your shoulder; so can an unexpected gybe if you are holding the mainsheet in your hand. 'Never cleat the mainsheet' goes back to our dinghy days: it is not valid for bigger boats.

Anchor chain can crush fingers or hands: I have a healthy respect for ours, which is very heavy. I keep my hands well away from it by looping a short length of codline through the links when I need to move it: this could be let go instantly if the cable began to run out unexpectedly.

You know those dinky little elastic sail gaskets with a plastic knob at each end? Release them with care, or they will knock your teeth out and probably break your glasses as well.

Body odour

This delicate matter must be mentioned, since the chronic water shortage often prevents normal bathing and showering.

First, be aware that your clothing affects your smell. Man-made fibres all engender smells in the smalls after a couple of hours. Cotton, wool and linen may be worn for much longer before they need washing. You may decide that the easy-care qualities of polyester-cotton mixtures are worthwhile, but you will have to wash them oftener thus using more water.

Canvas shoes need washing whenever you have access to a shore-side hose, otherwise the smell can become intense enough to glow in the dark; leather deck shoes of the Docksider type are more expensive, but kinder to your mates.

Personal hygiene can be assisted by moistened wipes. Do not, in the interests of economy, use those saved from restaurants on anything except your hands: I shudder to think of the effect of the lemon flavoured variety on tender portions of the anatomy. There are specially made ones such as Bidelle and Femfresh. For ladies, throwaway Brief Savers have their uses. My greatest contribution to cruising is probably the discovery that the Debutante brand plastic bowl (withstands boiling water and is graduated in pints and litres) fits exactly into the Lavac bowl to form a bidet. I was so excited by this discovery that I bought a second plastic bowl, but the first one has lasted ten years without breaking.

Bill is under the delusion that underarm deodorants are effective. Overuse can cause dermatitis.

Breaking nails

You need strong nails at sea. There are preparations to paint on and strengthen them, but you can also 'eat' them strong by including plenty of gelatine in the diet: eat straight jelly (Jello) cubes if you like, or dishes in aspic such as *ouefs en gelee*, brawn or pig's trotters. Wearing gloves can spare you damage: not the delicate little pair from the Yotte Shoppe, but a strong leather or plastic palmed pair, to prevent injury either when dealing with wire rope, or that popular French mooring system called the *Pendille*, where you pick up a fixed rope between the quay and a mooring buoy, and slide it through your hands to bring it to the forward anchor winch to make fast. As the rope spends a lot of time in the water, it is covered with coral and small, sharp crustacea. Those on shore can be heard tittering as you lacerate your hands and bleed into the scuppers.

Burns and scalds

Every cook must evolve her own way of coping with hot pans in a choppy sea. Some advocate seats and straps in the galley, but I prefer to be free to leap aside. With good fiddles it is not the pans that move, it is their contents, so it makes a lot of sense to have deep, tall pans, with well-fitting lids, and not to fill them too full. Pressure cookers are excellent because the lid stays on. Conversely, a wide-based kettle with a whistle closing the spout keeps boiling water in the right place. You need a safe place to put a hot pan down where it will not slide, and insulated pan and pot handles. A large cover-all apron of tough plastic will protect you from splashes.

Should you be unlucky enough to sustain a burn or scald, it is important to prevent dehydration. When Bill accidentally barbecued me four hours away from civilization, we were acutely conscious of this. Following instructions, he fed me lemon squash with a little salt in it, half a pint every half hour, and measured my output in the rain gauge — driving the boat at maximum speed all the time, I should point out. He also radioed ahead for assistance. On arrival (at an Eastern Mediterranean port with a hospital) we had waiting for us a French doctor, an English doctor, an English nursing sister, and an American nurse (all liveaboards or on holiday in yachts). All of them advised us not to go near the hospital, and were delighted with Bill's lemonade, now coming through me every five minutes, and tickled by the rain gauge. With such good care, my burns on thighs, arms and hands healed in no time, I remaining in the cockpit on a clean sheet the while.

Other crew members can get burnt if you have an on-board barbecue (usually the kind that gimbals on a stern rail). We know of two cases of burns caused by thoughtless use of methylated spirit: fire-lighters are much safer. We keep a fire extinguisher near the cooking stove in case of galley fires. (Firefighting in yachts is covered in Chapter 11.)

Ciguatera poisoning

This is caused by eating fish from coral reefs near the Equator. It manifests not only with the usual food poisoning symptoms — nausea, vomiting and diarrhoea; but can also produce tingling and numbness in the fingers, toes, lips and tongue; joint and muscle pains, weakness and cramps; fatigue, fainting and headaches; and itching made worse by alcohol. To confuse the issue even more, any or all of these symptoms may be present, and they may be so slight as to be barely noticed, or severe enough to include breathing difficulties. Some sources say the death rate (mostly from breathing difficulties) is 2-3%, others 1%; others say that it could be less as the milder cases are not reported.

In by far the majority of cases, unpleasant as these symptoms are they will go away in time, though muscular weakness may persist for quite a while.

Ciguatoxin is found in a small organism that attaches to the algae on certain coral reefs, where it is eaten by small fish. These are then eaten by larger fish, and as the food chain gets longer the toxin is concentrated until in the larger predatory fish it becomes a danger to those who eat it.

Distribution   This is the hard part, as the distribution of the affected reefs is sporadic and capricious: it is not yet understood what factors make some reefs harbour the organism, and others (though quite close by) not. So while one can say with truth that ciguatera is present in reefs in the Pacific, Japan, Queensland, the Great Barrier Reef and the Caribbean, that is not the whole story. North of Antigua in the Caribbean, ciguatera is present in some reefs. To the south, the Windward Islands and the Grenadines are free of it. French Polynesia is widely affected, Raratonga is not.

What is certain, in all the myth and rumour which abounds on this subject, is that the local fishermen, be they Polynesian, Caribbean or Floridans, know with fair exactitude which reef and which fish species to avoid. They will also volunteer much folklore on testing fish for poison, ranging from cooking it with a silver coin (which turns black if the fish is toxic) to trying it out on the Mother-in-law. No reliance can be placed on these methods, as only very sophisticated laboratory tests can detect whether the fish is affected. Neither heating or canning destoys the effects of the toxin. So what to do?

Local knowledge from a reliable source is vital. If in any doubt, do not eat the larger predatory fish: Grouper, Barracuda, Emperor, Sailfish etc. (One source describes over 10 kilos as large.) Do not eat Moray eel. Do not eat the roe, liver or other offal especially from large fish.

Research is going on in Queensland, Tahiti, Japan and Hawaii, among other places, to establish accurate tests for ciguatera.

Colds

Just go to sea. The virus disappears after a week to ten days.

Cystitis *(a urinary tract infection)*

If you are subject to this, make sure you drink a lot of water.

Dental problems

Some old Salt Horses, chiefly from the New World, suggest having all your teeth out before a long cruise. This seems to us a draconian solution. It should suffice to ensure that you are 'dentally fit' before you leave. Tell your dentist your plans, and he will be careful to miss nothing.

Thereafter, look after your teeth. I will not insult your intelligence by telling you how, since we are all over-exposed to dental hygiene. Here are some thoughts that might not occur to you, however. If you wear dentures, take them out if you feel seasick, they are too easily chundered overboard. Of course you will take a spare set in case of accidents.

A dental first aid kit should contain cement to repair bridgework, or even broken teeth. Lost fillings may be temporarily replaced by equal parts of oil of cloves and powdered zinc oxide. Mix this well, and work it into the well dried cavity. It will set in about a quarter of an hour, and last until you can get it seen to. Oil of cloves on cottonwool is a harmless local painkiller.

Departure stress

Leaving home and friends can be grievous. Husbands and lovers could help a lot by trying to understand how serious a bereavement this is; the male has no roots, it seems, certainly not the ones who go to sea, and feels less pain on upheaval. The tumbleweed male should allow plenty of time for his partner to adjust to transplantation (in the gardening sense). Unlike plants, this will be worst *before* the actual uprooting; on sailing day the relief will be balm to everyone's pain but the weeks or even months before you go will be hard. Bereavement is a sense of loss, of people and things that are loved and respected. It is not necessary for the people to actually die, or the things to be destroyed for you to feel bereft; bereavement is also caused by leaving treasures behind, whether human, animal, abstractions or objects. Bereavement is something to be reckoned with. It is a very germane consideration. Men come up against it with a jolt when they unexpectedly lose their jobs. Some people suffer severely from bereavement when they retire, and grieve for their lost jobs and status. If they have no absorbing hobby they can die of despair. In the same way women will grieve for family, friends and the house they leave behind.

Happy are they who are encouraged and comforted while they work their way through this painful stage. Grief is extremely hard work, and very time-consuming for the person undergoing it; and the support group will need great patience. He will need to check the urge to say: 'Aren't you making rather a meal of this?' or 'Dear oh dear, you are going on a bit.' Of course she is. That is how she will work through it.

Diseases, avoidable

'They fall sicke of one disease or another . . .'

Unless there are positive medical objections, it makes sense to acquire vaccination, immunisation, and inoculation against Smallpox, Tetanus and Typhoid (TAB).

Some parts of the world will not allow entry without an International Certificate of Vaccination, against smallpox and/or yellow fever.

It may also be advisable, according to where you intend to travel, to have shots against cholera and polio, and gamma globulin shots against hepatitis and some other viral infections. *Babies* should have the triple vaccine (diptheria, whooping cough and tetanus) unless your doctor advises otherwise. It is not considered advisable for babies under nine months to have Yellow Fever shots, but you may insist, in writing. *Children* should have the triple vaccine, plus immunisation against polio.

Discuss with your doctor the advisability or otherwise of all these precautions, and whether to include shots against tuberculosis and German measles for your children.

Detailed lists are available in a leaflet from your local Department of Health and Social Security. Try also the Hospital for Tropical Diseases and MASTA (Medical Advisory Services for Travellers) whose addresses will be found in the Appendix.

Ear itch

Many people get this infuriating complaint when swimming. Otosporin (on prescription) seems to work.

Eye damage

Whether you wear glasses or not, have your eyes tested before departure. You will need good sight by night as well as day, and if glasses help, wear them. Tell the optician your plans and discuss with him whether the lightness and toughness of plastic lenses outweighs their tendency to scratches. Take spare pairs and your prescription with you. Keep them on with chain, elastic or string: whatever suits you. *Do not* keep them in a breast pocket: I have seen many a pair of specs go to the bottom as their owner bent over a rail; otherwise they get broken. Fix a steel tag to them and you might get them back with a Sea Searcher magnet: we have rescued not only spectacles but keys, fountain pens, bolts and wing nuts, fish traps and bicycles.

When using the sextant for sunsights be extra careful not to glimpse the sun directly through the telescope. This is easy to do on days when the sun is fitful and can burn the retina, causing irreversible damage which may not be noticed at the time.

Professional seamen seldom wear sunglasses, preferring to train their eyebrows to jut like yardbrooms and to observe the world through slitted eyes. We feel that Polaroids can be helpful if you are looking up-sun. If bright reflections give you headaches, add a broad-brimmed hat or an eye shade.

> There's nothing that drives you out of your senses
> Like constantly losing your contact lenses.

Talk to your optician about the advisability or otherwise of using these at sea, and ask him to check for colour blindness, which would preclude unsupervised night watchkeeping. Eyes are priceless: guard them well.

Falls

Much of what was said under Bodily Damage is equally valid for falls. Apart from damage to fingers from tools, we observe falling to be the major cause of damage to yachtsmen, resulting in a wide variety of lesions, from bruises and scrapes to the very common cracked ribs, through broken bones of all kinds up to skull and vertebral fractures.

Good handholds and the right shoes go a long way to avoid these injuries. In weather when the ship's motion is very jerky, clip on and hold on, and only move when necessary.

Bill and I hold opposite views about cockpit cushions: I like plenty of them to cushion me when I get thrown off balance; Bill thinks there are too many, as he falls over them if they get dislodged.

A padded coat or lifejacket can save bruises to the upper part of the body. I sometimes inflate my pilot jacket a little to enable me to bounce off hard edges.

Your steering or seat should be difficult to fall out of, as well as comfortable to sit in.

> Mop, ah, mop those spills away,
> Before you crack your vertebrae.

Flip-flops are for wearing ashore only. They are highly dangerous. We knew a paraplegic who acquired his injury by catching the rung of a ladder between his toes and the sole of his flip-flops. He fell 30 feet.

Peeing over the side in a rough sea is an excellent way to lose crew, however alluring it might be not to have to go below. How about constructing a 'pig's ear' as the Navy calls it? Make a funnel from the top of a plastic bottle: an opaque one for aesthetic preference; attach it firmly to a length of hose which will reach over the side, then hang the business end within reach of the cockpit. A little ingenuity with the design of the funnel even allows us disadvantaged females to use it, instead of getting our bottoms splashed by the rollicking seas in the toilet bowl.

Heat exhaustion

This is nothing to do with sunstroke, it is caused by working in hot humid conditions. The danger arises with temperatures of over 27°C, 80°F, combined with high relative humidity. Increasing bad temper and bolshiness on the part of a normally cooperative crew is an indicator. A sufferer will be cool, sweaty, and pale. Prevention is a question of allowing the cook a heavier hand with the salt, and plying the crew with anchovies and highly seasoned salami. Keep cool and stay in the shade if possible. Stokers in the Navy used to be given pints of salty lemonade to prevent heat exhaustion.

Heatstroke, Sunstroke More catastrophic, but less common. The sufferer will *not be sweating*, and become very hot. Acclimatise yourself gently to hot weather and strong sun. Wear light clothing and a hat. Stay in the shade if you can, and keep decks and crew cool with buckets of sea water. Drink plenty and don't be mean with the salt.

Herpes (cold sores)

Avoid sun on the lips, as it excites the herpes virus into action. So does wind, dryness, and a raised body temperature. Wear a hat, use a sunscreen or Chapstick, which tastes better.

Hypothermia

'... not so much as a cloth to shift him, shaking with cold.'

In our young days, something vaguely termed 'suffering from exposure' attacked mountaineers, fell walkers, and shipwreck survivors. Old people and babies died, too, in their homes. After years of study and research, it is now called Hypothermia and is recognized as a killer. Not only in cold climates, take note. It is now suggested that yachtsmen at risk, whether in the water or in a liferaft, actually succumb to hypothermia oftener than drowning. If they are in the water, it is hypothermia which probably causes them to drown.

Since this is at present the most likely cause of death at sea, know the enemy. Hypothermia is a serious loss of heat from the deep areas of the body. If the inner body temperature falls below 32°C (87°F) the prospects are not good. Your clinical thermometer is no use for these deep body temperatures, which are caused by heat being leached away from the body without being replaced. This can happen when immersed in cold or even cool water, when exposed to wind without proper clothing, or, as in the case of the very old and the very young, through malfunctioning of the body's heat regulators.

The time it takes to get into this condition is idiosyncratic; if you are strong and physically fit, you will last longer than someone of smaller build who is equally fit. Fat people have an initial advantage as they store more heat, but lose their edge when they tire more rapidly and become exhausted. Children cool faster than adults.

Cold water leaches the heat away faster than cold dry air, and wind chills you very fast.

Prevention Your sailing clothes are important. They should protect you from wet and wind, and have some insulating (air-retentive) properties. The former is provided by waterproof foul weather gear, and the latter by wearing under it anything that will trap air, such as a knitted garment, or a foam lining. Those furry garments sometimes called Polar suits trap the air in the pile, and are comfortable. However as they are of man-made fibres, a woollen jersey over them is a good idea, as wet wool is a better insulator than wet nylon and actually generates a little heat.

Even on a warm night, a sudden strong wind can chill you rapidly. It is as well to have a windproof jacket and a woolly hat handy. Preventing loss of heat from head (20% heat loss is through the scalp), hands and toes becomes important in colder climates, and there is no substitute for wool. Wet nylon socks will not keep you warm, but having said that, once you get to survival level anything is better than nothing.

Signs to watch for

The person may not realize that he is dangerously cold.

He may be shivering. (This is beneficial, as it generates heat.)

He may be awkward and clumsy, and his movements and speech be very slow.

His mind may feel like porridge, and a state of lethergy can set in, preventing self-help.

If you suspect hypothermia, PREVENT FURTHER HEAT LOSS. Remove the person from the water or wind. Get him below. If possible replace wet clothes with dry ones, otherwise wrap him in a Space Blanket. Cover the head, mouth and nose with a woolly hat, and a closely wound scarf, to prevent heat loss from the lungs. Do not leave him alone, as he is capable of irrational behaviour, including removing all his clothes. Encourage a little activity if he is not exhausted. If he is conscious, give hot, sweet, drinks but NO ALCOHOL, which causes heat loss and a dangerous fall in the blood sugar.

It is much more important to *prevent further heat loss* than to try artificial warming by means of hot water bottles or baths, as this can bring the heat to the body surface at the expense of the deep organs. If the sufferer can get in the bath without help, it is safe for him to have one.

Survival in the water Float, don't swim. Swimming dissipates heat. If you are not alone cluster with the others, and try to roll into a ball, to reduce the heat loss from your body.

Infantile diarrheoa

This is probably the most dangerous thing that could happen to your baby or toddler, apart from severe sunburn. The baby becomes progressively dehydrated until he is seriously ill. To combat dehydration in children (and adults as well if need be) you can obtain a double-ended plastic spoon which has been developed for Third World mothers. Salt goes in one end, and sugar in the other, and both are stirred into a glass of water until dissolved. One glass for a child, and two for adults is taken after every diarrheoa. This cheap and simple device has saved more lives than kidney machines. The address to send for the spoon is in the Appendix, but if you encounter any difficulties here are the quantities: ⅓ coffee spoon salt, 1 level tea-spoon sugar, *dissolved in a glass of water*. (This is important because your body cannot use the salt otherwise.) Alternatively ask your Chemist for Dioralyte sachets, a ready-made mixture of sodium chloride (salt), potassium chloride, soda bicarbonate and glucose, for mixing with 200 cc (7 oz) water. They will be more expensive than the salt and sugar mixture, but can be used even for tiny babies.

Low morale

> 'For when a man is ill or at the point of death, I would know
> whether a dish of buttered rice with a little Cynamon, ginger
> and sugar . . . bee not better . . . than salt fishe . . .'

Sooner or later the time comes when nothing goes well, and every one feels low and grouchy. I have said earlier that food and drink are important: now is the time to break out something special for the next meal. In the meantime, splice the mainbrace or have a coffee with some rum in it, or eat a whole candy bar.

The aftermath of bad experiences takes its toll of all the crew, not always in the same way. Some talk a lot, some do not talk at all. Some sleep at once, some cannot sleep. Some are elated because it is over, others worry in case it happens again. All need comfort and reassurance.

If we found it hard to sleep after an exhausting (even frightening) experience, a tablet of Serene or Kwells was an effective calmer. If something stronger was needed 5mg of Diazepam usually did the trick, without fogging our heads in the morning as sleeping pills are apt to do. Usually, however, our practice after such events was to talk the shock away for an hour or two over a stiff brandy or gin, to cut the adrenalin. When we felt sufficiently unwound, we went to bed and usually slept like logs.

Morale on board is a delicate flower. It has to be nurtured and tended with care. We have met yachts where it seems to have broken down completely: everyone moving well away from each other in a heavy silence, speaking to us and other strangers without looking at us, in tones that are too loud. Someone is often crying down below; and you can bet she will be the first to recover.

I have said something already about mutual support between skipper and crew. This must extend, gentlemen, to allowing your ladies a good cry, after an exhausting or terrifying experience. Most women are immensely strong mentally and can also call on more physical strength than might be thought, if need be. They will do whatever is necessary, beyond what you could have hoped for. They will fight fires, pump valiantly, bail like demons, staunch the blood, and hang on to the uttermost.

They will cope, beyond the point of pain and exhaustion, like the human beings they are. When there is no more to be done, they are likely to burst into tears. Men react indignantly to this. They feel it as a reflection on their actions; but crying is no more a criticism of him than his heartfelt swearing at a sulky generator is a reflection on her. What is more, tears are as beneficial as a cold beer on a sweltering day. Better, since there is some evidence to show that a natural anaesthetic is released into the brain when someone cries. No wonder it is such a relief. Cry a bit more, chaps: it's good for you.

> After the storm is over
> Indulge in a real good cry,
> Swallow a whisky and water
> And dinner with lots of pie.
> Comforting words should be spoken
> Helping you sleep till morn,
> Harmony need not be broken
> After the storm.

Malaria

There are pills to prevent Malaria. You must start them in advance, and continue after you leave the areas where it is to be found. IAMAT, previously mentioned, has very good information. See Chapter Seven for dealing with mosquitoes.

Malnutrition and deficiency diseases

Most ocean passages last less than a month, so it is very unlikely that you are going to stagger ashore with Beri-beri or Pellagra at the end of your voyage, especially if you paid attention to the chapter on victualling. However, multivitamin pills take up no space at all and might be useful. One of the really long passages is that made by cruisers from Australia and New Zealand, who come across the Indian Ocean and up the Red Sea to the Mediterranean. The time for this is the dry Northeast Monsoon, which means that water is critically short and hard to replace. These folk sometimes arrive in the Mediterranean in poor shape, skinny (easily remedied) and with salt water boils and ulcers that are hard to heal. The protein-rich cereal mixtures in Chapter Nine could help to prevent these. For the Boils see Skin Problems, below.

Noxious diseases of all kinds

Your life will be changing completely. Would it be so hard to use the break to stop smoking? Apart from the good effect it will have on your health and finances (and you will not find low-tar and filter tips in the remoter areas) smoking in the confined space below decks of a small yacht is literally nauseating. Think about it.

Rabies

Get your ship's cat or dog vaccinated, (see Chapter Seven), and in areas where rabies is endemic warn the children not to pet animals they may find ashore. At the same time, they must understand the necessity to report bites, especially from 'oddly' behaving animals.

Seasickness

This above all can spoil your enjoyment of (anyway) the first two days of your voyage. There is much that can be done to minimise its likelihood and shorten its duration. You could be one of those who are never ill at all, or one of the unfortunates who are very sick indeed for a long time.

It is a comfort to know that on a long voyage the large majority of people are over it on the second day. Thereafter a sensible régime will prevent its recurrence, even in rough seas, unless prolonged galley or engineroom work are attempted.

To cut seasickness down to a minimum   Don't go to sea with a hangover.

Go into a rough sea with the stomach warm and comfortably full of something fairly stodgy: stew with lots of potatoes, or pilaf, or pasta or porridge.

Have an extra jersey handy; it is important not to get chilled and you might not want to go below for it. Best start off too warm: you can always discard.

Try not to get too tired. Do whatever is necessary, and rest between tasks, up on deck if you can.

Spell the helmsman, drive a bit. Drivers are seldom sick.

Take whatever remedy suits you in plenty of time: at least half an hour before you leave harbour if it looks rough outside. You should need only a couple to see you through the first day, if they are regular pills. The ones you stick behind the ear (Transderm) or on your wrist last for three days, but are available only in the US.*

If you can, keep eating. If you cannot face real food, nibble dry crackers or crispbread, and have an occasional sweet fizzy drink: a swallow or two of beer is surprisingly good, ginger ale not far behind; it's the fizz that counts.

* Now available on prescription under the name 'Scopoderm TTS'.

As a last resort, lie down below, for'd if running before the wind or aft if going to windward. (This takes one set of the semi-circular canals in your ear out of action, and so you feel less giddy.)

> Take in time your seasick pill
> Otherwise you will be ill.
> Tummy warm and full of food
> Helps to keep you feeling good.
> Too much booze the night before
> Makes you toss your cookies more.
> Cold your body, head and toes:
> Overboard your breakfast goes.
> Nibble, nibble, all the day
> To hold your queasy tum at bay;
> A gill of beer, or ginger ale,
> Will stay your stomach through the gale.
> Should you feel that death is near,
> Lying down you'll feel less queer.

Skin trouble

Ulcers and boils (gunnel bum, in the racing world) are caused by constant contact with salt water, such as occurs on the long run from Australia up to the Red Sea. With water so desperately short, none can be spared for washing to remove the salt from the skin.

It would be well worth taking a large quantity of travel tissues: the moistened kind; even one a day would get *some* of the salt off. Paper underpants make a lot of sense, too.

Stomach upsets

'. . . and then if their Victuals be putrified it indangers all'

Assuming that you have had your TAB shots, get further immunity by eating and drinking locally. Take the normal precautions of washing or peeling fruit and vegetables just before you eat them. Boiling the water we have not found necessary anywhere, but with a small baby you may feel it essential, or if you yourself are susceptible and worried about the water source. Purifying tablets are available, both for large and small quantities of water. All are based on chlorine.

Since a chronic water shortage leads to skimping the washing up, it is sensible to have two separate chopping boards. Keep one strictly for raw meat, fish or chicken and stow its appropriate knife with it. The other is for cooked meat, bread and cleaned raw vegetables for salads. It too has its own knife.

Stomach disorders are usually caused by one of the F's — food, flies or faeces, so keep the first clean and cool, murder the second merciless-ly (see 'Pests') and don't skimp the personal hygeine and hand washing. Put some medicated wipes in the heads instead of a towel, and a bin for used ones.

We ran into trouble with stomach disorders on our return from America, when we visited Tangier. We had obviously lost our resistance in the two years we had spent in the ultra-hygienic States, and Tangier is not a good place to be sensitive in. We suffered somewhat, but our Mediterranean immunity soon re-established itself.

Remember that alcohol is a great bug killer. 'Take a little wine, for thy stomach's sake, and thine often infirmities,' as St Paul advised St Timothy. Our eminent authority states that 'a little wine' can be reckoned as up to half a litre a day!

Stress

You have gone to a great deal of trouble to leave stress behind. Make sure that you also leave behind such lingering habits of the old life as hurrying to get somewhere, working from morning till night, or putting the engine on merely because it is faster. There will be quite enough to challenge you in the months ahead without looking for extra work. Use the lazy windless days to store well-being and energy, as well as learning how to cope when the weather turns foul, things go wrong and everyone is needed to the utmost. This is certain to happen, even if you neither girdle the earth or round Cape Horn. If you do decide that you want to do these heroic things, beware that a sense of compulsion does not creep in, and with it a loss of that carefree feeling that you are doing what you want and not what you must. That is not the way of laid-back cruising. Nor is the driving urge to 'get your ticket punched', as we have heard circumnavigation described: trying to do this in a limited time probably causes as much pointless hassle as staying in the cut-throat world of business or fighting for your job.

The way to circumnavigate or cruise without stress is to have no time limit and do it almost by accident, strolling from island to island and continent to continent.

> Blue sky and green water pour into your mind;
> The balm of the world, landsman's daughter,
> You sought so long to find.

Sunburn

Millions of words of warning are printed every year, yet one sees the boiled-lobster effect wherever there is a bit of sun and wind. Patience and a good sun-screen lotion (and the latter is not essential) are all that is required; you cannot get a deep water suntan in three days, you will merely have your skin crispy-broiled. Take a total screen cream: apart from prevention it can alleviate even a nasty sunburn. Protect noses, lips, bald pates and the tops of your feet. If you stayed in the shade for a fortnight in hot sunny weather, you would still achieve a pleasant tan and no burns.

Sun is not always beneficial. Even with a good protective tan you can get skin cancer. This is less likely if you are black, lucky thing.

Thrush (Vaginal candidiasis)

This distressing complaint can be discouraged by wearing loose-fitting cotton (never man-made fibres) next the skin. The Pill can predispose you to thrush.

Water contamination

Do not let the water hose fall in the dock. Keep the hose clean. Before you top up, direct a jet at the tap or standpipe to clean it: shore people can be very careless where they walk their dogs. 30 grains of stabilized chloride of lime to 100 gallons of water will destroy all organisms in it, but so will a little alcohol in your drinking glass and it tastes better.

The Medicine Chest

> '. . . also that his chest be well furnished bothe for Physicke and Chirurgery and so near as may be proper for the clime you go for.'

Here follows a list of what we took (after much discussion with our doctor and other authorities) and what we used it for; and whether we used it at all. In the fourteen years since our first departure many improvements and discoveries have been made, so I also give a 1990 update, and a list of additions that we found necessary. + means a prescription was necessary, 0 means that we never used it. Ampoules are for injections.

+ 0 Adrenaline: 1:10,000:   Shock or severe drug reaction.
+ Ampicillin: Broad-spectrum antibiotic. *1990* Amoxil.
Aspirin, soluble: Headache and colds, minor aches.
+ 0 Atropine: Narcotic, relaxes gastro-intestinal tract. *1990 update*: Pro Banthine.
+ 0 Benzedrine, 4 tablets: For emergencies requiring short-term prolongation of alertness.
+ 0 Benadryl Antihistamine: For allergic reactions. *1990 update*: Triludan.
Codeine compound tablets: Headache and colds. *1990* withdrawn from the market.
Cream of magnesia: Indigestion. *1990 update*: Aludrox.
Burrow's Solution: Fungus infections. *1990 update*: Canesten cream.
Chloramine: Water purifying tablets: *1990 update*: Sterotabs.
+ 0 Decadron: Severe allergies, shock and venom. *1990 update*: Piriton (and other antihistamines).

+ Diazepam 5mg: Tranquilliser (for sleeping in severe storms).
+ 0 Diazepam ampoules: Potent tranquilliser.
+ 0 Gelusil tablets: Antacid, for indigestion and wind. *1990 update*: Aludrox.
+ Mist. Kaolin Sed.:   'Concrete mixture', for diarrhoea.
+ 0 Lasix: Diuretic: for use after near-drowning in salt water.
+ 0 Lomotil: For severe diarrhoea.
Multivitamin tablets: To prevent difficiency diseases.
+ Nitrazepam, 5mg: Sleeping tablets.
Paracetamol: Moderate pain and toothache.
+ 0 Penicillin V.K. tablets: Antibiotic, replaced by Magnapen.
+ 0 Pethidine ampoules: Narcotic for pain relief.
Hyoscine hydrobromide: Seasickness. *1990 update*: we added Stugeron and Transderm.
+ 0 Septrin tablets: For those allergic to Penicillin. *1990 update*: Trimethaprim.
+ Tetracycline tablets: General antibiotic.
0 Senokot: Constipation. A rare condition, we found.
+ 0 Xylocaine ampoules: Local anaesthetic.
    Later we also added:
+ Tetanus vaccine.
+ Distalgesic: *1990 update*: Dihydrocodeine for moderate to severe pain.
0 Dioralyte: Against dehydration.
+ 0 Naprosyn: Muscular and skeletal pain (e.g. discs).

About one-third of this list was never used. The more heroic measures were there if they were needed, kept in a locked drawer (and we were told later that we would have been justified in using one of the narcotic pain-killing ampoules on one occasion) but it was run-of-the-mill remedies we mostly needed: antibiotics, paracetamol, kaolin mixture and so forth. As it should be.

Thorough discussion with a qualified person will be necessary, not only because you will need a prescription (and not on the National Health Scheme either) but also an explanation of how and when to use these things.

The First Aid Kit

Whatever you keep this in, it ought to be fairly near the cockpit (which tends to become the casualty centre) and easily accessible. A list of the whereabouts of more bulky items should be stuck into the lid or otherwise firmly attached (large dressings, bandages, and the applicators for the larger sizes of tubegauze, for example). This is what we took:
+ means we needed a prescription, 0 means it was never used.

Acriflavin ointment: For burns.
\+ Aureomycin ointment: Antibacterial, for cuts and abrasions.
Calamine cream: Minor skin itch, and sunburn.
Fisherman's Friend: Rubbing ointment (no, not the pastilles!) for sprains, wrenches and muscle pain.
\+ Furacin: Antibacterial, for burns or wounds.
Golden Eye ointment: For styes. *1990 update*: withdrawn from sale, substitute Chloromycetin ointment + 0.
Ice Pak: (added later) A once-only shake and apply ice pack for bad bruises. No need to store in the fridge. We got ours in the States, but now obtainable in the UK (see Appendix).
Mercurochrome stick: Used like Iodine, stays on better in sea water.
TCP antiseptic liquid: For disinfecting minor cuts.
\+ Neobacrin   Eye ointment: see Golden Eye ointment.
\+ Nystan ointment: Thrush and athlete's foot. 1990 Canesten cream.
Adhesive dressing strip.
Elastoplast (finger plasters):   We used hundreds of these.
Tubegauze bandages and applicators, in 4 sizes from toes to torsos. We used only the two smaller sizes. A particularly neat form of bandage.
Crepe bandages·   Could be washed and reused.
Butterfly sutures: Never successful, as the victim was always sweating and no matter how much we swabbed they would not stick.
Cotton Wool.
Sterile packs of wound dressings in several sizes. (Used 1 small one.)
Roll of adhesive plaster (tape):   The Bandaid type from America came unstuck within ten minutes: we were glad to get back to Elastoplast.
0 Eye bath: For washing out foreign bodies with saline solution.
0 Disposable hypodermic syringes, with needles.
Safety pins.
Scissors and tweezers—never to be taken away and used elsewhere!
Clinical thermometer.
Anti-sting cream: Mosquito bites, wasp stings, jellyfish.
    Later we added:
0 Prepacked sutures, already attached to needle. For closing wounds.
0 Sterile burn dressings: Sofra tulle, Opsite etc.
0 Aerosol burn spray: Now kept near the stove.
Nobecutane spray: Forms a sterile plastic coating over wounds or burns.
0 Disposable scalpels: After the fishhook episode.
Fever Tester: A temperature-sensitive plastic film; takes up no room, is unbreakable, but cannot be used rectally.
Sicatrin: Antibiotic for wounds.
0 Oil of cloves and zinc oxide powder: for temporary tooth filling.
    In addition we now take:
Disposable mini enemas (Microlax).
A rectal thermometer (Blue bulb):   for measuring Hypothermia.
Fluoroscein stain: for finding damage to cornea.
Labstix: for testing urine.

A Brooke Airway, for resuscitation.
A low voltage electric blanket. (Address in Appendix).

As you can see, we really needed nearly everything in the first list at least once. Murphy's Law being what it is, since we got the scalpels and sutures we have not required them again.

Epilogue

A night in harbour is a precious thing,
    No waves to rock the boat, a full night's sleep:
But we are wishful to be journeying,
    With islands yet unknown a tryst to keep.

They call and beckon, coax and draw us forth,
    A pull as strong as the relentless tide.
They draw us like a magnet, South and North,
    Their soft insistence cannot be defied.

We'll sail the ancient ways, the quiet ways
    By dolphin path, salty, and silver blue;
The saffron sun shall circumscribe our days
    Of hopeful travelling to Xanadu.

    A night in harbour is a precious thing,
    But when we go to sea again we sing!

Appendices

Book List

The following books may be of interest, although some are now out of print. We do not claim that the list is exhaustive.

The Boat Herself

Elements of Yacht Design by Skene, revised Kinney
Small Steel Craft by Ian Nicolson
Boatbuilding by Howard Chapelle. For wooden boats
Fitting Out Ferrocement Hulls by Rob Tucker
The Ocean Sailing Yacht by Don Street
Boat Electrics by John Watney
Metal Corrosion in Boats by Nigel Warren
The Complete Rigger, Wire and Rope by Brion Toss
Boat Owner's Mechanical and Electrical Manual by Nigel Calder
Trouble Shooting and Maintenance of Boat Engines by Peter Bowyer
The Care and Repair of Small Diesel Engines by Chris Thompson

Seagoing

The Cruising Life by Ross Norgrove
Cruising as a Way of Life by Thomas Colvin
After 50,000 Miles by Hal Roth
Cruising With Children by Gwenda Cornell
This is Cruising by J.D. Sleightholme. An introduction to the subject.
Cruising in Tropical Waters and Coral by Alan Lucas
Meteorology at Sea by Ray Sanderson
The Ship Captain's Medical Guide (HMSO)
Yachtsmen's Eight-Language Dictionary by Barbara Webb
Navigation for Yachtsmen by Mary Blewitt
Celestial Navigation for Yachtsmen by Mary Blewitt
Where There is No Doctor (pub. Teaching Aids at Low Cost)

The Yachtsman's Doctor by Dr. Richard Counter
Where There is No Dentist (pub. Teaching Aids at Low Cost)
Instant Wind Forecasting by Alan Watts
Instant Weather Forecasting by Alan Watts

Catering

Charcuterie and French Pork Cookery by Jane Grigson
The Best Bread Book by Patricia Jacobs
Mediterranean Seafood by Alan Davidson
Diet for a Small Planet by Francis Moore Lappé
Recipes for a Small Planet by Ellen Buchman Ewald

Some Useful Addresses (all in UK unless indicated)

Clubs and Associations

The Cruising Association   Ivory House, St Katharine Dock, London E1 9AT
The Ocean Cruising Club   Geoff Hales, 6 Creek End, Emsworth, Hants, PO10 7EX
Little Ship Club   38 Hill St, London W1X 8DP
Seven Seas Cruising Association   PO Box 2190, Covington, LA 70434, USA
Royal Yachting Association   Romsey Road, Eastleigh, Hants, SO5 4YA

Health Care

Hospital for Tropical Diseases   4 St Pancras' Way, London NW1 OPE
Institute of Child Health   30 Guilford St, London WC1N IEA
Intensive Survey of Medical Emergency Care   Suite 104, 25381 Alicia Parkway, Laguna Hills, CA 92653, USA
IAMAT (*International Association of Medical Assistance to Travellers*)   188 Nicklin Rd, Guelph, Ontario NIH 745, Canada
Teaching Aids at Low Cost   (Spoon, Books) PO Box 49, St Albans, Herts AL1 4AX
Ministry of Agriculture (*Animal Health Division*)   Government Buildings, Hook Rise South, Tolworth KT6 7NF
MASTA (*Medical Advisory Services for Travellers Abroad*)   Bureau of Hygeine and Tropical Diseases, Keppel St, London WC1E 7HT   Tel (01) 631-4408

Education

Worldwide Education Service   Strobe House, 44–50 Osnaburgh St, London NW1 3NN

National Extension College 18 Brooklands Ave, Cambridge CB2 1BR
Calvert School 105 Tuscany Rd, Baltimore, MD 21210, USA

Other

Royal Meteorological Society James Glaisher House, Grenville Place, Bracknell, Berks RG2 1BX
Hotcan Self-heating Meals Stadium Court, Mangham Rd, Rotherham, Yorks S61 4RJ
Dycem Ltd (non-slip table mats) Ashley Hill Trading Estate, Bristol BS2 9XS
The Good Book Guide 91 Great Russell St, London WC1
Cold Pack for bruises Mycoal Warmpacks Ltd, PO Box 43, London SW10 9BZ Tel (01)352-4056
Cold flex: Bruise strapping—Boots.
Low Voltage Electric Blankets: Griffin Products, Holland Way, Blandford Dorset DT11 7SO

Laurel and Bill's Starter Pack for Would-be Cruisers

'Here mayst thou learn the names of all ship's gear'

It has already been suggested that no one should embark on a long voyage or a life afloat without having acquired a minimum competence, which should be got not only by study but also partly by doing some boatwork. It is all very well to plan that the skipper will sail the boat to all intents and purposes as if singlehanded, and that his chosen crew will be entitled to consider themselves solely for catering and/or decorative purposes. It never turns out that way.

Circumstances will arise when it is a case of 'all hands to the something or other' and a certain basic knowledge of somethings-or-other would be no bad idea. Likely areas of difficulty are when berthing, or when others are berthing on you. There are occasions when sails will not do as they should, and no skipper, however brilliant, can see to both ends of a rope at once. People do fall overboard, they also fall in in harbour, especially from dinghies, and things do break or part.

Let us look at a checklist for the absolute novice so that he or she has, at the least, a basis on which experience can build.

Learn the names of important bits of boat or gear, so that you know what the skipper is talking about especially if he is excited or overwrought. Examples: bows, stern, jib, genoa, mainsail, mizzen, sheets, halyards, topping lift, forward, aft, port and starboard. Also: take a turn (or whatever term your own skipper uses to indicate bringing a rope to a cleat or winch), turn up, make fast, fend off, check or ease sheets, luff or bear away, haul, veer, cast off. Concentrate on the

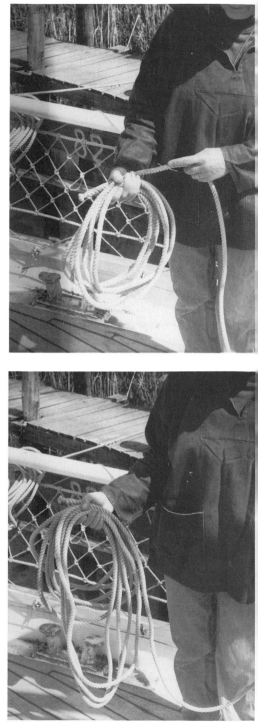

The ability to heave a line properly can be important. This sequence shows how to make one up for heaving, and the round arm throw with followthrough. Even without a monkey's fist on the end of the line, a good heave should reach nearly as far as the line's length. Note the standing end loosely, not tightly, round the left wrist so as not to get lost.

phraseology of your own skipper: it is more important to have certain communication than to have the precisely correct nautical jargon.

Learn to tie a few nautical knots. I suggest the bowline is very important. Then comes the rolling hitch, the round turn with two half-hitches, the clove hitch, the sheet bend and the figure of eight. The reef (square) knot may be better than a granny, but it is a bad knot except for tying reef points, and perhaps also for tieing two Boy Scouts together.

Learn well that in boats over 10 tons, on no account try to stop them moving with hands or feet unless you have an amputation impulse. A fender is best. Learn that when boats move towards a quay or each other there will be little or no damage if someone (why not you?) interposes a fat soft object (not your mother-in-law) so that the impact is absorbed. Learn that these fenders can be pre-positioned as a pre-caution and to save time, but that does not remove the need to see that in the event they are in the right position (where the impact takes place) and not too high or low.

Learn to heave a line. Most yachts in the sizes we are writing about can be controlled by rope capable of being thrown quite a long dis-tance. Remember to hold on to one end of it. If berthing, when you have thrown your rope to the quay and some kind soul has made it fast there, adjust your end so that the rope has no slack and take one full turn round the cleat. There is more to it than this, but that is a basically useful thing to do: if the skipper wants the rope hauled or veered (tightened or let out), or made fast, he will say so.

Learn to steer a compass course. It is not difficult and it gets easier with practice. It is a lovely feeling when you first master the art.

When you are able to cope with the above you will be very useful on board if you keep alert and use your loaf. Your typical Able Seaman is no great genius. He has a few basic skills, some basic knowledge, but most comes as he sails. A lot of the mystique is pure bullshit.

You will certainly not learn to be an Able Seaman from this book. There is much you cannot learn from any book, though a lot of background can be got from a good primer.

Basic Galley Equipment

In use daily:
2 Stainless steel saucepans
2 Non-stick frying pans
Asbestos mats with handles
2 Wooden spoons, 1 wooden 'turner'
Stainless steel tongs
Kitchen knives and cutting boards
Plastic measuring cups (though my standard measure is a 5 oz yoghurt pot)
Small jar containing salt and pepper mix (5:1).

In use weekly:
　Omelette pan
　2 Casseroles, enamel and lidded
　Pressure cooker
　Fireproof earthenware
　Large and small stainless steel bowls and dishes
　Plastic bowls (for mixing, and rising bread in conjunction with a large plastic bag).
　Potato masher
　Slotted spoon
　Ladle (with hook so it does not slip into the pan)
　Wood garlic masher
　Wall or hand tin-opener
　Hand egg-beater
　Bamix Magic Wand
　Non-stick loaf tins
　Strainer
In use less often, but worth their space:
　Hamburger press
　Huge paella pan, also good for frying enormous fish
　Huge pot for lobsters or rice/pasta for twenty

Transatlantic Food

My thinking went thus:
Meat for five people for supper for five weeks, using up the frozen meat first
SUPPER
First two weeks: Day 1, Hamburgers. Day 2, Chicken. Day 3, Tinned. Day 4, Pork chops. Day 5, Steaks. Day 6, Party night. Day 7, Rice or spaghetti.
Following three weeks: Day 1, Tins. Day 2, AFD Curry. Day 3, Tins. Day 4, Steak-and-kidney. Day 5, Rice or spaghetti. Day 6, Party night. Day 7, Tins.
To my great astonishment we caught a fish, so one night we ate that. Party night food had been thought of, and was tinned pheasant or frozen duck (Bill's birthday), or national dishes mostly Chinese or Italian.
LUNCH　These were bread (home-made when the bought bread gave up after the thirteenth day) and cold meats, galantines and pates, salami, etc with salad as long as it lasted (till the nineteenth day), cheese and fruit. If it was a cold day we added hot soup.
BREAKFAST　Very important, after everyone had done at least one and maybe two night watches. We used combinations of eggs, bacon, porridge, sausage and beans, bacon grill, and kippers, plus toast and marmalade, and hot drinks

NIGHTWATCH FOOD   Sweet biscuits, chocolate bars, cheese portions, wholemeal crackers, nuts and raisins, dried figs.

WHAT WE ACTUALLY USED (23 DAYS)
All the beer! All the fresh vegetables, and the following in tins:

Kippers 3	Steak-and-kidney 2	Roast beef 3
Bacon grill 3	Steak-and-onion 2	Roast lamb 3
Sausage-and-beans 4	Steak-and-mushroom 2	Sausages 2
Irish stew 5	Meatballs 1	Salmon 2
Corned beef 2	Stewing steak 1	Chicken breast 1
Chicken supreme 2	Pheasant 1	Game pie filling 1
Crab 1	Prawns 1	Chopped pork 1
Tongue 1	Ham 1	Haricot beans 3
Heinz beans 1	Pelati (tomatoes) 2	Spaghetti sauce 6
Peas 4	Pease pudding 3	Carrots 1
Brussels sprouts 2	Mushrooms 3	Lentils 1
Potatoes 1	Bamboo shoots 1	Water chestnuts 1
Bean sprouts 1	Soups 6	Ravioli 2
Fabada (Bean stew) 1	Cream 1	Raspberries 2
Pears 1	Jam sponge 1	

We had 2½ dozen eggs left, fresh fruit (oranges, lemons and grapefruit), and plenty of useful basic stores which stood us in good stead in the West Indies.

When we were within four days of Barbados the beer ration (jealously watched by the men) went up from one can a day to two, and then, to their great joy, to three.

The list of what we took follows.

Transatlantic food — What we carried

For five people. We already had on board pickles, jams, sauces, salt and pepper, stock cubes and other staples bought in Italy, France, Spain and Gibraltar.

TINNED MEAT (size and number of tins)

Hot dogs/			Meatballs	15oz	8 tins
frankfurters	15oz	6 tins	Irish stew	15oz	12
Stewing steak	15oz	18	Sausages	15oz	6
Breast of chicken	3½oz	6	Roast beef	7oz	7
Corned beef	7oz	12	Roast pork	7oz	7
Bacon grill			Roast lamb	7oz	4
6×12oz, 4×7oz			Pie fillings	15oz	
Tongue	1lb	6	Steak and		
Ham	1lb	3	kidney	6	
Steak-and-kidney			Steak and		
pie	15oz	2	mushroom	6	

322

Steak-and-kidney pud	15oz	6	Steak and onion		6	
Steak-and-kidney pud	7oz	12				

TINNED FISH

Kippers		9 tins	Crab	7oz	6
Prawns/shrimps	7oz	15	Mussels	3½oz	3
Pilchards	15oz	15	Oysters	7oz	2
Salmon	7oz	7	Sardines		12
Squid	7oz	3	Paella mix	3½oz	2
Tuna	7oz	6	Anchovies		2
Chopped clams	15oz	2	Herring roes		2

OTHER TINS

Chopped pork	7oz	6	Fabada (Spanish pork and beans)		1
Pork and beans	15oz	6	Paella		2
Sausage and beans	7oz	6	Ravioli, large		3
Pheasant	15oz	1	Cassoulet		1
Game pie filling	15oz	1	Fruit cake		1
Chinese goose	7oz	2	Assorted soups		12
Liver paté	3½oz	6	Oatmeal, large		1
Pate de campagne		3	Cheese biscuits	3lbs	1
Sweet biscuits	3lbs	1	Spaghetti sauce (Bolognese)		6
Spaghetti sauce (clams)		6	Spaghetti sauce (Matriciana)		6
Spaghetti sauce (mushroom)		6			

TINNED VEGETABLES

Pelati (tomatoes)	15oz	12	Brussels sprouts	15oz	12
Pease pudding	7oz	7	Ratatouille	20oz 2, 15oz 3	
Mushrooms	7oz	9	Red peppers	7oz	5
Leeks	15oz	2	Garden peas	15oz	8
Cauliflower	15oz	7	Petit pois	12oz	4
Spinach	15oz	7	Water chestnuts		2
Celery	15oz	4	Bamboo shoots		2
Beans, green	15oz	5	Bean sprouts		6
Haricot beans (natural)	15oz	12	Curried beans	7oz	4
Macedoine (mixed veg)	15oz	6	Heinz beans	15oz	3
Butter beans	15oz	3	Carrots	15oz	5
Beetroot	7oz	2	Sweet corn	10oz	12
Broad beans	15oz	2	Red cabbage	15oz	2
Chick peas	15oz	3	Lentils	15oz	4
New potatoes	15oz	12			

TINNED FRUIT

Pineapple	15oz	3
	7oz	4
Raspberries	15oz	4
Pears, large		3
Peaches, large		3
Fruit salad, large		3

FROZEN

2 Large pizzas
5 Steaks
10 Loin of pork chops
1lb Chicken pieces
2¼lbs Chicken breast
1 Duck
24 Beefburgers

IN FOIL

Cotechino (sausage)
Chicken curry, 12 portions
Minestrone

PERISHABLES

10kgs Potatoes
10kgs Onions
2 Cauliflowers
4 Cabbages
6 Aubergines
1kilo Green peppers
1½kilos Courgettes
10 Avocadoes
3kgs Sweet apples
3kilos Acid apples
4kgs Oranges
4kgs Green bananas
3 Melons
1kilo Red tomatoes
2kilos Green tomatoes
2kilos Cucumbers
1kilo Green beans
1kilo Carrots
1kilo Lemons
3kilos (10) Grapefruit
6 large White loaves
6 large Wrapped wholemeal
  loaves
12 Bread rolls

TINNED PUDDINGS

Syrup sponge	8
Chocolate sponge	2
Jam sponge	2

DRY GOODS

Plain flour	2kgs
Wholemeal flour	8×3.3lbs
Rice	2×5lbs
Spaghetti	10lbs
Chinese noodles	4pkts
Sugar	8kgs
Long-Life milk	36litres
Long-Life cream	12pkts
Nescafe	1½lbs
Tea bags	250
Dumpling mix	½lb
Batter mix	6pkts
Dried yeast	1tin
Paper towels	6×2 rolls
Toilet rolls	6×2 rolls

DRINKS

Beer	144 cans
Orange squash	½ gal
Lemon and lime squash	½ gal
Wine	40 litres

FRESH GROCERIES

3lbs Streaky bacon
16lbs Butter
5×7oz Vacuum packed bacon
3lbs Turkey galantine (whole)
3lbs 5oz Garlic sausage (whole)
2lb Ham
1½lbs Liver sausage
1 Pork boiling ring
2½lbs Cheddar cheese
1½lbs Double Gloucester cheese
2 boxes Cheese portions
8 dozen Eggs
36 bars Bournville chocolate
36 bars Kit-Kat chocolate
2 pkts Crispbread
Nuts and raisins 24 small packets
Wholemeal crackers in packets
  of 4   ×24

What to Buy Where

Gibraltar

Unit of currency: Pound Sterling.
Fruit and vegetables Much better now the border is opened, but still probably cheaper and better in Spain.
Imported goods English and Spanish. Mainly not expensive.
Frozen To good European standards.
Meat and fish Meat very good, fish variable, mostly frozen.
Bread Plenty of wrapped 'keeping' bread.
Restaurants and snack bars Not very cheap. Good fish-and-chips!
Groceries Pretty well everything.
Beer, wines and spirits You may do well if you buy duty-free, but compare carefully with Spain. Even if you qualify for duty-frees, it is not worth it for beer or wine.
Hard to get Some fresh vegetables and fruit, and dairy produce.
Fuel All obtainable (Cash payment only.)
Water Is in short supply. Do not waste it. Very expensive.
Stock up on Everything you need for your Transat except fresh fruit and vegetables, and fresh eggs, which you will find cheaper and more plentiful in Spain, Portugal, the Canaries or Madeira. Nothing much is obtainable in the Cape Verde Islands.
There is a Marks & Spencer's.

Tunis and Algeria

Unit of currency: in Tunis the Dirham, in Algeria, the Dinar (6D=£1, 1986). Being Muslim countries and with French influence, these are very similar to Morocco. Tunisia is the most sophisticated of the three, but only in the city. Diesel is cheap, and the water is good; but if you are at all sensitive drink mineral water in Algeria. Unsalted butter was very cheap in Tunisia, and if you have a freezer keeps better than salted.

Spain and the Canaries

Unit of currency: the Peseta.
Fruit and vegetables Cheap and very good
Imported groceries Those from all EEC countries are easily available. American goods are harder to come by.
Frozen To acceptable Western standards.
Meat and fish Good. Meat in the Med is rarely hung and benefits from a few days in a fridge, if you have one. The quality and variety of shellfish is excellent.
Bread For keeping, the wrapped Bimbo sandwich bread is fine for about five days: white or wholemeal.
Dairy Both fresh and Long-Life milk available. Eggs may be trusted.
Liquor Spirits are very cheap. There are many cheap (and often nasty)

imitations of well known liqueurs with deceptively similar labels. The cheapest locally distilled rum makes excellent cleaning fluid. The dearer wines are very good, but the range of both price and quality is very wide. The very cheap draught wines can be really rough. Beer, of the fizzy lager type typical throughout the Med, is cheap especially by the crate. In certain places bulk-buying spirits is possible, but this seems to be getting more and more difficult.

Fuel   Diesel, alcohol and bottled gas are easily obtainable. With the proliferation of bottled gas, paraffin (kerosene) is getting hard to find and often of doubtful quality.

Water   Easily available and of drinkable quality.

Restaurants   Very reasonable; the Tourist menus are especially cheap but not very copious or meaty.

Snacks   Alas, the *tapas* (bar snacks) that used to be free with your drink are now likely to cost more than your dinner.

Hard to get   Kettles do not exist and teapots are rare. Fresh cream takes some hunting down, and in the remoter places pet food and litter may be scarce.

Stock up in Spain on   Liquor, unusual tinned vegetables, tinned fish and shellfish, paella spice, fresh fruit and vegetables.

Portugal, the Azores, Madeira

Unit of currency: the Escudo.

Fruit and vegetables   Cheap, simple, straight out of the ground to the market.

Imported goods   Obtainable in larger towns.

Frozen foods   Not widely available except in the larger centres.

Meat and fish   The meat is not quite what you are used to, but the fish is excellent.

Bread   Good, and keeps.

Restaurants and snack bars   Very cheap. A meal with wine will cost about the same as buying the food and cooking it yourself.

Beer, wines and spirits   Reasonable to cheap.

Hard to get   Food is simple here, particularly in the Azores, so you will not find sophisticated pre-packed food.

Fuel   All obtainable.

Water   No problems.

Stock up   Port and Madeira.

Morocco

Unit of currency: the Dirham.

Fruit and vegetables   Patchy in quality, choose with care.

Imported goods   Will be French or Spanish.

Frozen   Don't bank on it.

Groceries   Many exciting pulses and cereals.

STREET MARKET, CIUDADELA, MENORCA

Meat and fish   Fish is usually good, but pricey. As this is a Muslim country you will not find pork or charcuterie. The lamb is better than the beef.

Bread   Very good, but based on French bread and does not keep.

Restaurants and snack bars   Choose a better class of place than you would elsewhere. Alcohol may not be served, but wine or beer is usually available if you eat in a hotel.

Beer, wines and spirits   In spite of Islam, these can be found, but you may have to look quite hard among the coffee houses to find the sort of bar that serves beer.

Hard to get   A good many things you might be used to. You will have great fun looking, though.

Fuel   All available. Diesel is very cheap.

Water   The only place in the Western Med where we were not completely happy about the water was Tangiers.

France

Unit of currency: the Franc.

Fruit and vegetables   Excellent, buy in the covered markets.

Imported goods   Those from other EEC countries are readily come by; the larger centres will have some US imports, at a price.

Frozen   Good and varied.

Meat and fish   Excellent but not cheap.

Bread   Delicious, but hard to find a wrapped loaf that will keep.

Country bread (Pain de Campagne) keeps well.
Restaurants Now very reasonable and of great quality. There is no need to go to the luxury places for very good food.
Beer, wines and spirits Average prices. Spirits are dearer than Spain and Italy, but supermarket wines can be a good buy.
Fuel All are available and expensive.
Water Available everywhere.
Hard to get Talcum powder does not seem to exist in France.
Stock up on Cheeses, charcuterie, tins of luxury items.

Italy

Unit of currency: the Lira.
Fruit and vegetables Very good. Look for the covered markets.
Imported goods Found in the larger supermarkets.
Frozen Varies, but mostly good.
Meat and fish Good, but fish tends to be expensive.
Bread Very good, but does not keep unless you can find *integrale* (wholemeal).
Beer, wines, and spirits Cheaper than France. Draught wine is very cheap and often quite good.
Restaurants Very expensive and not nearly as good as France.
Fuel Readily available. Can be got duty-free if leaving Italy.
Water Available everywhere, but it costs quite a lot as they are used to everyone washing their boats down before filling the tanks.
Hard to get In spite of being in the Common Market there is a very insular attitude to food; paté for instance is unknown in the south.
Stock up on Charcuterie, spaghetti sauces in tins, pasta of all kinds.

Yugoslavia

Unit of currency: the Dinar.
Fruit and vegetables Variable quality and sometimes limited variety.
Imported goods Even simple things are in the luxury class and will only be found with difficulty in the largest of tourist centres.
Frozen Hard to find and limited.
Meat and fish As with all Yugoslav shops and markets, you need to go very early to get any choice at all.
Bread The only country I have been where you may have to queue for bread.
Beer, wines and spirits Average prices.
Restaurants We found it better to look for simple food, since it was not only cheaper but better than the attempts at international cuisine at the classier places.
Fuel Available at the numerous yacht marinas, at a reasonable price.
Water No shortage.
Hard to get Luxury and sophisticated items, anything not produced in the country.

Stock up on The mountain ham, somewhat similar to Parma ham, is cheap though it can be a bit salty.

Greece

Unit of currency: the Drachma.
Fruit and vegetables Good, but not varied except in larger places. You will have a long hunt for mushrooms, for instance.
Imported goods Easier to come by now Greece has joined the Common Market.
Frozen Improving, but still apt to produce right-angled mullet.
Meat and fish Adequate to good, but the cuts (perhaps we should say collops) will be unfamiliar. Fish, as in most of the Med, is dearer than meat.
Bread Often still baked in a wood oven and very good. Ask for *mavro* (black), which is only a little darker than white bread and keeps better.
Beer, wines and spirits All local products are reasonable to cheap. Draught wines can be a good buy.
Restaurants You have to cultivate a more Eastern attitude to time in a Greek taverna. If you do not take the precaution of ordering some cheese and olives *'tora'* (now) you may be quite drunk by the time the food arrives. It will be simple and cheap if you do not choose shellfish or international style dishes.
Fuel Cheaper than Italy, but good fuelling places are not all that common.
Water Very scarce in the Greek islands and should be treated with the respect that a precious commodity deserves. Notices, in Italian mostly, beg you not to wash your yacht: heed them.
Hard to get Most things are available on the Greek mainland, but do not expect any but the simplest things on the smaller islands except perhaps on the day the ferry arrives.

Turkey

Unit of currency: the Turkish Lira
Fruit and vegetables Excellent; some may be unfamiliar e.g. black carrots.
Imported goods Obtainable only in the larger places.
Frozen Not yet very widespread or sophisticated.
Bread Good but does not keep.
Beer, wines and spirits The local beer and wine is reasonable; spirit (*raki*) is not dear but takes some getting used to. You can expect to pay a lot for imported liquor. A mainly Muslim country.
Meat and fish The fish is better than the meat, which is sheep, mostly of the Near Eastern fat-tailed variety, and rather thin cows. There is almost no pork, of course, which means no ham or charcuterie: try pastrami (spiced dried beef), however.

Restaurants The French influence makes the cooking considerably more *soignée* than in Greece, so it is dearer but a pleasure both to eye and palate. Very cheap food can be found at simple *Locantas*, mostly vegetables with a mouthful of meat and washed down with a glass of tea.

Fuel Available.

Water No difficulty.

Hard to get Pork, ham, sophisticated products. Sometimes shortages of such diverse items as light bulbs, sugar or coffee: Turkey is a huge country and the distribution trades are not very modern.

Bermuda

Unit of currency: the Dollar, linked to the US Dollar. Everything is available in Bermuda, but as most of it is flown in from the USA it is expensive. Local grown produce exists but is hard to find.

Fruit and vegetables Mostly the supermarket variety, so watch out for chilling.

Frozen Good and plentiful, but not cheap.

Meat and fish Meat is good, fish not so easy to find fresh; but plenty of frozen fish.

Bread Good. The wrapped wholemeal keeps well.

Restaurants and snack bars Very expensive but good.

Beer, wines and spirits Get it duty-free on leaving.

Fuels All available.

Water No problem, but go easy.

Hard to get Unchilled fruit and vegetables, new-laid eggs.

Stock up on nothing except essentials for passage. Everything will be cheaper in the Azores and Portugal. If you are going on to Gibraltar, English items will be cheaper there. The USA will also be cheaper.

The United States

Unit of currency: the Dollar.

Whether food is cheap here depends, of course, on the rate of the dollar against your currency, but it will be cheaper than Bermuda, and the same items will cost more after transport to the West Indies or the Bahamas.

Fruit and vegetables Obtainable everywhere in a wide variety. Choose carefully, as they are apt to be chilled and therefore short-lived. Iceberg lettuce is a very good keeper.

Groceries Some British goods are available in the better class supermarkets. You will find it very hard to find anything in its natural state: almost everything has been interfered with. Natural food can be found in Health Food shops at twice the price.

Frozen Very good.

Meat and fish Very good. The crabs and shellfish down the Eastern seaboard are especially good.

Bread A huge and bewildering variety is available. Wrapped bread keeps well.

Restaurants and snack bars You might as well use the cheaper ones (and some very cheap 'specials' are sometimes offered) since the cooking will not be any better in the dearer ones, unless you go sky-high.

Beers, wines and spirits Californian and other American made wines are good, but often too sweet to European palates. You need to pay more to find a dry wine. 'Dry' counties, on the other hand, are only too easy to stumble across. In these you cannot either buy alcoholic drink or be served with alcohol in a restaurant: they will offer coffee or soft sugary drinks, both equally bad for you and arguably more so than a glass of wine.

Hard to get Plain raw ingredients and materials, anything without sugar or sugar substitutes. Unchilled fruit, vegetables, and new-laid eggs. Thick double cream is unknown except as sour cream. Long-Life milk has only recently arrived and its distribution may be patchy. Curry ingredients, fruit squash. Marmite.

Fuels Bottled gas, petrol (gas) and diesel are all readily available and cheap. Prices vary. Kerosene (paraffin) should be looked for in the less urban areas.

Water No problems.

West Indies

Unit of currency varies from island to island: often tied to the US Dollar, as in the Virgins and the Bahamas.

Fruit and vegetables Variable in quality, at best very good.

Imported groceries All from the US. British and European goods are hard to find even in the ex-British islands, except for Martinique where many French foods may be found.

Frozen Not too good sometimes; it may be perfect at source but gets maltreated en route. You will know by the pool of frozen juice at one corner of the packet. Nevertheless, everyone lives on the excellent boxes of frozen chicken parts that come from the States.

Meat Not a lot of it and seldom hung. A few islands have a really good butcher, i.e. St Vincent and Martinique.

Fish Excellent. Buy it straight off the fishing boat and in remoter islands enjoy for a reasonable price the lobster that will cost you an arm and a leg in the restaurant. Ciguatera poisoning from reef fish need not concern you south of Antigua. North of there, put your trust in the local fishermen who know which reef and which fish are likely to be contaminated, or stop eating fish high in the food chain.

Bread Variable. In the wilder places be prepared to bake your own.

Dairy Packets of Long-Life milk have taken over from the once ubiquitous tins of condensed. Eggs are uncertain in quality and sometimes chilled; don't buy wet ones, and float them before use.

Liquor No local wines; everyone drinks rum, beer, lime or Coke, anything else is apt to be expensive. St Barts was the cheapest place we found for liquor.

Fuel Except in the large yacht centres diesel is not readily available. Bottled gas, alcohol and kerosene are found everywhere.

Water Expensive everywhere and not easy to come by except in the larger places. Mostly drinkable. Plenty of rain to collect.

Restaurants These are dear as most of their raw materials are flown in from the States. The local dishes are at an inflated price to match.

Snacks Can be excellent and cheap: look for somewhere good and ethnic.

Hard to get Fresh meat, milk, cream, British and European foods, new-laid eggs, pet food and litter.

Stock up in the West Indies on Rum, lime juice, bananas, coconuts, hot pepper sauce. Old-fashioned items that are useful on boats such as washboards and asbestos mats.

Great Britain

Unit of currency: the Pound Sterling.

Fruit and vegetables Buy them in the street markets, where they will not have been chilled if in season.

Imported goods Those from the EEC are widely available. From the USA, found in the larger centres.

Frozen Good and varied.

Meat and fish Meat is good and varied. Fresh fish is now expensive, depending on type, as we no longer have a fishing fleet to speak of.

Bread Everything except hot rolls for breakfast, as night baking is not allowed.

Restaurants Of every sort, more expensive than in most of Europe but cheaper than Italy. Comparable in price with the USA.

Snacks Macdonalds has arrived. But you might prefer the 'pub grub' which varies widely but can be excellent. Fish-and-chips is no longer a bargain, but still jolly good food.

Liquor Highly taxed and expensive.

Local and regional food It is easier to find ethnic restaurants from almost anywhere in the world than good British food, but it does exist. Again, try the pubs: some specialize in it.

Hard to get Dixie food (Hush puppies are something to wear), Granola bars, espresso type instant coffee.

Fuels are all available.

Water Britain is the only country in Europe where the water is not excellent. The EEC says so.

Stock up on Tinned meat, books (there is no Vat on books in the UK), duty-free liquor and cigarettes (but not from ferries or airports, where excess profits replaces much of the supposed saving on tax). (See below.)

Great Britain — Embarking Duty-free Stores

Duty-free stores may be shipped on pleasure craft of less than 40 tons subject to certain conditions: the intended voyage must extend beyond a line south of Brest or north of the north bank of the Eider River; and prior application to a Customs Office is necessary.

No Customs Officer will ever say how much you are allowed, or even admit that there is a scale, so a little game is now played. You say how much liquor and cigarettes you would like to take and the officer retires behind a door for a few minutes, returning to say Yes or No. The answer seems to be a function of the size of yacht, number of crew and distance of the voyage. Since the first two criteria are a matter of fact, it pays to be optimistic about the length of your voyage.

These stores (usually wine, spirits and tobacco, though other items may be shipped Vat-free) must now be obtained from a bonded warehouse and taken aboard at the last minute under Customs seal. It follows that you should have sealable lockers. If your lockers have finger holes, this is not too difficult. We put a lot of bottles in the bilge and bored neat holes in the floorboards to take the sealing wires: it is worth thinking ahead about this, as for a long voyage with a crew of six, as we were, the quantity was quite large.

You may break bond the minute you are outside the 3 mile limit, and we did so — and then had an emergency off the Channel Islands necessitating repairs in St Peter Port: there everything had to be resealed, except those bottles we had already started on.

If an emergency caused you to re-enter British waters, the Customs would have to be notified: an overhand knot in the Ensign gives prior warning, by ancient custom.

Sun Sight Reduction Form

A   Latitude nearest whole degree ▶ [° N OR S]

Local Date................ ▶ [ ]

B   Watch time in GMT.......... ▶ [h m s]

Date if changed for GMT
(Greenwich Date)........ ▶ [ ]

C   Watch error ±.................. ▶ [ ]

D   Calculate B ± C.................. ▶ [ ]

E   Declination...................... ▶ [° 'N OR 'S] ......Look up Declination for exact time D: in this case, interpolate.

F   Hour Angle...................... ▶ [° '] ......From Almanac, on Greenwich Date look up Hour Angle at time D hours: do not interpolate.

G   Hour Angle interpolation...... ▶ [ ] ......Obtain from back of Almanac for the minutes and seconds.

H   Calculate F + G.................. ▶ [ ]

I   Assumed Longitude............. ▶ [ ] ......The idea is to get a whole number of degrees by subtracting I from H if Longitude is West, or by adding I to H if Longitude is East.

J   Calculate H − I or H + I
as appropriate................... ▶ [ ] ......For numbers over 180° subtract from 360°.

Now consult Nav Tables and open for your Latitude (A). Choose side for Latitude either same name (N or S) as Declination, or contrary name.

Enter Table in column for Declination less than your figure (E). Opposite entry for Hour Angle (J) look up K, L, and M.

K   Altitude........................ ▶ [° ']   Q   Sextant reading.................. ▶ [° ']

L   Interpolation factor △......... ▶ [ ]   R   Index Error of sextant.......... ▶ [ ]

M   Azimuth .... ▶ [°]   S   Calculate Q ± R .... ▶ [ ]

N   From Interpolation tables in back of book use excess declination over that used to get KLM, relate it to factor L to get corr N... ▶ [° ']

T   1st Sun correction............... ▶ [ ]

U   Add S + T........................ ▶ [ ]

V   2nd Sun corr & monthly Corr ▶ [ ]

P   Calculate K ± N**
get CORRECTED ALTITUDE ▶ [ ]

W   U − V, THE OBSERVED
ALTITUDE....................... ▶ [ ]

X   Calculate the difference between P and W, the INTERCEPT............ ▶ ['] (OR MILES) TO* FROM*

Y   If sight is before noon re-enter M. If sight is after noon, subtract M from 360°, giving SUN'S TRUE BEARING.. ▶ [°]

*If W is larger than P, delete FROM, if smaller, delete TO (above right, the INTERCEPT)
**K + N if Declination same name as Latitude, K − N if opposite name.

Now, on chart draw in pencil position of Latitude (A) and Longitude (I), and mark with the symbol ☐

Draw in the bearing (Y), towards the bearing if TO, otherwise draw the reciprocal. Measure from the symbol ☐ the Intercept (X), marking it △

Through △ draw a line at right angles to the bearing (Y). Put an arrow head on each end of it. This is your position line at the time of the sight. Write that time along the line.

Position lines can be transferred by moving them in the direction of the Course Made Good, a distance of the Distance Made Good, and drawing the transferred line parallel to the original.

N.B. This form is suitable for use with British Admiralty and US Nautical Almanacs, and commercial Almanacs such as Reeds, MacMillans, and Browns. And for the Air Navigation Tables, HO 249, HO 214, HD 486, Spanish Publication Especial Num 4 and NP 401.

Index